Fishing in North America

1876-1910

Compiled by **Frank Oppel**

CASTLE

Fishing in North America

1876-1910

Copyright © 1986 by Castle, a Division of Book Sales, Inc. of Secaucus, NJ

Manufactured in the United States of America

ISBN 1-55521-124-0

The Castle logo is registered in the United States Patent and Trademark Office

87 88 89   9 8 7 6 5 4 3 2

CONTENTS

1
Fishing
in the
Rangeley Lakes
(1877)

SCRIBNER'S MONTHLY.

VOL. XIII. FEBRUARY, 1877. No. 4.

TROUT-FISHING IN THE RANGELEY LAKES.

TELLING FISH STORIES.

THERE can be no better text for a paper upon the big trout of the Rangeley Lakes than the representation of one drawn upon birch bark, an accurate engraving of which is given on the next page. The fish here reproduced, be it understood, is a genuine specimen of the speckled brook trout, or, to put it scientifically, of the *Salmo fontinalis*, and weighed *eight and a half pounds* when taken from the water by its captor, R. G. Allerton, of New York City. It had all the recognized peculiarities of brook trout,—the square tail, small head, mouth black inside (instead of white, as is the case with lake trout), and finally the bright vermilion spots which distinguish brook trout from all other species. This particular fish was captured June 5, 1869, in Lake Mooselucmaguntic. It was taken on a trolling line after a contest lasting forty-nine minutes. When landed it was entirely uninjured, and several days after when killed it was laid upon a piece of birch bark, and its outline traced, and then filled in by an amateur artist. The engraving has been made from this original drawing, which is reduced nearly five-sixths,—or, in other words, the figure here given is a little over one-sixth life size. In length this trout measured 25 inches, and at the thickest part its girth was 17 inches. There is nothing like accuracy in a "fish story," and as this

3

trout is by no means the largest which has been captured in the Rangeley Lakes, and is one of thousands of this species ranging from half a pound to ten pounds which have been taken in these waters, it only remains to add that the legend this drawing bears—*hic jacet*—refers entirely to the fish whose obituary is here written, and not at all to the statements about his fellow-denizens of the Rangeley Lakes, some information about which it is the purpose of this paper to present.

Thoreau, to be sure, described it in a general way years ago, and so did Theodore Winthrop, but their accounts made it appear like a *terra incognita*, full of difficulties when it was once reached. Now, however, the railroad excursion fiend has fixed his fangs upon the district. Excursion tickets from Boston to the Rangeley lakes and return by various routes are sold by the different railroads; photographers have

HIC JACET.

Mooselucmaguntic, Molechunkemunk, Welokenebacook, Cupsuptuc, and Rangeley, are the names carried by the individual members of a group of lakes which are yet destined to be as familiar in the literature of the American sportsman as the salmon rivers of Canada or the trout streams of the Adirondacks. These lakes lie in the western part of Maine, near the New Hampshire boundary line. The White Mountains are some thirty miles distant, a little to the west of south, and Moosehead Lake is about sixty or seventy miles to the north-east. It may be absolute incredulity as to the fish stories which are told of these lakes,—it is hard for one who has not seen a speckled trout weighing ten, eight, or even six pounds, to have faith in the existence of a fish of this size and species,—or it may be despair of defining his destination when the sportsman reads the unpronounceable names which these lakes bear; but whatever the cause, the number of visitors to this region has thus far been comparatively small.

been through the Lakes taking views of the various camps and of picturesque localities in general; at least one guide-book has been issued, and since the last barrier to the exclusiveness of the district has thus been broken down, there can be no breach of trust in giving to the readers of SCRIBNER'S MONTHLY an accurate account of one of the most picturesque and attractive regions east of the Rocky Mountains.

Maine is so profusely dotted over with lakes as to suggest the thought that the State has not yet been well drained or that a slight tilting of the continent might depress the general level of this region so as to submerge it in the Atlantic. But the fact is that the lakes which have just been named are between fourteen and fifteen hundred feet above the sea-level, and are embosomed in mountains, some of which reach a height of two, three, and even four thousand feet. Approaching from the south-east by way of Farmington and Phillips (see map, page 436), you first strike Rangeley Lake at its extreme eastern end, and here the entire group is generally spoken of as the Range-

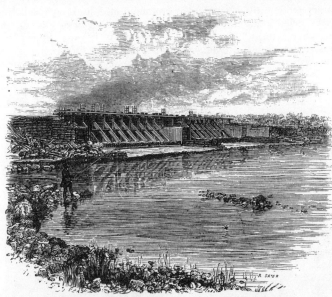

UPPER DAM. (FROM PHOTOGRAPH BY C. A. J. FARRAR, BOSTON.)

whence stages run three times a week—Monday, Wednesday and Friday —to Andover, eighteen miles distant. There at the Greig House you will find in "Charley" Cushman a "guide, philosopher and friend," who will not only give all necessary information as to the accommodations for fishermen upon the lower lakes, but in an emergency, as I can bear most cheerful witness, will see you safely to your destination, and make it certain that you are well provided for. To reach the "Arm" a twelve-mile ride on a buckboard over a difficult road must be undergone, and thence by a small steamer

ley Lakes. Coming from the other direction, by way of Andover, Welokenebacook is first reached, and in this region one hears the group spoken of as the Richardson Lakes, although this name is properly applicable only to Welokenebacook and Molechunkemunk. But the tourist and the fisherman will appreciate the advantage of explicit directions regarding the precise routes which it is desirable to follow in reaching the Lakes.

Portland is the point where one must decide whether he shall approach the Lakes from their southern or from their north-eastern extremity. If he wishes to go by way of Umbagog, he must take the Grand Trunk Railroad to Bethel. Taking supper at the Bethel House, the traveler goes to Upton by stage the same evening, accomplishing the distance — 26 miles — by eleven o'clock. The next morning the little steamer "Diamond" will take you through Lake Umbagog to the "Inlet," a distance of twelve miles. Leaving the "Diamond" at this point, a row-boat conveys you to the "Rapids," a mile and a half further. Here is a "carry" of four and a half miles, over which the luggage is hauled by a team, while the fisherman foots it, and you are at the Middle Camp Dam, which is about the middle of the western shore of Welokenebacook, whence access is easy to Molechunkemunk and Mooselucmaguntic.

Or a shorter, and in other respects a preferable route, is to stop at Bryant's Pond,

the Middle or Upper Dam may be reached. Communication by either of these routes, however, is not so regular, sure or easy as by way of Farmington and Phillips, and as this is the direct route to the camp of the Oquossoc Angling Association, which is by far the best

"GLAD TO SEE YOU, UNCLE JOHN!"

managed organization of its kind in this region, the tourist or sportsman will generally give it the preference. Leaving Portland a little after one o'clock, you arrive at Farmington about six. There "Uncle John" Pickens takes charge of all your "traps," and stows them with conscientious care in the boot of his capacious Concord coach. A supper at the Forest House fortifies you for an eighteen-mile ride to Phillips, and this is materially shortened by Uncle John's famous "bear story" and other characteristic narratives. Stopping overnight at the Barden House, or at the Elmwood House, kept by Mr. Prescott, you take an early start the next morning, and after a stage ride of twenty miles reach Kimball's

singularly commonplace and civilized, but formerly it was quite as well off as its neighbors. Originally it was known as Oquossoc Lake, but about fifty years ago a wealthy English squire, Rangeley by name, having wearied of the civilized tameness of his Virginia estate, decided to settle in this northern wilderness. He cleared a broad tract at the outlet of Rangeley Lake, built a dam across the stream, erected extensive saw and grist mills, and expended large sums of money in other improvements. His supplies of all kinds were transported from Phillips or Farmington, a distance of thirty

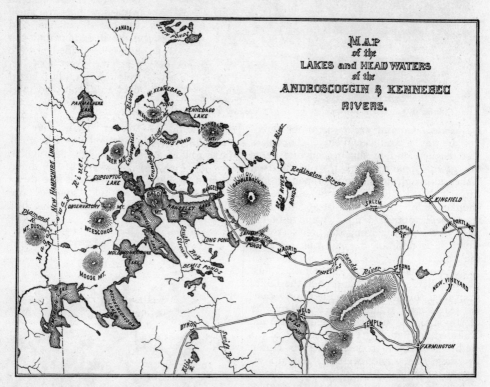

Hotel, at the head of Rangeley Lake, by noon. Taking dinner here, and after it the "Molly-chunk-e-munk," one of the little steamers which have recently invaded the sanctity of these lakes, you are in an hour and a half landed at the foot of Rangeley. Here there has just been erected a hotel known as the Mountain View House, which is open to all comers, and near it is the private camp of Theodore L. Page,—Lake Point Cottage.

In comparison with the unpronounceable Indian names which the contiguous lakes bear, that of Rangeley appears

to fifty miles, and he was compelled to haul his lumber a hundred miles to find a market. For twenty years Squire Rangeley lived here, pushing his business enterprises with great energy and more or less success, and enjoying the field sports, of which he was passionately fond. Moose, caribou, deer, bears and wolves were his constant neighbors; ducks, geese, partridge and smaller game were so abundant that shooting them could hardly be called sport; and brook trout weighing six, seven, eight or nine pounds could be taken by the score from the stream which ran past his front door

When Squire Rangeley, for reasons which tradition does not record, gave up the enterprise which he had pushed for a time with so much energy, his mills and buildings were all abandoned, and the clearings which he had made were rapidly seeded down by

tries" there is little that is noteworthy about the town, and the sportsman misses nothing which he has cause to regret in the fact that his route does not take him to the "city."

Until two years ago the trip through Rangeley Lake to its outlet was made either

CAMP KENNEBAGO. (FROM PHOTOGRAPH BY C. A. J. FARRAR, BOSTON.)

the hand of nature; pines, spruces, juniper and fir springing up everywhere in place of the ancient monarchs of the primeval forest which he had cleared away at the cost of so much labor. Ten years ago, the frame and roof of the massive old mill were still standing, but in 1866 these were pulled down and the solid pine timbers of the structure were incorporated in the new dam which was then built for the purpose of floating logs through the outlet in the early spring. Of the old homestead, which occupied a commanding site on a beautiful knoll, only the decayed foundation timbers remain. Enough of the "Potash" building still stands to give a passable shelter to the benighted angler. With these exceptions, Squire Rangeley's "improvements" have all disappeared. The township which he once owned, however, still bears his name. Nearly all of the lake lies within its limits. The town of Rangeley— or the "city," as the natives call it—is half a mile back from the extreme eastern end of the lake. Most of the male inhabitants of the village devote themselves to "guiding" throughout the entire fishing season, and spruce gum in its native state is one of its chief exports. Apart from these "indus-

in Captain Crosby's sail-boat or in row-boats. Rangeley Lake, by the way, is 1,511 feet above tide water. Its breadth is three miles and its length nine miles, and few more picturesque scenes can be imagined than a fleet of six or seven of these row-boats, each with a small United States flag floating from its bow, rapidly moving down the lake, carrying one or two sportsmen on the way to the head-quarters of the famous Oquossoc Angling Association.

Leaving the steamer "Molly-chunk-e-munk,"—the name of which has thus gallantly been metamorphosed and Anglicized from the Indian appellation of Lake Mole-chunk-e-munk,—members of the angling association named or visitors to their camp cross a two-mile carry from the foot of Rangeley Lake to the junction of Kennebago Stream with Rangeley Stream, where is Camp Kennebago. A wagon takes the baggage, while the sportsmen themselves walk across through an excellent wood road, which, however, is marshy enough in spots to make very careful stepping or very thick boots indispensable. Indian Rock—a locality famous even in the aboriginal annals of Maine, as its name indicates—is on the left bank of the stream, directly facing Camp

Kennebago. Tradition relates that this spot was a favorite haunt of the Indian long before the white man ventured so far into the forest, and that as late as 1855 they made visits here from Canada each season.

The lakes of the Rangeley group are so located with respect to one another that it is extremely difficult for the visitor to get a clear idea of their relative positions. Nothing does this so effectively as an ascent of Bald Mountain, which is one of the most prominent objects in this whole landscape, since it rises seventeen hundred feet above the level of the lake. The ascent may be made with comparative ease by any one at all accustomed to mountain climbing, and there are several paths to the summit. Bald Mountain is in reality a peninsula. Its base is washed by Rangeley Lake, Rangeley Stream, Cupsuptuc Lake and Mooselucmaguntic. A narrow strip of land on the south connects it with the main-land. Once on the summit, looking eastward, you see the Rangeley, its graceful form deeply outlined, and every indentation plainly marked. Old Saddleback, rock-ribbed and bare, and rising four thousand feet, faces you. Still further east are the twin Bigelows, Mount Abraham, and the East and West Kennebago Mountains. That thread of silver in the immediate foreground is the wide and rapid Rangeley outlet, which falls twenty-five feet in the two miles intervening between the point where it leaves the lake and its junction with the calmer and deeper waters of the Kennebago. At this point can be clearly distinguished the grounds and buildings of Camp Kennebago, with the stars and stripes waving from the tall flag-staff. Something more than words is necessary to do full justice to the exquisitely varied panorama of lake and mountain, the beauty of which could be hardly more than indicated by the catalogue of names necessary to identify them. Few finer views can be found in the English lakes, among the Trossachs, or even in Switzerland, than this from the summit of Bald Mountain.

Before describing Camp Kennebago in detail, it may be as well to give in brief a sketch of the history of the Oquossoc Angling Association, of which organization this camp is the head-quarters. So long as thirty years ago, a sportsman now and then worked his way through the wilderness to these lakes, but it is only within the last fifteen years that the Rangeley, Kennebago and Cupsuptuc Lakes, with the upper end of Mooselucmaguntic, have become at all well

MEETING OF THE WATERS—JUNCTION OF RANGELEY AND KENNEBAGO.

known to anglers. The Richardson Lakes—Welokenebacook and Molechunkemunk, with Umbagog, forming the lower lakes in the great chain whence the Androscoggin River derives its mighty power—have for the last thirty or forty years been frequented by a score or more of Boston and New York gentlemen. These sportsmen were invariably found at "Rich's" "Middle Dam," Mosquito Brook, or the "Upper Dam." Hundreds of spotted beauties, weighing from two to eight pounds, were captured by these anglers year after year, but they wisely kept their own counsel, and if an item occasionally found its way into the New York or Boston papers chronicling the arrival of a six or eight pound speckled trout, those who claimed to be best informed dismissed the paragraph with a sneer at the ignorance of editors who did not know the difference between brook trout and "lakers." In 1860, Henry O. Stanley, of Dixfield, now one of the efficient commissioners of fisheries for the State of Maine, organized an expedition to penetrate to the lakes from the upper end. Twenty years before, Mr. Stanley's father had made the survey of much of the lake country, and discovering the extraordinary size of the trout, had frequently repeated his visits. The son now and then accompanied his father on these trips, and

GEORGE SHEPARD PAGE, PRESIDENT OF THE OQUOSSOC ANGLING ASSOCIATION.

with such a preceptor in the gentle art, and with such opportunities for its practice, it is not strange that Mr. Stanley should have achieved the distinction of being the champion fly-fisher of the world. His record of brook trout weighing from three to nine and a half pounds, all taken with the fly, reaches many hundred. The party which Mr. Stanley headed on the occasion alluded to made its way to the lake, *via* Dixfield, Carthage, Weld, Phillips, and Madrid, striking first the upper end of Rangeley. One of its members, Mr. George Shepard Page, of New York City, was so delighted with his experience upon this trip that in 1863 he made a second journey by the same route. He returned from this trip, bringing with him eight brook trout weighing respectively 8⅜, 8¼, 7¼, 6½, 6, 5½, 5, 5—total, 51⅞ lbs., or an average of nearly 6½ lbs. each. William Cullen Bryant, Henry J. Raymond and George Wilkes were presented with the three largest, and made acknowledgments duly in the " Evening Post," the " New York Times," and the " Spirit of the Times." Then there broke out an excitement among anglers altogether without precedent. Scores of letters were sent to the papers which had presumed to call these brook trout,—some of them interrogative, others denunciatory, others theoretical, and others flatly contradictory. The Adirondacks had never yielded a brook trout which weighed more than 5 lbs., and that, there-

fore, must be the standard of brook trout the world over. But Mr. Page had foreseen the violent scepticism which was sure to manifest itself, and had sent a seven-pounder to Professor Agassiz, who speedily replied that these monster trout were genuine specimens of the speckled or brook trout family, and that they were only found in large numbers in the lakes and streams at the head waters of the Androscoggin River, in North-western Maine. In 1864, several New York gentlemen visited Rangeley, among the number Messrs. Lewis B. Reed, R. G. Allerton, and L. T. Lazell. Upon their return, they fully corroborated the report made by Mr. Page the year previous, and brought back with them several trout which weighed from three to eight pounds. In 1867, Mr. Page again visited Rangeley in company with Mr. Stanley, and ten days' fishing by these two gentlemen and Mr. Fields, of Gorham, N. H., showed these extraordinary results:

No. of Trout.	Weight of each in lbs.	Total weight. lbs.
3	2	6
1	2¼	2¼
3	2½	7½
2	2¾	5½
5	3	15
5	3¼	16¼
3	3½	10½
2	3¾	7½
1	4	4
2	4½	9
1	4¾	4¾
3	5	15
1	5¼	5¼
1	5½	5½
2	5¾	11½
5	6	30
2	6¼	12½
1	6½	6½
1	7	7
3	7¼	21¾
3	7½	22½
2	7¾	15½
2	8	16
1	8¼	8¼
1	8½	8½
1	8¾	8¾
1	9½	9½
1	10	10
59		293

Average nearly 5 lbs.

In 1868, the number of anglers visiting the lakes had so rapidly increased that it was decided to organize an association for the purpose of leasing ground, erecting buildings, and purchasing boats. Messrs. Bowles, of Springfield, Mass., Lazell and Reed, of Brooklyn, N. Y., George Shepard Page and R. G. Allerton, of this city, Hon. W. P. Frye, of Lewiston, Me., W. S. Badger, of Augusta,

Me., and T. L. Page, of New Orleans, who were all in adjacent camps at the outlet of Rangeley Lake, formally organized the Oquossoc Angling Association by the election of Mr. G. S. Page as president and Mr. L. B. Reed, secretary. In the year following (1869), the association purchased the buildings, improvements and boats belonging to

May 25 to October 1, when the law prohibits the capture of trout save for scientific purposes by written permission of the fish commissioner. During the first month and the last three weeks of the fishing season, guests are only admitted upon the invitation of members, since the camp accommodations are then likely to be overtaxed, but be-

INTERIOR OF CAMP KENNEBAGO—THE BIG FIRE-PLACE.

C. T. Richardson (now superintendent of the association) at the junction of the Rangeley and Kennebago, and immediately began the erection of Camp Kennebago. Meantime the membership rapidly increased, and in 1870 the association was formally incorporated under the laws of the State of Maine. The membership of the association is limited to seventy-five. There are now, however, a few vacancies. Shares are $200 each, and the capital stock is $10,700, which is invested in camp buildings, furniture, boats, etc., etc. The annual dues are $25. Camp charges are $2 per day for board, $1 for board of guide, and 50 cents per day for use of boats. The best guides receive $2 per day, making the total cost per day while in camp $5.50, unless two persons choose to fish from the same boat, when, of course, the expense of guide, board for guide and hire of boat may be shared. The fishing season extends from about

tween June 20 and September 10 the camp is open to all visitors upon the same terms as to members. Ladies and children are also admitted between the dates named. A roomy building with separate apartments is specially reserved for them, and as two or three female servants are constantly employed in the camp, they are sure to be quite as comfortable as in ordinary country hotels.

Without drawing any invidious comparisons, it may be stated in general, that there are few organizations of the kind in the country the *morale* of which has been so carefully guarded as has that of the Oquossoc Angling Association. The present board of trustees consists of George Shepard Page (president), J. W. Kimball, of Bath, Maine (vice-president), L. B. Reed, New York (secretary), J. A. Williamson, Jersey City (treasurer), L. T. Lazell, Brooklyn, Dr. F. N. Otis, New York, Hon. W. P. Frye, Lewiston,

Maine, and A. P. Whitehead, Newark, N. J. The names of these gentlemen are an emphatic guarantee of the prudence with

HIS HEAD.

which the affairs of the association are managed, and also of the fact that everything looking toward the dissipation which is likely to exist in camps where sportsmen congregate is rigidly prohibited. It would be difficult, and indeed impossible, to name a similar locality where the guides are so steady and so thoroughly respectable. Perhaps the Maine Liquor Law has had something to do with this result, for most of the guides have at one time or another acted as river-drivers; and it is not so very many years ago that in the lumbering-camps and on the "drive" a common proportion of supplies was a "barrel of rum to a barrel of beans." The Maine Liquor Law has certainly put an end to this *régime*, and with it have disappeared to a very great extent the drunkenness, profanity, and kindred vices which at one time degraded the brave men who season after season risked their lives by exposing themselves to the dangers of river-driving.

There are some peculiar features in the arrangement of the camp buildings which will be of interest to those who are not familiar with such institutions. The main camp is a substantial board structure 100 feet long by 30 feet wide. At its extreme westerly end is a well-equipped kitchen, and adjoining it is a dining-room. Then comes the main apartment, which is occupied as a sleeping and sitting room. This room takes the full width of the main building (30 feet), is about 60 feet in length, and from the floor to the gable is 30 feet in the clear, giving it a most spacious appearance and securing thorough ventilation. There are no partitions in this apartment, but twenty-five or thirty beds are

ranged along its sides, and at its extreme easterly end is a large open fire-place, around which the weary anglers gather after their day's sport, and entertain each other with the rehearsal of their experiences and exploits. As one huge log after another blazes up,—for the nights are seldom so warm that a fire is oppressive,—story after story passes around. It rarely happens that some one of the circle has not captured a six or eight pound trout during the day, and the one who has been so fortunate is of course the hero of the hour. With what kind of fly the fish was captured, how long it took to land him, the narrow escape which the lucky angler had from losing his prize just as the guide was netting him, are points which must be rehearsed over and over again. Could one-tenth of the fish stories which have thus been rehearsed around this famous old fire-place in Camp Kennebago be put on record, they would make a book which would throw far into the shade any volume of piscatorial experience that has ever yet seen the light. Before eleven o'clock the weary anglers are all in their beds, and the camp sinks into a silence which is undisturbed save by some obstreperous snorer, at least until daylight the next morning, when some fisherman who has had poor luck the previous day starts out with a desperate determination to retrieve his fortunes by testing the virtue of early fishing.

A tour around the upper end of Lake

ALLERTON LODGE.

Mooselucmaguntic discovers a number of snugly constructed buildings, some owned by private parties and others by members of the Angling Association, who spend several weeks consecutively at the lake during the fishing season. Prominent among the latter are those of Hon. W. P. Frye at the Narrows, and that of R. G. Allerton at Bugle Cove, just at the foot of Bald Mountain. Allerton Lodge is a thoroughly built house, fully equipped with all the comforts of civilization. It is located upon a rocky bluff twenty feet or more above the level of the lake, and commands a magnificent view. Since Bugle Cove is one of the best fishing-grounds on the lake, its proprietor, who is one of the most enthusiastic and persevering of anglers, never fails to make up such a score during his visits in June as to excite the emulation of all other visitors during the rest of the season. Exactly what Mr. Allerton has accomplished during his eight successive annual visits to the lakes is summarized in the following table:

C. T. RICHARDSON, SUPERINTENDENT OF THE OQUOSSOC ANGLING ASSOCIATION.

RECORD OF BROOK TROUT CAUGHT BY R. G. ALLERTON IN RANGELEY LAKES, MAINE, FROM 1869 TO 1876—SPRING SEASON.

1869..	247 Trout, weighing	234¼ lbs.
1870..	124 "	"	172½ "
1871..	218 "	"	135 "
1872..	130 "	"	285¾ "
1873.	149 "	"	205½ "
1874..	175 "	"	231 "
1875..	157 "	"	177½ "
1876..	136 "	"	182¼ "

Total.. 1,336 "   "   1,623¾ "

Averaging about 1 lb. 3½ oz. each.

WEIGHTS AND NUMBERS OF ABOVE OF TWO POUNDS AND UPWARD.

38 Trout of	2	lbs. ea.	3 Trout of	5¼ lbs. ea.
14 "	2¼ "	4 "	5½ "
33 "	2½ "	1 "	5¾ "
14 "	2¾ "	13 "	6 "
29 "	3 "	9 "	6½ "
1 "	3¼ "	2 "	6¾ "
17 "	3½ "	7 "	7 "
4 "	3¾ "	1 "	7¼ "
15 "	4 "	1 "	7½ "
1 "	4¼ "	4 "	8 "
14 "	4½ "	2 "	8½ "
13 "	5 "		

Making 240 trout, weighing 891¾ lbs.; averaging about 3 lbs. 11½ oz. each.

But it need not be imagined that it is only the practiced anglers who are successful in the Rangeley Lakes. There is in Camp Kennebago a record-book in which each visitor is expected to set down his score when he finishes his stay. This exhibits some catches nearly as remarkable as that which has been set down above. In 1869, eleven members of the association in six days' fishing, besides a large number of smaller fish, captured 30 trout weighing as follows: three of 4 lbs. each; one 4¼ lbs.; two, 4¾ lbs. each; three 5 lbs. each; one 5¼ lbs.; four 5½ lbs. each; two 6 lbs. each; two 6¼ lbs. each; two 6¾ lbs. each; two 7 lbs. each; one 7¼ lbs; one 7½ lbs.; three 8 lbs. each; one 8½ lbs.; one 9 lbs.;—total, 181¾ lbs., averaging over 6 lbs. each. Then the ladies find the locality a wonderful one for great "catches"—of trout. Mrs. Theodore Page has taken several weighing between 6 and 9 lbs. each, and even the young folks are fortunate. Masters Harry and Allie Page, aged respectively 5½ and 3½ years, it appears from this record, during one visit caught 57 trout weighing 37 lbs. Ten averaged 1 lb. each, and one weighed 2 lbs. Lest these large catches should provoke remonstrance against such wholesale slaughter of this beautiful fish, it should be stated that it is the almost invariable rule to return to the water all uninjured trout weighing less than half a pound. Those hooked so deeply that they cannot live are kept for consumption at the camp. The larger fish as soon as caught are deposited in the car which each boat always has with it. Upon the return to camp at night, the living trout are carefully transferred to a larger car,—which in this case is the name given to an ordinary dry-goods box with slats on the bottom and sides, admitting the free passage through of water,—and at the end of his stay each angler, if he desires to take a box of trout home with him, selects the largest and releases all the others, which speedily find their way to the deep waters of the lake again. Thus the actual destruction of fish is by no means so extensive as it would at first appear that it might be.

In general, the early spring fishing and the late fall fishing are decidedly the best and most enjoyable. The pestiferous black flies do not appear until June 10, but their attentions can be warded off by a liberal application to all exposed parts of the neck, face and hands of a mixture of tar and sweet oil in equal parts. Oil of pennyroyal in sufficient quantity to make its odor plainly perceptible is thought by many to render this preparation more effective. By September, with exemplary regularity, the black flies disappear, and with them goes the only hindrance to complete enjoyment of out-door life.

As regards methods of fishing, it need only be said that the high-toned angler will not tempt his intended victim with anything but a fly at any season. The best fly-fishing is to be had in the streams in the spring and in the lake in the fall. Those who go to the lakes in the spring and early summer determined to catch the biggest fish at all hazards must seek them with live minnows for bait, still-fishing, or by trolling in deep water. In either case, the law rules out all gang hooks. The "single baited hook" only is permitted, and any one infringing upon this wise restriction exposes himself to severe penalties. A larger hook, with a heavier leader than is used in ordinary brook trout fishing, is called for in these waters; but upon such points and with reference to the varieties of flies which are most available, advice may be had at any of the fishing-tackle stores. In general, however, give preference in making your selection to the

more subdued colors, and do not permit yourself to be stocked up with an immense variety. Five or six kinds well selected will be more than enough to give the fish ample range for choice.

AN EXPERIMENT IN NATURAL PHILOSOPHY.

As I have already stated, these big trout are caught either in the lake or in the streams which feed it, according to the season; and each kind of fishing has its peculiar incidents and surprises. Both Kennebago and Rangeley streams are too deep and swift to be waded in the orthodox style, although at certain seasons they are so shallow in places as to make their navigation even by boats of the lightest draft an undertaking of no little difficulty. Rangeley Stream, between the famous dam at the outlet of Rangeley Lake and Indian Rock, a distance of perhaps a mile and a half, abounds in pools which the big trout love to frequent. These particular waters have been so steadily and thoroughly fished, that the association, with a degree of self-sacrifice which speaks well for the true sportsman-like spirit in its members, lately secured the passage of a law by the Maine Legislature prohibiting any fishing there for a term of five years. When that time has elapsed, it will be worth a trip to Maine to cast a fly under "the dam" or in the "eddy." It is not unusual for the more enterprising fishermen to work their way up Kennebago Stream four, five, or even six miles. This trip involves hard labor by the guide in poling or in pulling the boat over the frequent shallows, and great caution is necessary to guard against such a mishap as the pencil of that enthusiastic and thoroughly scientific sportsman, Dr. F. N. Otis, has re-produced, where an unexpected push by the guide's pole or the sudden striking of the

"THERE GOES MY ROD!"

boat's bow upon the pebbly bottom sends the surprised fisherman, heels over head, into the bottom of his boat, while his leader and flies are sure to become securely hooked in the loftiest overhanging branch within reach. Still, the discomforts of these excursions up the Kennebago or Cupsuptuc streams are sure to be rewarded with some rare sport.

Nor is the fishing in the open lake without its occasional surprises. I very well remember an incident which happened upon the occasion of my first visit to Camp Kennebago, when I was a tyro in trout-fishing, and had not been fully initiated in the use of the fly. My boat was at anchor some distance below "Stony Batter," and with humiliation I confess that I was angling with a minnow. For a half hour or more there had been no sign of a trout in my vicinity, and I had carelessly laid my pole across the boat, with the butt under the thwart. Suddenly there was a "strike." Before I could seize my pole, the trout had carried the line directly under the boat with such a rush as to snap the rod,—which I ought to say, in justice to the professional makers, was a cheap store rod,—into two or three pieces. The trout escaped, as he deserved to do, and for once I could not help confessing myself outgeneraled. This mishap, of course, put an end to my fishing for the day; but fortunately it occurred quite late in the afternoon, and thus left me at leisure to enjoy a scene which was in itself singularly beautiful, and which was an appropriate setting for a striking incident. As the sun was sinking behind the hills, close under which

we were fishing, it threw their long shadows far out on the lake, while the waters on the eastern shore were still bright with the golden light of the gentle June evening. In the distance we descried three specks upon the water, which gradually grew in size as they steadily approached us, until we made out three batteaux laden with the "river-drivers," who were returning from their perilous and tedious journey down the Androscoggin with the great log-rafts, —the results of the previous winter's lumbering. The first sound which disturbed the Sabbath-like stillness of the lake, as the batteaux came nearer, was the steady thump, thump, thump of the sweeps in the row-locks. Then we heard the sound of voices, but at first too indistinctly to determine whether it was the echo of boisterous talk, or some river-driver's song, with which the oarsmen were keeping time. But soon the sounds, as they became linked together, grew into that grand old tune "Coronation," and the words:

"All hail the power of Jesus' name!"

came to us over the peaceful waters, sung with all the strength, steadiness, and fervor which might be expected in a congregation of religious worshipers. Nothing could have been in more perfect harmony with the scene, and yet nothing could have been a greater surprise than to hear this tune, and the words with which it is so inseparably connected coming with such zest from the throats of men who have gained an undeserved reputation for roughness, not to say profanity, of speech.

During the extremely warm weather, the trout naturally run deep in the lake, since there only can they find the cold water in which they thrive; but even then the streams afford good sport; so that the angler cannot spend a week at the lake during the fishing season without certainty of getting better sport, and more of it, than can be found in any other resort in the country. Another fact that adds greatly to the pleasure of fishing in the Rangeley Lakes is, that with the exception of the land-locked salmon lately introduced, they contain no other fish besides the trout and the smaller fish upon which he feeds. Of the latter, there are three varieties,—the chub, the sucker, and the minnow or "red-fin," as they are locally termed. All these exist in countless numbers in the streams and at the outlets of these streams into the lake. There is still a fourth variety called by the natives the "blue-back" trout, the *Salmo Oquossa* (so named because it is peculiar to these waters), which is also generally supposed to furnish food to the monarchs of the lake. These are never seen before October 10, when they appear in the Rangeley Stream and in three or four other localities for the purpose of spawning. Then they come in an immense army, actually filling the streams here and there with a dense struggling mass, which the natives capture by the bushel and by the barrel in nets, buckets, and

observations, made under the auspices of some of the practical pisciculturists belonging to the association, have developed results full of interest and of much practical value. For instance, in reply to queries as to the probable age of the mammoth trout found in the Rangeley Lakes, Professor Agassiz emphatically declared that "no man living knew whether these six and eight pounders were ten or two hundred years old." To get some light upon this question, Mr. Page conceived an ingenious device, which he at once proceeded to put in execution. Platinum wire was obtained, cut into one and a half inch lengths, flattened at one end, and various numbers were stamped on the surface from $\frac{1}{2}$ to 4, also the numbers 70, 71, 72, to denote the year. As trout were captured they were weighed, one of these tags

CATCHING A FIVE-POUNDER IN THE LAKE. (FROM A SKETCH BY DR. F. N. OTIS.)

pails; even scooping them out by hand and throwing them on the bank. They are salted down and preserved in the same way as mackerel are cured. These blue-back trout have never been found more than nine inches in length, nor less than six inches. In flavor they are quite as rich and delicate when cooked as the brook trout. After spawning, they return to the lake just as suddenly as they appeared; and notwithstanding the numbers in which they are captured during their brief stay in the stream, they do not diminish in multitude year after year. It is inferred that their regular haunts must be in the deepest waters of the lake, since their capture by the enticements and appliances which prove irresistible to the speckled trout, is almost unknown.

Numerous experiments and continued

was passed through the skin just under the adipose fin and securely twisted, and then the fish was liberated. In the course of the two or three years named a large number of these trout were thus labeled. Of course, the chances that any of them would be caught seemed infinitesimally small, yet in 1873 one of them reported. In June of that year, Mr. Thomas Moran, the artist, captured a fine, vigorous trout weighing $2\frac{1}{4}$ lbs. Upon taking him from the landing net the platinum tag flashed in the sunlight. Upon examination, the mark, "$\frac{1}{2}$—71," was discovered, thus establishing the curious fact that this particular fish had gained $1\frac{3}{4}$ lbs. in two years.

The entire influence of the association has uniformly been thrown in favor of a rigorous enactment of the laws protecting the trout in the spawning season and regulating the mode of capture. More than this, it has taken the most active measures in the direction of increasing the supply of fish in the waters to which it has access. Land-locked salmon have been introduced (this is one of the very few species which co-exist with the trout), and a large number of the young of the sea salmon (*Salmo salar*) have also been put into the lakes. Last season, several land-locked salmon two years of age, and weighing half a pound, were captured. This year those of this same growth will probably have reached a pound, and in the course of two or three years these fish, which some anglers regard as even more "gamey" than the trout, must become very abundant.

Some of the earliest and most successful

"STONY BATTER."

efforts in trout culture are connected with the annals of Rangeley. In October, 1867, Mr. Page transported two live trout—one a male weighing ten pounds, the other a female weighing eight and a half—from Rangeley to his home in Stanley, N. J., a distance of nearly five hundred miles. An oblong box of forty gallons' capacity, lined with sponge which was covered with muslin, and having an air pump attached so as to make constant renewal of the air easy, had been carefully prepared. This box was carried from the head of Rangeley on a spring wagon to Farmington, a distance of thirty-five miles, and thence by railroad to its destination in New Jersey. Three days were occupied in the journey, but by unremitting care night and day the magnificent fish, both alive, were deposited in the pond at Stanley. Unfortunately, the weather was unusually warm for the season of the year. The temperature of the pond could not be

reduced below 65°, and the larger of the two trout lived only eight hours. The female survived six days longer. Thus the attempt to propagate Rangeley trout in New Jersey by natural means failed. The larger of these trout was unfortunately not weighed when first captured, but when dead balanced the steelyards at precisely ten pounds. It is a well-known fact that all fish lose in weight after capture, and Professor Spencer F. Baird and Professor Agassiz both gave it as their opinion that when taken this trout weighed at least eleven and a half pounds. He measured 30 inches in length and 18 inches in circumference. His tail spread 8 inches and his jaws 6½ inches. He was mounted by one of the most skillful taxidermists in the country, Mr. Dickinson, of Chatham, N. J., and has since occupied a prominent place in the private office of Mr. Page at 10 Warren street, New York. This is admitted to be the largest authenticated brook trout on record since the time of Izaak Walton, and as such it well deserved the place of honor which was assigned it in the department of Fish and Fisheries in the Centennial Exhibition.

About this time (1867), Mr. Seth Green's attempts to propagate trout artificially had begun to attract attention, and anticipating the possibility of failure in transporting the live trout so great a distance, Mr. Page, to make assurance doubly sure, had secured 30,000 trout eggs which had been impregnated by the milt of the male in the method now so well understood. These had been carefully packed between layers of moss, and immediately upon their arrival at Stanley were deposited in the hatching-houses. After the usual interval of six weeks, Mr. Page had the gratification of seeing the newly hatched trout. In due time they were fed, and when they had attained a suitable size were liberated to stock the stream below the hatching-houses. Thus we have the history of one of the earliest and perhaps the first attempt in this country to take eggs from wild fish, transport them 500 miles, and successfully hatch them.

The determination of the members of the Oquossoc Angling Association fully to maintain the superiority of their fishing-grounds is conclusively manifested by the arrangements for artificial propagation which were made on Bema Stream, at the extreme south-eastern extremity of Lake Mooselucmagmtic, under the direction of Messrs. Page and L. L. Crounse. Nearly three years ago, these gentlemen leased the beautiful spot where this stream empties into the lake, and here they erected a series of private camps spacious enough for themselves and their families, including a large cooking and dining camp. The next step taken by Messrs. Page and Crounse was to secure the privilege of controlling the waters of the adjoining township for the propagation of trout. Three miles up Bema Stream, at the foot of a bold mountain, there bursts out from a rocky bed a series of remarkable springs, which in the spring and fall furnish much of the water that flows down the rapid stream to the lake. The water of these springs rarely falls below 45°, or rises above 49°, and is therefore peculiarly adapted to the propagation of trout. The smaller trout from the lake, weighing two pounds and under, make these springs and the stream in the vicinity their spawning-grounds, and in the month of October they crowd the waters in great numbers. Mr. Stanley, while securing fish for spawn, has actually dipped up as many as six trout of an average weight of a pound each at one scoop of his dip-net. As is their habit, the males always come up in advance and clear off the beds, and in a few days the female follows. So strong is the instinct which leads them to the spawning-beds, that the trout, like the salmon, will force themselves over shallows in the stream where there is not depth enough to permit them to swim. Just at the spawning-beds, and over the little branch which carries the water of the springs to the main stream, the gentlemen above named erected a hatching-house. In return for this privilege, they agreed to place in the waters each season from 50,000 to 100,000 young fry, recompensing themselves for their trouble, if they could, by taking out spawn for use in other waters. In the seasons of 1873 and 1874, they were able to deposit in the streams more than the maximum of spawn agreed on. In 1875 and 1876, Mr. Stanley's duties as fish commissioner prevented his giving this matter the necessary attention; but the young fry were so successfully hatched the first two seasons, that a sudden increase

THE DAM ON RANGELEY STREAM.

of small trout has been noted in the stream itself, and as far up as the Bema Ponds, four miles above the hatching-houses. Some of the spawn were successfully transferred to other waters,—the eggs had to be carried out in December, on the backs of men, nine miles through the woods,—and Mr. B. B. Porter, the pisciculturist of Crystal Springs, New Jersey, can now show Rangeley trout double the size of any other variety of trout of the same age.

The method of capturing trout for their spawn was either to dip them up near the springs with an ordinary net, as they came up to deposit the spawn, or to take large trout in the lake chiefly with the fly in advance of their ripening, and to "car" them until they were stripped, when they were restored to the lake. At one time in the fall of 1874, Messrs. Stanley and Hayford, who were in charge of the operation, had in a large car at the mouth of Bema Stream over two hundred of these famous trout weighing from one pound to six pounds each,—a sight which could not be paralleled in any other waters in the world.

The camps at Bema look out over the broad expanse of the bay which opens toward the north-west and are very prettily situated. The very remoteness of the camp secures its freedom from the visits of miscellaneous tourists, while the beauty of its location and the excellent fishing to be found in its immediate neighborhood

"CLEFT ROCK" AT BEMA.

these mammoth trout. If he misses the fly, a second cast almost invariably provokes the fated fish to a more eager rush. Rising through the topmost curl of the wave, his side, brilliant in purple and gold, gleams in the sunlight for an instant. But this time he is fast, and there is a thud as if a locomotive, under full headway, had been hooked. With a mad rush, he strikes for the depths of the lake, but the light rod yields like a thing of life. Whether the trout weigh one pound or eight, the lance-wood or split bamboo is faithful to the trust placed in it. With a pertinacity almost human it clings to the frantic fish, steadily drawing him to the surface until after a contest which may have lasted only ten minutes, or which may have been prolonged through two hours, the landing-net of the skillful guide deposits him in the boat.

Apart from the risk of losing your trout because of the difficulty of landing him while the boat is tossing on the waves, this fishing in rough water has its perils, which add to its excitement if they do not increase its pleasures. One bracing September morning I was industriously casting my fly from my boat, which was anchored three or four hundred yards from the sand-spit at the mouth of Bema Stream. The "Spirit of Mooselucmaguntic" (an effigy which the ingenuity of some of the campers had constructed from the gnarled roots which the waves had cast up on the beach

amply justify the wisdom shown in its selection by the gentlemen who control it. They and their immediate friends here enjoy a coveted seclusion and keep clear of intruders by a lease of three miles of the shore which covers the entire southern end of Bema Bay. Its position, however, exposes the bay in its front to the north-west gales which prevail to a greater or less extent through the whole season. Those who are accustomed to wait for the traditional "fly breeze," will receive with incredulity the statement that the largest trout have been taken in these waters when a north-west gale was driving the spray from the white-capped waves, and when the persevering angler found a seat in the bottom of his boat the most comfortable position from which to cast his fly, if, indeed, the fly can be said to be "cast" when the wind carries the line so straight from the rod that it is difficult to keep the fly on the surface of the water. Yet the keen-eyed trout, at this very time, rushes the most unwarily upon his imaginary prey. A sudden splash from which the spray flies in the face of the wind betrays the presence of one of

A WATERSCAPE.

and worn into incredibly fantastic shapes) looked upon the scene with a grin which foreboded some dire disaster. My guide, in despair at the determination which persisted in casting a fly in such a gale, was fishing from the bow of the boat with a drop line. A sudden exclamation from him, a start and a sharp twitch, indicated that he had hooked a large fish. I turned to see him pull a beautiful three-pounder over the thwart, which he had depressed to the level of the water to save the trouble of using the landing-net. But our triumph was of

either of us to cut it and let the boat drift ashore. Fortunately, however, another boat happened just at this crisis to be starting out upon the lake. By his vigorous yells my guide attracted the attention of those in the other boat, and in a few moments it

"MATCHING" A SEVEN-POUND TROUT.

short duration. No sooner had the victim been deposited in the boat than we both, in an instant, found ourselves pitched out of it and struggling in the water of the lake. Unnoticed by either of us in the excitement of the moment, our boat had swung around into the trough of the sea, and a huge wave had dashed in, completely filling it and tipping it so nearly over that as the water came in we went out. Confident in my own swimming powers, I called to my guide, as soon as I came to the surface and grasped hold of the boat, that I could take care of myself, and not to be alarmed on my account. But a desperate series of flounderings on his part indicated to me what I had never before suspected, that, notwithstanding the fact that he had been a guide upon these waters for thirty years, *he could not swim a stroke.* His frantic efforts to insure his own safety quickly tipped the boat bottom-side up, and again sent us both under. When I came to the surface he was seated astride of the bow in comparative safety while the second submersion had so water-logged my heavy winter clothing that I found it impossible to do more than hang on to whatever part of the slippery bottom of the boat I could best clutch. Then it began to look as if our strait was desperate. The anchor-rope held our boat with the same firmness upon which we had before congratulated ourselves, and I fear that it would never have occurred to

was alongside. My guide easily stepped from his place of refuge into the rescuing boat, nearly upsetting that in his precipitancy, and then it came to my relief. But I could neither lift myself over its side nor could those who were in it pull me in without imminent risk of capsizing. There was no other way but to tow me ashore ingloriously. As soon as my feet struck bottom, I waded to the beach, and then for the first

THE SPIRIT OF MOOSELUCMAGUNTIC.

time realized how completely my strength was exhausted, and for how short a time, in all probability, I could have sustained myself in the perilous position from which I had so happily escaped. A blazing camp-fire and a dry suit of clothes quickly restored my equanimity, which was, however, completely destroyed again by the reflection, which in an instant burst upon me, that my three rods, including a new split bamboo, together with a carefully prepared box of fishing tackle, which contained my fly-books, were at the bottom of the lake and in water at least twelve feet deep. At first it seemed as if my sport for that trip at least had been completely and disastrously terminated. One of our guides, who was an expert swimmer, comforted me by the assurance that he could easily recover the more important articles by diving for them, and for a time it appeared as if this would be the only chance until it occurred to us that one of the most enterprising and ingenious of our party had a day or two before constructed a square box with a pane of glass in the end, with which, after the manner of the sponge and pearl divers, he had been studying the bottom of the lake to discover, if possible, the localities which the trout were the most likely to frequent. Taking this out with us the next day, we found that the contrivance worked to a charm. Thrusting below the ripple the end of the box which contained the glass and excluding the light as far as possible from the other end, every object on the bottom of the lake, at a depth of even fifteen or twenty feet, could be clearly discerned. A little patient labor with this and a large landing-net with a handle of sufficient length was finally rewarded with the recovery of every article of any value. The fly-books, however, were both destroyed and part of their contents were seriously damaged; still these were trifling offsets to my own fortunate escape and that of my guide.

An incident in strong contrast with this unfortunate beginning terminated this same eventful fishing trip. Mr. Page, although the most expert and enthusiastic fisherman of our number, had devoted himself so assiduously to caring for the comfort of his guests that his own chances at catching the big trout had been seriously lessened. It was our last afternoon together, and as the hours waned toward sunset, the surface of the lake became as smooth and as brilliant as burnished steel. Our three boats were anchored within a short distance

BREAKING CAMP.

of each other, and we were condoling with our friend upon his lack of luck, when suddenly a few rods away there was a quick swirl and splash which told of the presence of a big fish. "That's my trout!" exclaimed Mr. Page, as he ordered his guide to haul anchor and scull him quietly over the spot where the fish had appeared. Two or three casts of the fly, and in an instant, with a ferocious rush, the trout had hooked himself so firmly that his final capture became only a question of time,—but of what a time! After two or three desperate struggles, during which he was met at every turn with the skill of a practiced fisherman, he settled sulkily at the bottom of the lake. Meanwhile a gentle east wind had sprung up with the setting sun, and Mr. Page's boat began to drift with it gently to the westward. Fifteen minutes, half an hour, three-quarters of an hour passed, and from our anchorage we could see that the trout showed no signs of yielding,—nor did Mr. Page. As it gradually grew too dark to "cast" with satisfaction, my companion in the other boat and myself decided to haul up anchor and "go to see the fun," which, at our distance from the scene of conflict, seemed to be growing decidedly monotonous. By this time Mr. Page had drifted fully half a mile to the westward, and not once had the trout given any sign of yielding. When we came up with Mr. Page it was quite dark, and the contest, which did not seem so very unequal after all,—for it was yet doubtful which would get the best of it,—had stretched out to a full hour and a quarter. Then at last the trout showed signs of exhaustion, and, yielding to the inevitable pressure of the elastic rod, was once brought near the surface, but not close enough to net. Settling again to the bottom, he had apparently made up his mind to stay there; but the gentle, steady persuasion of the faithful seven-ounce Murphy split bamboo fly rod again proved too much for him, and straining his tackle to the utmost, Mr. Page brought his victim gradually toward the surface. The three boats had now come so close together that the fish was shut in on all sides. But it had become so dark that it was difficult to discern objects with any distinctness, and to shed all the light we could upon the puzzling problem which was at last approaching solution, we got together all the matches we had with us, and made in each boat a miniature bonfire. Soon a commotion upon the surface of the water showed that the

critical moment had arrived. There, with his back fin as erect as ever, was a magnificent trout, which was soon in the landing-net, and in a moment after in the boat, after precisely an hour and a half of as steady and persistent a fight as a fish ever made for life. But his capture was a full reward for all the time and trouble it had cost, since he weighed by the scales full seven pounds.

This trout, and one weighing eight pounds which had been taken by Mr. Crounse, were among the magnificent trophies which were carried away from Bema when we broke camp a day or two afterward. And the scene upon that memorable morning was one to which it is difficult to do justice with pen or pencil. There was the batteau laden with all the camp paraphernalia, including the pet dog Prince. As passengers, there were the two leaders of the party, Messrs. Page and Crounse, each with his two boys, while the guides pulled the oars. "Dan" Quimby, the faithful cook and profound philosopher, whose "corn dodgers" had been in steady demand and in unfailing supply during the whole time of our stay in camp, was starting off for a ten-mile tramp overland to Madrid, leading the cow which he had brought in with him by the same route a month before, and the "spirit of Mooseluc-maguntic" stripped of its blanket seemed to be dancing in wild glee at the prospect of being left in undisturbed possession of his wild domain. Two or three of us remained behind to catch a few more trout, and in the hope of a less boisterous passage to the main camp. After a day or two we followed, taking with us delightful memories of the camp at Bema, and trout enough to excite the envy of the less successful anglers at the other end of the lake.

THE NET RESULT.

2
Salmon
Fishing on
Snake River
(1895)

SALMON FISHING ON SNAKE RIVER.

By Frank C. Read.

ALMOST anywhere along the windings of the Snake River, from where it joins the Columbia to its head-waters in Wyoming, it is possible to catch the salmon.

According to some authorities, what I have designated as salmon are really salmon-trout, which feed in fresh water and do not return to the ocean. Whether they are salmon or salmon-trout, they are game, and vary in weight from ten to forty pounds.

I was spending a holiday in Idaho, when my host, Bob, introduced me to the Judge and to salmon fishing as practiced in the West. The run of fish began about the end of December.

It took thirty minutes' rowing and towing to get the boat one-half mile up the swift current of the river, and then we were at the fishing ground. The whole procedure was new to me, and I had formed but little opinion about the utensils of war and the mode of operating them ; but I accepted everything quietly, until they produced lines with two or three-ounce sinkers dangling from the end; then I wanted to start for home. I explained that I had come to capture a game fish and not to angle on the bottom, as if for suckers or sturgeon. My friends did not pitch me out of the boat, as later developments showed they should have done; but my friend Bob took a long and, apparently, pitying glance at me and then said: "Just wait, Sonny! If you hook a good big salmon to-day you will think you have game enough." And I waited.

We each had an unjointed bamboo pole, to which was fastened a reel containing from two hundred to three hundred feet of braided silk line. Attached to each line were a sinker and a treble hook, i. e., three hooks soldered together at such angles that when a fish has once gorged the thing, disgorgement is almost an impossibility. The bait used was salmon-roe.

After baiting our hooks, tying on the roe with pink-colored thread, we drifted with the current some three hundred yards to where an eddy began; then we turned in toward the river-bank, so as to strike this eddy and let us return nearly to the starting point.

"You must keep your sinker just above the bottom," said Bob.

The sinker is about two feet above the hook; when it is just grazing the bottom you may be reasonably sure that the hook is tumbling around over the gravel and stones of the river, where the salmon look for food.

I consumed most of the time of the first float feeling for the bottom with my sinker, so that my hook might "find the bottom" as instructed. We caught no fish. Then we returned and tried it again.

This time, after two or three cautious locations of the bottom with my sinker, I suddenly felt a tug on my pole and I struck. Away went my line up-stream at a rapid rate, while my reel sang a merry tune. I had him set down for at least a forty-pounder, the pull was so great. Then came an extra surge and the pole snapped, but I grasped the line with my gloved hands and drew it in slowly and steadily, until I knew he was nearing the surface; then, gaff in hand, I waited, until from the green of the deep water there emerged—about fifteen pounds of the river mud and a pair of dead-men's shoes. At least I supposed they were dead-men's shoes because, subsequently, I angled up his coat and trousers, and the Snake is much given to disgorging an unfortunate prospector at irregular intervals.

My hook had caught on the stones at the bottom, and the tugging at the line was caused by the current driving our boat down-stream faster than the reel could run out. What I had thought to be my line scurrying up-stream was, in fact, the boat rapidly drifting from the place where my hook remained fastened to the bottom. When I realized all this, I passed a number of remarks, in rapid succession, my companions keeping surprisingly quiet. They afterwards confided to me that they remembered we were close to town, and that I knew the way there.

I was rowed ashore, where I repaired my fishing pole while the others made two or three runs, during one of which the Judge hooked a ten-pounder and had hauled him into the boat before the fish realized that anything was wrong.

Presently, I tried it again. This time I did not feel so assiduously for the bottom and got along better. I saw the Judge make a strike. His line ran out a little and then slackened. The fish had got off the hook.

Then Bob made a strike, and just as I opened my lips to tell him that he had hooked him, I felt a tug at my own line. I struck hard and—whew-w!—I knew it was not shoes this time.

There was a mighty swirl of the water, a broad fin and tail flashed into view, then away sped my line across the stream, with the water flying from in front of it. How the reel did sing! And how he did pull! My pole was about fourteen feet long, but it was bent so that I could reach out my hand and nearly touch the tip. I put the brake on the large reel, and also pressed the line, where it left the reel, hard against the pole. A hole was burned in my glove and my hand was blistered as the line ran out, but still the fish sped on. Some one hundred and fifty feet away a shining, silvery body sprung high into the air and fell back, with a loud splash, and amid a cloud

of spray. Then he went to the bottom and sulked.

I was not sorry; it gave me an opportunity to replenish my reel. Fifty feet more of a run, and he would have been gone, for my line was nearly out and, once the end was reached, it would no more have held him than it could have held a young bullock. So I reeled up with alacrity, as the judge rowed us over to where my catch lay sulking, and not until I had taken up all the line did I feel master of the situation again.

Then I began to pull my prize around a bit to see if he was tractable. He was not. When ready, he took a spurt down-stream that would have done credit to a 'varsity crew for speed. Just then Bob's fish (I had been entirely too busy to watch his manœuvres) concluded it would go up-stream, and there we were! Strung out between the two salmon, with our reels being rapidly emptied and no means at hand to stop it. The boat could not follow both fish at once to prevent our losing line, and it was equally certain that unless something was done, very shortly, the end, both of the line and the episode, was at hand.

Something of this sort came into my mind, and I was trying to calculate how much of my tackle the salmon would take with him as we parted company, when Bob took a quick glance at my nearly spent reel, then turned to his own and stopped it dead, at the same time that he gave a heavy surge on his pole. There was a sharp ping of the line and then it lay limp and still on the water.

Praise be given unto this friend of mine! He had seen that my line was nearly out, and rather than that I, the enthusiast, with his first salmon well hooked, should lose that prize, he had deliberately broken his tackle and allowed his own catch to escape. If he have transgressions, may Heaven shrive him!

Away sped my salmon, actually towing the large boat. He kept up the gait for, perhaps, a quarter of a mile down the river, and then again he shot out of the water, twice his own length, and again sounded to the bottom and sulked. This time we allowed him no interval for rest. I reeled up and we immediately began to break him to lead. Vim had departed from him

They say if a fish runs with the current any distance he suffocates. As to this I do not know, but I do know that this one never had the same amount of energy after his down-stream run. I pulled him around for a time and he made a weak run or two, but I was always able to prevent him heading away from me, and it is only in this straightaway pull that they can exert their strength. Then they can lean up against the hook, very much as a horse settles into the collar for a hard pull, and snap your line in an instant, if you do not let it play out to them. This fellow would flash from side to side of the boat as far as the forty feet of line would allow, but I kept him snubbed up too closely for him to get a start, so we had no great difficulty in gradually worrying him down, until he permitted us to tow him to the bank. The Judge waded out, gaffed him, and then my first salmon was securely captured.

After this we sat on the river's bank and smoked the pipe of contentment. I, perhaps, more than the others, for they were in haste to return and secure more salmon. I was not—I had had enough for the time; had drunk to satiety, and intuitively felt that, though I should catch unlimited numbers of far finer fish; though I should struggle with them stoutly and long, smash tackle and have a generally uproarious time, I would never again feel the same thrill of unadulterated joy that was mine when I had this magnificent creature on the end of a two-hundred-foot line, and he conducting himself as if he were lord of the earth and the waters thereof.

I was now content to turn my tackle over to Bob and sit down and row the boat, while the others fished, so we rowed up to the fishing ground once more and settled down to work.

My two friends were veterans in the sport and took things more coolly than I had done, so, as I sat and watched them, I learned some things and unlearned others. The Judge, I noticed, did not use his reel more than was absolutely necessary. He seemed to be out for fish and nothing else; the appetite of the chase was upon him. When he hooked a salmon, his only thought seemed to be to get it off his

hook so that he could capture another. It was in his way. He would make them fight for every inch of line they took and, if possible, would drag them into the boat before they knew they were caught.

Fewer fish escaped from him than from Bob, but somehow I liked the latter's way the better. So long as a fish possessed the power to pull and the disposition to do so, Bob was indifferent to its being this one or some other yet in the river. He would allow them to take line according to their weight, and then have it out with them on a more equal basis.

And sometimes one would take line without his permitting it, for you do not know how large a salmon is until you have felt the strength of him, and then it is often too late. You find you should not have allowed him latitude, because by it he is beyond your control. After a salmon reaches a certain weight, say thirty pounds, there is no reason for being lenient with him. He will amuse you enough without your feeding him line to play with, and will keep you very busy preventing him from smashing things and severing all connecting ties between you.

The fish on this occasion bit freely, and my two companions kept me busy rowing to the shore with them, where they could wade out and gaff their prizes. At one time the Judge and Bob each had a fish hooked at the same time, but no complications arose; the Judge quickly pulled his into the boat and got it out of the way of other prospective victims, and Bob could not coax a vigorous run out of his fish.

A mishap which befell the Judge ended the sport.

The Judge is much given to periods of abstraction, during which he sometimes performs some peculiar acts. The fish, during one particular float, were biting voraciously and the Judge, having caught one and unhooked it, was in great haste to secure another. He was wondering if Bob would hook one before he could get back to his fishing again; and, as he wondered, he baited his hook, fastened on the bait with the thread, picked up the scissors and, instead of cutting the thread on the bait, he deliberately cut his line just above

Painted for OUTING by Marc Lucas.

"STRUNG OUT BETWEEN TWO SALMON."

the sinker and nonchalantly cast hook and sinker overboard. As they left his hand he awoke from his abstraction enough to realize what he had done; then, with eyes straining to watch the downward course of his baited hook, he said: "There, that's gone!" That was all. He was too used to himself to be surprised at anything he might do. We had started so late in the day that by the time a new sinker and hook could be prepared it would be nightfall, so we concluded to go home. They had eight salmon in all—enough for any reasonable minded person, I think, though none of them weighed more than eighteen pounds.

Up in the other end of the boat I had one—one only—but far too fine to associate with such fry as they had caught, so I kept him aloof and free from taint of association. I will not say how much he weighed—you would not believe me.

3
A Bit
About
Bass
(1900)

A BIT ABOUT BASS.

By E. W. Sandys.

WHEN soft June airs rustle the leaves of uncounted growths, when birds are busy with their young, when lakes flash like gems, and the larger streams run clear and slow, then come the days of the bass fisher. They are, indeed, halcyon days, when it is good for a man to be out of doors, enjoying to the full the glorious sunshine, the bursts of bird music, and the beauty of the 'world at its best.

There are two varieties of the black bass, the small-mouth and the large-mouth. Both are good, and both are game upon any sort of tackle. There have been many discussions over the relative merits of these two fish, but to my mind the small-mouth bass is much the better fighter, and far superior to his cousin upon the board.

Both varieties of bass are widely distributed. The waters of the Great Lakes system abound with them, and one or the other may be found in most of the important lakes and rivers of the Northeast, East, and Southeast. In Southern waters the bass is frequently termed " trout," but it is hardly necessary to say that he bears no resemblance whatever to the jeweled beauty of which so much that is true and false has been written.

While I and many other anglers may be safely set down as admirers of the brook trout above all other fresh-water fish, it does not follow that the bass is greatly, if at all, inferior to the spangled beauty of storied fame. The trout is an aristocrat of his race, a gaudy gallant, a swell fellow in fish circles, yet game and clever as your highbred gentleman should be. The bass may be taken to represent the sturdier upper class. Grim, stout, and self-reliant, he prefers to depend upon his own fearlessness and rather rough and ready methods to carry him through. He goes into a scrimmage as though his heart were in the right place, and his hurricane tactics and defiant struggle never fail to command respect.

When in the humor no fresh-water fish will bite more freely or force the fighting faster. All he asks is a fair field and no favor, and when he yields to a skilled hand the successful angler has every reason for a little self-gratulation.

But the bass, while a voracious feeder, is frequently capricious over his choice of food. What he will greedily take one day, he may, for no apparent reason, refuse the next ; hence he frequently is a puzzle to all but the most resourceful of anglers. This uncertainty about appetite is one of his marked peculiarities, and to get the better of it may tax the angler's skill to the utmost.

To judge from my own experience, I should class the natural baits, as crayfish, minnows, and worms, for all-round effectiveness in order as named. The white larvæ of the cockchafer and the bee frequently prove deadly. Grasshoppers caught near the stream often prove irresistible, while a small, green and lively frog is by no means to be despised. Plump worms are good, if the hook be liberally supplied, and a big bumble-bee may land a trick.

I use the standard bass hooks upon fine gimp or heavy gut. These are large and strong and admirably adapted to their purpose. In baiting with worms I put on plenty, looping them here and there and leaving a half inch of head or tail free. When using minnows (shiners are the only reliable ones), I pass the hook in at the mouth, then out through the gill, and finally bed the barb in the flesh just above the tail. This is the reverse of the usual way ; but I find it answers very well. I keep the bait moving in a natural headforemost manner by means of a slight turning of the wrist. A bass seizing this bait, will either grab it crosswise or by the tail, and then bore toward his stronghold before swallowing. If given plenty of time he will flirt the minnow around so as to take it head first in swallowing. This is natural, but I do not wait for it.

Upon the first twitch I strike sharply and trust to luck. The bass has the minnow either crosswise or tail first in his first grab, and in either event the hook has two chances of taking hold. Two to one is good odds, and I trust to it. If given time the bass will reverse the bait, and in so doing he may find either the hooks or the gimp, and promptly reject the imagined dainty. When hooked head upward the minnow plays in a natural manner ; if hooked merely through the lips it may be taken without giving a chance to plant the barb firmly, and good minnows are scarce. If hooked first through the lips and then through the skin of the back, or the back fin, there is still a goodly portion of it at which a fish may grab with impunity. Therefore, I hook the bait as described, and strike at the first sign, without giving any chances for gorging at. leisure and subsequent trouble in removing a fairly swallowed hook.

When using white grubs I pass the hook in at the mouth, or just below it, and on to the tail. This gives a natural curve, which few bass can resist. When the bait is crayfish I pass the barb in at the mouth and through to the tail. This also gives the important natural curve, and a bait so rigged and sent down with Mr. So-and-So's compliments, is well-nigh irresistible.

Another important point is that baits so rigged may serve two or three times. This is no trifling matter, when fish are biting freely. As a rule, crayfish, frogs, minnows, and so on, are difficult to secure in numbers, and the more service one can be made to render, the better. And furthermore, a bait so rigged will almost invariably slide up the gimp, or the gut, at the fish's first rush, and so be preserved to do another turn. This, too, is important.

When using a frog I pass the hook first through the lips and then through the skin at the juncture of the legs with the back. In this position the frog can kick out and swim more or less, and in so doing make himself the more attractive. The grasshopper and the bee may be hooked crosswise behind the wings, and so serve their purpose.

The rods, reels, and lines for this bait fishing may be selected from the stock of any first-class tackle-shop. Tell the dealer what you want the tools for, and he will consult his own interests by properly supplying you with the best he has. Creels are an abomination for bass fishing. If one be fishing from a boat, raft, or, as often happens, from the shore, his best plan is to string his fish upon a stout cord with a suitable crosspiece fastened to one end so as to prevent escapes. This string can be fastened to the boat, or to whatever root or snag may prove convenient, and the tethered fish may be kept alive and moved at will until the day is done.

The fly-fisher will probably find his best sport during the latter half of June, before the sun has warmed the water too much. Useful flies include the following : Rube Wood, Furgerson, Henshall, Seth Green, Chubb, Chenee, Coachman, Silver Doctor, Lord Baltimore, Polka, Oriole, Grizzly King, Montreal, Magpie, and Parmachenee Belle.

Various spoons and artificial minnows, too, occasionally prove deadly when trolling, or whipping with the rod. The best way to prove their merit upon a certain day and water is to try them. If they prove attractive, well and good; if the reverse, try something else. Bass are capricious.

Trolling with the long hand-line is, upon many waters, a deadly method. For this I use a braided line and the standard silver and gold spoons—the former for bright and the latter for dull days. If one can hire a rower, so much the easier, but he is not a necessity. I usually do my own rowing and take a turn of the line about the right leg, above the knee, where it will be within easy reach of the right hand.

By this method the hands are left free to manipulate the oars, while one cannot fail to feel any attack upon the spoon. And here let me say that the slightest pull upon the line should receive prompt attention. It may be caused by a fish, a snag, a weed, or by touching bottom. If a fish, well and good ; if a snag, at once check forward motion, then back up to the hook and free it ; if a weed, as is frequently the case, pull in and clear the hooks, for there is no use whatever in dragging the smallest fragment of green stuff, as no sane bass will take a hook so decorated.

My favorite craft for trolling is a canoe, as it is easily managed by one who knows the peculiarities of the craft. I attach my paddle to a stout cord so that it may be dropped and recovered at will. The line is made fast to a thwart and looped about either wrist, or when not smoking, which is seldom, is held between the teeth. A bass is so impetuous that he is almost certain to hook himself and to afford plenty of time for the hands to assume control.

The size of the bass taken depends more or less (usually *more*) upon the imagination of the fisherman.

"THIS PLACE LOOKS BASSY, EVERY FOOT OF IT."

Some of the finest bass I have ever seen were taken on trolls from lakes St. Clair and Erie, and, perhaps, the very largest of these may have weighed six pounds, and this by careful estimate. I have killed fish which weighed plump five pounds upon tested scales, and this some hours after the fish had been taken from the water, which means that, had they been truly weighed at the moment of capture, they would have scored a bit more. Taking the statements of recognized authorities upon this subject, the superior limit of weight of the small-mouthed bass may be set at about eight and one-half pounds. The large-mouthed variety runs much heavier, twenty odd pounds being quite possible. If those who speak positively of small-mouthed bass of eight pounds or so would only bear in mind the fact that such fish must needs be about two feet long, there would be fewer exaggerators.

Another matter about which many misleading statements have been made is the leaping power of the bass. Some writers speak of leaps four or five feet high, as if these acrobatic performances were common occurrences. This is all wrong. The small-mouthed bass certainly can and does leap freely, both when at play and when struggling upon the hook, but I have yet to see a hooked fish rise more than at most three feet above the surface, except it be whizzing shoreward at the end of some novice's tackle. The large-mouthed fish will rise to the surface and thrash about, but I have never seen one leave the water in any considerable leap.

Now let us glance at one of many golden days in which the bass have played the leading and the writer the misleading part.

Imagine a perfect June morning, with the air full of sunshine, song, and sweetness. It is not so very early, for I am lazy anyway, and bass are not much better. Fly and bait tackle, and plenty of worms dug the night before, are in the canoe, the old dog leads the way, and presently we are off, the dog in pure content, I in flannel shirt, old trousers, soft hat, and broken shoes. There is no cramping style about our outings. We are out for the fun, and we are going to have it or find out why.

The canoe slides rapidly for a mile before the first likely spot is reached. The dog can translate *Quo Vadis*, and

could he talk English would say, " I know—you put in under yonder tree, and you try the big, half-submerged log." He, being captain, must be obeyed.

While the rods are being shipped up, some big fish strikes at an unseen quarry, and makes broadening circles upon the oily water. This settles the matter of fly or bait, and soon the daintier tool is sending the feathered deceits over the promising spot. Fly after fly is tried in vain, then an artificial grasshopper is substituted. This provokes a rise, but the fish is only curious, and has no intention of taking hold. Presently the fly-tackle is laid aside, and the bait outfit brought into service. Fat worms are strung upon the hook, and sent to where they should do most good, but they tempt nothing, and presently the canoe glides on.

This trying of point after point along a pretty stream is to me the best of bass fishing. The nature of the fish impels it to ambush itself in the shelter of sunken stuff, piles, big stones, and the like ; and from these hides it lances forth upon whatever prey may happen within range. An oily roll upon the surface, or a faint, swift streak in the water may betray the lair of the black buccaneer ; the next thing is to find out what he is after. It most frequently is a minnow. Try one; should it fail, try something else, and, if needs be, keep on trying until you light upon the popular item.

The crayfish should do the work when nothing else will tempt. This bait hides under sunken stuff, stones, etc. Why it craves seclusion might be explained by any sizable bass. To secure the crayfish, cautiously raise sunken stuff until the nipping fellow is revealed upon the bottom, then steal a hand toward him until he can be secured. There is an art in this which can be mastered only by practice. The nip of a crayfish is a trifle which cannot hurt any hand fit to wave the wand of a true angler. Do not worry about the crayfish which escape and go darting tail first to deep water. They, if they be wise in their generation, will soon come hustling back, for a big-mouthed black peril haunts the outer shades.

The canoe glides on to another promising spot where a sunken tree is overhung by the canopy of a sturdier mate. This place looks bassy, every foot of it, and worms are sent farther and farther from the tree until the accessible water has been covered. Then a halt is called for fifteen minutes' smoke upon the bank, during which everything quiets down. Meanwhile, eyes are busy watching the water and deciding where the next trial shall be.

A medium-sized crayfish is selected, artistically impaled, and sent upon its mission. And now comes bass-fishing that is bass-fishing! A dusky demon has been lurking out there all this while, and he hoists his piratical flag and clears for action.

Zip! Whish! The lithe rod curves almost to the breaking-point, the silk cuts the water in a fierce zig-zagging, the restraining thumb is lifted from the reel, and its thin, metallic voice rises in that grand old song which only a good reel can sing. Now for it! Away he goes, and yard after yard of line hisses through the guides. Check him! You might as well try to check a wild engine with a pack-thread. This first mad rush is all his and he *will* have it. Forty yards away he pauses for a moment to consider. Long distances are not his forte. He is getting away from his favorite lair, so he suddenly concludes to come back.

This is a critical moment, for woe be to the rod's chance if he can get slack. Rapid reeling and the wonderful spring of the dainty wand prevent this. Again and once again he steams away, only to be steadily hampered by that delicate yet persistent force which, though ever yielding, never yields outright.

He comes to the surface and lashes the water into a snowy spume and fails. For an instant his massive shape is plainly revealed; then, like a glancing light, he is off again. This time his run is shorter, for he knows such tactics will not avail. Another pause, a couple of savage jerks, and then he bores down and down in a desperate endeavor to reach the friendly bottom where he can rub from his jaw its troublesome jewelry. But the steady lift of the rod halts him, and baffled once more, he decides to try his best ruse. He is mad all through, and he will find out who or what dares to thwart his royal will.

Zip! Up he comes as though flung from some submarine torpedo. There are a swish and a splash, a scatter of shining drops, a glimpse of a gleaming bronze shape a yard above the surface, then a plunge, a sullen wallop, and he is gone. Next he remembers his favorite shelter and darts for it. Once there, among the twigs which so often have sheltered him, he surely will get rid of the thing which is driving him frantic. Vain hope! The unseen power drags and drags at him: do what he will, he can go so far and no farther. It is outrageous, it is monstrous, and he will now see about it once and for all!

Up he flashes and for the first time sees the cause of the trouble. "It" *is* outrageous and it *is* monstrous. Something awful is standing upon his favorite log. It is bigger than the lazy old sturgeon which he once met in the lake below. It has terrible eyes which glare with ferocity; its tail is all split up and it stands on the two tips; its fins are long and utterly unlike any fins he has ever seen!

For the first time in his life he experiences fear. What! Go near that hideous monstrosity? Not for all the crayfish and shiners that ever lived would he again look at that damnable form which stands there like a tree and waits.

In his terror he forgets all his tricks. Any way, and any place rather than nearer that thing, is his thought as he darts to and fro and strains for dear life. The crayfish, the accursed cause of all the trouble, slips from his jaw and rises above him, but he cares naught about the loss. He jerks and backs, snapping at the curious affair which clings to his jaw; he sweeps his broad tail from side to side in a life or death effort; then a deadly numbness steals over him and soon a glare of light tells him he is at the surface, yards from his dearly-loved retreat.

Through a film of water he sees the thing again. He is dimly conscious that it is moving now and that it appears ten times worse than it did before; then, with a despairing, gasping shudder, he turns upon his back too weak for further struggle, too terrified to more than wiggle his fins in feeble protest.

He feels some crushing things close between his gills; he misses the life-giving water, and in a mingled agony of fright and rage he strives to rouse himself for one more effort. He stiffens his late invincible armament of spines in vain. Something rasps between his gills ; again he feels the water, and weary and faint of heart as he is, he can yet endeavor to reach his home. Vain hope. Some all-powerful restraint holds him, and after sullenly tugging for a while, he gives up and awaits his final end, like the heart-broken captive king he is.

No more sport for the present at this place, so the canoe glides on for a hundred yards or more. This time it pauses at the mouth of a small stream famed for its bass. A brace of good fish are killed here, and then, stage by stage, from one well-known point to the next, the sport is continued.

In time a rest is decided upon, and man and dog seek a soft, grassy slope, where they divide their lunch. Then follows a period of sweet content, while the two lie there in brotherly peace. With his shapely nose resting upon his master's leg, the dog sees through half-shut eyes the sleepy river, the creeping shadows, and the birds flitting to and fro. His sensitive ears twitch in response to the plash of a leaping fish or the hiss of a rapid wing. Not for worlds would he move, for this to him is heaven, so far as his grand nature can understand it.

And the man—he just lies there, seeing through faint wreaths of smoke the beauty and the glory of it all. He, too, hears the plashing fish and by its sound he knows its name and lineage. The fluting of birds, the hum of insects are in his ears, and from all the sweet confusion he can identify every sound that floats upon the scented breeze.

Hark ! From some field above comes a mellow piping, " Bob-white ! Bob-bob-white ! " Dog and man hear it together. The smoke ceases curling upward, while the dog half raises his head. " Bob-bob-whi-te ! " Louder and clearer rings the call, and the dog's grand eye rolls round till it catches the amused glance of his master. The mute exchange of glances is pregnant with meaning. No further movement is made, for the leaf must turn and that call be changed before the full magic of it can assert itself.

The shadows creep on and on, until, at last, the man moves. Like a flash the dog is upon his feet and fairly dancing in sheer delight. Fain would he go to further investigate the cause of the whistling, but a word restrains him. Once more the canoe is pushed off, her shapely nose this time pointed homeward.

On and on she steals, faint music whispering from her bow and from the trailing bass astern.

" The day is done, and the darkness
     Falls from the wings of night."

The raven broods the earth, but still through the scented glooms bird-vespers are sighing soft farewells to what has been a perfect day. The dog is curled up in lazy content, the man kneels in the stern, sending the slow paddle stealing along the side. Behind him floats a filmy wreath, rich with the subtle spice of his offering to Diana, then canoe and all vanish into velvet shades, the queen-star dances on a fading wake, and my golden day is over.

4
Anglers
of the
Wharf
(1902)

OUTING

VOL. XL   JULY, 1902   NO. 4

THE ANGLERS OF THE WHARF

By LEONIDAS HUBBARD, Jr.

AS the streams are to the country, so are the docks on its water front to every great city. Thither go the anglers when the itching to fish comes over them. There are boys in America, men too, I suspect, who doubt whether the docks were made for steamer landings or for the accommodation of fishermen. Most steamer lines have a great deal of sympathy for the anglers and allow them full use of their landings. The dock fisherman, like the man who goes to the streams, finds varying luck in different regions. At Chicago, Detroit, Cleveland, or any one of a hundred smaller cities of the Great Lake waters the angler takes perch, fine ringed fellows that average a pound in weight. Now and then, too, he takes a bass or pike; and tales cling about the fishermen's haunts of sturgeon and muskallonge captured in other generations.

The coming of the carp was a boon to the dock fishermen of inland waters. Expert anglers, professional fishermen, and patriotic icthyologists may complain as they will of the carp nuisance; the dock fisherman will be glad. When the farmers who started in to make their fortunes by carp culture grew tired of the experiment and drained their ponds, carp poured into the tributaries of most of our inland waters. Now they are numerous, and will bite rather readily at bread crusts or little balls of dough, which, if held together by cotton, make very good bait. As a result it is not infrequent that the man out of work or the small boy will carry home a fish big enough to make dinners for a family for three days.

But, after all, the fish taken count little in the thronging of the docks, except that it adds to the self-respect of some of the fishermen to show returns for the time spent. If the angler can show a good catch or has hopes of making one he will look you squarely in the face. Otherwise he will look out on the water or down at the plank. The fishermen on the Manhattan docks have little real hope; so if you walk among them as a stranger your presence will cause uneasiness. The red faced man with the sandy mustache will puff harder at his cigar. The scholarly appearing young man will take pains to hint that he is out for the air. The well-to-do-looking man will gaze away in feigned abstraction. The young barkeep will yawn and say, "Awh, t'ell wid such fishin'!" Your departure will bring rejoicing; yes, and shame, too, for away down in his heart every one of them will feel that he has been guilty of cowardice in offering an apology for his love of the water.

It is a shameful state of affairs that makes us take this apologetic attitude when caught fishing. The trouble all lies in the old sophistry that men who like to sit on the bank of stream or lake and watch a float or wait for the feel of a bite must necessarily be of the shiftless sort. This planet is covered with sordid men who demand that he who spends time fishing shall show returns in fish. And we have very foolishly attempted to answer them on their own premises. I know a man who will leave his work, drive ten miles, pay boat hire, buy minnows, and generously tip the stable boy, to go home at night with an average of half a dozen bass. And he honestly explains these excursions with the statement that he is procuring food for his family and friends. One day

"T'aint the lyin' out nights an' gittin' cold I mind. It's the goin' home without fish. My wife don't want me to go, and when I don't get fish my life's hell."

Into such predicaments does our false position lead us. It is time we declared our independence of the sordid ones, and announced to the world that we do not care a rap for the fish or for their opinion, that we like to sit on the bank, or to wade the stream, or stand in the bow of a boat, and that the reason is *because*.

When the shad are running and men in

"All fish on in peace."

Photograph by Jas. Burton.

I sat on a log in the midst of a Michigan pine slashing and looked at a big bony graduate of the lumber woods who sat on the other end. We had been caught the day before fifteen miles from a house by rain and a cold wave, had lain out all night in a swamp, and now, after five miles of running over natural obstacles, had seen the lumber train round the bend on the side toward civilization. There had been no supper nor breakfast, and now the big man weakened. In a voice that made me wonder why the tears did not come, he wailed:

boats are bringing them in from the nets, one auburn haired youth of Manhattan preys upon this weakness of fishermen for financial gain. He meets a boat and then walks down the docks with a string of fine shad in each hand. He approaches a group of anglers to say:

"Here, gents, have some fine shad to take home to your wives."

His visit is well timed. The sun is low and every angler dreads an empty-handed homegoing. The well-to-do-looking man and the red faced man with the sandy mustache buy fish at twenty-five cents each.

Photograph by Jas. Burton.

" The happy old ' regular.' "

If you come to know the auburn haired youth he will confide in you that, " Youse can buy 'em at the boats for ten cents, but these gents is easy." One can very easily imagine the return of the purchasers of shad, and the admiration of their fond families. Some day a well-to-do-looking man will present a shad to a wife who knows enough of fishes to be certain shad never bite the hook, and in that day there will be looks that make words seem tame and inadequate things.

that has not trout, but suckers, catfish, and eels. That creek is calling and calling, and he wants to go. But the stream is a hundred or a thousand miles away; so once in a year he breaks away from the things that are conventionally proper and takes his place with the fishers at the docks. You may always know him by the light bass rod which has seen service on lakes and streams. Then, too, he casts with the swing of a man who would drop a minnow lightly in an eddy where a bass is lying.

" Below the railroad track."   Photograph by Jas. Burton.

The well-to-do-looking man goes to the docks once a year. He lived in the country when a boy. Now when the leaves come out he begins to think about the creek. Then he forgets his engagement to lunch, and instead of reading his paper on the way down town in the morning sits looking away off into infinite distance. If his early home was in the mountains he sees a trout stream that tumbles over stones and dashes out of sight under an arch of overhanging cedars. If he lived in a level country he sees a more sluggish stream

The red faced man reels in his line, takes his rod in both hands, and, whirling around, sends the half-pound sinker flying through the air like a missle from a sling, until it drops in the water, with a mighty splash, a hundred feet away.

Fishing, for the red faced man, begins not as a pleasure, but a duty. Therefore, he begins early in the day. You may see him in the morning making his way to the docks below Riverside Drive. He carries a rod in one hand and a little bag in the other. A bag looks more respectable than a pail. He has been too long in business at "The Place," and the doctor says he must stop drinking and get out of doors or he will have trouble. He has money and might go to the country, but he has not been off Manhattan Island for so long that he does not really know there is a country. He goes to the tackle store and selects a rod. He despises the light things the dealer shows him first and selects one made for deep sea work on the banks, with a reel to match. It is the sort of rod a

first hour or two he wishes for a bite. Then he does one of two things. He jumps up, says, "Doctors be damned," and goes straight away to business, or else he begins to like this sitting by the riverside. In this latter case he takes to looking out upon the water through half closed eyelids, feeling a charm in the fresh air from the ocean and knowing the spell that makes anglers anglers and not common men.

The well-to-do-looking man and the red

"The aristocracy of the docks."

Photograph by Jas. Burton.

facetious dealer, who cannot reconcile the twenty ounce rod with the six inch lafayette, calls the "lobster rod," basing his nomenclature not on the use of the rod, but on his estimation of the user.

The red faced man, if he has a pull—and his specialty is pulls—goes to one of the volunteer lifesaving stations and gets a seat on a little private platform, where he has a chair and finds fishing reduced to its easiest form. The first day is by all odds the best on which to observe the red faced man. It is a critical occasion. For the

faced man are the aristocracy of the docks. You can always tell an aristocrat from one of the common herd because he carries a rod. Members of the herd have no rods. Instead, each has a little wire line-holder. On one end of this is a screw, and on the other end a bell. At the middle is a notch for the line. When the screw has been driven into the dock and the line caught in the notch the angler may forget that he is fishing and think of things far away, for the least tug of the line rings the bell. Sometimes, in midsummer, the anglers turn crab fishers; then the aristocrats bring little wire crab traps which open out on hinges and lie flat on the bottom. When the owner thinks a crab may be nibbling at the beef tied to the centre he pulls; the sides of the trap rise up to form a box, and the crab is landed. The multitude have no traps, but a piece of beef tied to a line does nearly as well, for a crab will hang on until you can draw it to the dock, if you are not too abrupt.

Perhaps an apology is due the angling fraternity for speaking of an aristocratic class. The distinction is purely an external one of appearance and equipment. Down in their hearts there is no caste among anglers. Go down to the docks of the Hudson and watch. The well-to-do-looking man, the red faced man, the young barkeep, the man-out-of-work, and all the rest fish on in peace and mutual sympathy. How can there be caste among men who trade bait and hooks? And how can there be snobbishness among men who understand? If you doubt the mutual understanding, take your own rod or line or crab trap and join the fishermen. The fresh winds from the ocean fan your face. The ripple of the water comes up from the foot of the pier. The sunshine starts new currents of life in your being. Some way you only half remember the fishing, and like a man charmed by music you sit and feel. Now you know why all the others are here. You know why they speak in low tones. You know why peace and goodwill and, above all, common understanding, make these men fellows; fellows, forgetful of difference in wealth or culture or station, as they sit here charmed by the magic spell of wind and sun and waters.

You know why the young barkeep spends his day-off at the river, why the well-to-do-looking man finds it a substitute for the creek of his boyhood, why the man-out-of-work prefers it to the barroom, and why the poor woman now and then comes with her son or her grandson. She does not go to the docks where men congregate, but to the rock piles below the railroad track, somewhere between the Soldiers and Sailors' Monument and Grant's Tomb. You understand, now, the "regular," the poor old "regular" or happy old "regular," as you choose to consider him. His fellows do not call him "regular"; that is the designation given by the workmen, the

lifesavers, and the dock police. Every dock has its "regular" or two. He has been there every day since a time which the dock police do not remember. He comes in midforenoon and goes away at sunset. Sometimes he wears a blue coat, and you know that a pension gives him leisure to indulge his fondness for angling. Again, I regret to say, there is no such mark of honor, but ragged garments speak of stress, financial stress, entirely incompatible with so much enjoyment of the waterside. You cannot help suspecting that he is a confirmed man-out-of-work, and a dejected countenance and long delaying at the day's close tell only too plainly that he dreads an interview with the mistress of his household. He is the Rip Van Winkle of the Metropolis. An idler, you call him; an idler he is called at home; but he is more than that. A mere idler can haunt the barroom or the park more easily than the dock. He is an *angler;* there is in him something of the Waltonian spirit; he knows the charm of the waters and must be admitted to the angling fraternity. Last year a "regular" walked off a dock into the Hudson. When the lifesavers had fished him out one said: "Been here every day for three years. Bad case of nutty." Maybe the lifesaver was right. Genius is a form of insanity.

The "regular" is a good man from whom to seek information. He is never too much interested in fishing to answer questions. He seldom seems interested at all, but puts out his line and spends much time walking up and down the dock, hands in pockets.

"Are they biting?" you ask.

"Not much," answers the "regular," as he has answered other men for years.

"What have you caught?"

"Couple o' eels an' a 'tommy'!"

If you seem interested he unrolls a paper, or brings a pail or a basket or a box—the "regular" long since passed the genteel stage that requires a bag—and displays two eight inch eels and a seven inch "tommy-cod."

"Are they pretty good to eat?"

"They're lots better'n the big ones. Sweeter and tenderer. An' then the eel skins is good for rheumatism an' sprains." Habit is strong, and he is justifying himself on the old lines.

"Do you catch anything but eels and 'tommys'?"

"Bass an' lafayettes, sometimes. A man caught a bass up above here about three weeks ago half as long as my arm. Ain't gettin' any lafayettes this year. They don't run but once in three years, and they come thick last summer."

The docks of Manhattan will never attract the game butcher, nor the man whose delight in fishing is in the mere handling of a big fish on the line. The docks tell the same story day after day, year after year. The spell of the river is on the anglers. Then comes the tinkling of a tiny bell. The young barkeep grabs his line. His fellows turn their heads without a word.

"Must be a 'tommy,'" mutters the young barkeep. But he must pull in the line hand over hand to the very end before he knows, for the half pound sinker would nullify the stoutest "tommy's" struggles. Half an hour later the red faced man reels in, as fast as he can. His fellows turn their heads in doubt as to whether this means a bite or merely a new cast. It is a bite. Another "tommy" flops on the dock beside the heavy sinker. Later on the small boy with a piece of beef tied to his sinker pulls up, very, very gently. There is a crab at the meat. Can he raise it to the dock before the thing lets go? Here is the first real excitement of the day. Breath is held, and all eyes are glued upon the boy and the crab. There! it is on the dock. Now every one walks over and looks at the crab. If it is soft-shelled, the man-out-of-work tells the boy, "It'll make fine eatin'."

When the crab has been dropped into a shoe box which the boy carries, the fishers all turn again to the river. What they have said has been spoken in low tones, the tones of men who listen to music. No one speaks until the well-to-do-looking man turns to the other small boy, the one with the hook and line, and says:

"Here boy, they don't seem to like that fat meat. Try a sandworm." He offers his bait box. Sandworms cost ten cents a dozen, and small boys must often be content with less expensive baits.

After a while a trace of uneasiness comes over the fishers. The whistles are screeching from here and there on both sides of the river; the sun is low in the sky, and the time for homegoing has come.

"Just one more try," says the red faced man, as though he had really been trying all day for fish and was waiting for a bite. When the cast has been made he turns to the small boy and says:

"Here boy, want these worms?"

Then he winds up his line and walks away. There is no talking now. It is as though every one wanted to spend these last few minutes drinking in the fresh air and the ripple of waters before returning to the close city atmosphere and the roar of rushing cars.

One by one, the man-out-of-work, the small boy, the young barkeep, and the rest go their way. The last to leave is the well-to-do-looking man. After the others have gone he sits looking into the west till the lights come out on the other shore. The Hudson has narrowed to the creek; the water's ripple is a distant cowbell, and he is wondering what mother will say when he gets home late for supper, with no fish.

5
Fishing
for a
Cat
(1905)

FISHING FOR A CAT

By FRANCIS W. MATHER

DRAWINGS BY HY S. WATSON

THERE is a great deal written as to how to catch trout and bass, with all their cousins and aunts of game fish included within a Highland Scotch relationship, and epicures have frenzies of anticipation over the delights of fried crokers, broiled pompano and baked red-fish, while all pass by with scorn an humble fish of our Southern waters, which for gameness in fight, toothsomeness and general all around qualities of frier, baker and broiler, is hard to be surpassed—the catfish.

Don't laugh, for that displays ignorance of his excellent qualities, but seriously incline thine ear and learn of the wisdom of cat fishing and how to cook after having caught—of the variety of his tribes, and then hie thee with pole and pan to the streams that flow into Lake Maurepas, and if you have learned your lesson in fishing, and have made due and acceptable sacrifice to the gods of palate and appetite—you shall sit down to a feast of fish that will last long ere satiety come.

The catfish that inhabit the waters of Amite, Tickfaw, Blood, Natalbany and Ponchatoula rivers are in their order of inferiority, the small yellow and black "mud cats," the slender built, quick-striking, hard-fighting blue, or "channel" cats, and the broad-headed, big-mouthed, heavy-bodied and rather sullen "Opelousas," or "Tabby cats;" last so called on account of the peculiar marks and spots which give it

He keeps up the fight until landed.

a resemblance to a tortoise-shell house cat. These fish are found in all of the streams of the southland, but in greater quantity, and of infinitely more edibility in those streams that empty into land-locked salt lakes, such as Lakes Pontchartrain and Maurepas. There is no doubt that their alternate sojourning in the saline lake waters and the cold spring waters of the upper portion of these streams, vastly improves their flesh, and when they are eaten with hot corn bread and strong black coffee—gormandizing becomes almost a virtue. The natives of these parts do not as a rule fish for the mere sport ; it's fish to eat they are after, but if the most ardent rod and reel man who has killed pike, pickerel, salmon or trout would be lucky to hook a ten or twelve pound "blue cat," he'd have a fight on his hands that would amply satisfy his sporting blood.

In Tickfaw River the blue cats are the fattest, finest and gamiest; and where the stream narrows naturally, or where saw logs have been thrown in to await the down-rushing flood that will bear them to the boom at tide-water—in these swift waters the catfish, especially the blue cats, gather to the feast of little fishes who try to run the gauntlet of their swift striking jaws. Almost any kind of bait will tempt them, but in the full green leaf of spring there is a peculiar, large caterpillar, found only on the Catalpa trees (where it feeds on its large, juicy leaves that resemble the mulberry leaves) and so is known as the "Catalpa worm," and the catfish never has been hatched yet that could resist taking a snap at this bait. The big red earth worms, large as lead-pencils, and found in old stables, offer plenty inducement to a hungry catfish, and the intestines and white stomach of perch are a tidbit with which to tempt a partly gorged "tabby cat." The last are not often hooked, for the very good reason that the blue cats are too swift in striking, but when one takes hold, the experienced fisherman knows at once what kind of a fish is at the end of his line. There is a rush, a swift dart for the bottom, one or two plunges, and, except for a sullen backward pull, the fight is all over and one is sure of his fish if the line holds. Not so with the blue cat—he fights to the last, flops like mad when he is landed on the bank, and the fisherman is never sure of his

game until he has him on a string, back from the water. And beware of those sharp side fins when the hook is being extracted!

On Tickfaw River at the big "cut off," a few miles below Centerville, in Livingston Parish, the writer fought a sixteen-pound blue cat for nearly two hours. The pool was at the foot of a steep bank twelve feet high, and as there were several old sunken saw logs in the pool, Mr. Blue had the fight in waters of his own choosing. He made rushes to right and left, with sudden dashes at the bottom to get under one of the logs and snap the line, with occasional leaps out of the water like a salmon, when he would savagely shake his head in an endeavor to get free of the hook. That was his undoing, for it wrapped the line round and round his gills and each struggle drew it tighter and seemed to choke the very life and spirit out of him—until finally he rolled over and lay gasping. A companion of the fisher climbed down the steep bank and with a long hooked stick drew his blue majesty out of the water.

But when you are out for meat, there are two preferred methods of taking the cat, one with the "trot line," and the other with set hooks. The trouble with the former is, that after it has been baited for a few days the gars find the place and take off the bait almost as fast as the fisher can put it on. So the location has to be changed frequently. If a spot cannot be readily found where the line can reach across the stream, a good plan (and one which the writer has found successful and prefers) is to fasten one end of the line high up on a tree on the bank, then weight the other end of the line heavily and carry it in a boat diagonally down, not up stream, and drop the weighted end in deep water. With hooks strung on short lines and baited with small perch, there is something to tempt the fish at every depth of water, from a few inches below the surface to the bottom, where the gars seldom hunt. They seek their prey nearer the surface, and for this reason are so troublesome about a straight-across trot line.

And a word just here about the gar—the shark of fresh waters—is very apropos. He is an ugly brute, sly and cruel, but if he runs all the catfish away from your line and gets caught himself, eat him out of revenge, and the next time you catch one of his brethren you'll fry and eat the second one because the first was so succulent. The meat is snow-white, firm and deliciously toothsome, and it is surprising that the meat of this fish—though he be of mon- for a rain that has muddied the water and caused a slight rise in the river. Then the catfish begin to swim up stream, feeding along close to the banks in little bays and eddies where the smaller fish have taken refuge from the rush of waters. Set out

Beware of those sharp fins when extracting the hook.

strous ugliness—has not yet found its way to the tables of epicures.

The most catfish are taken on set lines tied to swinging limbs, which give play to the fish that are hooked. Choose a dark night, for catfish are shy of biting at baits that they can see distinctly, or better wait your lines before dark so that you can see how to choose well the location of each hook, if they are to be visited during the night, and bait the hooks with small perch. Fasten the hook through the fleshy part of the perch's back, just in front of the dorsal fin. This will not hurt him, and a perch so fastened will swim and play around for hours, and proportionally offer a more attractive bait to the feeding catfish. Another excellent morsel is spring-frog, artistically put by being hooked through the back with his hind legs tied with a string to the shank of the hook, thus giving the frog the appearance of having just dived into the water. Catfish thinks so—makes a rush and a gobble, and—well, he's your meat if the line holds.

If one is hard put to it, woodpeckers, sparrows, any kind of birds, plucked and quartered, make good bait, but the intestines of a chicken strung on a hook during the "fall rise" will break up catfish families in a surprising manner. It is well to visit your set hooks and swinging lines at least once during the night, and as soon after daylight as possible, as man is not alone in his love for its delicate flesh. Gars and turtles quickly find when a fish is helplessly hooked and tear it to pieces, and water snakes will also attack them. Only a few days since, the writer, while passing along the banks of a big ditch, tributary to one of the small streams of this section, witnessed a curious sight. A large moccasin had swallowed a little catfish, head first, until his mouth reached the side and back fins

which the fish had erected in self defense. There he lay, unable to swallow or to disgorge, while a small snapping turtle was busy at the tail of the unfortunate fish, biting lumps of flesh from its wriggling body. A stout stick broke up that dinner party, but the catfish was mutilated beyond hope of life.

Most lovers of catfish like it fried in corn meal and boiling lard, with adjuncts of corn bread and hot coffee, but stuffed and baked, *a la* red fish, the meat has hardly a superior among fresh-water fish. Sliced and broiled, with a basting of butter, black pepper and salt, and served with egg sauce, it is simply delicious; or if one's taste runs to court bouillon or stew, it is equally good. Catch a few and try them.

How big? How many? Well, this is a tale of veracity, but "tabby cats" have been taken from the Tickfaw and its kindred streams, that weighed fifty-four pounds in one instance, and over seventy in another, while there are plenty of catfish of twenty and thirty pounds weight. But don't catch a big fish; catch some of his smaller brothers that pull down the scales to ten, twelve or fifteen pounds. Then fry, bake, or stew them—sit down and eat, and thank your gods for the feast.

6
Two Weeks
with
Newfoundland Salmon
(1895)

Painted for OUTING by Marc Lucas.   "Two Weeks with Newfoundland Salmon."

READY FOR THE GAFF.

TWO WEEKS WITH NEWFOUNDLAND SALMON.

By Pendetti.

"ALL aboard!"
The sound of hurried feet, a vibration in the ship from heel to toe, the splash of a rope falling short into the water, and we were off for the land we had so often dreamed of. During the long, slothful winter our fancies had conjured up bright visions of the lusty salmon fighting his spirited battle for freedom and life in the cold rivers of the sea-beat land.

Let me here explain that "we" consisted of only Will and myself. Down Halifax harbor we steamed, past the forts, where the guns looked grimly down upon us; past the various small craft and pleasure boats, from some of which fair hands waved kerchiefs and sweet voices bade "Bon Voyage," as we sped on our way; on to Chebucto Head, and the broad Atlantic.

Soon our gallant ship began to pitch and roll, and we, contrary to the captain's stoutly expressed "No one is ever sick on the *Harlaw*," concluded that we should be more comfortable below. We did not venture again on deck until sunrise next morning, when a lovely day greeted us! And how pleasant it was to loll about the deck basking in the sunshine, breathing the fresh, invigorating air, with never a thought of business interrupting the moment's enjoyment.

That day we passed through the lovely Bras d'Or lakes—the delight of the tourist, the heaven of the artist—and at dark reached Sydney, the chief town of Cape Breton Island. Leaving Sydney we headed straight north to the extreme point of the island, which is most appropriately named Cape North, and having left this in our wake we turned a point east and made for St. Paul's Island, which is considered about half way between shore and shore.

On the third morning after leaving Halifax we reached Channel, the first point on the Newfoundland coast at which the *Harlaw* touches. Then passing along the shore and doubling Cape Ray we reached Cod Roy. From the landing to the river of the same name, and in which there is excellent fishing, the distance is about seven miles. But we did not wish to stop here now.

The Humber river was our goal. So on we went, past Bay St. George to Bay of Islands, into which the Humber flows, and we began already to feel the rod in our hands, and to see the salmon leap from the stream in mad endeavor to free himself from the hook. We had telegraphed to a man named Nicholls—who with his family are the only people on the river—to meet us at the Bay of Islands, and he was waiting our arrival. But, to our intense disappointment, he told us that we were too early for the fish. "A fortnight too early, sir; the first of July is about the time for fish up the river. What you had better do is to go up the river and wait about until the fish arrive." We did not relish the idea of wasting a solid fortnight in this manner, so after a few moments' debate, we decided to return to the Cod Roy, have a week's fishing there, and then go up the Humber. We therefore remained with the *Harlaw* as far as Boune Bay, where we landed, to await the return of our ship which went a little farther north.

The coast along here is magnificent. Large fiords make inland, the bluff on either hand rising boldly from the water's edge. In places we would see the hills rising inland, their summits capped with snow, and glistening in the sunlight like furbished silver.

It was Sunday morning when we again boarded our ship, and a most charming day. The water like a mirror, save when now and then a cat's-paw ruffled its surface, the air soft and sweet as the balmiest day in spring.

At five o'clock next morning we arrived at Cod Roy, and immediately proceeded to get ourselves and baggage transferred to the shore. I say transferred, for there are no wharves there, and passengers and baggage are all taken from the steamer in the good old-fashioned manner of being rowed ashore in boats. Cod Roy is a mere hamlet. We stayed no longer than was necessary, and having procured a Jehu and team drove to Cod Roy river. Here we stopped at a house kept by Miss Siers, who it seems is accustomed to see fishermen, for we had no sooner told our errand than she volunteered to procure men for us, and after a short absence our hostess returned, bringing with her two men named respectively Mike and Denis, who signified their willingness to "gang along wi' us" up the Cod Roy.

That evening we reached a pool called the "Overfall," where we decided to camp for the night. It is only a second-class pool, but I was sure there were salmon in it. It was too late, however, to cast a fly that night, so we pitched our tents and had supper. After disposing of this we sat about the fire smoking and talking, and as we talked our fire burned low, bats and moths fluttered about our heads, the stars came out one by one, and their images, caught in the ripples of the stream, went dancing along the water. The hoot of an owl came like a ghost from the darksome woods and was lost in the murmur of the river, and then we turned in to dream sweet dreams. But such were not to be mine that night, for I tossed and turned on my rubber bed until the "wee sma' hours." It was my first night out that year, and I could not keep myself warm. I had about the traditional "forty winks," when I was roused by the stir of the men making up the fire for breakfast, and soon we were ready for the fray.

It was glorious to feel the old Castle-Connell in one's hand again, and see the silver doctor glancing through the stream. Ah, the glories of the sport of a salmon-fisher! What can equal it? See him, as with rod held back over his shoulder, the tip doubled forward, his ear filled with sweet music of the whizzing reel, his eye lighted with the joys of anticipated victory, he plays the first salmon of the season! I had scarce made half a dozen casts when I had a

rise from what seemed to be a good-sized fish. After waiting a moment I cast again, and at it he came with a rush. A bar of silver leaped from the stream, was caught for a moment in the bright beams of the morning sun, and then sank again. I had him hard and fast. "By Jove! what a whale he must be!" I thought. Yard after yard of line went flying out. There was no stopping him. He again leaped from the pool. Ah! what is that? Fouled in the tail, as I'm a sinner! And not such a large fish after all. It often happens in fly-fishing that a fish will be fouled in some part of the body like this. He will jump at a fly, and from some cause—such as being too eager—will overshoot the mark, and the hinder part of his body will foul the fly as he is going down. When a fish is hooked in this manner the fisherman must steady himself for a tiresome struggle, for he will not land the prize until after many a run is over. He has not the control over his fish as when it is hooked in the mouth. I have seen a salmon hooked foul fight for hours, and, had the same fish been hooked in the mouth, it would have been landed in twenty minutes. As it was I had a two hours' fight with this fish. He dashed about the pool, taking out yard after yard of line as though it were a mere trifle. Time after time would I wind in fifty or sixty yards, when, with a mighty rush, he would be off again, and it would all go spinning out. How tired my arms got! At one time I could scarcely hold my rod up, and I almost wished that the fish would break away that I might get a rest, and then I set my teeth and determined that I would kill that fish if I had to play him for a week. I had wound in my line pretty well once and was thinking that Denis might risk a trial of gaffing, when, just as the fish was coming within distance, a new freak seized him and he dashed off at an awful rate straight down stream. My line was whizzing out like lightning, and in a few moments would be gone. So I decided we must follow him. "Up, Killock Denis," I cried, "and after him!" and soon we were dashing down stream in pursuit with about five yards of line on the reel. Presently he slowed up and I reeled in, hoping to get him this time. Vain hope! for he was off down stream again on another cruise. And so we fought on for two mortal hours, and when at length I did capture him, he had taken us a full mile from where he rose. That fish weighed only ten pounds, but I had got fight enough out of him for a fish three or four times his weight. My companion, Will, landed two good fish and lost another while I was down stream.

We now struck camp and proceeded up the river, wishing to have the afternoon's fishing in the real pool, "Salmon-Hole," — a most suggestive name, truly, calling up many memories.

The river here is shallow, and not much more than a hundred yards in width. It lies about midway between two parallel ranges of hills, apart from each other a distance varying from one to three miles. The crests of some of these hills are covered with snow the greater part of the year. It was a pretty piece of country, the river valley full of ferns and a luxuriant growth of wild grasses, with here and there a few of the earlier wild flowers peeping out.

As we came up to the pool—Salmon Hole—we disturbed a large eagle. He was sitting on an old tree, but when he saw us he took wing and began mounting the air in those strong sweeping circles that always suggest to me grand power and a desire for space. I have a strong liking for these birds, they seem capable of such large ideas. What is height, depth, distance to them? A day's tramp for us is but a matter of a few moments to them. If there is any bird or beast that can grasp the idea of infinity, I think it must be the eagle.

Wishing to change the fly on my cast before beginning operations here, I put my hand to my pocket to take out my fly-book, when horror! I found that my pocket was empty. Now, losing a fly-book at this time in the trip was a serious matter. It meant a good many fish, for there was no way of replacing the snares as we had no feathers.

"Will," I said to my companion, "you haven't seen my fly-book anywhere, have you?"

"What! No!" he answered. "You haven't lost it?"

"I'm afraid I have," I replied.

While trying to think what could have happened to it, and wondering would it be worth while to walk back a short distance to see if I had dropped it, Will broke in and said:

"You didn't leave it on that rock away back there?"

And then I recollected that I had sat down upon a rock, about a mile and a half down stream, and taken out my book to select a new casting line. And there I must have left it. It was a broiling hot day, and I was tired, so it was with no enviable feelings that I trudged back to look for that book. After half an hour's tramp I found the rock upon which I had been sitting, and, sure enough, there was my open fly-book.

I was too exhausted to swing my heavy rod when I got back to Salmon Hole, so I made a little nest for myself among the willow saplings and Balm of Gilead trees, and, sinking down, watched Will thrashing the pool. For a while the hope of seeing him kill a fish kept me watchful, but gradually my weariness, the sweet odors of balm trees, the gentle breeze, the soft murmur of the waters, were too much for me, and I fell asleep, to dream of snaring a monster salmon with the strap off of my fly-book. I was about to tell Denis to stand ready to gaff the fish, when I was awakened by Will shaking me, and asking if we had better not camp for the night on this pool instead of going on to the next. We decided to do the former, as it had for some time been threatening rain and, anyway, we might as well have the evening's fishing in Salmon Hole. We took four fish out of this pool, the largest weighing twenty pounds.

Just before sunset the ominous-looking clouds on the horizon dispersed, and the sun shone brightly for a few minutes. We heard an owl hoot and remembered the old adage:

"And owls that mark the setting sun, declare
A starlight evening and a morning fair."

This night I slept very well, except that I was troubled for a while by one or two flies that worked their way through my mosquito netting and began operations on me. Will was better fitted out in this respect, having a framework covered with muslin which he stretched about his bed, and through this no fly could penetrate. In the morning we would often find them perched by hundreds upon the netting.

The flies on the Cod Roy are of four distinct varieties. The largest is the deer-fly, or, as it is sometimes called, the copper-headed fly. This fellow worries the deer a great deal and is very vicious, drawing blood like a leech. He is gray in color, and is a half-brother, I think, to our horse-fly. Then there are two grades of mosquitoes, the large and small, the former nearly an inch long and much more formidable looking than he really is; the latter is much the same as our own mosquito and bites like a fiend. The third and fourth varieties are our own black-fly and the small sand-fly—the "biteum no seeum" of the Indian. These are never "slothful in business" when opportunity is afforded them.

Our faith in the saying of the owl was not vain, for next morning broke gray and still, with a slight mist which soon lifted and disappeared under the influence of the sun.

We had the morning's fishing here and each succeeded in capturing another fish, and then we journeyed on up the river to the "Forks," the best pool on the Cod Roy, formed at the junction of the two branches of the river. It is a lovely, long pool, very suggestive of twenty pounders. We fished all along the river as we ascended, but did not do much except in the pools, of which there were only three or four. The bed of the river is continually changing, and one often finds a place holding a few fish that in former seasons was nothing but a plunging rapid. But those pools which I have named are always certain to hold fish if there are any in the river. At the "Falls" we tented on an old camping ground that had been used for several years.

It did not take us long to get to work on the pool. Ah! that fellow was touched. No! there he was again. I had him this time. At the same moment a shout from Will told me that he had hooked a fish. And how those two fish cut about the pool, and played duets upon the musical reels! I never found a pool better stocked with fish in my life. One after another would come up from the same "lair," and make the line sing as they rushed about. I forget how many fish we took here the first day, but it was an astonishing number, and next day the pool seemed as well stocked as ever.

Day after day we fished, not wishing to give up such good sport for the uncertainty of that in the Humber river. Day after day we rose before the sun and worked the pool. Then a late breakfast, a ramble about the country, or perhaps an excursion for trout for our larder, or a trip down stream to the nearest house for fresh eggs, butter, etc., and the morning would wear to the afternoon, and then the evening fishing over, a hearty meal, and a pull at the pipes as we stretched out with our feet to the blaze—made more for pleasure than comfort—and listened to the yarns of the men, would end the day.

So through those long, sunny days we gathered rich stores of health and happiness and forgot all but the enjoyment of the moment. And then, the nights. He who knows not nature in the wilds, and by night, knows not her better half.

7
A Day
with the
Black Bass
(1895)

A DAY WITH THE BLACK BASS.

By Francis J. Lynde.

To lovers of bass fishing few fields offer more attractions than the lake region of Minnesota. During the fishing season, the climate is at its best, and all nature habited in that luxuriant garb of vegetation which, in the far north, attains a profusion and vivid coloring peculiarly its own. The air, laden with the perfume of wild flowers, is an elixir infusing new life into heart and brain. I know, then, of no more alluring land in which to spend a day, a week or a month, and I mark those days with a white stone when business or pleasure has taken me thither.

Meeting my friend, Dick Carter, one day in Chicago, we arranged to make a flying trip to a chain of lakes in central Minnesota, and the evening of a day a week later found me in St. Paul awaiting the arrival of my companion.

When the train from Chicago came rolling into the station, my single, short-jointed rod and modest box of accessories were quite put to shame by the diversity and quantity of fishing paraphernalia with which my friend was burdened. As he descended to the platform, I queried with a laugh if he usually carried such an equipment for a single day's fishing.

"Never you mind, my boy," he replied, handing me a spare rod and an immense landing net. "When you want anything, you want it just as badly in a day as you would in a week, and I don't depend upon a country store to supply deficiencies."

"Apparently not," was my rejoinder, as I led the way to the train that was to carry us on to our destination.

"Yes," resumed Carter, as we settled down for the night ride, "I always go prepared to fish forty miles from the nearest store if necessary, and, speaking of distance, you haven't told me yet where we are going and when we will get there."

"We are going to Douglas county; our station is Victoria, which boasts of a two-by-four platform in lieu of a railway station, and a good hotel, which two structures comprise the town; and we should arrive at three o'clock to-morrow morning."

"Three o'clock!" exclaimed Carter, in a tone of great disgust, "and what will we do at three o'clock? Go to bed?"

"Most certainly not. We'll get the early morning fishing, and to make sure, I've telegraphed the boat-keeper to leave a boat and a bucketful of live minnows where we can get them."

"Well, you're just a simon-pure crank, that's all," said Carter, putting his knees up against the seat-back in front of him, and subsiding into the uncomfortably doubled-up position affected by old travelers; "and if I could find the handle I'd turn you around a few times for getting me out on such a trip. I supposed we were only going a few miles out into the country. Three o'clock! Why I'll wager a large, iron dollar that we don't catch a fish before breakfast."

After a while he straightened up and said, "Well, if we've got to make a night of it, here goes," and opening one of his valises, took therefrom a rubber pillow, which he inflated, and, placing it under his head, was soon asleep.

Being particularly wakeful, I amused myself for a while by letting the air out of the pillow at intervals, and managed to extract quite a fund of quiet enjoyment for myself and for other wakeful passengers out of Carter's vigorous abuse of the "miserable, good-for-nothing, leaky wind-bag." We had a most vigilant brakeman on the train who seemed to be in continued fear lest someone be carried by his destination, and when the pillow joke had become somewhat worn, I called the attention of this railroader to my friend Carter as the man who wanted to get off at the next station. Accordingly, as the train slowed for the next stop the brakeman came through shouting "Long Lake," with an emphasis that awakened everyone in the car save my somnolent friend. Stopping opposite Dick, he again yelled the name of the station accompanying the words with a rough shake, and "This is Long Lake, come, hurry up, you'll be left!" To help matters along he began to gather up the luggage. Dick stared vacantly at the man and asked, sleepily, if there was a fire somewhere. "Fire? No. But this is Long Lake; hurry up!" "Oh, it is," said Dick, now thoroughly awake. "Well, what do you suppose I care if it is Long Lake? Kindly let my baggage alone, and give your voice a vacation."

By this time the train had stopped, the brakeman was frantic, while the passengers at our end of the car were convulsed with laughter.

"This-is-Long-Lake," again shouted the man. "Don't you want to get off at Long Lake?" "No, I-don't-want-to-get-off-at-Long-Lake," yelled Carter, now thoroughly incensed, "and if you don't go away and let me alone, there'll be a murder committed right here."

A shout of laughter from the spectators greeted this speech, and the brakeman backed away from Carter looking as if he were sure that he had an escaped lunatic for a passenger, while Dick once more inflated his pillow and throwing himself down upon it with the remark that it had never been his misfortune to travel with such a lot of idiots, was soon snoring again. When we finally reached Victoria I could scarcely make him believe that he was not being victimized again. We were on the little platform surrounded by our baggage, and the lights of the train had disappeared around a curve, before he fully realized what had happened.

Gathering up our parcels we made our way through the silent woods to the lake shore, where we found the boat and bait awaiting us, and as soon as we were fairly embarked my friend forgot the discomforts of the night in the ardor of a true sportsman, and, as I took the oars and pulled slowly along the shore, he mounted his rod and tried casting in shallow water. As it was very dark, this method was not successful. After Dick had lost two hooks and about one-half of one line in the trees which overhung the margin of the lake, we pulled out into deeper water and tried still fishing. This was also unsuccessful, Dick remarking that "the fish had more sense than to bite at such a time o'night."

As soon as it became light enough to enable us to steer clear of the shallows and obstructions, we again tried casting and trolling along the shore, and I confidently believe that, with the patience of a true fisherman, I pulled not less than fifteen miles around that lake shore before we gave up in disgust and headed for the hotel and breakfast.

Our host jeered us unmercifully for our ill luck but we repaid him by eating enough breakfast for four men, after which we renewed the bait and caught a few small frogs before starting out again.

The so-called black bass of the Minnesota lakes, which, by the way, is not the black bass at all, but a big-mouthed cousin of his, is somewhat peculiar in his tastes and the greatest variety of bait often fails to tempt him to strike after the first few days of the season. In the early summer he takes young frogs with great avidity and a little later he will rise quite promptly to a live minnow or a gray "doctor," but after this he loses his voracity and will take a spoon or a piece of red flannel as readily as the most tempting fly or live minnow, but quite as frequently will not strike at anything. The largest bass I ever landed was caught upon a hook baited with a bit of the red gill of a perch which I was using in sheer desperation after having tried every fly in my book without success. The bass will sometimes take frogs again later in the season.

After giving the minnows another trial without success we began experimenting with the frogs, and Carter's efforts to cast with them, after having used minnows, were laughable. His first attempt landed the frog in the branches of a convenient tree and his next whipped the bait off entirely and sent it spinning out into the lake.

He got the "hang" of it, however, after a few trials and landed nicely over into a bed of rushes with a good long cast. Before the line had fairly settled down a magnificent fish sprang clear out of the water for the bait, and the reel shrieked as he struck and darted off through the reeds.

Carter was as keen as he had a right to be after a whole morning without a single bite, but he kept cool while I took the oars and prepared to assist as might be needed. The fish first made a quick rush for the bank and then, turning, darted directly for the boat. A light pull on the oars let him pass astern and the slack which Carter had managed to get in went out again like a flash as the quarry made for deep water. "Give him his head," I shouted, as the line spun off the reel and Dick stood like a statue watching the flying silk and the rapidly diminishing coil in terror lest the fish would not stop in time to save the tackle. On he went until only a few more turns were left, when suddenly the reel stopped and the line slackened. Hastily reeling in all the slack he could get, Carter waited in anxious suspense for another rush. It came presently, and far out in the lake a splendid fish sprang clear out of the water describing a graceful curve as he descended and darted off at right angles to his former course.

A few quick strokes with the oars saved the tackle, then the fish sounded and, after sulking for a full minute, took another turn and made directly for the boat. I couldn't get out of his way this time and the good bamboo rod fairly creaked with the strain as it bent double under the boat. "Pass the rod over the stern," I said as I endeavored to turn the boat so as favor the manœuvre, and Carter cautiously worked the line aft. It was nearly accomplished when the line unexpectedly slackened and, with a frantic clutching at the air Carter went out of the boat backward while the fish swam slowly out into the lake again, towing the rod behind him.

Carter was up in a moment, puffing and spluttering and abusing me roundly for my untimely levity, for I was laughing so that I couldn't help him for the moment, and when he finally clambered into the boat and sat down in the stern, his teeth chattering with cold, and the water running in little rivulets from his clothing, I went off again in an uncontrollable fit of merriment.

"That's it, s-s-sit there l-l-like a gibbering idiot and l-l-lemme freeze to death, w-will you? N-n-nice way to t-treat a man, ain't it?"

"My dear boy, I couldn't help it, if you could only see how woe-begone you look—"

"D-d-don't have to see, I g-guess I can feel."

Resuming the oars I pulled after the rod which was still moving slowly out into the lake and securing it, the fish was landed with little further difficulty. It was a fine specimen but Carter was too miserable to be very enthusiastic, so I pulled the boat back to the hotel and put him to bed while his clothes were drying at the kitchen fire.

After dinner we concluded to try it again and as we wished to go to a lake some ten miles distant by water, I asked our host if we could get a sailboat.

"Yes," he replied, "there is one up at the other landing, but she's not much of a sailer."

"It will do for us if it will sail at all," said Carter, as we started off to look for the boat.

We found it to be a very clumsy old tub, but we decided to try it, and loading our tackle were soon speeding down the lake with the wind directly aft.

"Don't see but that she sails all right," said Carter, as we bowled along, "and this beats rowing out of sight," to which, having done all the rowing so far, I agreed heartily.

We soon covered the distance and cast anchor on a famous bass-bar.

"Now Dick," said I, "let's see if your ducking has changed our luck." Something had, certainly for the sport for the next hour was fine and at the end of that time we had a goodly string, every fish of which had been game to the finish.

"Hadn't we better be working our way back?" said Dick, looking at his watch, "It's nearly four and we don't know yet how this tub will sail with a head wind."

"That's a fact," I replied, "and I guess we'd better begin to find out. We've more fish than we know what to do with now."

Carter got the anchor up while I hoisted the sail and as the boat fell off and took the breeze, which had freshened into half a gale, the course was set as close to the wind as possible and the little craft, burying her nose in the seas, made good time across the lake.

As we put about on the other tack I remarked to Dick that we'd soon know what progress we were making. We found out sure enough, for when we tacked again we were exactly on our former anchorage.

"Let me take that tiller," exclaimed Dick, "I don't believe you know how to sail a boat, anyway."

Once more we stood across and back with precisely the same result.

"It's of no use, Dick, we'll have to row back," and I went forward to lower the sail while Carter got out the "sweeps," as he called them. Then we settled down to work and just four hours later beached the boat in front of the hotel.

"My back is broken in four places," said Dick with a groan, as he gathered up the tackle while I dragged out our fish, "and I don't suppose we can get any supper to-night, but we've had a glorious day just the same."

We were agreeably disappointed, however, for our host had anticipated our trouble with the boat and we found an excellent supper awaiting us to which was shortly added some of own bass, broiled to a turn.

8
The
Primitive
Fish-Hook
(1883)

8
The
Primitive
Fish-Hook
(1883)

THE PRIMITIVE FISH-HOOK.

I HAVE before me an illustrated catalogue of modern fish-hooks and angling implements, and in looking over its pages I find an *embarras de choix*. I have no need for rods, for mine, like well-kept violins, have rather improved by age. A lashing may be frayed, or a ferrule loose, but fifteen minutes' pleasant work will make my rods all right again. Lines are sound, for I have carefully stretched them after use. But my hooks! They are certainly the worse for wear. I began my season's fishing with a meager stock. Friends borrowed from me, and in replenishing my fly-book in an out-of-the-way place, the purchase was unsatisfactory. As I lost more than one fish from badly tempered

69

or worse fashioned hooks, I recalled a delightful paper by Mr. Froude. Rod in hand, he was whipping some pleasant trout-stream, near an historic site, the home of the Russells, and, breaking his hooks, commenced from that very moment to indulge in the gloomiest forebodings as to the future of England.

Fairly familiar with the general character of fishing-gear, either for business or amusement, I see in my book, Kirby, Limerick, Dublin, O'Shaughnessy, Kinsey, Carlisle, Harrison, Central Draught, as somewhat distinct families of hooks, used for sea or river fishing, and from these main stocks there grow many varieties, with all conceivable twists, quirls, and crookednesses. I discard all trap-hooks, infernal machines working with springs, as only adapted for the capture of land animals. Somehow I remember an aggressive book, given to me at an early age, which, containing more than one depressing passage, had one of extraordinary malevolence. This was couched nearly as follows: " Suppose you were translated only some seven hundred years back, then pray what would you be good for ? Could you make gunpowder? You have, perhaps, a vague idea that sulphur, saltpeter, and charcoal are the component parts, but do you know where or how they are procured?" I forget whether this dispiriting author was not equally harrowing in regard to the youthful reader's turning off a spectroscope at a minute's notice, or wound up with the modest request that you should try your hand among the Crusaders with an aneroid barometer of your own special manufacture.

Still this question arises: Suppose you were famishing, though fish were plenty in a stream, and you had neither line nor hook. What would you do ? Now, has a condition of this kind ever occurred? Yes, it has, and certainly thousands of times. Not so many years ago, the early surveyors of the Panama route suffered terrible privations from the want of fishing implements. The rains had rendered their powder worthless : they could not use their guns. Had they only been provided with hooks and lines, they could have subsisted on fish. Then there are circumstances under which it would be really necessary for a man to be somewhat of a Jack-of-all-trades, and to be able to fashion the implements he might require, and so this crabbed old book might, after all, act in the guise of a useful reminder. There was certainly a period, when every man was in a condition of comparative helplessness, when his existence depended on his proficiency in making such implements as would catch fish or kill animals. He must fashion hooks or something else to take fish with, or die.

Probably man, in the first stage of his existence, took much of his food from the water, although whether he did or not might depend upon locality. If on certain portions of the earth's surface there were stretches of land, intersected by rivers, dotted by lakes, or bordering on the seas, the presence of shell-fish, the invertebrates or the vertebrates, cetaceans and fish, to the exclusion of land animals, might have rendered primitive man icthyophagous, or dependent for subsistence upon the art of fishing. But herein we grapple at once with that most abstruse of all problems, the procession of life. Still it is natural to suppose, so far as the study of man goes, when considered in relation to his pursuits, that in the early dawn of humanity, animals, birds, and fish must have been synchronous.

After brute instinct, which is imitativeness, then came shiftiness and adaptiveness. The rapid stride of civilization, considered in its material sense, is due solely to the use of such implements as are specially adapted for a particular kind of work. With primitive man this could never have been the case. Tools of the Paleolithic or Neolithic age (which terms indicate stages of civilization, but are not chronological), whether they were axes, hammers, or arrows, must have served river-drift or cave-men for more than a single purpose. People with few tools do manage, by skill alone, to adapt these to a variety of ends. The Fijian and the Russian peasant, one with a stone adze, the other with a hatchet, bring to their trades the minimum of tools. The Kafir, with his assegai, fights his battles, kills cattle, carves his spoons, and shaves himself. It was only as man advanced that he devised special tools for different purposes.

According to our present acquaintance with primitive habits, if man existed in the later Miocene age, and used a lance or spear for the killing of land animals, he probably employed the same weapons for the destruction of the creatures—possibly of gigantic form—inhabiting the seas, lakes, and rivers. The presence of harpoons made of bone, found in so many localities, belonging to a later period, may not in all cases point to the existence of animals, but to the presence of large fish.

Following, then, closely the advance of man, when his fishing implements are particularly considered, we are inclined to believe that he first used the spear for taking fish; next the hook and line; and lastly, the net. There might have been an intermediate stage between the spear and the hook, when the bow and arrow were used.

Interesting as is the whole subject of

primitive fishing, we are, however, to occupy ourselves principally with the form of the primitive fish-hook. To-day there are some careful archæologists who are not willing to accept that particular form which is presented below. I believe, from the many reasons which can be advanced, that this simple form was the first device used by man in taking fish with a line. The argument I shall use is in some respects a novel one.

STONE FISH-GORGE, FROM THE VALLEY OF THE SOMME. (NEW YORK MUSEUM OF NATURAL HISTORY.)

These illustrations, exactly copied as to size, represent a small piece of dark, polished stone. It was found in the valley of the Somme, in France, and was dug out of a peat-bed twenty-two feet below the surface. The age of this peat-bed has been variously estimated. M. Boucher de Perthes thought that thirty thousand years must have elapsed since the lowest layer of peat was formed. The late Sir Charles Lyell and Sir John Lubbock, without too strict an adherence to date, believed that this peat-bed represented in its formation, "that vast lapse of time which began with the commencement of the Neolithic period." Later authorities deem it not older than seven thousand years B. C.

Wonderful changes have come to pass since this bit of polished stone was lost in what must have been a lake. Examining this piece of worked stone, which once belonged to a prehistoric man living in that valley, we find it fairly well polished, though the action of countless years has slightly " weathered " or disintegrated its once smooth surface. In the center a groove has been cut, and the ends of the stone rise slightly from the middle. It is rather crescent-shaped. It must have been tied to a line, and this stone gorge was covered with a bait. The fish swallowed it, and, the gorge coming crosswise with the gullet, the fish was captured.

The evolution of any present form of implement from an older one is often more cleverly specious than logically conclusive ; nevertheless, I believe that, in this case, starting with the crude fish-gorge, I can show, step by step, the complete sequence of the fish-hook, until it ends with the perfected hook of to-day. It can be insisted upon even that there is persistence of form in the descendants of this fish-gorge, for, as Professor Mitchell writes in his " Past in the Present," " an old art may long refuse to disappear wholly, even in the midst of conditions which seem to be necessarily fatal to its continued existence."

In the Swiss lakes are found the remains of the Lacustrine dwellers. Among the many implements discovered are fish-gorges made of bronze wire. When these forms are studied, the fact must be recognized at once that they follow in shape and principle of construction the stone gorges of the Neolithic period. Now, it is perfectly well known that the early bronze-worker invariably followed the stone patterns. The Lacustrine gorges have had the name of *bricole* given them.

BRICOLE, FROM THE LAKE OF NEUFCHATEL.

This is a faithful copy of a bronze bricole found in the Lake of Neufchatel. It is made of bronze wire, and is bent in the simplest way, with an open curve allowing the line to be fastened to it. The ends of the gorge are very slightly bent, but they were probably sharpened when first made.

The bricole below varies from the rather straight one found in the Lake of Neufchatel, and belongs to a later period. It is possible to imagine that the lake-dweller, according to his pleasure, made one or the other of these two forms of fishing implements. As the double hook required more bronze, and bronze at first was very precious, he might not have had material enough in the early period to make it. This device is, however, a clever one, for a fisherman of to-day,

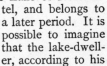

BRICOLE OF A LATER PERIOD.

DOUBLE HOOK, FROM THE LAKE OF NEUFCHATEL.

who had lost his hook, might imitate it with a bit of wire. Had any member of the hungry Isthmus party mentioned above known of this form of Lacustrine hook, he might have twisted some part of a suspender buckle, providing there were no thorny plants at hand, and have caught fish.

When we compare the four forms, showing only their outlines, the evolution of the fish-hook can be better appreciated. Returning to the stone fish-gorge, the work of the Neolithic period, it is evident that the man of that time followed the shape handed down to him by his ancestors ; and as this fashioned stone from the valley of the Somme is of a most remote period, how much older must have been the paleolithic fish-gorge of rough stone ? It might have been with a splinter of

PREHISTORIC FORMS.

flint attached to some tendril in lieu of a line, that the first fish was taken.

It is very curious to learn that in France a modification of this gorge-hook is in use to-day for catching eels. A needle is sharpened at its eye-end, a slight groove is made in the middle of it, and around this some shreds of flax are attached. A worm is spitted, a little of the line being covered with the bait.

Not eels alone are taken with this needle, for M. de la Blanchere informs us that many kinds of fish are caught with it in France.

Any doubts as to the use of the Neolithic form of fish-gorge must be removed when it can be insisted upon that precisely this form of implement was in use by our Indians not more than forty years ago. In 1878, when studying this question of the primitive hook, I was fortunate enough to receive direct testimony on the subject. My informant, who in his younger days had lived among the Indians at the head-waters of Lake Superior, said that in 1846 the Indians used a gorge made of bone to catch their fish. My authority, who had never seen a prehistoric fish-gorge, save the drawing of one, said that the Indian form was precisely like the early shape, and that the Chippewas fished some with the hook of civilization, others with bone gorges of a primitive period.

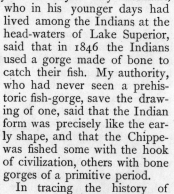

SHARPENED NEEDLE USED FOR CATCHING FISH IN FRANCE.

BRONZE FISH-HOOK. (MAYER COLLECTION.)

In tracing the history of the fish-hook, it should be borne in mind that an overlapping of periods must have taken place. By this is meant, that at one and the same time an individual employed tools or weapons of various periods. To-day the Western hunter lights his fire with a match. This splinter of wood, tipped with phosphorus, the chlorates, sulphur, or paraffine, represents the progress made in chemistry from the time of the alchemists. But this trapper is sure to have stowed away in his pouch, ready for an emergency, his flint and steel. The Esquimau,

the Alaskan, shoots his seal with an American repeating rifle, and, in lieu of a knife, flays the creature with a flint splinter. The net of the Norseman is to-day sunk with stones or buoyed with wood,—certainly the same devices as were used by the earliest Scandinavian,—while the net, so far as the making of the thread goes, is due to the best modern mechanical appliances. Survival of form requires some consideration apart from that of material, the first having much the stronger reasons for persistence. It is then very curious to note that hooks not made of iron and steel, but of bronze, or alloys of copper, are still in use on the coast of Finland, as I have quite recently obtained brass hooks from Northern Europe, such as are commonly in use by fishermen there.

The origin of the double hook having been, I believe, satisfactorily explained, to make the barb on it was readily suggested to primitive man, as he had used the same device on fish-spears and harpoons.

DOUBLE HOOK, BARBED. FROM SWISS LAKES.

This double-barbed hook from the Swiss lakes is quite common. Then, from the double to the single hook the transition was rapid. Single bronze hooks of the Lacustrine period sometimes have no barb. Such differences as exist are due to the various methods of attaching the line.

In Professor A. A. Mayer's collection there is a Lacustrine bronze hook, the shank of which is bent over parallel with the stem of the hook. This hook is a large one, and must have been used for big fish—probably the trout of the Swiss lakes.

Hooks made of stone are exceedingly rare, and though it is barely possible that they might have been used for fish, I think this has not been conclusively shown. Wilson gives,

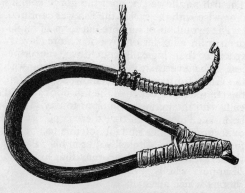

ALASKAN HALIBUT HOOK.

in his work, drawings of two stone hooks, which were found in Scandinavia. Though the theory that these stone objects were fashioned for fishing is supported by so good an authority as Mr. Charles Rau, the archæologist of the United States National Museum at Washington, it does not seem to

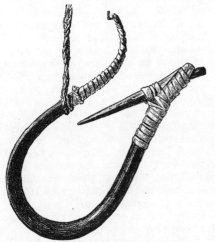

ALASKAN HALIBUT HOOK.

me possible that these hooks could have been made for fishing. Such forms, from the nature of the material, would have been exceedingly difficult to fashion, and, even if made, would have presented few advantages over the primitive gorge.

This, however, must be borne in mind: that, in catching fish, primitive man could have had no inkling of the present curved form of fish-hook, which, with its barb, secures the fish by penetration. A large proportion of sea-fish, and many river-fish, swallow the hook, and are caught, not by the hook entering the jaws of the fish, but because it is fastened in their stomachs. In the Gloucester fisherman's language of to-day, a fish so captured is called " poke-hooked "; and accordingly, when the representative of the Neolithic period fished in that lake in the valley of the Somme, all the fish he took must have been poke-hooked. A bone hook, excellent in form, has been found near the remains of a huge species of pike (*Esox*). Hooks made of the tusks of the wild boar have also been discovered with Lacustrine remains.

In commenting on the large size of the bone hook figured in Wilson's work, its proximity to the remains of large fish was noticed. When the endless varieties of hooks belonging to savage races are subjects of discussion, the kind of fish they serve for catching should

always be cited. In the examples of hooks which illustrate works of travel, a good many errors arise from the simple fact that the writers are not fishermen. Although the outline of a hook be accurately given, the method of securing it to the line is often incorrectly drawn.

In THE CENTURY MAGAZINE for July, 1882, an Alaskan halibut-hook is represented. The form is a common one, and is used by all the savage races of the Pacific; but the main interest lay in the manner of tying the line to this hook. Since the fish to be caught was the halibut, the form was the best adapted to the taking of the *Hippoglossus Americanus;* but, had the line been attached in any other way than exactly as represented, this big fish could hardly have been caught with such a hook.

In the drawing, the halibut-hook hangs but slightly inclining toward the sea-bottom, the weight of the bait having a tendency to lower it. In this position it can be readily taken by the fish; but should it be suspended in a different way, it must be at once seen how difficult it would be for the fish to swallow it. In this Alaskan hook must be recognized the very first idea of what we call to-day the center-draught hook. A drawing is also given of a steel hook of a peculiar form, coming from Northern Russia. The resemblance between the Alaskan and this Russian hook is, at first, apparently slight, but they both are, nevertheless, constructed on the same principle. When this Russian hook is seized by the fish, and force is applied to the line by the fisherman, the point of the barb and the line are almost in one and the same direction. Almost the same may be said of the Alaskan hook. Desirous of testing the capabilities of this hook, I had a gross made after the Russian model,

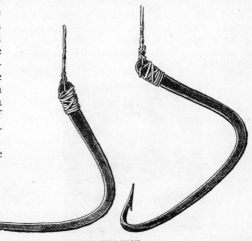

RUSSIAN FISH-HOOK.

THE BEGINNING OF A SHELL-HOOK. (WEST COLLECTION.)

and sent them to Captain J. W. Collins, of the United States Fish Commission, stationed at Gloucester, requesting him to distribute them among the fishermen. While writing this article, I am in receipt of a letter from Captain Collins, informing me that these hooks are excellent, the captains of fishing-smacks reporting that a great many deep-sea fish were taken with them.

A study of these hooks—the Alaskan and Russian—with reference to the method of attaching the line, explains, I think, the peculiarity of certain shell-hooks of great antiquity found in California, which have puzzled archæologists. These hooks, the originals of which are to be found in the National Museum, at Washington, are shown in acompanying engravings. The notch cut in one of the hooks seems to show that the line was attached at that place. Hang the hooks in any other position and they would catch no fish,—for one could hardly suppose that the blunt barb could penetrate the mouth of the fish.

If there be some doubt entertained by American archæologists as to the use of these shell-hooks (page 904), there can be none in regard to their having barbs. The barbs turn outward, in which respect they differ from all the primitive European hooks I have seen. In confirmation of the idea advanced as to the proper place of attaching the line, Professors C. C. Abbott and F.

W. Putnam, in a chapter entitled "Implements and Weapons made of Bone and Wood," in the United States Geographical Survey, west of the hundredth meridian, write, referring to these hooks: "These hooks are flattened, and are longer than wide. * * * The barbs in these specimens are judged by fishermen of to-day to be on the wrong side of a good fish-hook, and the point is too near the shank. By having the line so fastened that the point of tension is at the notch at the base of the shank, instead of at the extreme end of the stem, the defect of the design of the hook would be somewhat remedied, as the barb would be forced down, so that it might possibly catch itself in the lower jaw of the fish that had taken the hook." The summing up of this is, I think, that in an imperfect way the maker of this Santa Barbara hook had some idea of the efficiency of a center-draught hook. As the first step in manufacturing this hook, a hole was drilled in the shell, and the hook finished up afterward by rounding the outside. Dr. West, of Brooklyn, has a whole series of such primitive work in his collection.

It is quite obvious that, in a study of this

SHELL-HOOK. (NATIONAL MUSEUM, WASHINGTON.)

character, it becomes necessary to understand the implements now in use by uncivilized man. To advance the idea that in all cases hooks have been improved by slightly increased culture among semi-civilized races, would be a source of error. It is quite possible that, in many instances, there has been retrogression from the better forms of fishing implements once in use. This relapse might have been brought about, not so much by a decrease of intelligence, as changes due to fortuitous causes. A fishing race might have been driven away from a shore or a river-bank, and replaced by an inland people ignorant of fishing.

Some primitive races still use a hook made from a thorn, and in this practice we find to-day a most wonderful survival. On the coast of France hooks made of thorns are still used to catch fish, the fishermen repre-

SHELL-HOOK. (NATIONAL MUSEUM, WASHINGTON.)

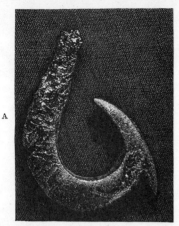

SHELL-HOOK FROM SANTA BARBARA. (NATIONAL MUSEUM, WASHINGTON.)

these are laid in grooves cut into the stone. It must have taken much toil to perfect this clever artificial bait, and, as it is to-day, it might be used with success by a clever striped-bass fisherman at Newport.

In this necessarily brief study of primitive fishing I have endeavored to show the genesis of the fish-hook, from the stone gorge to the more perfected implement of to-day. Simple as it may seem, it is a subject on which a good deal of research is still requisite. "It is not an acquaintance with a single series of things which can throw light on any subject, but a thorough comprehension of the whole of them." If in the Swiss lakes there are found bronze hooks of a very large size, out of proportion to the fish which swim there to-day, it is but just to suppose that, many thousands of years ago, long before history had its dawn, the aquatic fauna

senting that they possess the great advantage of costing nothing, and of not fouling on the sea-bottom. The Piutes take the spine of a cactus, bending it to suit their purpose, and very simple barbless hooks of this kind may be seen in the collections of the National Museum at Washington.

Undoubtedly, in primitive times, hooks of a compound character were used. Just as men tipped a deer's antler with a flint, they combined more than one material in the making of their hooks, lashing together a shank of bone or wood with a bronze barb. It would be almost impossible in a magazine article to follow all the varieties of hooks used and the ingenuity displayed in their manufacture. Occasionally a savage will construct a lure for fish which rivals the daintiest fly ever made by the most fastidious of anglers. In Professor Mayer's collection there is an exceedingly clever hook coming from the North-western coast, which shows very fine lapidary work. A small red quartzose pebble of great hardness has been rounded, polished, and joined to a piece of bone. The piece is small, not more than an inch and three-quarters in length, and might weigh an ounce and a half. In the shank of bone a small hook is hidden. It somewhat imitates a shrimp. The parts are joined together by lashings of tendon, and

SHELL-HOOK. FROM SANTA BARBARA. (NATIONAL MUSEUM, WASHINGTON.)

were then of greater bulk than in 1883. Considerations on the primitive form of the fish-hook must even comprehend examination of prior geological conditions, differences of land and water, or such geographical changes as may have taken place. Then ichthyology becomes an important factor, for by the character of the hook the kind of fish taken, in some instances, may be understood. We are fast coming to this conclusion : that, putting aside what can only be the merest speculations as to the condition of man when he is said to have first diverged from the brute, he was soon endowed with a wonderful degree of intelligence. And, if I am not mistaken, primitive man did not confine himself in his fishing to the rivers and lakes alone, but went out boldly to sea after the cod ; and so the fishing instincts of the men of Cape Ann to-day go backward to that indefinite period the exact date of which is so far distant that no human mind has yet been able to fix it.

Barnet Phillips.

ARTIFICIAL STONE SHRIMP. (MAYER COLLECTION.)

9
Goin'
Fishin'
(1905)

"AT LAST YOU WERE OFF"

GOIN' FISHIN'

BY EDWIN L. SABIN

WITH PICTURES BY FREDERIC DORR STEELE

T was twenty feet long, and cost ten cents—a whole week's keeping-the-woodbox-filled wages. To select it from amid its sheaf of fellows towering high beside the shop entrance summoned all your faculties and the faculties of four critical comrades, assisted by the proprietor himself.

"That 's the best of the lot," he encouraged, not uninfluenced by a desire to be rid of you.

So you planked down your money, and bore off the prize; and a beautiful pole it was—longer by three feet, as you demonstrated when they were laid cheek by jowl, than that of your crony Hen.

Forthwith you enthusiastically practised with it in the back yard, to show its capabilities, while the hired girl, impeded by its gyrations, fretfully protested that you were "takin' all outdoors."

Your father viewed its numerous inches and smiled.

You clothed it with hook and line, an operation seemingly simple, but calling for a succession of fearful and wonderful knots, and a delicate adapting of length to length.

Thereafter it always was ready, requiring no fitting of joint and joint, no adjustment of reel, threading of eye, and attaching of snell. In your happy-go-lucky ways you were exactly suited the one to the other.

During its periods of well-earned rest it reposed across the rafters under the peak of the woodshed, the only place that would accommodate it, although in the first fever gladly would you have carried it to bed with you.

HALF the hot summer afternoon Hen and you dug bait, for you and he were going fishing on the morrow. Had you been obliged to rake the yard as diligently as you delved for worms you would have been on the verge (for the hundredth time) of running away and making the folks sorry; but there is such a wide gulf betwixt raking a yard and digging bait that even the blisters from the two performances are totally distinct.

With a prodigality that indicated at the least a week's trip, you plied your baking-powder can—the cupboard was continually stripped of baking-powder cans, in those days—with long, fat angleworms and short, fat grubs; and topping them with dirt to preserve their freshness, you set them away till the morning.

Then, with mutual promises to "be on time," Hen and you separated.

"I suppose," said father, gravely, to mother, across the table, at supper, "that I need n't order anything at Piper's [Piper was the butcher] for a few days."

"Why so?" asked mother, for the moment puzzled.

"We 'll have fish, you know."

"Sure enough!" agreed mother, enlightened, and glancing at you. "Of course; Johnny 's going fishing."

From your end of the table you looked keenly at the one and at the other and pondered. If the show of confidence in you was genuine, how gratified and proud you felt! But was it? Father went

"'JUST A BULLHEAD!'"

on soberly eating; mother, transparent soul, smiled at you, as if in reparation, and winked both eyes.

You grinned confusedly, and bent again to your plate. Yes, they were making fun of you. But who cared! And you had mental revenge in the thought that perhaps you 'd *show* them.

You turned in early, as demanded by the strenuous day ahead. To turn you out no alarm-clock was necessary. The sun himself was just parting the pink hangings of the east, and on earth apparently only the roosters and robins were astir, when, with a hazy recollection of having fished all night, you scrambled to the floor and into your clothes.

Mother's voice sounded gently outside the door.

"Johnny?"

"Yes; I 'm up."

"All right. I was afraid you might oversleep. Now be careful to-day, won't you, dear?"

Again you assured her. You heard her soft steps going back down the stairs. She never failed to make your rising her own, both to undertake that you should not be

disappointed and to deliver a final loving caution.

Your dressing, although accompanied by sundry yawns, was accomplished quickly, your attire for the day being by no means complicated. Your face and hair received what Maggie, the girl, would term "a lick and a promise," and kitchenward you sped.

To delay to eat the crackers and milk that had been provided was a waste of time; but you had been instructed, and so you gobbled them down. On the kitchen table was your lunch, tied in shape convenient to stow about your person. It was a constant fight on your part with mother to make her keep your lunches at the minimum. Had she her way, you would have traveled with a large basket; and what boy wanted to be bothered with baskets and pails and things?

Upon the back porch, where you had stationed them in minute preparation, had been awaiting you all night the can of bait and the loyal pole. You seized them. Provisioned and armed, you ran into the open and looked expectantly for Hen.

From Hen's house came no sign of life. You whistled softly; no Hen. Your heart sank. Once or twice before Hen had failed you. Affairs at his house seemed to be not so systematized as at yours.

You whistled louder; no Hen. You called, your voice echoing along the still somnolent street.

"All right," suddenly responded Hen, sticking his head out of his window.

He was not even up!

You were disgusted. One might as well not go fishing as to start so late and have all the other fellows there first; and you darned "it" gloomily.

After seemingly an age, but with his mouth full and with other tokens of haste, Hen emerged from the side door.

"Bridget promised to call me and she forgot to wake up," he explained.

Had Hen *your* mother, he would have been better cared for. But, then, households differ.

At last you were off, your jacket, necessary as a portable depository, balanced with lunch, and the can of worms snugly fitted into a pocket, over the hard-boiled eggs; your mighty pole, become through many pilgrimages a veteran, sweeping the horizon; and your gallant old straw, ragged of contour and prickly with broken ends, courting, like some jaunty, out-at-the-elbow, swash-buckler cavalier, every passing breeze.

As you and Hen hurried along, how you chattered, the pair of you, with many a brag and "I bet you" and bit of exciting hearsay! How big you were with expectations!

"By jinks! I pity the fish to-day!" bantered "Uncle" Jerry Thorne, hoe in hand in his garden patch, stiffly straightening to watch you as you pattered by.

You did not answer. Onward stretched your way. Moments were precious. Who could tell what might be happening ahead at the fishing-place? Busier cackled the town hens, into view rolled the town's sun, from town chimneys here and there idly floated breakfast smoke. The town was entering upon another day, but you—ah, you were destined afar and you must not stay.

To transport your pole, at times inclined to be unruly, with its line ever reaching out at mischievous foliage and its hook ever leaving butt or cork and angling for clothing, was an engineering feat demanding no slight ingenuity. The board walk, which later would be baking hot, so that the tender soles of barefooted little girls would curl and shrink and seek the grass, was gratefully cool, blotched as it was with dampness from the dripping trees. When the walk ceased, the road lay moist and velvety, the path was wet and cold, the fringing bushes spattered you with diamonds, and the lush turf, oozing between your toes, gave to your eager tread.

Rioted thrush and woodpecker and all their feathered cousins; higher into the silver-blue sky climbed the sun, donning anon his golden robes of state; one last impatient halt, to extract your hook from your coat collar, and now, your happy legs plashed knee over with dew and clinging dust, you had reached your goal.

You and Hen were not the first of the day's fishermen. As the vista of bank and water unfolded before your roving eyes you descried a rival already engaged. By his torn and sagging brim, by his well-worn shirt, by his scarred and faded overalls, draggling about his ankles and dependent upon one heroic strap, you recognized a familiar. It was Snoopie—Snoopie Mitchell, who always was fishing, because he never had to ask anybody's permission.

Snoopie's flexible life appeared to you the model one.

"Hello, Snoop!" called you and Hen.

"Hello!" responded Snoopie, phlegmatically, desisting a moment from watching his cork, as he squatted over his pole.

"Caught anything yet?"

"Jus' come," vouchsafed Snoopie. "They ain't bitin' much. But yesterday —gee! you ought to 've been here yesterday!"

No doubt; that usually was the way when you had to stay at home.

You tugged your bait from its tight

"'BITIN' AGAIN?'"

lodgment; you peeled off your coat and tossed it aside as you would a scabbard; with feverish fingers, lest Hen should beat you, hopeful that you might even outdo Snoopie, you unwrapped your gallant pole of its line, and selecting a plump worm, slipped it, despite its protesting squirms, adown the hook.

The favorite stands at this resort were marked by their colonies of tinware—bait-cans cast away upon the grass and mud, some comparatively bright and recent, many very rusty and ancient, their un-fragrant sighs horrifying the summer zephyrs. You sought *your* stand and threw in.

From his stand Hen also threw in.

An interval of suspense ensued. The placid water was full of delightful possibilities. What glided therein that *might* be caught! You besought your bobber with a gaze almost hypnotic; but the bobber floated motionless and obdurate.

"Snoopie 's got a bite!"

At the announcement you darted ap-prehensive glances in Snoopie's direction. You were greedy enough to harbor the wish—but, ah!

"Snoopie 's got one! Snoopie 's got one!"

Snoopie's pole had energetically reared upward and backward, and, as if at its beckoning, something small, black, and glistening had popped straight out from the glassy surface before and had flown high into the brush behind.

Snoopie rushed after, and Hen and you discarded everything and rushed, too.

"Just a bullhead!"

So it was, and quite three inches long. Snoopie ostentatiously strung it on a bit of cord and tethered it, at the water's edge, to a stake. Then he threw in again and promptly caught another.

Somehow, Snoopie invariably did this. He was lucky in more respects than one.

From each side Hen and you sidled toward him and put your bobbers as near his as you dared.

"G' wan!" objected Snoopie, with shrill emphasis. "What you kids comin' here for? Go find your own places. I got this first."

Presently, to your agony, Hen likewise jerked out an astonished pout.

"Ain't you had any bites yet?" he fired triumphantly at you.

"How deep you got your hook?" you replied.

Hen held his line so that you might see. To miss no chances, you measured accu-rately with a reed. Once more you ad-justed your cork, moving it up a fraction of an inch, and you spat on your baited hook.

Again you threw in, landing your now irresistible lure the length of your pole and line from the shore.

"Quit your splashin'!" remonstrated Snoopie. "I had a dandy bite, an' you scared him away. Darn you! can't you throw in easy?"

The ripples caused by your bobber widened in concentric circles and died. You watched and waited. A kingfisher dived from his post upon a dead branch, and rising with a minnow in his bill to show you how easy it was, dashed away, laughing derisively.

With a quick exclamation, Hen swished aloft the tip of his pole.

"Golly! but I had a big nibble! He took the cork clear under!" he cried.

You wondered fiercely why *you* could n't have a nibble.

As if in answer to your mute prayer, your bobber quivered, spreading a series of little rings. An electric thrill leaped through your whole body, and your fingers tight-ened cautiously around the well-warmed butt, which they had been caressing in vain.

"I 've got a bite! I 've got a bite!" you called gleefully.

Hen and Snoopie turned their faces to witness what might take place.

Then your cork was stricken with inter-mittent palsy, and then it staggered and swung as though it had a drop too much. Your sporting blood aflame, you bided the operations of the rash meddler who was causing this commotion.

The cork tilted alarmingly, so that the water wetted it all over. With a jump and a burst of pent-up energy (no cat after a mouse could be quicker), you whipped the heavens with your great pole; but only an empty hook followed after.

"Shucks!" you lamented.

"Aw, you jerked too soon!" criticized Snoopie.

"Darn him! he ate all my bait, any-how!" you declared. "See?"

With utmost speed you fitted another

worm and very smoothly let down exactly in the same spot.

Scarcely had the cork settled when it resumed its erratic movements. Its persecutor, whatsoever he might be, was a persistent chap.

"Bitin' again?" inquired Snoopie, noting your strained attitude.

You abandoned your pole; you plunged after him. Upon hands and knees you wallowed and grappled with him. With fish instinct, he was wriggling for the deeps and safety. You grasped him. He slid through your clutch. You grabbed at him again and obtained a pinching hold on his tail. He broke the hold and was off.

"'IT 'S NOTHIN' BUT A SNAG!'"

You nodded; the moment was too vital to admit of conversation.

"I got him! I got him! I—"

You had exulted too soon. Out like a feather you had whisked the meddlesome fellow, but in mid-air, unable to maintain the sudden pace, he parted company with the impaling steel. Down he dropped, and while the lightened hook went on without him he dived into the shallows where mud meets water.

"Get him!" shrieked Snoopie.

"Get him!" shrieked Hen.

Desperately you scooped up the slime. Once more you had him. He stabbed you with his needle-like spines, but you flinched not. You hurled him inshore and tore after, not allowing him an instant's respite.

There! He lay gasping upon the drier bank. He had lost, and out of his one piggish eye not plastered shut he signaled surrender.

Of the two parties to the wrestle you were much the muddier.

"How big?" queried Hen, anxiously.

"Oh, 'bout as big as the first one Snoop caught," you replied, which was strictly the truth.

You devoted a few seconds to squeezing your pricked thumb; then pleasantly aware that several new arrivals were viewing your success, you gingerly strung him and deposited him, thus secured, in his native element. Here he flopped a moment, but finding his efforts useless, sulked out of sight.

You baited up; you were more contented.

Two pole-lengths from shore occurred a quick splash and a swirl.

"Gee!" burst simultaneously from the three of you; and you stared with wide eyes at the spot where the bubbles were floating.

"What was that?" ejaculated Hen.

"A big bass, I bet you," averred Snoopie.

Nobody—within your memory, at least—ever had actually caught a "big bass" in these haunts, but upon various occasions, such as the present one, he had made himself known. To doubt his existence was heresy. He was here; of course he was. Nearly to see him was an exploit accomplished by many; nearly to catch him was accomplished by only a few less: but really to haul him out had been accorded to none.

In the meantime he cruised about, in his mysterious way, and now and then made a rumpus on the surface, to wring a tribute of hungry "Gees!" from the astounded spectators of his antics.

You gripped closer your pole and barely breathed. Perhaps he was heading in your direction; perhaps, at last, he would accept your worm, and, glory! *you* would be the boy to carry him through town, and home! Could anything be more deliriously grand?

On the other hand, misery! perhaps he was heading for Snoopie or Hen. However, he might turn aside.

Silence reigned; the atmosphere was tense with expectation. Another swirl, a small one, off a brush-pile nearer the shore, just to your left. Cautiously you tiptoed down there and craftily introduced your tempting hook.

The cork vibrated. For an instant you lost your breath. The cork dipped. You poised, rigid but alert, daring to stir not even a toe. The cork righted, dipped again, and slowly, calmly sank into the pregnant depths.

Furiously you struck. Your good pole bent and swayed. You were wild with excitement.

"Say! Look there! Look at John!" exclaimed Hen.

"Hang on to him! Don't let him get away!" bawled Snoopie.

Spurred by your down-curving pole and your violent endeavors, they scampered madly to your succor.

"Don't you give him slack!" instructed Snoopie. "He'll get loose!"

"Don't bust the pole, either!" warned Hen.

As for you, you were fighting with all your strength. The line was taut, sawing the water, as valiantly you hoisted with the writhing tip. Your antagonist yielded a few inches, only to demand them back again. You were in deadly fear lest the hook would not hold. You hoped that he had swallowed it. But who might tell?

At any rate, you were determined that he should not have a vestige more of line if *you* could help it.

"Can you feel him?" asked Hen.

"Uh huh," you panted affirmatively.

"Gim*me* the pole," ordered Snoopie.

You shook your head. You wanted to do it all yourself.

Little by little, in response to the relentless leverage that you exerted, your victim was being dragged to the surface. Higher and higher was elevated your pole, and the wet line followed. The cork appeared and left the water. Victory was almost yours, but you would not relax.

"It's nothin' but a snag!" denounced Snoopie.

You would not believe. It was—if it was not the big bass, it was something else wonderful.

A second—and up through the heaving area upon which were fixed your eyes broke a black stem. Swifter it exposed itself, and suddenly you had hoisted into the sunlight an ugly old branch, soaked and dripping, wrenched by your might from the peaceful bed where it long had lain.

Amid irritating jeers you swung it to shore.

"Well, I *had* something all right—and

it was a bass, too; and he snagged my hook on me. He took the bobber under in less 'n no time, I tell you!" you argued defensively.

That was a favorite trick of the "big bass" and other prodigies of these waters —to be almost caught and to escape by cleverly snagging the hook.

Hen and Snoopie returned to their stations. You ruefully twisted your hook from the rotten wood and tried in a new place for bullheads.

You tired of this location and changed to a log; and tiring of the log, you changed to a rock; and tiring of the rock, you changed to a jutting bank; and tiring of the bank, you waded into the shallows, where, at least, the flies could not torment your legs. In the course of your wanderings your can toppled; you snatched at it, but it evaded you, gurgled, and gently sank beneath. You borrowed bait from more or less unwilling brethren, or appealed

"YOU LUXURIOUSLY DINED"

to the most respectable of the riffraff cans scattered about. From the zenith the sun glared down upon your neck, and from the water the sun glared up into your face, and neck and face waxed red and redder; turtles poked their heads forth and in-

spected you; and dragon-flies darted at your bobber and settled upon it, giving you starts as you thought for an instant that you had a bite. You pricked your fingers on the "stingers" of vengeful victims, and you cut your feet on tin and shell and sharp root and branch; you luxuriously dined on butter-soaked bread and saltless eggs (the salt being spilled), and you drank of water which, in these scientific later days, we know with horror to have been alive with deadly bacilli; and Snoopie, lying on his back, with his hat over his eyes, tied his line to his big toe and went to sleep.

Finally, spotted with mud and mosquito-bumps, scarlet with burn and bristling with experiences, in the sunset glow homeward you trudged, over your shoulder your faithful pole, and your hapless spoil, ever growing drier and dustier and more wretched, dangling from your hand.

"Mercy, John! What *do* you bring those home for!" expostulated mother, from a safe distance surveying your catch, none thereof longer than a clothes-pin.

"Why, to eat," you explained.

And she fried them for you, her very self.

10
Fishing
for
Mountain Trout
(1910)

·FISHING FOR MOUNTAIN· ·TROUT· BY SAMUEL G. CAMP

Photographs by the Author

TO the accustomed trout fisherman the words "mountain trout" have a definite significance. Do you remember — or is it so very long ago that you have forgotten—the little mountain stream where you took your first trout and your first lessons in trout fishing? No need to describe your tackle and methods at that time—"boy tackle," but, withal, a pretty keen little angler behind it. It was not long before you knew where to look for trout, and how to float down your garden-hackle where it would do the most good. That was some time before you took up dry-fly fishing. If, to-day, you are more than ordinarily successful as a trout fisher-

man, that little mountain brook and the days you passed along its banks are three-quarters of the reason.

Quite recently, at the Upper Dam, Rangeley Lakes, Maine, "the place, of all others, where the lunacy of angling may be seen in its incurable stage," a genuine brook trout, *Salvelinus fontinalis*, weighing twelve and a half pounds was captured. This trout, authenticated beyond doubt, was not taken by an angler but by some hatchery men for breeding purposes. At the same place, in the fall of 1908, a brook trout scaling nine pounds seven ounces was taken on the fly by Mr. Raymond S. Parrish, of Montville, Connecticut, concerning whose prowess as an angler— "Parsons the furtive fisherman" — the reader is referred to Henry Van Dyke's story, "A Fatal Success."

Some little time ago, at the biennial session of the General Assembly of a certain State, a bill making seven inches the length of trout to be legally retained came up for consideration. Whereupon, the Honorable Member from—but that might identify the State—at any rate, the Honorable Member arose and, with tears in his eyes, protested that in his county, although there were several trout streams, many trout, and a well-established industry devoted to their capture, there was not at that time in that county, or ever had been at any time in that county, a trout measuring seven inches! Wherefore the injustice of such a measure to his constituents was palpable, etc., etc. The bill did not pass.

Trout fishing may mean one thing, and it may mean another. It is a fact that in many parts of Vermont, Massachusetts, and Connecticut, and doubtless other States, trout fishing such as that described by the Honorable Member— of course, he exaggerated a little as becomes all Honorable Members, orators, and anglers—is the rule and not the exception.

Where average fishing may be had it is a very poor plan, one finely calculated to spoil sport, to fish the small mountain streams. These little brooks act as feeders for the larger streams and rivers. In the fall the trout of the larger streams ascend these brooks to spawn, and the little trout remain in them from the fry to the fingerling stage, when they seek the deeper and more extensive streams. "Skinning" the small brooks merely means that the stock in the larger ones will surely de-

teriorate in numbers and in size, and eventually poor fishing or none at all will be the rule.

But if the small feeder brooks are religiously protected, the stocking of the larger streams is more or less automatic no matter how hard these may be fished; this is especially true where the little feeders are stocked by the State or by individuals. It is manifestly futile to stock the little brooks and at the same time allow them to be fished. And stocking is most successful where the fry or fingerlings are planted in the small tributary streams where they are free from the larger trout and the generally strenuous life of the rivers.

But where little brooks and small mountain trout obtain exclusively, where heavier fishing need not be taken into consideration, fishing for the little charrs of the mountain brooks is a legitimate sport—and not a half bad one. With trout fishing, as, in fact, with any sport of the rod and gun, especially in these days when light creels and hunting-coat pockets are the rule—the law in most localities jealously looking out for this— and when the camera plays so important a part in field sports of every nature, the country to be fished or hunted, whether attractive or commonplace, is a primary consideration. It would be difficult to find a more pleasant field of action than that afforded by the typical mountain trout stream.

When you go fishing for mountain trout you seek the country of the ruffed grouse and the woodcock, the gray squirrel and the white-tailed deer, the pines and hardwoods, and, withal, a rather strenuous country. Following the brook you pass through deep ra-

WHERE A TROUT WEIGHING A QUARTER OF A POUND IS A MONSTER.

THE FIRST SIGHT OF THE LITTLE BROOK—WITHAL, A
SOMEWHAT STRENUOUS COUNTRY.

the brook and, if you are at all lucky and quiet, you may see the trail makers. Incidents of this sort, with fair success with the little rod, will surely serve to make your day a pleasant one. In such streams a trout weighing a quarter of a pound is a monster, and the average is less than that. But sport with any game fish is largely a matter of the tackle used, and presumably you will use light tackle.

The little trout of the mountain streams, unless in very secluded brooks which have been fished little or not at all, are not in the least foolish or uneducated. Anglers are wont to associate extreme sophistication with the two-pounders of the big rivers. When considering the typical mountain trout it is well to remember that with them size is small indication of age or degree of education.

The size of brook trout is a matter of range-extent and food supply, and the charrs of the little brooks of the hill country are small because the food supply is limited, the "swim" is limited, and the little fellows have to work hard for a living. So the six-incher of the narrow, shallow, and rapid mountain brook may be even as highly educated as the two-pound brown trout which, in a more extensive stream, rises only to the fly cast "dry and cocked." At any rate, if you find a well-worn angler's path along the little brook, you will have to use some finesse and no little patience and ingenuity in order to make a very heavy showing.

Fishing for mountain trout has its "know how" equally with the sport on larger streams and weightier fish. The primary essential for success and sport is light tackle—the very lightest. Fly-casting in any true sense of the words, because of the confined and brushy nature of the stream, is out of the ques-

vines strewn with green, moss-grown rocks, steep, slippery, moist, and prolific of mosquitoes, tumbles, tackle smash-ups —and trout!

You work through little alder swamps, almost impenetrable tangles of close-growing alders interspersed with bogs, mud- and sink-holes, where there is nothing to see but the work ahead, and nothing to do but to do it—and catch trout. But, however difficult may be the local habitation of the mountain trout, it is sure to have the virtues of picturesqueness and freedom from monotony, and to offer many opportunities for the camera as well as the rod.

Working quietly along the little stream you will sometimes flush a ruffed grouse and will often hear them drumming. Later in the spring perhaps a woodcock will get up within the rod's length of you. Where deer are at all common you will see their tracks along tion. So the tackle need not be selected with a view to casting any distance, and this permits the use of a small caliber line. An enameled line size G is exactly the sort. This line may properly be used on a little four-ounce fly-rod eight feet in length or thereabouts.

A very small single-action reel should be used, the smaller the better, since a small reel will not foul in the brush as often as a larger one. A very good plan is to wind an additional guide between each of the guides on the rod when much brush fishing is to be done. This will keep the line close to the rod at every point and there will not be slack loops between the guides to catch on branches. The thing to aim for in the whole outfit is to avoid loose ends. Leaders should be short and fine in caliber—short so that the flies may be reeled in close to the rod tip when landing a trout through brush.

Under normal conditions flies and bait are about equally successful for small brook fishing. While it is a fact that real fly-fishing is out of the question, still, the mountain brook is no place for the duffer with a fly-rod. Indeed, a small stream of this sort demands a deftness, skill, and versatility of expedients in handling rod, line, and flies that is unknown on the larger streams out in the open where free casting is the rule. The problem is to get out the flies from fifteen to twenty-five feet without casting them, and it is not always an easy one.

Small flies of modest colors are best, such as coachman, Cahill, cowdung, Beaverkill, and other gray- and brown-winged flies, and also the various hackles. The smallest sizes should be used, tens, twelves, and even at times the midges.

More than two flies should never be used and it is better to use only one.

As a matter of fact it is seldom that more than one fly can be laid on the water and fished properly owing to the difficulty of casting and the smallness of the stream; also, two flies are just twice as apt to get fouled as one. If two flies are used they should be attached to the leader quite close together, say about a foot apart, so that both may be fished at once in the small pools.

The angler will save himself much trouble and annoyance by forgetting to bring a landing net. The use of a net on a seven-inch trout is at best of questionable propriety or necessity—something like using a ten-gage on rail— and on the brushy mountain brook it is the most versatile trouble-maker you can bring along. A very playful little trick of the net fitted with an elastic cord is to catch on a branch, stay behind you to the elastic limit of the cord when you go ahead, then break loose and snap forward into the small of your back

"STRINGING-UP" AT THE HEADWATERS OF THE MOUNTAIN-TROUT HOME.

CLOSE WORK IN THE STREAM THROUGH THE ALDERS.

with considerable velocity and some penetration.

The "smashing effect," however, is usually ultimately upon the net. You do not mind it—much—the first time. You can even condone a second offense. But the third time starts the fireworks in earnest. Instead of the net pack a little pocket ax; it is far more useful.

Perhaps the greatest factor for success in this sort of fishing is the faculty of going slowly, never hurrying by places which look a little difficult to fish and consequently have been neglected by other anglers, and carefully fishing out all fishable water. Here and there you can make short casts in the usual man-

ner; in other places the flies may be got out by simply swinging them over the water as you would fish a garden-hackle.

Often the only way to get out the flies is to make a "snap cast," using a line about the length of the rod, grasping the end fly between the thumb and forefinger of the left hand, pulling straight back so as to get a good bend in the rod, and then letting go, always carefully avoiding the possibility of hooking yourself in the fingers. In this manner very accurate casts, in difficult places, may be made with a little practice.

When a trout is hooked, if the banks are so brushy that you cannot beach or swing—not throw—him out, the fish

HERE AND THERE YOU CAN CAST IN THE USUAL MANNER.

should be slowly reeled in up to the leader knot, taking pains to avoid reeling the knot through the tip guide and thus fouling the line, and then brought in through the brush by moving the rod backward, keeping it down low. Many trout will be lost by attempting to land them in this way and the method should only be used as a last resort in the worst and most brushy places. Move slowly and quietly, keep as far back from the brook as possible without using too long a line and thus inviting disaster, and use deliberation in the choice of methods for fishing the various little pools, falls, and shallows. The first cast is the one that counts.

When brush fishing a good point to remember is not to strike upward but, rather, backward or toward you. If you strike upward a missed strike always means a hang-up, but if you strike by pulling the rod quickly toward you, always keeping it down low, line-fouling is in great measure obviated. An effective method is to strike not with the rod but by quickly pulling in the line through the rod guides with the left hand. The two-handed caster who habitually uses the slack-line cast soon becomes very expert at striking small trout in brushy streams in this manner.

As a general thing, and as above stated, you will not ordinarily find trout

NO ROOM FOR FANCY CASTING IN THIS WATER.

IF YOU DON'T SAVE THE SMALL ONES, YOU DON'T SAVE ANY.

exceeding seven or eight inches in the small mountain streams, but conditions vary and a good many times you may take or see taken a trout weighing a pound or even more. Many small brooks, although they are not wide, may be comparatively very deep. Little brooks flowing through meadow lands and swamps, with sandy or muddy bottoms, are apt to be of this sort; often they are not over two or three feet wide but there will be many places, particularly at the bends and below little falls, where the depth is from three to four feet with fine shelters for trout hollowed out beneath the banks by the current.

There is a brook of this sort, well-known to the writer, which flows partly in Massachusetts and partly in Connecticut. Its average width is not over five feet and the bottom is muddy. Mostly it runs through an alder swamp with a little open fishing in the clearings.

Men who have ambition and sand enough to fish through the swamp— football is child's play in comparison— show "strings" of trout that would drive the average angler crazy; many times the creels show from a dozen to twenty trout, not a single one much less than a pound and running from that up to two pounds and a half. This is not a fish story alleged but one experienced. Not long ago a friend of the writer's took two trout from this stream which weighed just five pounds.

In view of this it is a good plan to find out from local anglers whether the stream you are going to try has a reputation for an occasional big trout, and outfit accordingly. It is rather disconcerting when you are sure that seven inches is the limit for the stream to have a pound fish roll up to your flies; and always a rattled angler means a lost trout.

11
The Trout
of the
Nepisiguit
(1904)

SCRIBNER'S MAGAZINE

VOL. XXXV   JUNE, 1904   NO. 6

THE TROUT OF THE NEPISIGUIT

By Frederic Irland

PHOTOGRAPHS BY CHARLES D. JOSLYN AND THE AUTHOR

A TROUT river ought not to be too easy of approach. Now for instance, there is the Au Sable, in northern Michigan. One railroad crosses near its source, and another at its mouth. All you have to do is to take the train and go to Grayling, put a boat into the water close by the railroad station, and float without effort on the smooth, strong current all the way to Lake Huron, unless you get mixed up with the overhanging cedars that sweep the river in many places. If you run afoul of them you will upset, and then you will find how chilly is the water best adapted to the health of trout. The piscatorial favors of that river are at the disposal of anyone who cares to accept them. So, during the open season, this wonderful stream is crowded with fishermen. It is rather disquieting to know that at any moment, while you are casting over a likely pool, a stranger may hook you firmly in the neck.

Last June my friend the Fish Commissioner, who has a cottage on the banks of the Au Sable, invited me to visit that beautiful but delusive stream. We spent several days in submitting fine specimens of the flytier's art for the inspection of the capricious fish. Nineteen times out of twenty, if a trout took any notice at all, he would dart out from under a sunken log, give one sharp look at the fly to ascertain the maker's name, flirt his tail disdainfully, and return whence he came, the whole thing being over in about a second. The Commissioner does not always fish. In the closed season he may be found hypnotizing courts of last resort; but the occupation he most enjoys is the educating of trout. He is exceedingly proud of the intelligence displayed by his apt pupils in differentiating live insects that fall on the water by accident, from spurious creations at the end of a string, cast on the surface by design. If a hundred trout rush out of their lairs to look at his flies in the course of a day's fishing, and only five of them are deceived, he feels that his protégés are entitled to a credit mark of 95 per cent. If the sky is murky, and the breeze makes ripples on the water, so that seventeen fish out of one hundred fall victims to their own inadvertence, he feels chagrined that his scholars are becoming dull-witted. He hopes some day they will attain a proficiency of one hundred per cent. Then they will be safe from honest men.

After a day when the trout had shown unusual discernment, and I had taken just two that were above eight inches in length, I told the Commissioner we ought to go to a place where the fish were as the heathen in their blindness, but where they made up in size and recklessness what they lacked in discrimination. I said he had developed the intelligence of the Au Sable trout to a point where they could care for themselves, and that he ought to bestow some of the blessings of civilization on other watery multitudes far away. So in a self-sacrificing missionary spirit he consented to go, and in August, when we knew the black flies would not be very troublesome, we got on board a sleeping-car and rode a thousand miles to New Brunswick.

A relative of mine who gets his geography lessons from western railroad folders once told me he did not see why anyone should go to New Brunswick to fish, because the map he looked at did not show any rivers; but if you will examine a large and accurate map you will see that the face of that good old wilderness is seamed with hundreds of wrinkles. Every wrinkle is a stream, and some of them are so crooked you can scarcely tell which way they run. Their sources seem inextricably tangled. A Massachusetts college professor has devoted his vacations for several years to the unravelling of these watery labyrinths, and his amateur surveys are of great value to the crown land office. He says that a long time ago the upper waters of the great St. John River used to flow across New Brunswick into the Bay Chaleur; but that afterward the backbone of the country was elevated, so that part of the river was compelled to reverse its direction, and the water cut a new channel to the Bay of Fundy. This curious geological performance ultimately had a queer political result. The

The trout that died happy.

map-makers of the eighteenth century, who lived in London, had never seen the country, and did not know that some of these far-away rivers in Canada had broken in two and taken the back track. They knew there were some rivers that flowed into the St. Lawrence, and some that fell into the sea. They reasoned that there ought to be a range of mountains running through the centre of the country; and because the mountains ought to be there, they put them on the map. After the Revolutionary War the peace commissioners agreed on this imaginary mountain range as the boundary line on paper between Canada and the United States. The unhappy surveyors who were

sent to find the mountains could not locate them, because they were not there. This enabled Daniel Webster, when he was Secretary of State fifty years afterward, to keep the upper half of Maine as a part of the United States; and for this piece of statecraft his reputation in New Brunswick is damaged to this day. But the result of this proceeding was that when the Intercolonial Railway was built, being a military highway it had to take a very circuitous course around the edge of the Province, to keep away from American soil, and so the centre of New Brunswick, instead of being opened up to settlement, was left as it now is, a complete wilderness.

The trip planned by the Commissioner and myself was a journey by canoe, from the Maine border clear across New Brunswick to the Bay Chaleur. Two fine streams, the Tobique, gliding westward, and the Nepisiguit, tumbling toward the east, are cradled in lakes which are only three miles apart, and the neck of land between them has been an Indian portage from immemorial time. The eastern woodland Indian sticks to the water. The idea some people have that he goes through the forest as a crow flies through the air, in a perfectly straight line, is entirely incorrect. If there is one thing the Indian knows better than another it is that in the woods a straight line is not always the shortest distance between two points. His idea of woodcraft is to go up one river and down another wherever he can; and nobody knows how many hundred years ago the Micmacs and Milicetes of New Brunswick, taking the otter-trails for their guidance, cleared the bushes off the path leading from one watershed to another. The Indians are nearly all gone now, and it is a good thing for the moose and caribou.

Ready for a fresh start.—Page 644.

At the Forks of the Tobique, fifty-five miles above the place where it falls into the St. John, four streams unite to make the main river, and here the Tobique Salmon Club has its house. This is occupied during the fishing season, but beyond it nobody lives, and you do not see another human habitation until you reach the head of the settlement on the lower Nepisiguit, one hundred and twenty miles away. The Tobique is a famous salmon stream, and thanks to the vigilance of Superintendent Tom Allen and his young men, who watch over the salmon like as a father pitieth his children, nobody goes up river to fish unless he has a right to do so. The Upper Nepisiguit is too far away from the settlements to be disturbed by poachers. No one thinks of fishing much for trout in a salmon country anyway, and the result of this combination of circumstances is that the pools of the Upper Nepisiguit conceal trout large enough to swallow young ducks. These waters, including the nest of lakes where the river is hatched, are leased for fishing purposes by an enterprising young man

named George E. Armstrong, who lives down at Perth, on the St. John. So lightly are the privileges esteemed, because of the remoteness of the water, that he got the whole thing for ten years, for fifty dollars a year.

The Commissioner's daughters can cast a fly almost as far and fine as he can, and because Mr. Armstrong said that within the memory of the oldest inhabitant of New Brunswick no woman had ever taken the canoe trip across, and because the waters of the Nepisiguit are very wild and beautiful, these young ladies prevailed upon their father to let them go with him.

There is a railroad that runs up the Tobique twenty miles to a place called Plaster Rock, where lives a feudal baron who charges passers-by twenty dollars for the use of a spring wagon for one day, to take them to the Forks. But the country in which he lives is so beautiful that five minutes after you leave him you forget all about his mediæval way of doing things.

Armstrong had been notified to have five

canoes and four young men of the country at the Forks, ready for our journey. It was in the haying season, and men were not easy to get. "When they know you have got to have 'em, they hang back," said Armstrong. But after a pleasant day at the club-house enough polers and canoes came so that we made a start. The Tobique Salmon Club placed at our disposal the whole fishing of the Little Tobique on our way up; and we took from its pools enough beautiful fish—ten and

The old Indian portage.—Page 642.

The amphibious canoe.

twelve pounders—to show that the salmon were there. Senator Proctor, of the Club, told us afterward that the members rarely or never fish the Little Tobique, and he thought we were entitled to the fishing by right of discovery. The other branches are considered superior. More than four hundred fine salmon were taken with the fly last summer in the water leased by this club. The branch we ascended was full of parr under five inches in length, brilliant in the

iridescent markings that give the young salmon his distinctive baby name.

The first afternoon we fished, the Commissioner killed a fine little twelve-pound salmon on a six-ounce rod. He had an appliance that was new to me. A salmon requires a long line, for he will often run fifty yards on the very first rush after he is hooked. The line required, if all one size, makes a large and clumsy reel necessary. But the Commissioner had a moderate-sized trout reel containing thirty yards of heavy casting line, and beneath that, spliced on, fifty yards of hard fine running line, that took up very little space on the reel, yet was strong enough for any strain. With this outfit he killed his first fish in a very short time. And when his eldest daughter hooked a fifteen-pound fish—that is a chapter by itself.

The Tobique is full of holes that look like splendid salmon pools. Yet the fish pass by many of them year after year, and are found only in others that seem less hospitable.

A fishing camp on the Tobique.

Salmon pool on the Upper Tobique.—Page 644.

Who knows the way of the eagle in the air, or of the salmon in the sea? Of all fish the most tantalizing, he has been the life-study of thousands of men. Yet how little anyone really knows about him, and how conflicting is the testimony as to what is known! If you want to get the idea that there is no such thing as abstract truth, you can form that opinion quickly by sitting in front of the fireplace in a fishing club some evening when the most experienced members are present and feel like talking. There is scarcely any proposition connected with the life history of this fish upon which any two men of forty or fifty years' experience in salmon fishing will agree. The biography of the fish is filled with puzzling blanks. You catch a glimpse of him in his infancy. He mysteriously disappears, returns during adolescence, and

The Nepisiguit near its source.—Page 650.

then is gone again until, on his third appearance, the infant has grown to be fully mature. Who would think the childish smolt of a few ounces, that slips quietly down river in the early spring, could come back the same summer in the pride of youth as a three or four pound grilse? And the next time he goes, upon what meat doth he feed, that he jumps to maturity and ten pounds' weight? What ports does he visit while he is off on his deep-sea cruise? Where does he keep the chart by which, after his far-away wanderings, he unerringly returns to his birthplace? And why do many grilse come to some rivers and comparatively few or none to others? In Miramichi waters there are in August ten grilse to every full-grown salmon. In the Tobique there are scarcely any grilse at all.

Many are the ways of propelling watercraft; but none, I think, so interesting as poling a canoe up a rapid stream. In comparatively slow currents and in crossing lakes the paddle is always used, but on a roaring, rocky river, full of bowlders, where the current is swift and full of turns, the pole is indispensable.

Although the canoe is still the universal means of summer transportation in the larger part of North America, and although, except the raft, it is the oldest type of watercraft in use, there are such variations in its form in different places that an experienced Canadian traveller, if he came down from a balloon, could tell pretty nearly where he was as soon as he saw a canoe. On the Miramichi the pine pirogue, or dugout, thirty feet long, is in very general use. On the streams of that water system there is little or no carrying, and the weight of the canoe is of small consequence. The Micmac birch-bark of the Nepisiguit can be recognized half a mile off by its high, bulging centre. The canoe on the Tobique is a home-made product, but the model is borrowed from Maine. It is like the birch-bark in all except the outer skin. That is of canvas, stretched and painted. One of these canoes, twenty feet long, will carry a surprising load, and a man who knows how can stand in the stern and push it up stream against a tremendous current. To a person unfamiliar with the setting-pole it is a demon of perversity, and the canoe acts worse than a frightened pig. It dodges first one way, then the other. It tries to turn round, to back, to roll over. The pole catches between sunken bowlders, or slips on a smooth rock, or dives deep

The Commissioner and the loon.—Page 653.

into an undiscovered hole at the foot of a rapid, where pole-bottom is most needed. Generally the new poler goes out into the water. I have done some hard work in this line. On the way up Tobique I poled the Commissioner's canoe some of the time. He is a heavy man, but he got a board and put it across the gunwales for a seat. This procedure altered what experts call the metacentric height of the canoe, and my friend has not yet grown tired of telling what happened. It was the finest illustration of unstable equilibrium I have ever seen. One day I felt strong and spurted ahead of the other canoes. Soon we came to a place called the Ledges, where the water runs swiftly and silently over rocks smooth as glass. I could not get the pole to hold on the bottom. First the canoe stood still; then it began to sidle across the river and to settle back, in spite of my most earnest efforts. The four other canoes, manned by experienced young men of the country, who had poled boats since they were four years old, all filed by me in stately procession, climbing the liquid hill with effortless ease, while I remained stationary, to the great enjoyment of the spectators. I felt humiliated and short of breath. The Commissioner has a vivid recollection of this event, and he tells it circumstantially. Some day I will get him out where the water is very deep, and will capsize the canoe. But the trouble is, he can swim farther than I can. Anyway, I know more about the physical peculiarities of that river than he does.

Strangely enough, the Tobique is not worth mentioning as a trout stream.

Miles of white water—Nepisiguit River.—Page 654.

Though it is pretty certain that its head waters were once connected with the Bathurst lakes that now form the sources of the Nepisiguit, the latter are filled with trout, but the Nictor lakes have few or none. After we left the salmon pools we caught enough fish for an occasional meal as long as we were on Tobique water, but the real trout fishing was on the other side.

There are a few deserted lumber camps on the way up the Little Tobique. Some people may think an old clearing is a good place to pitch a group of tents. Nothing could be further from the truth. A clearing soon grows up to tall grass, that shelters mosquitoes and gnats. It is filled with bushes, that are troublesome to cut away. The wood supply is generally poor, and the clearing is exposed to the wind. The very finest and easiest place to make camp when travelling is on a level spot in the woods where not a tree has ever been cut, and, if possible, in a grove of birches.

Here a few strokes of the axe clear away all the underbrush. The birch makes a lovely night fire. There are balsams for boughing the beds, and tenting on such a spot is the luxury of out-door life.

A week from the time we left the Forks of the Tobique we reached Nictor Lake, where rises the great bald dome of Sagamook Mountain, the second peak of the Province in height. A storm had been entangled in the hills for days, and at Nictor Lake we saw its ineffectual efforts to escape. The clouds sailed down the valley, rolled up against Sagamook, and came curling over the top in great white blankets that tucked the mountain snugly away to sleep. Night slowly fell. The rain beat a long tattoo upon the tight canvas of the tents. The glowing logs outside, in the third and best stage of a birch fire, sent out tiny puffs of steam where the drops of water struck, exploding the film of ashes, and producing that little miracle, which no one will believe who has not seen it, the fire that burns more brightly because of a steady pour of rain. The perfume of the woods filled the air. The warmth of the fire soothed weary limbs. The melody of the raindrops was accompanied by the harmony of the wind-swept tree-tops and the waves on the lake shore. From the ladies' tent came little chirps and gigglings, like the chatter of young swallows in a chimney. By the guides' fire somebody was droning an oft-told narrative. How much better story-teller is the primitive man than the busy, newspaper-reading dweller of the town! To the dull senses of the sleepy ones the voice of the tale-teller seemed to float on and on, getting fainter and more distant, till it was lost in the murmur of the forest sounds. That was when sleep came.

Then, as the night passed, the wind went down and the rain ceased. The fire burned lower and lower, and the chill of the dampness crept into the tent. It grew cold, and the lightest sleeper began to dream of walking barefoot in the snow. Miles and miles he trudged over arctic wastes, world-without-end. Then, after what seemed to be hours of shivering, he woke to wonder if anyone would fix the fire. The callous roustabouts in the guides' tent, would they be frozen first? Not they. Not at two o'clock in the morning. So the awakened dreamer rose and threw on logs without stint, till the bright flames shot up and flashed far out on the lake, and a foolish loon, frightened by the blaze, shouted hysterically to her mate that the woods were burning up. How quickly it got warm again! The canvas steamed. Sleep once more, and the next thing, the sun was peering over the corner of Sagamook, and the wilderness was wide awake.

Perhaps there is no country within moderate distance from New York that shows the tremendous results of glacial action so well as central New Brunswick. The upper end of Nictor Lake is filled with huge bowlders that mark the terminal limit of some ancient ice-stream, which laid down there, one by one, the rocky burdens it had carried as far as it could. These piled-up rocks fill the lake almost to the surface of the water; and as the canoe floated over them, it gave one a creepy sensation to think what would happen to the unfortunate who fell in among

them, and got his leg caught in some slippery crevice. Even the best swimmer would have a poor chance. More than one New Brunswick lake is bounded by a curved dike that looks like as if it was dredged up; but these embankments are of glacial origin.

On the shore of Mud Lake, next above Nictor, and the last water on the Tobique side, Adam Moore, a famous guide, has a cabin that he uses in moose-hunting time, but leaves deserted the rest of the year. It was while we were looking at this cabin that one of the polers began waving his arms to attract our attention. When we went down where the canoes were, he showed us a moose in the water up to its neck, feeding on pond-lily roots. Every few minutes it would reach down into the mud, and be entirely out of sight. Two of the boys took a canoe and paddled between the moose and the shore, on the windward side, where it would smell them, and so be driven out into the lake toward the main party. This programme worked well, and the moose waded and swam away from the one canoe, straight toward the four others that it had not winded. Going through the water the moose stretched its neck forward in a ridiculous attitude. When it reached the shore it was not more than a hundred feet away from the nearest canoe. As it was about to enter the woods the man who had the camera hastily secured a picture, consisting mostly of the bow of his canoe. These little episodes make wilderness photography enjoyable.

Twenty-five years ago this spring an old Indian and his two sons killed one hundred and sixty moose near the head of the Tobique, and started down the river with the skins on a raft. When they got into the strong water of the Tobique Narrows the raft struck a rock and was upset, and the Indian lost all his cargo. The moose were pretty scarce for awhile under such treatment; but thanks to the enlightened game laws of the Province they have increased so wonderfully that probably there would be little difficulty in repeating that Indian's performance at any time when the snow is deep in the spring. It is also pretty certain that anyone attempting the experiment would go to jail for the rest of his natural life.

From Mud Lake the old portage runs to the first Bathurst lake, the source of the Nepisiguit. This forest path begins in a balsam swamp, and rises a little toward the

The consummation of canoeing.—Page 656.

The vanishing moose and the intrusive canoe.—Page 650.

lake, through a spruce forest. The Commissioner enlivened the three miles by frequent halts to knock gum off the trees with a pole, spying the inconspicuous little excrescences on the brown trunks with the precision of a professional gum-picker, an accomplishment he learned when a boy in Vermont.

There are few places in North America as beautiful as Bathurst Lake. In every direction there is a wilderness of low mountain peaks, covered with unbroken forest. A number of small streams pour down into the lake, and in August the trout gather in the cooler water opposite the mouths of these rivulets. As soon as we reached the lake, and while we were waiting for the canoes to be carried across the portage, we began to see evidences in the air that there were fish in the water. Fishhawks, cranes and kingfishers were abundant, and there were more loons on the lake than was good for the trout. The Commissioner made a remarkable shot at a kingfisher, killing it with a .30-30 rifle at fully a hundred yards. He hates the birds that prey upon his pets.

Armstrong has a camp on Bathurst Lake, and as soon as we reached it, the girls went

Harry running a rapid.—Page 657.

fishing. There were nine people to fish for, and all hungry. Two canoes moving slowly, and not getting a quarter of a mile from the camp, took forty trout on two rods in less than an hour. The fish were very uniform in size, most of them being about half a pound in weight. Such fishing was too good to be fun. All the smaller ones were promptly put back in the water, but even then it was too soon over. Most of the time both rods were bent. Only a cast or two, and a trout was hooked. Sometimes he broke away, but there was no time to mourn. Another promptly took his place.

It had rained at some time during every day but one since we started; but the next day there was an exhibition down-pour that no one can conceive of unless he has seen it rain on a mountain lake. It always seems to be raining harder on the water than over the land anyway. During one of the lulls I paddled the Commissioner out after loons. In the days of the slow-velocity rifle, with smoking powder, it was of little use to shoot at a loon on a large lake. The creature would dive before the bullet struck,

and reappear a long way off, diving again as soon as he took one breath. But the high-power smokeless rifle is too quick for him. He cannot dive soon enough. We were only out a few minutes, and came back with two dead loons. The guides would scarcely believe it when the Commissioner called to them to come out of the camp to look at the great birds. That one morning's work preserved the lives of more trout last summer than all the fish that were taken by all the people who fished in the lake. Two men had been there before us, but they had gone.

Some people think the loons, kingfishers, fishhawks, sheldrakes, cranes, otters, minks, and other creatures that prey on the fish do no harm to the supply, because they only catch the slower and feebler ones, and thus keep up the standard of vigor among them; but the trout destroyed by their forest enemies, in such a lake as Bathurst, must amount to many thousands every year. Fishing with the fly, a few days each season, is about the same as taking a bucketful of water out of the lake each morning, so far as the supply is concerned.

111

We stayed a couple of days in camp, while the Armstrong brigade were carrying all the freight across the portage. The girls made blueberry pies and red raspberry short-cakes; so that the Commissioner and I lived too high. Then we started down the Nepisiguit, and day by day we saw the life history of a river, from its cradle to the sea. Perhaps it would be hard to find a more typical Canadian stream. Rising in a group of spring-fed

Canoe surgery—mending a break.

Hauling over a cedar jam.

mountain lakes, it has a goodly volume of water from the start. All the way down it is broken, at frequent intervals, by long reaches of bowlder-strewn rapids. Sometimes it is compressed between perpendicular walls, where a glacier long ago threw up a barrier that turned it from its former bed, and then the river slowly cut back to the channel it liked best. In two or three places the process is yet unfinished, and a cataract, without

haste and without rest, is gnawing at the solid rock, century in and out.

Armstrong only sees his river about once a year, and none of the guides except himself had ever been down the Nepisiguit. One of them had been a sailor, and he talked every day of seeing the salt water again. Sometimes when I heard their stories of the lumber camps, and the animals in the woods, and the pride of their strength, I wished I had been born where they were. If they say of a person in that country, "He is a mighty able man," they always mean that he is physically strong. The craft of the lawyer, the wisdom of the statesman, do not much appeal to them. But they are fine fellows, of the same ancestry as our-selves, and they ought to be Americans. But their wilderness is better as it is. If New England had remained British, there might be moose among the Berkshires yet and salmon in the Connecticut.

The boys had all heard about the im-petuous waters of the Nepisiguit, and were greatly impressed with the responsibility of bringing their passengers through safely. The continued rains had raised the water, but in that country, no matter how high the flood, the rivers remain clear. Armstrong said the high water made the fishing poor, but at that it was the most wonderful thing in the way of trout that I ever saw. The heaviest fish we took from the Nepisiguit was caught by a girl, and it weighed four and three-quarter pounds. We did not waste one fish on the whole trip. It was a touching thing to see the Fish Commis-

Great Falls of the Nepisiguit.—Page 657.

Gorge below Great Falls of the Nepisiguit.—Page 657.

sioner, after hooking just one more three-pounder, and exhausting the poor fish till it could not sit up straight, hold the trout right side up with one hand in the water, in order that it might breathe more easily, and smooth its ruffled fins with the other hand, till the trout suddenly revived and shot away!

But the greatest fun of all was running the heavy rapids. I had for a poler a boy named Harry, who I think would try the Whirlpool Rapids below Niagara if anyone dared him to do so. At the first white water we struck, after all the canoes had gone down in safety, and Harry, coming last, had picked out a channel for himself, the Commissioner said, "Harry, I would give five dollars to get a photograph of your canoe

coming over that rapid." "I'll run it over again for a dollar," said Harry. So we took the canoe back over the portage, and ran down again. All the rest of the way down river Harry was looking for rapids to run, that no one else wanted to try, till the people whose baggage was in our canoe came and insisted that the freight be carried elsewhere. They said they did not so much mind two fools being drowned, if that was what we wanted, but they did not wish to have their clothes lost.

There are two ways of running through rough water among bowlders. One is to keep checking the canoe and to drop down easily. The other is to pole vigorously, and by going faster than the water keep steerage-way. Harry always waited at the head of a rough stretch till the other canoes were well out of the way, and then ran down at full speed.

My camera is an experienced traveller. Twice on other trips it has floated down river in capsizes. This year, because everybody was watching to see us swamped, nothing happened. The only upset on the whole trip was once when Fred Watters, who carried freight only, was bringing his craft down a *décharge* after the luggage had been carried around. We were all watching him, and as he shot over the last pitch into a smooth pool, he brought his paddle down flat on the water with a slap, and the handle broke off short. Of course he went out; but he was back again in an instant.

All the way down river we drove ahead of us flocks of young fish-ducks, that could not yet rise from the water, but beat it with their wings, giving them their local name of flappers. On the more frequented rivers these ducks are known as the Poacher's Friends, because they always flee from an approaching canoe, and so give timely notice of the coming fish-warden. But on this wild stream we saw neither poacher nor warden, nor any other stranger, till we got to the end of Armstrong's lease, at the Great Falls. Here we waited for the stuff to be portaged a mile around the gorge of the falls, and when we looked up from a game of four-handed cribbage it gave us a curious start to see, standing twenty feet away, a man who manifestly was no guide of ours. It was the warden of the lower river, come from town to give us the key of the deserted club-house a little way below. The news had gone around the Province that there was a fishing party coming across, and he was there to welcome us; also to see that we did no meddling with the salmon, for the season had closed. Trout were yet a legal prey, but not the big jumpers.

The Great Falls of the Nepisiguit, one hundred feet high, would furnish an immense water power. Some people wanted to put a pulp-mill there, and when they went to see how much the salmon fishers would take for their rights, they found out. The owners of the fishing privileges would take two hundred thousand dollars. The pulp-mill project languishes; and may it die the death and be eternally damned!

We had brought with us a special case of Fishwarden's Joy, for the promotion of diplomatic relations with strangers. When we offered some of this to the guardian of the Nepisiguit he would have none of it. That evening after supper the boys asked him his nationality, and he said he was a Methodist. We concluded that the salmon of the lower Nepisiguit were pretty safe, so far as we were concerned.

The next day we began to see places where people had cut the wild hay along the river, and at noon we came to a crew of men building a wing-dam to keep the logs in the channel at the Pabineau Falls. Then, as we ran down, we surprised a farm-house on the river bank. We had reached the head of the settlement.

We shot beneath the high spans of the railroad bridge, portaged around the last rock-bound rapid, and met the little floating bits of sand that marked the incoming of the flood tide. An hour later we stepped ashore at Bathurst, and heard that the *America's* cup was still in New York.

That night there was a grand sale of slightly worn canoes, and the guides grinned at the prices they received. But it is fair for a Tobiquer to get the better of a Bathurst man any day. The next morning the boys started home by rail; and because there is no short cut across, it took them two days to go around. May the man be paralyzed who plans a railroad to destroy that lovely wilderness!

12
A
Rondeau
Muskallonge
(1895)

A RONDEAU MUSKALLONGE.

By Ed. W. Sandys.

RONDEAU Harbor, on the Canada side of fussy Lake Erie, was, not so many years ago, an ideal place for sport with rod and gun. Unfortunately, overshooting has nearly exterminated several varieties of game which formerly abounded, but it is still by no means to be despised as a camping and fishing resort. The "Round Water" will well repay a trial, providing the visitor is not one of those semicranks who believe that all of fishing consists of catching fish, and all of catching fish consists of catching *trout*.

To-day, instead of being what it once was—a capital shooting ground, where duck flocked in countless thousands—it is rather a sort of disappointing mirage. There are duck in plenty, of various kinds, in the proper season, but visions of flocks are about all there is of it. Merciless persecution has made the fowl shy and wary to a degree, and while a man can yet bag his half-hundred duck on a very favorable day, such days are few. The glorious sport with big duck is a thing of the past, and all that remain, to remind old-timers of what they used to enjoy, are pleasant memories of full many a jolly outing, and beggarly remnants of the great rafts of fowl which formerly made the Eau their chosen abiding place.

Of the teal which used to whistle past the sportsman's blind, but enough are left to hint that they once frequented the place, and where ten years ago the beautiful wood-duck followed the windings of the creeks, or fell in response to the sudden, deadly challenge of the lurking gun, there is naught but a lonely silence, broken only by the croak of a frog or the plunge of a musk-rat.

In the heavy timber bordering the marshy shores there used to be plenty of grouse, but their day has passed. In certain localities where the marsh waters trespassed far into the forest, mak-ing the black mold softly treacherous to unwary feet, the woodcock used to dose away the sunny hours in drowsy comfort, 'neath the blended shadows of giant trees and drooping fern fronds. The presence of these peerless birds was unsuspected, save by a few keen nimrods who knew the mysteries of those woods. But the pot-hunter finally grasped the possibilities, and the beginning of the end was apparent. Guns that knew not how to spare roared all day long among the stately elms and over the grassy marshes, thundering the doom of the game. A few short seasons did the work, and the Eau relinquished its premier position as a shooting resort.

But with the fishing it was different. Deep down in the cool depths of a water miles long and miles broad, lurked uncounted black bass, pike and lesser quarry, and through the narrow reach which connects this natural harbor with Lake Erie passed many a mighty muskallonge, to range at will the broad inner limit, or to take prey at every creek's mouth or channel through the shoreward marshes.

The expanse of the Eau, perhaps nine miles long by four broad, is too great for fishing in perfect safety, except upon calm days. Any approach to a stiff breeze is sure to kick up a nasty, chopping sea, rough enough to make an ordinary skiff or canoe a decidedly ticklish craft to handle.

At the head of the Eau is a narrow strip of sand-bar, separating the harbor proper from Lake Erie. Through this sand a channel has been deepened and protected by a crib-work, so as to form an entrance to the harbor, and the sand upon one side of the channel is styled "The Bar," and upon the other side "The Point." In this channel the water is deep, and about the inner end of the crib-work lurk the finest black bass. Now and again a giant muskallonge is killed, but these cases are comparatively rare. At the foot of the Eau, where the weeds and rushes extend far out into the shallows, any decent performer with the rod can kill, in half a day's

Painted for Outing by Hermann Simon

"THE TUG-OF-WAR." (*p. 137.*)

"whipping" with minnow bait or small spoon, plenty of pike of good size.

The catch may also include a few pickerel and bass, but such sport is rather tame. I have tried it many times, more to keep my hand in than anything else, but, whenever the water is right, the sport, *par excellence*, is to troll half round the harbor, some seven or eight miles, and then to finish off with a few hours' work with the rod at the channel into the lake.

A trip of this kind is almost certain to yield a good string, and, on more than one occasion, I have killed some very large fish. The major portion of the captives comprised black bass, rock bass, pike and pickerel, but there was always the chance of hooking a muskallonge to cheer one up. Time and time again I had essayed to capture one of these great northern pike, and as often I had failed; but the longest wait must have an end, and my day came at last.

A little railway was under construction down to the Eau, and I was constantly traveling back and forth on ballast train or engine, as the case happened to be. Upon such trips the trolls invariably accompanied my outfit. From the terminal pier of the railway to the inlet to the Eau was, perhaps, five miles, and this stretch, when the day was right, was my favorite water.

One glorious autumn morning, about half-past six, the rickety old engine clattered down to the water's edge and discharged her crew of engineer, fireman and fisherman. They, having other fish to fry, merely amused themselves, for an hour or so, by catching small rock bass and sunfish near shore. I was intent upon nobler quarry, and was presently stealing over the rippling water towards the Bar.

It was a grand morning for the sport; a faint breeze whispered among the rushes and ruffled the surface just enough and no more, and I felt that the chances for a rousing catch were good.

I trolled, as was the fashion on that water, kneeling in the canoe with the line gripped between my teeth, the spare end being twisted around my leg. For a quarter of a mile I slid steadily along, the light canoe making

no sound, and the braided line trailing away behind to where the silver Delaney fluttered through the haunts of bass. Presently I passed along a fringe of reeds, and, looking down into the clear depths below, could see a tangled mass of trailing weeds which, doubtless, covered many a fine fish.

Tug! and the trembling of the line ceased, and as my hand seized the cord I knew that a good one had struck the spinning spoon.

Hand over hand he was hauled in, the strain growing greater with every foot gained; a good one indeed, and, as the pressure told on him, he made a couple of dodging rushes, then resorted to the old, old trick of the black bass, and leaped two feet clear of the water. But the triple hooks were too well planted to be easily gotten rid of, and in a couple of minutes he was alongside.

"A good three-pounder," was my mental comment, as I watched him resting a bit, preparatory to the final struggle. Of course, I could have lifted him in then and there, but there was no particular hurry, and I always like to get all the fun out of them I can. After a time he renewed the fight, pulling this way and that, and boring down under the canoe in a fierce effort to rid himself of his painful jewelry, but all attempts were vain, and up he came dead-beat.

Following the time-honored custom, I ran a stout whip-cord through his gills and towed him behind, and presently he had a companion in misery. This method of disposing of captured fish possesses the merit of keeping the victims fresh and sweet, instead of having them dry up in the bottom of the canoe.

A little farther on the fish bit freely, and for two hours I did little but strike and haul in. Black bass, some of them rattling good ones, followed in rapid succession, and now and then a pike, rock bass, or pickerel signified its willingness to be added to the lengthening trail of captives behind the canoe.

It was clearly an angler's day, and when I reached the Bar there were about thirty mourners on the string. But my mind was occupied with visions of the giant muskallonge. Might not a long array of disappointments be obliterated in a crowning triumph now? Compared to the grim pike, the really good catch seemed but a mockery.

At the Bar, the string of fish was safely tied in a cool pool, and I set out for the channel, determined to put in a couple of hours, if need be, in trying for a muskallonge.

Up and down, back and forth, I paddled, trying every likely place for full two hours, but the great fish gave no sign of his royal presence. In the deep water, every now and again, I hooked big bass, but they were no longer regarded with favor. However, patient and persistent effort counted for naught, so at last I gave it up, and, once more securing my string of fish, started for the engine which was to take me home.

For about four miles I drove the canoe along at a rapid clip, as the boys might be awaiting my arrival; but, when I neared my destination I saw them busily working, and so guessed that there was time to spare. The speed of the canoe was accordingly relaxed, the spoon was tossed overboard again, and I trolled over the water where the sport had been so good in the morning. Fish took the lure greedily, and for a time it seemed as though the supply was inexhaustible. At last, for some unexplained reason, they stopped biting, and no more could be taken. The canoe was headed for the landing, though the lure was dragged behind so long as fishable water remained.

Now, I had been disappointed about my big fish, and had done a lot of hard work, and had accepted the inevitable with a good grace, and in so doing had presumably touched the heart of that fate which rules piscatorial matters and had made her relent.

A surprise of the biggest and most unexpected kind was coming, and it came with a jerk. The canoe was traveling at a rate too fast for bass, when on a sudden I struck a snag—a clean, dead stop, and no mistake, for the line went from between my teeth with a jerk, letting ivories together with a snap that promised future work for some dentist. I hastily backed water, for the line was stretched until it fairly twanged, and the hitch around my leg cut deep into the flesh.

"How the devil did I strike a snag out here?" was my first thought; then I thrilled with a sudden start of glorious excitement, for there came a powerful tug at the line which explained the mystery.

"A muskallonge, by the great horn spoon!" Naught else could yank a line like that, and I hung on with the grip of desperation.

To get some slack line aboard was the most important thing. Luckily, the canoe was light and she spun round in response to the strain. In a few moments I was straightened up and breathed freer, and then began a mill royal. Foot by foot the line was gathered in, until there was enough secured to provide against a sudden rush.

"Now, my friend, we'll just fight it out!" And I proceeded to business. The big fish woke up and made things remarkably lively. He was evidently determined to force the fighting, and dashed this way and that with amazing strength. The cord zipped through my fingers, fairly burning the skin as the royal tug-of-war went on, he pulling for dear life, I striving for glory, and both of us fighting for every inch of tether.

Once my hair rose as he sped straight away, taking every foot of line, but the fact of the cord being fast to my leg eased the strain and the good canoe helped me out by following lightly in his wake. At the end of twenty minutes there was a very weary fish at the one end of the string and a very excited man at the other, but the fight continued, though with abated vigor.

Five minutes later he was close alongside, and for the first time I saw his splendid proportions and also saw something else which made me quake. His gills were wide-spread and his mouth ditto, and hanging from the lower jaw was the little spoon with but one hook fast, and that one holding by a mere shred of skin, as far as a hasty scrutiny showed.

Another rush would surely give him freedom, and but one thing could be done. Gaff I had none, and to attempt to lift such a fish upon the line was but to make certain of losing him.

It was a case of now or never. He was resting and would surely make another dash, so, firmly but gently I drew in the string until he was at the surface. A cautious lift, and he rolled over on his side, and I shuddered as I looked at the terrible array of teeth, which, like the tusks of a dog, flashed at me from beneath strong jaws. But there was no alternative ; my hand stole down till my fingers closed in a fierce grip inside his gills, and I had him and he had me !

For a moment there was an awful splashing and commotion, and my hand felt as if it was being run through a set of cog-wheels. But he came up over the side of the canoe, for I would have suffered my arm to be chewed off rather than relinquish the prize so fairly in hand. A moment later he was thrashing about on the foot-boards and I thumped him with the paddle in vindictive glee, for it was questionable who had got the best of it.

13
Notes
on
Salmon Fishing
(1876)

NOTES ON SALMON FISHING

GASPÉ BASIN, CANADA EAST.

ALTHOUGH the salmon is the acknowledged king of fishes, and the taking of it the most royal of sports, yet comparatively few indulge in the pastime. There are most certainly many, and those too among the foremost men of our country, who concede fully the benefits to be derived, not only from open air life and exercise, but from having some pursuit or specialty outside of business and profession,—call it hobby if you will,—which, while it gives rest to certain faculties of the mind, equally exercises and strengthens others. They realize truly that life is better than fame, and sound lungs and good diges-

tion than a fat purse, but the difficulties in the way of taking salmon turn most of these in a different direction for their recreation.

The three principal hinderances to salmon-fishing in this country are : the great trouble in obtaining either a lease of a stream or a permit for the best part of the season ; the great distances to be traveled, and consequent loss of valuable time ; and the large expense as compared with other sorts of out-door amusements.

The region where salmon can at the present day be taken in sufficient numbers to reward one for the attendant trouble and ex-

127

pense, is a circumscribed one. Beginning at Quebec and following down the river St. Lawrence, the salmon-streams are very numerous upon the northern shore, and extend far away to the Labrador coast. Among them are the well-known Laval, Godbout, Trinity, St. Margaret, Moisie, St. John's, Magpie, Mingan, Great and Little Romaine and Grand Natashquan Rivers. In the last named, the Governor General of Canada and party killed, some years since, 202 salmon in seven days. On the Godbout, Comeau, the river guardian, is said to have done the best fishing on record in this or any country,—killing between July 8th and 31st, 365 fish, weighing 3873 lbs. This was but an average weight of about 10½ lbs., so that the fish were "mere sticklebacks."

The range of mountains on the north shore runs within a few miles of the St. Lawrence, and hence the rivers upon that side are very short and rapid, giving but few good pools, and are, as a general thing, very difficult to fish. Only a few good streams are found on the south shore, among which are the Rimouski, Grand Metis and Matane. Passing down the Gulf of St. Lawrence we come to the Basin of Gaspé, into which flow three admirable streams, and farther on upon the north shore of the Bay of Chaleur, and at its western end, are some of the best, including the famous Restigouche, fished yearly by Englishmen who cross the Atlantic for that express purpose; also the Cascapedia, made more noted through Mr. Dawson's most charming letters written from there, where, at a good ripe age, he had taken his first salmon. The Nipissighuit on the south shore of the Bay of Chaleur and the Mirimichi on the eastern coast of New Brunswick are the last salmon-streams of any account until we come to Nova Scotia, where there are a few upon its south-east coast below Halifax. Mr. Hallock of the "Forest and Stream" seems to be the only one who has been favored with much sport in the Nova Scotia rivers.

Some years ago while searching for good salmon-fishing, I was advised by a noted angler who is somewhat of a wag, to apply to a certain lawyer whom we will call Brown. The angling wag said that Brown had spent a year or so near the streams just mentioned above, and could fully post me on those matters. Presuming upon the spirit of good-fellowship which pervades all salmon-anglers, I, although a stranger, addressed Brown upon that topic, telling him that I was informed that he spent some time formerly in the vicinity of Halifax. Brown replied that while in Nova Scotia he was so *closely confined* that he had neither time nor inclination for angling. My waggish friend informed me soon after, that lawyer Brown, for some violation of the letter of the local laws, *without any wrong intent*, had been in jail for nearly a year in the region about which I had questioned him.

In Cape Breton there is a single good river, the Margarie. Here and there small streams are found in other parts of New Brunswick and in the Island of Anticosti, but practically, salmon-angling is confined to the rivers of Canada East and those of the northern part of New Brunswick, which includes the Mirimichi.

But few of the rivers we have mentioned debouch near a steamer landing, and all others are difficult of access. To reach these latter the angler must manage in some way to get transportation for many miles over a rough country where it is difficult to find horses, wagons, or roads; or he must charter a small sailing-vessel and run along a most dangerous coast, carrying with him both canoes and men. The Restigouche and Matapedia are reached with comparative ease from Dalhousie, a landing-place of the Gulf Port steamers. This line of steamers also touches at Gaspé Basin, leaving one just at the mouths of the three streams flowing into it. These are the York, St. John, and Dartmouth, called by the natives the South-west, Douglasstown, and North-west. These rivers are among the best stocked in Canada. The scenery about them is most varied, and in this respect unlike most other parts of Canada, where one tires of the monotony of mere grandeur and longs for the picturesque. They flow chiefly through deep gorges, or cañons, and between mountains, which occasionally rise to the height of a thousand or fifteen hundred feet. Beautiful lakes, filled to repletion with brook-trout, are found on the high land between the rivers, which for quite a distance flow within a few miles of one another. These streams are very rapid, and in early spring are almost torrents, and yet they have very few falls around which a "carry" must be made. Comfortable houses have been erected at some trouble and expense every ten or twelve miles on those parts of the York and St. John which abound in good pools.

The Canadian Government exercises complete control of the principal salmon-streams, both in their tidal and fluvial parts. Leases are commonly given for several years, but occasionally a schedule of vacant rivers is published, giving "upset" or minimum prices at which season permits will be granted. These vary from $20 to $500 in gold. The one giving the largest advance upon these prices gets the permit. The very fact that such advertisement is made indicates of it-

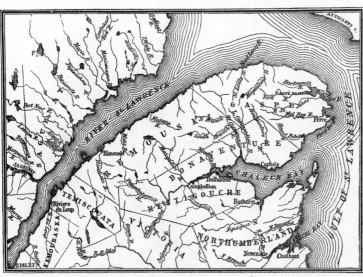

MAP, SHOWING SALMON-RIVERS AND GASPÉ BASIN.

self that the rivers are not, for some reason, very desirable. The best rivers are leased for eight or ten years, and upon the likelihood of a vacancy, numerous applicants bring influences of all sorts to bear to secure the chance at once.

It is understood that as a general thing leases of the better class of streams are not to be given to the "States" people, as they call us of the United States. Our political anglers often remark that it is more difficult to lease a good salmon-stream than to secure an election to Congress. A thousand dollars has been paid for the use of the fluvial part only of a first-class stream for a single season, this including, of course, all the fittings and canoes, etc. Add to the cost of a "permit," the traveling and camping expenses, and the price of good salmon tackle, which is always of the most expensive sort, and you swell the sum total of a summer trip to quite an amount.*

---

* From the report for 1875 of W. F. Whitcher, Dominion Commissioner of Fisheries, we learn that the total sum accruing as rents under leases of angling privileges for the year was $4,685.00, and that the salmon caught by anglers with artificial flies number 2,780. The outlay of the anglers upon thirty-four leased rivers was estimated at about $37,200.00.

While the Canadians are so tenacious of their leases, and naturally desirous of keeping the best streams for themselves, yet they are most generous and kind to their "States" friends. Often, one is not only accorded a permit to fish, but receives an invitation to make, for the time being, all the accessories and fittings of the stream his own, including houses, canoes, and cooking-utensils. My invitation, some years ago, from that genial sportsman, Mr. Reynolds, of Ottawa, was to make the York my own, paying simply for my men and provision. His guests kill every year many salmon to his one, and he enjoys their successes far better than his own. An Indian would wish him, in the happy hunting grounds, the exclusive right of the best stream. We can only express our heartfelt wish that for a score of years to come he may continue yearly to take his 47-pound salmon in his favorite stream.

To the cost of stream and tackle must be added the great uncertainty of getting fish. One may secure the best stream, purchase the best tackle, and travel a thousand miles to no purpose, for *salmo salar* is a very uncertain fish, and the worst sort of a conundrum. Sometimes he comes early and sometimes late; sometimes he goes leisurely up the rivers, lingering accomodatingly at the pools, and seemingly in good mood for sporting with flies, and sometimes, as last season, when kept back by the ice of a late spring, he goes for head-waters at once, only stopping when compelled by fatigue, and then having no time to waste upon flies. Last year with scores of salmon, by actual count, in the different pools, often not more than one in a pool could be tempted to rise to our flies. All these combined causes make the number of salmon-anglers small.

A stream being secured, the selection of tackle is an easy matter. A water-proofed American-made silk line of about three hundred feet, tapering gradually at each end, so that it may, when worn, be changed end for end, is the only one much used in this country, except, perhaps, a new sort of oiled silk introduced by Bradford & Anthony, and just coming into favor. A simple reel with click is the only one worth taking, and it may be of hard rubber or metal, as preferred. If of metal, it is usually nickel or silver-plated. In olden times the Scotch salmon-angler strapped around his waist a roughly made wooden reel of large size, called a pirn. It was entirely unconnected with the rod, along which the line was carried by rings, beginning quite a distance above the hand, as is shown on the poacher in the cut. In old Scotch works upon angling, we read of the gaffer singing out to his laird, " Pirn in ! pirn in ! you'll be drooned and coot " (drowned and cut), by which he meant, " Reel in, or your line will bag and be cut off by getting around the sharp edges of rocks."

The Scotch poaching angler suspends by straps under his outer garments a capacious bag of coarse linen for concealing his salmon, while he carries in his hand quite innocently a string of trout. Lord Scrope once caught a poacher with a salmon in his bag, and demanded how it got there. The reply was, " How the beast got there I dinna ken. He must ha' louped intil ma pocket as I war wading." His clever answer so amused Lord Scrope that he let him go scot-free.

The leader, of seven or eight feet nearest the hook, is of the best selected silk-worm gut, which should stand a test of four or five pounds strain. This gut is made by taking the silk-worm just before it begins to spin its cocoon, and soaking it in vinegar some hours. The secreting glands of the worm are, at that time, filled with the mass of glutinous matter from which the silk of the cocoon is to be spun. One end of the worm after it is thus soaked, is pinned to a board, and the other stretched out some eight or ten inches and secured. When this is hardened it becomes the beautiful white round gut of commerce, which, when stained water color, and dropped lightly in the pool, will not attract the fish as having any connection with the gaudy fly displayed before him.

In the matter of rods, the conservative man still clings to a well-made wooden one of greenheart or other approved wood, of which the taper and strength are so accurately proportioned that the addition of but a few ounces at the end of the line carries the main bend or arch nearer the butt end. Those not so conservative, and who are

fond of lessening in every practicable way the somewhat tedious labor of casting the fly, choose a rod of split bamboo, which weighs about two pounds. My own weighs but twenty-seven ounces, although nearly sixteen feet long. No one will risk himself

"HE MUST HA' LOUPED INTIL MA POCKET."

upon a stream without extra rod, reels, and lines, and if he takes a greenheart and split bamboo he has two as good rods as are made. One who has long used a heavy wooden rod has at first a feeling of insecurity and a distrust of the slender bamboo, which can, if necessary, be wielded by a single strong arm. It is said an old Scotchman handling one of these rods for the first time, exclaimed : " Do ye ca' that a tule to kie a saumont wi' ? I wad na gie it to my bairnies to kie a grilsie wi'." It should be explained, that a grilse is a young salmon just returned from a first trip to the sea. After its second trip, it returns a salmon proper, with all the characteristic markings. It often happens that a grilse (called by the Scotch " gilsie," or salmon-peel) is larger than a salmon one or two years older, the varieties differ so in size. The young of the salmon are first called parrs, and have peculiar spots and dark bars, or " finger marks," as they are called. At eighteen months, they are some six inches long, and the following spring silver scales grow over the bars and spots, when they are called smolt, retaining that name until they go to sea. For a long time the parr was held to be a species of trout and entirely distinct from salmon. Lord Scrope, the author of "Days and Nights of Salmon-Fishing," a work now extremely rare, held long and animated discussions with James Hogg, the "Ettrick Shepherd," upon this subject, which was settled practically by a Mr. Shaw, of Drumlanrig, who tagged a parr and identified it again as a full grown salmon in 1836. In 1839, Sir David Brewster announced that the fibers of the crystalline lens of the parr were arranged like those of the salmon, while trout of all sorts showed an entirely different arrangement. Figures 1 and 2 show front and rear view of the lens of a salmon, and Figure 3 the arrangement of the

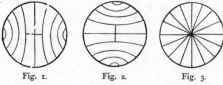

| Fig. 1. | Fig. 2. | Fig. 3. |

CRYST_LLINE LENSES OF SALMON AND TROUT.

fibers in the lens of a trout, according to Brewster.

The manufacture of a fine rod of split bamboo is a work requiring great skill and judgment, not unlike that required to make the far-famed Cremona violin. The rods are made usually from Calcutta bamboo, as it has a larger proportion of enamel with tough fiber and long growth between joints. In the Japanese bamboo the fibers follow the joints too closely, and so must be cut into in straightening the pieces. Our American cane is lighter, and the enamel is very hard and elastic, but the inner woody fiber is soft as well as brittle. Sometimes several invoices of Calcutta cane will not contain one suitable piece for rod-making. The canes mildew on the passage, and this injures the fibers. Sometimes they are injured in being straightened over a fire, and often a single worm-hole ruins the entire piece. Just as our forest trees have the thickest and roughest bark on the north side, so the bamboo has thicker and harder enamel upon whichever side was exposed to storms. In making fine rods not only the best cane is selected, but the best side of this selected cane is preferred.

The split-bamboo rod is an instance in which nature is successfully improved. The cane in its natural growth has great strength as a hollow cylinder, but it lacks the required elasticity. The outer surface or enamel is the hardest of vegetable growth and is made up largely of silica. The rod-maker, by using all of the enamel possible, and by his peculiar construction avoiding the central open space, secures great strength with lightness, and nearly the elasticity of steel itself.

In making a rod, some ten or twelve feet of the butt of the cane is sawed off and split into thin pieces or strands. These pieces are then beveled on each side so that when fitted together they form a solid rod, of say half the diameter or less of the original hollow cane. This beveling is done with a saw or a plane if preferred, but more expeditiously by having two rotary saws or cutters set at an angle of 60° to each other, in case the rod is to be of six strands. The strip is fed to the cutters by means of a pattern which, as the small end of the strip approaches, raises it into the apex of the angle formed by the cutters. This preserves a uniform bevel and still narrows each strand toward its tip end so as to produce the regular decrease in size of rod as it approaches the extreme end. These strips can also if desired be filed to a bevel by placing them in triangular grooves of varying depths in a block of lignum-vitæ. The

MAKING SPLIT-BAMBOO RODS.

pieces are then filed down to the level of the block which is held in a vise during the operation. In the accompanying illustration, some pieces are being thus worked out by hand, while others are tied ready for gluing, and still others glued and ready for the ferrules. For this sketch I am indebted to Mr. Leonard, to whom every angler in America owes thanks for what he did as the pioneer in this art and for what he is constantly doing in perfecting these excellent rods.

The six or twelve strips as required, being worked out, and each part carefully tested throughout its entire length by a gauge, are ready for gluing together, a process requiring great care and skill. The parts should be so selected and joined that the knots of the cane "break joints." The parts being tied together in position at two or three points, the ends are opened out and hot glue well rubbed in among the pieces for a short distance with a stiff brush. A stout cord is then wound around the strands from the end glued toward the other portions, which are opened and glued in turn, say eight or ten inches at a time. A short length only is glued at one time so that slight crooks in the pieces can be straightened, and this is done by bending the rod and sliding the pieces past each other. During the gluing all inequalities and want of symmetry must be corrected or not at all, and so the calipers are constantly applied to every side at short intervals, and any excess of thickness corrected by pressing the parts together in a vise. Figure 1 shows a section of a length of bamboo cane from which the strips indicated by spaces marked off are to be sawed. Figure 2 is an end view of the six strands properly beveled and glued together. This

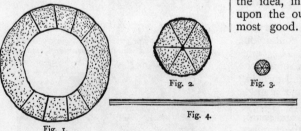

Fig. 2.

Fig. 3.

Fig. 4.

Fig. 1.

SPLIT BAMBOO SECTIONS.

length or joint of the rod is made up of six sectors of a circle whose diameter is greater than that of the rod, and hence it is necessarily what in common parlance might be called six-cornered. It must now be filed round, taking off as little of the enamel as possible in so doing. Figure 3 is an end view, natural size, of a six-stranded salmon-rod tip at its larger end ; and Figure

4 is a longitudinal view of a piece of a Leonard trout-rod tip of *twelve strands* now lying before me. This figure gives the size as accurately as the calipers can determine it, and shows what vast amount of skill, patience, and untiring industry is required in the art we have been describing.

It is at once evident that the larger the number of strands the less the amount of enamel to be filed off. The ferrules are water-tight and expose no wood in either the socket or the tenon part. Bamboo is so filled with capillary tubes that water would be carried through the lengths and unglue them, if it could once reach the ends where the joints of the rod are coupled together, and hence the necessity of careful protection at this place. The entire rod when finished is covered with the best copal coach varnish. By taking care to renew the varnish from time to time, no water need ever get to the seams.

In spite of the prejudice against what has been called a gentleman's parlor rod, they have steadily gained in favor, and although it is but five or six years since a perfect rod of this sort was made, yet this year Leonard sends out over two hundred. Twenty years ago, Alfred & Sons, of London, made split-bamboo rods, putting the enamel inside. They were imported and sold in limited numbers by Bradford & Anthony of Boston. Naturally enough, with the soft part of the cane exposed to wear and weather, and nearly all the enamel sacrificed, they did not find favor in the eyes of thoughtful or scientific anglers, at least. Mr. Phillippi, living at Easton, Pa., conceived the idea, in 1866, of putting the enamel upon the outside, where it would do the most good. Next, Mr. Green and Mr. Murphy put their heads together, and made rods of this sort of four strands, and finally the old well-known firm of A. Clerk & Co., New York, introduced into the market the Leonard rod of six and twelve strands, and have since been supplying Europeans with all they get of this article.

I have taken not a little pains to get, as far as possible, a correct history of this somewhat remarkable invention. My own rod of this kind has been used in both rain and shine for two seasons, and is now in perfect order, in spite of all the warnings of conservative angling friends, who pronounced such things a delusion and a snare. In careful tests, I have never yet seen a rod of its weight, or of its length and any weight, that could throw a fly quite as far; and, light as it is, it brought last year to gaff in twenty minutes a thirty-five pound fish, which my friend Curtis gaffed for me, off the high rock at the "Big Salmon Hole" of the York. Any rod with which one has killed many and large fish is, naturally, held to be perfection upon the stream; but the rod we have been describing is beautiful as an *objet de vertu*, and in the library becomes a source of joy to every admirer of skilled workmanship, though he be not familiar with its use.

The cut on page 776 shows the angler who has kept just strain enough on the rod to prevent the hook from dropping out of the mouth of the fish,—which measured forty-eight inches in length,—while his friend, after having skillfully hooked him with a prodigiously long gaff, is drawing him forward so as to use both hands in lifting him upon the rock. As skillful surgeons, like Nélaton, of Paris, performed even the delicate operation for a cataract equally well with either hand, so must the successful salmon-angler become ambidextrous. In casting he must be able, of course, to use either hand forward at will, and when one arm has become lamed by holding the rod, as it rests against the waist in playing a fish, and takes nearly all the strain while the other manipulates the reel, he must be able to change the position of the reel upon the rod, and work it with his left hand while his right manages the rod. This left-handed arrangement is shown in the figure with the reel on top in its proper position, and the right hand taking all the strain.

Conservative anglers still play the fish with the line and reel upon the under side of the rod just as in casting; and, beside constantly fraying the line and pulling off the rings, only get a bearing upon the rod at the ring attachments. The scientific angler, as soon as the fish is hooked, turns his rod over and brings his line uppermost, so that it hugs and strains the rod equally at every inch of its length, leaving to the rings their proper function of simply guiding the line. It may be noticed, too, that the conservative man still " gives the butt," as it is called, when he wishes to exert the greatest possible power of the rod upon the fish; that is to say, he extends the butt in nearly a direct line *from* himself and *toward* the fish, throwing the bend of the rod over his shoulder or at one side, while Young Amer-

ica tests the matter accurately with his scales, and finds that with the butt toward himself and the main part of the rod extending toward the fish at an elevation of about forty-five degrees, and his thumb pressing the line firmly against the rod just above the reel, he utilizes all the elasticity of his rod, and, with less danger to it, pulls fully a half-pound more.

Having, through Mr. Curtis's kindness, received an invitation from Mr. Reynolds, as already mentioned, to fish his river, the York, accompanied by any friend whom I might select, I provided myself with a Norris greenheart and a Leonard bamboo in the way of rods, and with an assortment of proper flies made by Forest & Son, of Kelso, Scotland. Not but that excellent flies are made in our own country, but the composition of an artificial fly is an art like that of making a bonnet, and as ladies have their favorite milliners, so anglers have their favorite fly-makers. Forest's flies, moreover, are tied by the deft fingers of Scotch lassies, and that gives them an additional charm.

It is, however, in the selection of friends to accompany us that we find the greatest difficulty connected with a projected excursion for salmon. One may have plenty of friends who would make camp-life delightful, and whose presence at the festive board " would make a feast of a red herring;" but they cannot be ordered for a trip, like tackle. For various reasons of their own, they may not wish to go; and, too, they may not have the capacity to enjoy such recreation. Your choice must, as a matter of course, be very much restricted. You will never trust yourself in camp with your best friend unless you have seen him under fire; that is to say, unless you know how he will stand the thousand and one annoyances incident to long journeys with poor conveyances and still poorer hotels; with black flies, sand-flies, mosquitoes, fleas, and worse. The best companion of the library, the drawing-room and the watering-place, although possessed of the most kindly attributes, oftentimes becomes absolutely unendurable when quartered for a day or two in a Canadian forest, with limited cuisine, unlimited numbers of insects and poor luck at angling. Never go with one who is painfully precise and who wishes to have everything his own way and at once. Such a man might as well stay away from Gaspé, where the natives always have their own way, and never, under any circumstances, hurry. Never go with one who is over-excitable or enthusiastic, for it isn't just the thing to have a man standing on his head in a birch-bark canoe every time he gets "a rise," or the canoe takes a little water running down rapids. The experienced angler chooses a friend who is deliberate, and takes all ills philosophically, and, if possible, one with that fortunate disposition which permits him to keep both his head and his temper under all circumstances. Other things being equal, he selects an admirer and follower of Brillat-Savarin, for he has ever remarked that one who fully enjoys and appreciates the best of dinners is just the one to endure with equanimity the worst, if no better is attainable.

To be eighteen miles from main camp when fish are rising as fast as they can be killed, and to have but three pieces of pilot bread for the angler and his two men, and be forced to go without supper and breakfast or else give up the sport and return, will bring the bad out of a man if it is in him. Apropos of this : In June of 1874, Mr. Monk, of Montreal, fished after food and drink were both out; didn't even scold his head man for not packing more supplies, but killed his eighteen heavy fish at "The Narrows," or upper falls of the York; floated them down on an extemporized catamaran, and came into camp half starved, and yet was happy.

Your companionable angler need not always take things quite as coolly as did a well known

GAFFING AT BIG SALMON HOLE.

editor who once upon a time, while engaged in pulling in a blue-fish, after sawing his fingers with a hundred or two feet of line, was seized with hunger and fatigue, and taking a hitch about a cleat, satisfied his inner man with sardines and crackers. To the surprise of all his companions, after finishing his lunch and resting his fingers, he pulled in the fish, which had swallowed the hook so far down that it had to be cut out. Of course the first few feet of the line was wired so that it could not be bitten off.

A little farther on we show a sketch of a jolly English gentleman, whose peculiarity consists in getting thoroughly disgusted every time he loses a fish. He then, without saying a word, quits the business, puts his back against a smooth tree, and takes a short nap, leaving others to thrash the pools. It is worthy of note that one need never fear meeting snobs, swells or disagreeable people fishing for salmon. The air of a first class stream seems fatal to all such.

The last of June, 1874, found Mr. Lazell and the writer tired out with close attention to duties, and with barely frame-work enough left " to veneer a decent man upon," rendezvousing at the office of Fred. Curtis, Esq., in Boston, preparatory to setting out for Gaspé Basin, Canada East. An idler cannot appreciate fully the enjoyment we felt in anticipation of several weeks entire freedom from business of any sort. To get so far from civilization that no irascible inventor can find you and argue his case until your head seems ready to burst; no client bore you for hours without giving a single important fact in his case ; and where you will hear of no impecunious creditor's paper going to protest,—is worth a large amount of preliminary toil.

After having, as Lazell asserted, taken an outfit sufficient for a whaling voyage, we devoted still a day to getting little odds and ends which Curtis's experience had taught him to provide—things which seemed superfluous, and in fact almost absurd, and yet worth their weight in gold when one is thirty miles from a settlement. Lazell finally, getting a little out of patience, sarcastically insisted upon our taking a crutch, in case any one should lose a leg. Six weeks later, when my unfortunate friend, after cooling off too suddenly from a twelve-mile walk on a hot day, found himself unable to use one leg, and hence deprived of his turn at the distant best pool, we turned back the laugh by suggesting the crutch which we had failed to bring. The only desirable thing we did forget was a box of Bermuda onions. These could not be procured in Canada, and were ordered thither from Boston by telegraph. They only reached us ten days after our arrival upon the stream, and if a tippler longs for his drams as we did for the onions after a diet of fish and salt meats, we pity him.

To one about to make a trip to Canada East we would say: Start in all cases from New York, even though you live in Boston. Take express trains direct from New York to Montreal without change, and then the Grand Trunk Railway or night steamer to Quebec. We started twice from Boston, going once by Portland and the Grand Trunk, and once by the Passumpsic Railroad. One can on these routes endure waiting from six or seven P. M. until ten P. M., and then, after two hours' additional travel, waiting from midnight until three A. M. at Newport, Richmond or Island Pond; and at Richmond being crammed in a small room packed with French-Canadian laborers who never heard of a bath—I say one *can*, but he doesn't wish a second experience of the same sort. The Frenchman's remark, that all roads are good which lead to victory,

THE PHILOSOPHICAL ANGLER.

didn't console us when we arrived in Quebec on time.

A day in the quiet, quaint old city of Quebec is not without pleasure and profit. One goes away feeling that, after all, heavy taxes with progress and improvement are not such objectionable things. The quiet of Quebec is broken but once each day— upon the departure of the steamer for Montreal.

In Quebec salmon-anglers get their supplies, usually from Waters of John street, Upper City, who from long experience needs only to be told the size of your party, the time of your stay, and approximately, the limit as to expense. When you go aboard your steamer, everything will be found there admirably packed, with not an article wanting,—not even extra corks for stopping opened and partially used bottles,— and the genial old countryman himself, with bill of lading in hand, awaiting your coming to wish you good-bye and galore of sport and salmon.

Tuesday, the last day of June, 1874, at two o'clock P. M. we set sail in the "Secret," formerly the fastest of the Southern blockade runners. The officers of this line are unusually courteous and accommodating. The steward —quite an intelligent Frenchman—wrote his bills of fare correctly in his native tongue, but as a compliment to his "States" guests, he prepared one or two copies in English. It is quite easy to manufacture bad spelling, and so, to avoid exaggeration, I copy *literatim* from the bills now before me: "Frechs Salmon—Curned Beef and Tung—Bold Mutton—Chickine Pie—Potatos Rost and Bold—Mach Torneps—Plum Pouding—Almens and Raisin—Crakrs and Chees."

We were due in Gaspé Basin at four A. M. Thursday, but were delayed by storm, and did not arrive off the Cliffs until one P. M. For quite a distance before reaching Gaspé Head, which is at the immediate entrance of the Bay, we sailed past long lines of small boats anchored at intervals of a few hundred feet. Into these boats we could with a glass see the cod-fish pulled at rapid rates. This cod-fish is a small variety, of fine and sweet meat, rarely exceeding five or six pounds weight, and sent principally to the Mediterranean. Very few of them reach the United States. Although caught in immense numbers near the rocky shores where they come to spawn and feed, yet the quantity seems not to be appreciably diminished from year to year.

The last few miles of sea-coast is a rugged, nearly perpendicular cliff, in some places over eight hundred feet in height, and resembling somewhat the Dover Cliffs, but more remarkable in appearance. As we

THE DISGUSTED ANGLER.

turned Gaspé Head the sun shone out warm and bright, the water became more quiet, and our lady passengers were able to get on deck, and, for the first time since leaving Quebec, have an enjoyable hour.

Until the establishment, a few years since, of the Gulf Port Line of steamers, Gaspé was almost a *terra incognita*, from which intelligence came only at intervals by small trading vessels, or the long and tedious overland mail route. The Gaspé rivers, perhaps taking all things into account as good as any in the country, were put down in Norris's "American Angler" in 1865 as "untried with the fly." As we sailed up the Basin, we could see here and there among the mountains little silver threads in relief against the beautiful green. These were the streams upon which we were to take our first salmon.

So well had our kind friend Reynolds arranged matters that all our men, with horses for taking us with our luggage up the stream, were awaiting us at the wharf. Old William Patterson, Mr. Reynolds's head-man, who had for several years managed the river, took entire charge of everything, even to provisioning the men. Young Miller, who had most satisfactorily served Earl and Countess Dufferin earlier in the season, was to be our cook; and for courier we had the ubiquitous George Coffin, who had more Young America in him than a dozen of the ordinary *habitans*.

We delayed a little to receive the honest welcomes of a score or more of the inhabitants, who, having learned that friends of Mr. Curtis had arrived, lost no time in paying their respects. Our friend Curtis has a way of going around the world, dispensing favors right and left, and but few prominent persons in Gaspé had not at some time received the much coveted permit for a day's fishing, accompanied with flies and leaders, or something else equally desired. We were now to reap the reward of his thoughtfulness about little matters. It was known also that we were the intimate friends of Earl and Countess Dufferin's friends; and so universally popular and truly beloved are they in all parts of the Dominion by both the highest and the lowest, that even *friends of their friends* are favored.*

* All Canada seems to feel that no such worthy and intelligent Governor has been sent them for a long time. The French-Canadians think that he is partial to them because he is cultivated and is a lover of the arts, while all lovers of out-of-door life and sport (and this class comprises nearly all well-to-do English, Irish and Scotch) claim him as especially their own. All seem grateful to the Mother Country for sending them such a man in place of foisting upon them some favorite who needs a good place. He spends annually, in entertaining and amusing Canadians, a sum equal to, or larger than his salary. The Countess Dufferin shares with the Governor the universal affection and admiration of the people.

One can be made uncomfortable by a thousand little annoyances, and he will be, if in any way he gets the ill-will of the people near his stream. If he acquires a reputation for bargaining and paying small prices for services rendered, he had better at once give up his stream and seek another as far from it as possible. Accompanied with the honest hand-shake of some of the hardy fishermen was their assurance that they should as usual expect all our worn-out flies and frayed leaders upon our return from the river, and also any spare fish we thought not worth sending home. Their universal " so long" in place of good-bye amused us not a little, but why they use it or whence it is derived we could not conjecture.

In the next cut we have shown one of the native youngsters using one of our worn-out flies; he is dressed as Mrs. General Gilflory might say, " in the costume of the *pie-ese* " (*coutume de pays*).

Half a mile from the landing we stopped upon high ground near the residence of Mr. Holt (our efficient Consul at Gaspé), to enjoy our surroundings.

At our feet was the Bay, by common consent scarcely less beautiful than the Bay of Naples, which it resembles when seen from a certain point. In the hazy distance was the indistinct line of the Gaspé Cliffs, and our steamer rapidly making her way to the Gulf. The sun lighted up most beautifully the intense green of the forests which were broken here and there by neat white cottages and their surrounding patches of still brighter green. Although the very last of June, the foliage was not yet burned by the summer's sun, and the grass was but just greening.

Six miles from the settlement the road became a mere path, and we took to our saddles, which the thoughtful George had stowed in our two-horse wagon. Two miles farther and we were at the first pool of the river called the High Bank Pool. We determined at once to try it and throw our virgin fly for salmon. Setting up our rods, we scrambled down the steep gravel bank with the enthusiasm of school-boys. Insects of various sorts were there long before us, and soon we were compelled to send Coffin up the bank for our veils. The veils used are of the thinest silk *barége* in form of a bolster-case open at both ends, which are gathered upon rubber cords. One cord goes around the hat-crown and the other around the neck under the collar. These veils perfectly protect the face from insects, but do not allow smoking, and interfere slightly with the vis-

ion; I therefore discarded them and now use a brown linen hood with cape buttoning under the chin. The pests were so persistent that we were glad to put on linen mitts which tie around the elbow and leave only the finger-tips exposed. Finally, the little brutes drove us to anointing our finger-tips with tar and sweet oil, a bottle of which usually hangs by a cord from a button of the angler's coat. A philosophical friend

"THE COSTUME OF THE PIE-ESE."

once insisted that it only required the exercise of strong will to endure the pests, and that protection was effeminate. The second day he looked much the worse for wear, his handsome face disfigured with swellings, and his eyes almost closed from the poison of the bites.

We now worked away in comparative comfort until I saw Lazell, who was a few hundred feet distant, suddenly dash off his hat and commence slapping his head with both hands as if determined to beat out his brains. I concluded that he must have had a rise, and that contrary to his custom he had become excited. Going to him, I found that the black flies, baffled at all other points, had found the ventilating eyelet-hole upon each side of his hat-crown, and had poured in through them in hordes upon the top of his unprotected head. Getting no rise, I climbed up the bank to await my more persevering friend. (It may be noted in passing that we learned a few days later that we had not cast within several hundred feet of that part of this pool where salmon usually lie.) Soon my friend's head appeared over the bank with apparently a good stout stick thrust completely through it, hat and all, as if some stray Micmac had shot him with a roughly made arrow. "The times have been, that, when the brains were out, the man would die;" but remembering Alexis St. Martin who, with a cannon-ball hole in his stomach, had lived in Canada so many years for the benefit of medical science, we concluded that in the clear bracing air of that country people had a way of going about with seeming mortal wounds. The solution of this conundrum was that Lazell had plugged up the holes in his hat with two pieces of a broken rod, and thus cut off the flies from their favorite foraging grounds. The moment I fully comprehended the true situation my anxiety was allayed.

It is a fact not generally known that the farther north you go, the larger and more venomous are the mosquitoes. According to the late lamented Captain Hall of Arctic fame, one knows little of the annoyance of these insects who has not been in Greenland during the summer months. After a summer upon the Gaspé streams, a person of even large inquisitiveness doesn't long for any more information upon that branch of natural history. They are so troublesome there that, to fish comfortably, it is necessary to protect the face and neck, and cover the finger-tips with a mixture of tar, sweet oil and pennyroyal. Gaspé insects seem fond of new-comers and our blood afforded them a favorite tipple. Many a time have I seen one stand up to his knees in culexifuge and bore away until he first struck oil and then blood. Seriously, however, we were not much inconvenienced, as we took every known precaution against them, and not only had our rooms thoroughly smoked with smudges, but kept large smoldering fires around the houses the greater part of the time. When ladies fish, a smudge is kept burning upon a flat stone in the canoe. One night, an insect of some sort raised so large

a lump upon one side of Lazell's forehead that the only way he could make his hat keep a dignified perpendicular was by putting a champagne cork under the side opposite the swelling to preserve symmetry.

We reached our comfortable quarters at House No. 1 at nine P. M. while it was still light. We found our house clapboarded, and

A STRATEGIC ANGLER.

with two comfortable rooms; one contained berths like a steamer's which were furnished with hair mattresses and mosquito bars; the other served as sitting and dining room, and had a large bar suspended over the table to enable us while eating, reading, writing and smoking to be free from flies. A large log house adjoined and was furnished with a good cooking-stove, while a tent was already pitched to serve as quarters for our men—five in number. Stoves and furniture are permanent fixtures of the houses at the different stations, as are the heavier cooking-utensils, so that in moving up the stream one has merely to carry crockery, provisions, blankets and mosquito-bars,—which latter are of strong thin jute canvas. Above the first house, the men make your beds of piles of little twigs of the fragrant fir-balsam, whose beauties have been recorded by every writer upon angling. Near each house is a snow-house dug into the hill-side and thickly covered with fir-boughs and planks. The snow is packed in them in winter by the men who go up for that purpose and to hunt the caribou that frequent the hills adjoining the river. The snow lasts through the season and is more convenient than ice. If one drinks champagne, he has but to open a basket upon his arrival and imbed the bottles in the snow, and he has at any moment a *frappé* equal to Delmonico's best. No salmon-angler would commit the indiscretion of thus cooling his claret. The fish as soon as killed are packed in the snow, as are the butter, milk, and eggs when brought up every two or three days by the courier, who remains at the Basin ready to start for you at any moment that letters or telegrams arrive. Our courier delighted in surprises for us like baskets of native strawberries and cream for our dessert. Ten cents at Gaspé buys quite a large basket of this exquisitely flavored wild berry.

I have been thus minute in describing our surroundings because I believe more comfortable and complete arrangements are found on no other stream. It is all very well to camp out under an open "lean-to" or tent, and exceedingly healthful and enjoyable, but we had long ago outgrown the sentimentality of roughing it, and rather enjoyed this comfortable way of living. Standing for six hours or more daily while throwing a fly or killing a fish is hard work for one of sedentary habits, and gives enough exercise and oxygen to entitle to good living and quarters; and with this open-air life one may indulge his appetite with impunity if he can get the food, for his digestion and assimilation are at their best.

The cut on page 783, while not absolutely true to nature in every minute detail, yet gives, quite faithfully, a scene upon the St. John River in July, 1873, when the Governor General of Canada and Countess Dufferin, together with Colonel and Mrs. Fletcher and the Countess's brother, were guests of Mr. Curtis, the then lessee. Lady Dufferin here killed her first fish, which weighed 26 pounds and was gaffed by Mr. Curtis. The difference between the temperature at midday and midnight in the mountainous regions along the Gaspé salmon-streams is notable. One day last season the air at nine A. M. was 74°, at two P. M. 84°, and at half-past seven P. M. 51°. We were anxious to get approximately the temperature of the water of these northern streams to compare with the water of streams farther south, which had been stocked with young salmon by Professor Baird—United States Fish Commissioner—and so made the best observations possible with a couple of ordinary thermometers. At the bottom of one pool in the York, near the mouth of the Mississippi Creek, which is a roaring little branch of the York coming down from the snow of the neighboring mountains, the water at midday was but 40½° Fahrenheit, while the air was 78°. In other pools on this river we found the temperature at noon to be 44° at the bottom, and 44½° at the surface, with the air at 60°. This was well up among the mountains, thirty-five miles above the mouth of the river. Lower down the stream, 48° bottom, 48½° surface; and sometimes after a very warm day, 47½° to 48½° at eight o'clock P. M. Ten or fifteen miles distant, upon the Dartmouth, which flows through a less mountainous country and has longer and more quiet pools and less shaded banks, we found the pools varying from 55° to 59° when the air was 60° to 70°. The first time our thermometers were sunk in the pool our men indulged in their only pleasantry by asking if we took fish in the States with a ground bait of thermometers, and assuring us that it wouldn't work at all in Canada. Of course, with our temperature of pools we always took that of the air simultaneously and made a record of the weather.

Upon the first morning of our arrival we *did not* get up at three A. M., when the day was just dawning, and order up our men to get breakfast. We had been in northern latitudes before, and took the precaution to hang our rubber overcoats over the windows to darken them, thus keeping out the early morning light and securing a long night's sleep. Our first day opened with a drizzling rain which forbade fishing. After coming a thousand miles and with but six days' "permit" upon our stream, a rainy day seemed like a misfortune.

About ten o'clock, the sun came out for a time, and a Mr. Eden, son of the Gaspé harbor-master, rode up and told us in apparent seriousness, that a fish had followed him all the way up the stream, and was waiting in the pool directly in front of the house, where he intended to gaff him for me, and in fact that he had come over to our camp from where he was at work, expressly to help me kill my first salmon. Our men all laughed at him, for just in sight of the house and where the canoes were constantly disturbing the water was not the place to expect a salmon; certainly not, when for years none had been taken there. I concluded to humor the good fellow and practice casting with both hands as well as get used to standing in a cranky canoe. Soon a fish rose and hooked himself, only making it known by spinning off a few feet of line as he dropped back to position at bottom of pool. A fish will thus hook himself nine times in ten if the fly comes slowly over him, with a taut or at least straight line behind it. More fish are lost by too quick striking them, than by other bad management. The steel-like tip of the rod upon the slightest pull at the fly springs forcibly back and fixes the hook at once. I had resolutely determined never to strike and have never done so. I may have lost a fish by it, but am sure more would have been lost by striking. Of course, a strong, quick pull is given after the fish is hooked and has started the reel, in order to imbed the hook more firmly. Soon my reel was furiously whirling. I had read about the "music of the reel" and all that sort of thing *ad nauseam* as I had often expressed it; but somehow, after hearing a salmon in his first fierce run upon a reel with a stiff click, the wonder was that people had not written more about it.

One cannot afford entirely to ignore book teaching. Having read and re-read every standard author on salmon-angling, my rod-tip was at once, and without thought lowered when this lively little fellow made his first leap in the air, showing the beautiful silver of his sides. It was done just as the fingers strike the proper key upon a musical instrument, when the player's mind is too far away perhaps to name the tune he has unconsciously run into. Of course, if you do not lower your rod-tip, the fish, falling upon a taut line, will break himself loose. This fish showed no disposition to leave the pool for the rapids below, but went first to one side, and then to the other, sweeping around by the farther shore, and jumping clean from the water each time he turned. It was impossible to keep below him, so rapidly did he change place. In spite of all the strain which could be safely put upon him, he would now and then get a hundred feet below the rod and rest there in comparative ease, with the force of the current balancing my strain upon him in an opposite direction. When you can keep abreast of your fish, or a little below him, the current, weight of line, and your strain of two or three pounds all in the same direction will soon tire him out.

Most anglers greatly miscalculate the force exerted by the rod and will speak of using many pounds strain. An actual test with scales upon various rods showed that rarely is a strain of three pounds put upon the fish, and, in fact, few rods can raise a four-pound weight at the end of a line.

As my fish became tired and slowly passed Eden, he tried to gaff and missed. This goaded the fish to more desperate running and plunging in the direction of a pro-jecting tree-trunk lying upon the water. If he could have reached it he would have run under and then jumped back over it, leaving the line fast while he broke himself free. Soon his runs were shorter and his jumps less frequent, and finally, from very weakness, he would turn upon his side. I swung him gently toward Eden, who in his eagerness had waded nearly waist-deep into the pool. In an instant the fish was struggling at the end of the cruel gaff, making hard work for even Eden's brawny arms, and in a moment more he was laid upon the shore, where old William Patterson gave him the *coup de grâce* with a stout short stick carried for that purpose in every canoe. Just at the moment of gaffing many fish are lost; for if more strain is exerted than usual the hook breaks out of the well-worn hole in the jaw, and if the strain is relaxed a moment before the gaff is in, the slack line lets the hook drop out of the enlarged opening.

My trip and trouble had not been in vain, as my first salmon had been hooked and played to gaff without the slightest assistance. Before putting him in the snow, I lighted my pipe and sat quietly down to admire and talk to him. It seemed wonderful that the little thread of silk-worm gut could have conquered so brave a fish. There was no need to sing,

"Backward, turn backward, O Time, in your flight,
Make me a child again, just for to-night:"

I *was* a child again as far as delight and enthusiasm could make me.

Finding but few fish in the lower pools, we broke camp on Monday and set out for House No. 2 at what is called the Big Salmon Hole. The men assured us that it would be impossible to pole the canoes with ourselves and provisions over the shoal rapids, and that in several places they would have to unload and make a "carry." In order then to favor our men, Mr. Lazell and I set out to walk the distance, with the cook to show the way and carry our tackle. We could risk the wetting of our extra clothing and provisions, but did not care to have our rods floated down the stream, in case of an overturn. Of itself, a twelve-mile walk is not objectionable, but when one must climb over a dozen fallen trees at every hundred yards, it becomes tirefully monotonous. Six miles from camp we came to the North Fork, a roaring brook of perhaps eighteen inches in depth. Lazell, with his wading-boots, stalked triumphantly across, while the cook and I went down a quarter of a mile to cross upon a tree which some years ago had fallen and formed a natural bridge. There was no path along this wind-swept gorge, and trees were piled upon trees, giving not the windfalls of a year or two, but of many, to be gotten over. At the end of a long half hour we came back to where Lazell was awaiting us. Could we have met the man who said there was a "pleasure in the pathless woods" he would have fared badly. The truth was that the dead wood of the bridge had broken under our weight, and we were wetter than if we had waded the branch: Often upon this trip we touched, with our rod-cases or gaff, the partridges which unconcernedly flew up and lighted on the lower branches of the trees. We reached the pool and killed a fish before the canoes arrived. The next morning, Annette, Lazell's gaffer, came tumbling down from a tree where he had been sent to point out where the salmon were lying, and ran to the house yelling as if crazy, " Mr. Lazell has got his first fish and he's a whopper!" Sure enough he had on a fish and it commenced sulking at once. He had lighted his pipe and taken his seat just where one of Mr. Reynolds's friends in 1873 took his breakfast while holding his sulking fish with one hand. Having gone to the pool with my light bamboo, to which he was unaccustomed, he was unprepared for heavy fighting as he felt insecure, and had a dread of breaking it. Now and then, by rapping on the metal butt of the rod with a stone, the vibrations of the line would start the fish into making a short run and lazy jump. The men all put the fish at 35 pounds, and they are rarely more than a pound or two out of the way. Soon the fish began quietly working for the deepest part of the pool, and in spite of all the strain

my friend was willing to put on him, finally got there under the edge of a sharp ledge. The canoe men could not reach him with their setting poles and we didn't wish the entire pool disturbed by throwing in stones. The salmon commenced sawing upon the line whenever a strain was brought to bear, and this necessitated giving line at once. After working for one hour and forty minutes the leader parted.

Without a word Lazell took his own greenheart rod and in a few minutes was busily casting at the very upper end of the pool above where he had hooked the first fish. As good fortune would have it, he soon hooked a large one which came down the pool and tried the same game, but he managed to stop him and slowly swing him away from the center of the pool each time. Quite soon the fish ran and jumped enough to

COUNTESS OF DUFFERIN POOL, ST. JOHN RIVER, GASPÉ, C. E.

MY FIRST SALMON.

weaken himself, and was brought up to the gaffer, who was so excited and anxious for Mr. Lazell that he came near losing the fish. This was my friend's first salmon and it weighed 33 pounds.

The skill of our men in gaffing struck us as remarkable, for during the season they missed for us but a single fish. Not the same romance attaches to them as to Indians, and they do not present that statuesque appearance while gaffing, but they are a thousand times more reliable, and always know better where the fish lie, and how quickest to aid you to circumvent and kill them. The Gaspé men can give even the best of anglers a valuable hint occasionally, which it is quite safe to follow, as it often saves a fish. They come from that good old stock, Scotch-English, and are as true as steel. Money and jewelry were safer in our camps than at home in the way of our servants. They never touch a drop of liquor, and work faithfully from morning till night. Even after long and tedious hours of poling up rapid streams under a hot sun, they are ready to anticipate your slightest wish. Old Mr. William Patterson, our head man, seemed to know every stone in every rapid on the rivers, and when running down these rapids at the rate of fifteen miles an hour, such knowledge often saves an overturn or a broken canoe. Although over sixty years of age, no one could tire him poling or equal him in quick, graceful gaffing. All the men ask for beside fish, is pork, hard-bread, sugar, and black tea. Without the latter they are good for nothing. At every halt of even half an hour a fire is at once kindled and the black tea-kettle soon steaming over it. They make the tea in the tea-kettle itself, and drink several large tin cup-fuls at a sitting. Following this by a five minutes' pull at a pipeful of navy plug

tobacco, they are ready for work and apparently as fresh as in the morning.

While the season for fishing brings to us great enjoyment, it brings to them bread and butter in the shape of a dollar, or a dollar and a quarter a day, and this is about all the money they get during the year. In fact a large part of the cash which finds its way to Gaspé is left by the dozen or more anglers who yearly visit the rivers. The large firms, like Bouthillier, the lobster pack-ers, and Lowndes Bros., lumber dealers, for whose kindness all American anglers are indebted, pay their help mostly in goods or "orders." It does good for one reared in our country of luxury and extravagance to see these hardy sons of toil, in a land where life is a constant struggle for existence, and where summer is no sooner begun than win-ter follows at once. In 1874, the cold spring and terrible floods prevented planting until too late to raise any crop at all, and the people of the north shore of the St. Law-rence had to be supplied charitably with food the next winter. Dried fish and hard bread, with occasionally a little pork, is about all they get, and last winter some of our faithful canoe-men ran out of this meager supply, and we were appealed to for aid. As I am writing this,—June, 1876,—I learn that Gaspé people have run out of hay and flour, and are killing their domestic cattle.

In favorable seasons the big salmon-hole of the York is good for two or three fish daily, and as Lazell was unable to walk by reason of cooling too rapidly after our twelve-mile walk, it seemed best to leave to him the exclusive use of this and the other pools near House No. 2. On Wednesday, therefore, I set out for the Narrows, near which are the last and best pools of the river, leaving two men to come with the canoe and luggage, and taking one with me. We arrived before noon, and, after lunch, carefully inspected the pools. By crawling quietly to the edge of low cliffs, or climbing trees, we could count the fish by scores, lying quietly behind small stones or just at the edge of the current, with heads up stream. At first one unaccustomed to it only sees large numbers of dark, smooth stones, as he expresses it; but soon a little wavy motion of the lower end of the object is seen, and you find that they are all salmon, only the dark backs being visible as you look down upon them. Conversation with many Canadians who have fished numerous streams, induces the belief that in no other pools can so many salmon be readily seen and watched. They rest in these pools for several days, to gain strength for leaping the falls just above. Often one hundred and fifty have been counted in

Before entering the Gaspé streams they gorge themselves with capelin, a small fish resembling our smelt. Quite often fish which we killed at the lowest pools had undigested parts of capelin in their stomachs. As their digestion is known to be very rapid, this indicates a high rate of speed against a swift current, up fierce rapids and over falls. A bit of dried leaf seems to amuse them as much as an artificial fly. Dropping a leaf quietly off a tree into a pool, we could see a salmon rise and take it, and after getting to the bottom open his mouth and let it float up to the surface again, when other fish would take it, one after the other, apparently enjoying the sport like kittens at play. So distinctly could we see the salmon that we easily traced the scars of the nets, which are found on large numbers. Many we take have an eye entirely blinded from the wound made by the twine. At one time, just under the upper falls, I was for some fifteen minutes so near a salmon that I could have touched him with the end of my rod. The water was shallow and clear, and gave a good opportunity of closely watching the king of fishes as he majestically sailed around, probably wondering whether he would succeed in his leap over the falls. Dozens of his fellows were coming up at intervals to look at the falls, but not one could be tempted to take the slightest notice of any fly in our books, although we were out of their sight and threw our flies within a few inches of their noses.

We had with us rods, reels, gaffs, and, unfortunately, a new and untested package

PERCÉ ROCK, SOUTH OF GASPÉ BASIN, CANADA EAST.

the lower or long pool at the Narrows, and frequently not more than a single one will take the fly.

The matter of taking a fly seems to be one of sheer sport. It is a well established fact that salmon eat nothing during the several months they remain in the rivers.

of leaders. The run of the first fish hooked parted a leader. A second leader shared the same fate; and a third was taken by a salmon who determined to leave the pool and go down the rapids below. Testing our leaders with the pocket scales, we broke them at a pound or pound and a half strain, although they had previously received a thorough soaking. We were in a bad predicament—salmon everywhere; pools full of them, and seeming eager to rise, and no suitable leaders with which to take them. We made the best of

THE PATIENT ANGLER.

it, and with what patience we could summon up, awaited the canoe with our large fly-books containing new gut. From this we afterward tied leaders which stood a strain of five pounds, and were soon engaged in trying to overcome a strong, lively fish.

Presently Patterson sung out, "You must lose your fish or get a drenching." A small dark cloud came over the near mountain, traveled rapidly down the gorge, and before one of the men could bring a rubber coat from the house, a few hundred yards distant, the rain was pouring upon us. The rapidity with which heavy showers follow down the gorges and course of the streams at Gaspé is somewhat startling to a new-comer. Of course, the fish must at all hazards be killed; and, of course, this particular fish was not in half the hurry to come in out of the water that we were, but tried our patience in many ways, sometimes taking us in the canoe where we couldn't wade, and sometimes through quite deep

water where we did not wish to take the canoe and disturb the pool. It was thirty-five minutes before faithful old William had him quiet at the bottom of the canoe. He, as well as all our men, preferred to get us into a canoe before gaffing, when practicable, for they then felt much more sure of the fish. The Gaspé-built canoes are very long, and if the angler passes one of the men and steps to the extreme end, he can with perfect ease swing the fish to the gaffer at the other end, always taking great care not to reel in his line beyond its junction with the leader. If he does this and the gaffer misses, or the tired fish gets up life enough for a short spurt, then the knot sticks in the tip ring, and good-bye to fish and tip. It is with some reluctance that we differ with so good an authority as Norris, in his "American Anglers' Book," but we prefer canoe gaffing. We were all thoroughly soaked with rain, and I was additionally uncomfortable from having gone over the tops of my rubber wading-stockings in water which at two P. M. was only 42° Fahrenheit. As there were but three hours more of this the last day of our permit, we could not afford the loss of a moment. As soon as the sun came out, I hooked a second fish, and worked away busily until in the three pools I had killed five, when I stopped, wearied as well as satisfied with salmon-fishing, resisting Patterson's most urgent entreaties to "kill another', and make it a half dozen." I have never made a large score or killed a *very* large fish, but this work of three hours and a half was quite satisfactory, and is here given:

1	Fish of	22 lbs.,	Fairy Fly.		
1	"	" 22	"	"	"
1	"	" 24	"	Jock Scott Fly.	
1	"	" 21½	"	Silver Doctor Fly.	
1	"	" 23	"	Silver Gray	"
5		112½	Average, 22½ lbs.		

The healthful excitement as well as open-air exercise enabled us without ill effects to endure this three and a half hours' wetting. Coming up the stream for a single night only, we had taken no change of clothing, and must perforce retire while our men dried the wet ones we wore.

At half past four A. M. next day, the canoe went down with the fish, and I walked to Middle House, where I found Lazell in good spirits over one thirty-three pound fish and other smaller ones. Hastily packing, we set out in our canoes for House No. 1, where we took in additional fish and luggage. Running down the rapids between sharp rocks, both out of the water and under its surface, where all your safety depends upon the accuracy of your men's knowledge, their nerve, and the strength of rather slender spruce setting-poles, is quite exciting to a novice. At the word "check her" from old William at the stern, young James throws his entire weight suddenly upon his pole in the bow. Several times the pole broke, and necessitated quick work in dropping the pieces and grasping a second one, which is always kept within reach in running rapids. Upon breaking a second one, in all likelihood we would have got an extremely unlucky dipping.

We reached Gaspé the same day, having made thirty-five miles since half-past four A. M., and were in time to have our fish packed in snow and forwarded by the afternoon steamer for Quebec. For transportation, the fish are first "drawn" through the gills, then filled with snow and packed two in a box. The snow is then rammed solid around them until it resembles in consistency a cake of ice, and the box is placed inside of a much larger one. The space between the two boxes is now filled with sawdust. At Quebec the boxes are examined by the accommodating and courteous agent of the Canadian Express Company, Mr. Scott, who orders them refilled with snow, if necessary, before forwarding by rail. Our fish left Gaspé Thursday, were in Boston in good condition the Tuesday following, and were served at the Somerset Club just a week after they were killed. With ice in place of snow, the packing is usually a failure.

Finding a letter at Gaspé inviting us to fish the Dartmouth, we went over to that river, July 10th, taking horses to a place called by the *habitans* Lancy Cozzens, which we presumed to be a corruption of *L'anse aux cousins*, or Black Fly Cove. From this point we proceeded by an invention of our own. One of the three canoes had a small sail, and holding another canoe by our hands upon each side of it, we voyaged very independently until we tried to tack under a very stiff breeze,—a performance which (in round-bottomed canoes) didn't take place exactly to suit us. Reaching the narrower part of the stream, we took our setting-poles in orthodox fashion, and soon reached camp, where we found a commodious wall-tent ready pitched, and all needed cooking-utensils, as well as a salmon for supper, left in the house by our departing friends, Messrs. Guild and Barnes of Boston.

The sea-trout had just commenced running up the river, and gave us most serious annoyance. The sea-trout is anadromous and follows up the salmon some weeks later. An old trout-angler believes you not quite sane, and much less serious and truthful, when you positively assure him that oftentimes before you can reach a salmon you must play to gaff a half dozen or more sea-trout, varying in weight from one to five pounds. That a five-pound trout can be an annoyance, and a serious one at that, isn't readily comprehended. You can't hurry a large trout, but must play and tire him out. Occasionally your man from a tree-top will tell you just where a fine salmon is lying, and, perhaps, that he started for the fly and missed it at your last cast. The next cast, a sea-trout, which is quicker than a salmon, snatches your fly the moment it strikes the water, and in the next few min-

AN IRASCIBLE ANGLER.

utes flounders all over the pool, putting an effectual estoppel to salmon-fishing. Now is the time for self-control,—for quietly lighting a cigar and strolling back to camp. Sometimes an irascible angler seizes the trout the moment he is off the hook and hurls him vindictively against the cliff.

This same abused sea-trout, however, when broiled before the fire in an open wire broiler, with a bit of salt pork clamped upon him, or rolled in buttered and wetted papers, and roasted under the embers, is preferable to salmon, and is more often eaten by the Gaspé anglers. The sea-trout and the common brook-trout, *Salmo fontinalis*, are taken side by side in the same pools, and so great is the apparent dissimilarity, that it seems impossible that they are one and the same species, the sea-trout merely being changed by his trip to sea, as some naturalists assert. The spots on the brook-trout are much more clearly defined, and have the light color upon their edges, while the markings of the sea-trout seem not to be distinct spots, so much as irregular markings akin to those of the mackerel. This is as it appears to us who are not naturalists. At the suggestion of Professor Baird of the Smithsonian Institution, I brought home some good specimens of different sizes, in alcohol, and we are awaiting the settlement of this vexed question authoritatively by Professor Gill, who will soon publish an exhaustive paper on the Salmonidæ.

It is notable that although the three Gaspé rivers flow into the same bay, and for long distances within a few miles of each other, yet the fish are so different as to be readily distinguished one from another by the natives. The fish run up earliest in the York, and those taken even in the lowest pools are of larger size than those of the other streams. Of course those that are strong enough to get to the upper pools early in the season before the river has run down, are extremely large. The last runs of fish in the York are perhaps a trifle smaller than the general average of the St. John, where the early and late runs are of more nearly the same average size. So the fish of the Tay, in Scotland, are a month earlier than those of the Tweed, and presumably in this case because the snow gets out of the former much the sooner. The fish of the St. John are slightly shorter and fuller than those of the York, resembling more nearly the *Salmo quinatt* of California. A few seasons since the St. John was so jammed with the logs of a broken-up lumber raft, that the fish were blocked out of it, and that year its peculiar fish were taken in the York. The next year the St. John was clear and its fish went back to it. A few seasons later, grilse and young salmon were taken in the York which

slightly resembled the St. John fish. The parent fish returned to their own stream. Their offspring, which were hatched in the York, remained in that river.

On the Dartmouth, the extreme northern of the three rivers, the so-called nightingales are singing continually, commencing at three A. M. at the first gray of the morning. These birds are probably a kind of sparrow, and by no means true nightingales; but so sad and sweet were their plaintive notes, that by a sort of fascination we would lie awake to listen, at the expense of some hours of needed sleep. During two seasons upon the other two rivers, only a few miles distant, not one was heard. After some practice in imitating them, we thought the following musical notation gave a very good idea of the song, which varied slightly with different birds, and at different times with the same bird. Between each double bar is a single song. Numbers 1 and 2 are different songs of one individual, and numbers 3 and 4 are songs of another individual.

BIRD-NOTES.

It was the close season and we dared not shoot a single specimen even to take home to our ornithologists of the Smithsonian.

The terms of lease of a Canada salmon-stream require the lessee to maintain a guardian upon the river at his own expense. A comfortable log-house of a single room is usually built just below the first pools, and the guardian occupies it during the few months of the angling and spawning season. This expense is quite light—sometimes only a hundred dollars in gold. In addition, the Government appoints and pays overseers, who are assigned to special districts, and are expected rigidly to enforce the law regulating the net fishing in the tidal part of the rivers, and particularly to see that the nets are taken up over Sunday. The Monday and Tuesday fishing up the streams is somewhat a test of this latter enforcement. The Gaspé rivers flow through so wild and inaccessible a country that it is impossible for poachers to reach the pools and carry away fish in large quantities except in canoes, which must, of course, pass the guardian's house. It is, then, practically impossible to do much poaching without the collusion of guardians and overseers.*

If the Government would offer a bounty for every sheldrake killed it would greatly aid in keeping the streams better stocked. In the stomach of a young sheldrake will be found sometimes six or more *parr*, as the young of salmon are called. When we consider the numbers of broods raised each year on a stream, and that both young and old are gormandizing parr all day long, we see that thousands upon thousands of fish are yearly lost in this way alone. These little parr, by the way, often bite at the fly, which is so large for them that they can only grasp some of its feathers, and hang on so well that you throw them several yards as you withdraw to make a fresh cast. The finger-marks or bars identify them at a glance.

One evening while on the Dartmouth, we were surprised by a visit from the guardian and the overseer, who came to dine and spend the night with us. They bragged a little of a big fish the overseer had captured in an unaccountably short time. Upon examining the tackle we found that the line practically ended at the reel, where it joined a worthless cord, and that even this apology for a line had not been wetted. The rod was a shaky affair that couldn't possibly kill a lively five-pound trout. The hook was covered thickly with rust. In their canoe we found a fish of over 30 pounds. One eye was covered with an opaque substance which had grown over it on the line of an old net scar. The other eye had across it a recent cut, which had totally destroyed its sight. The fish was then totally blind, and in all likelihood had broken out of a net a few nights before. These cunning jokers had made a sharp and well-defined cut in the jaw where fish are usually hooked, but they had entirely for-

VIEWING THE AURORA

gotten that during the play of a fish the corners of the cut are rounded and sometimes worn ragged. They had gaffed him as he lay unable to see the approach of the canoe. We were glad that they had thus saved the fish from a lingering death sooner or later by starvation ; but raising a blind fish to a fly and killing him with a rickety bait rod and worthless line was too much for our credulity. We never informed them that we had seen through their little fish story and presume that they had many a laugh at having made " States " men believe that blind salmon could be taken with a fly.

The displays of the Aurora Borealis upon this stream far exceeded in splendor anything we had previously seen. We sometimes sat about a roaring camp-fire until midnight watching them, although a temperature of 40° made indoors more comfortable. An Aurora looks best at such times (it is said) when viewed through the concave lens in the bottom of a glass tumbler in which some hot fluid has been previously placed for a short time to expand the glass properly ; sometimes this extemporized lens seems to enlarge the view and even to double the number of the streamers.

Wednesday, July 15th, found the usually quiet and sleepy little settlement of Gaspé in great commotion. Some people were out on the house-tops with spy-glasses, and others rushing down to the wharf, where a goodly number had already collected. Going to the upper rooms of the Gaspé Hotel to which we had just come from the Dartmouth, we saw a beautiful yacht coming rap-

---

* We are delighted to learn that the Dominion Fish Commissioner proposes to thin out the stands of salmon-nets fished at Gaspé. If he does so we can confidently expect better fishing in the rivers there. As it is, the wonder is that any fish ever manage to get up these streams except on Sunday when all the nets are supposed to be up.

idly up the Basin under full sail. Soon she was abreast the wharf, giving all a view of her exquisite proportions, and passing slowly up where the York merges itself in the waters of the Bay, gracefully swung into po-

"IT CAWNT BE DONE!"

sition and dropped anchor. She was the "Palmer," well known in both this country and Europe for her victory over the "Cambria," and famous as well for being the winner of numerous other races. Soon we received a call from her owner, Mr. Rutherford Stuyvesant, who was to have the York the rest of the season, and was even then pushing on to House No. 1 to take a fish that evening. We met a little later the rest of his party and were invited to pass the evening on board the yacht. It was nearly a month since our eyes had been gladdened by the sight of any of our countrywomen and the invitation was accepted with eagerness. The ladies had braved a ten days' voyage from New York, and part of it in very rough weather off what sailors call the "nastiest of coasts," and were to brave the mosquitoes and black flies as well,—hoping to rival the Countess Dufferin, who had a few weeks before thrown her own fly, hooked and played to gaff a large fish upon the St. John. The evening we passed in the society of these most agreeable and accomplished ladies was marked with a white stone. After reaching home we learned that both Mrs. Stuyvesant and her friend Miss Beach took a fine salmon, and tied, if they did not outscore, the Countess.

We returned home by the "Secret," leisurely stopping at various points, as our fancy dictated. While at a certain place, the steamer touched with the mail, and was to remain two hours. Could the mail be opened at once, and we receive our letters, we might wish to hurry on by that very steamer. We therefore brought all our forces to bear upon the obdurate postmaster to induce him to open the small pouch with mail for his office, and give us our letters at once while the steamer was still at the landing. His constant reply was: "It cawnt be done. Government business cawnt be hurried. The mail is too lawge, too lawge." Exposure of the folly of one manufactured excuse merely brought out a dozen more. Of course he couldn't change his mind; he could die more easily. We were not unmindful of the fact that in mountainous, cold countries, people are naturally conservative, and that when ideas do, with difficulty, reach them, they take deep root, as do the trees in the clefts of their rocks; and yet we didn't expect to find a postmaster in this progressive age who opened mails at his leisure when he had nothing else for amusement.

When the steamer arrived, he was the first to board her. He chatted consequentially with the officers for more than an hour. They were all on our side, and tried apparently to shake him off. Finally, with the little pouch (which he wouldn't intrust to his clerk—also on our side) under his arm, he slowly and with the firm, determined tread of a militia captain on training day, moved off toward the post-office. Fifteen minutes would have sufficed to distribute the mail; but not until the steamer's last whistle blew did he put the letters into the boxes. He reckoned without his host, however, for a friend was quietly watching, and in an instant took our letters and started for the steamer at full run, yelling at the top of his voice. Good old Captain Davison just then remembered that he had forgotten something, and took time enough with the steamer's agent to enable us to glance hastily over our letters, and ascertain that we could go by that steamer.

In 1874, Mr. Curtis exchanged his old river, the St. John, for the Dartmouth, in order that the former might be set aside for the Governor General. Earl Dufferin having been called to England in the summer of 1875, it fell to Mr. Curtis's lot to have the use of both streams, and I accompanied him to them for a few weeks' recreation. We found the season unusually late; few fish up, and the river too high for comfortable canoe-poling. We were again delayed twelve hours in reaching Gaspé, as the dense smoke from forest fires around Ottawa had blown down into the Gulf of St. Lawrence, and compelled us to anchor for an entire night. Mr. Curtis was also accompanied by young Mr. Douglass, son of Sir Charles Douglass, of London, England, —a most genial and companionable gentleman, who had, since graduation at an English University, been shooting alligators in Florida, and buffaloes in the West. Like other young Englishmen, he was well " up " in all outdoor manly accomplishments.

To reach our stream we were obliged to take ourselves and all our luggage across the swollen York by repeated trips in a small dugout, at a place some six miles from its mouth. After crossing, our provisions and luggage were taken in large boxes mounted upon stout timber sled-runners; this being the only

We arrived at our house at nine P. M., and hungrily awaited the coming of our provisions and luggage two hours later. If one expects to enjoy any part of first class salmon-fishing, in the luxurious and dilettant style of anglers at the Thousand Islands, a single trip will not fail to disabuse him of all such notions, particularly if in going up his river he has to get out in the water and help the men pull the canoe around the corner of a small fall.

The fishing of 1875 was comparatively a failure, less than twenty being killed by three of us during a week on the St. John. Douglass one day hooked an ugly fish, which played him all known pranks, and seemed, in addition, to extemporize a few for the occasion. The fish leaped out of water enough to make it exciting, but not enough to tire himself out. He tried pulling constantly backward and forward in quick, short jerks, which is the worst thing a fish

Trolling at the Thousand Islands.　　Helping with the Canoe on the St. John River.

DILETTANT AND PROFESSIONAL SALMON-FISHING.

conveyance that would stand a nine-mile trip over a slightly widened forest trail. We took saddle horses, but yet found the trip most tedious by reason of the " windfalls " which had to be cut away by our canoemen, who carried axes for the purpose, and by the swamp mud through which we frequently had to wade our horses. Black flies and the like seemed more hungry and persistent than usual.

ever does. This makes the coolest angler nervous and anxious, for unless line is upon the instant given, the hook is pulled out, or the gut broken. The fish came down in view of the house, when, comparing the pluck and strategy of the fish with the skill of our friend, we counted the fish a trifle ahead. Of course when near either bank the men took care to keep on the shore side of the fish, so that when he suddenly rushed

EQUAL TO THE EMERGENCY.

for deep water he would not pass under the canoe and break loose. In spite, however, of all precautions, the fish made a dash to run under, and one of the men gave a quick, powerful push on his setting-pole, which unfortunately rested upon a flat, slippery rock. The next instant our view was cut off by an immense pair of caribou hide boots, which seemed suspended in mid-air. The fish was just at the canoe, and the greenheart was taking the last possible ounce of strain. The line could not run out fast enough to relieve the rod, and we awaited its snapping. Equal to the emergency, Douglass, remembering an old trick

"A LITTLE O' YER FLY-ILE."

of Curtis's, threw the rod behind him, and with the reel end in the water and the tip ring resting on the edge of the canoe, the

line ran safely and swiftly out. Douglass then tired and killed his fish, which weighed fifteen pounds—about the average of the St. John fish. In the York, my average of all fish taken is twenty pounds.

The non-angling reader by this time surmises that the only way to bring a salmon to the gaff is to tire him, by keeping a constant steady strain upon him, with the shortest practicable line. The greatest dexterity and skill of the angler and his men are required to keep the canoe always in such a relation to the fish as to make this possible. Half your score depends upon the quickness of the men, who must, if you are on shore, be so near you with the canoe that if the fish starts down a rapid, they can take you in upon the instant, and follow him. How patiently would our faithful fellows sit on the cross-bar of the canoe, watching our every movement, and only now and then, when the flies and mosquitoes were unusually troublesome, break silence with : " Mr., I don't care if I do take a little o' yer *fly-ile*."

To give the general reader an idea of the way in which anglers make up their scores for distribution among their friends, we give an old one which still stands among the best made in America :

F. Curtis's Score of Salmon-Fishing, York River, Lower Canada, for one evening and the following day, 1871.

TWO HOURS, THURSDAY EVENING, JULY 6.

| 1 fish, 18 pounds weight. . . . . . .fly, Jock Scott. |
| 1 " 22 " " . . . . " Robin. |
| 1 " 25 " " . . . . ". Robin. |
| 1 " 26 " " . . . . " Silver Doctor. |

FRIDAY, JULY 7.

| 1 fish, 34 pounds weight . . . . . . .fly, Curtis. |
| 1 " 32 " " . . . . " Curtis. |
| 1 " 26 " " . . . . " Robin. |
| 1 " 31 " " . . . . " Robin. |
| 1 " 17 " " . . . . " Robin. |
| 1 " 22 " " . . . . " Silver Doctor. |
| 1 " 24 " " . . . . " Silver Doctor. |
| 1 " 23 " " . . . . " Robin. |
| 1 " 26 " " . . . . " Robin. |

Total weight for both days, 326 pounds.
Thursday's average, 22 3-4 pounds.
Friday's average, 26 1-9 pounds each, and gross weight 235 pounds.
Whole average, 25 1-13 pounds.

Mr. Reynolds took, some seasons since, in the York, a fish of 47 pounds, which stands now as the largest ever taken in Gaspé with a fly.

The score on the York for the first part of July, 1876, comes just as this article is being put in type:

On Steamer "Mirimichi," July 14, '76.

My dear Wilkinson :—Our score just made, in the face of bad weather and very high rough water, will interest you, not as to number, but as to weight of fish :

		fish		lbs.		average	
Earl Dufferin (3 days)	8	fish	197	lbs.	average	$24\frac{5}{8}$	
Countess "	......	2	"	45	"	"	$22\frac{1}{2}$
Capt. Hamilton	...	6	"	148	"	"	$24\frac{2}{3}$
Mr. Grant (1 day)	....	1	"	27	"	"	27
Mr. Molson	....	14	"	326	"	"	$23\frac{2}{7}$
Mr. Middleton	....	50	"	1094	"	"	$21\frac{22}{25}$
Mr. Reynolds	....	29	"	633	"	"	$21\frac{24}{29}$

110	2470 gen. ave.	$22\frac{5}{11}$

Yours very sincerely and truly,
THOS. REYNOLDS.

Sunday is the only day in camp when all are sure to be at home for an early dinner, and in condition to enjoy and appreciate a good one. On week-days, the cook, who never leaves camp, does not serve dinner until half-past seven P. M., so as to give all time to return from the pools, which are often a few miles distant. If one gets a sulking fish late in the afternoon, he may be detained until long after the dinner-hour, and it is by no means a very rare occurrence to have a fish gaffed by the light of a birch-bark torch.

When the dinner-hour comes, and an angler is absent "*on l'attend comme les moines font l'abbé,*" that is to say, we never wait for him at all,—monks being proverbially good feeders, and never delaying a mo-

LATE TO DINNER.

ment after the dinner-bell strikes, even to await their abbot. Canada fishing-laws forbid throwing a fly Saturday evening after six o'clock, but of course must allow killing a fish previously hooked. It is therefore reckoned quite desirable to get hold of a lively one just before that hour. On Sunday all are somewhat rested, and appetites are always keener after the day's rest which follows excessively hard work out-of-doors. Again, every canoe-man is a natural as well as practiced cook, so that on Sunday, when all have leisure to assist in preparing the dinner, they do not, according to rule, "spoil the broth."

On Sunday, July 4th, 1875, Mr. Reynolds, who was upon his own river five miles or so away, sent over one of his men to say that with three friends he would come over and take dinner with us on our glorious Fourth. As his name is a synonym for hospitality, we were quite anxious to show no shortcomings ourselves in that direction. Our six men and the cook were assisted by Curtis himself, who undertook the unheard-of thing of making a loaf of cake on a salmon-stream. How he succeeded is best told by his own letter to his sister, who had given him the cake recipe :

"I used every available dish in camp—spilled the flour all over my clothes and the floor, and then rubbed it well in with butter, of which latter I melted one mess too much and the other too little. Took a vote and found a majority of one for stirring it with the sun. Think after all I stirred it the wrong way, and certainly put in too much egg-shell to make it settle well, for all the plums, currants, citron, &c., nearly settled

A MAJORITY OF ONE.

through the bottom of the small wash-bowl in which I baked it, while some large lumps of sugar failed to get crushed at all. The cake was however quite passable. To be sure I forgot to butter the dish, and had to dig the cake out in small pieces and glue them together; but that was a mere trifle, and my success was greater than could be reason-

FALLS AT THE NARROWS OF YORK RIVER.

ably expected from so *doughty* a matter. The cow which I had driven up from the settlement and put in our old and now unused snow-house, *so as to keep her*, came to grief by breaking her leg going down the steep rocky river-bank to get water."

Our admirable courier came up from the Basin early in the morning with a clean pocket-handkerchief full of lettuce leaves, the size of a silver dollar, which he had procured from the minister's wife, who had raised under a cold frame the only lettuce in the settlement. Coffin complained bitterly of the imposition of the lobster-dealer, who, learning that his purchase was for "States" men, charged him ten cents each for lobsters of about five pounds weight, while he sold them commonly to Bouthillier, the packer opposite Gaspé, for fifty cents a hundred, large and small as they run. So plentiful are lobsters around Gaspé Basin that a few moments suffice to get a basketful hooked up with a peculiar sort of gaff made expressly for the purpose.

A heavy shower overtook our friends between the two rivers. They had, in honor of the special occasion of a Fourth of July dinner with their American friends, dressed themselves in gorgeous apparel of white flannel. What with the rain which had soaked them and beautifully distributed the usual face dressing of tar and sweet oil over large geographical surfaces, the stains of tree-drippings and the wadings through the marsh at the end of the lake, they presented a sorry appearance. Nothing could induce them to remain and dine in such plight, and so after a little rest and a modest lunch of crackers and cheese, they left us. Our bill of fare, which in accordance with camp custom we had written on bark, was as follows:

St. John's River, Gaspé,
July 4th, 1875.

DINNER.

Soup.
Dried Vegetable with Beef Essence.
Salmon Chowder.

Fish.
Boiled Salmon, Anchovy Sauce.
Broiled Brook-Trout.
Lobster Salad, Mayonnaise Sauce.

Meats.
Boiled Mutton.
Boiled Ham.

Vegetables.
Potatoes. Bermuda Onions.
Canned Sweet Corn and Tomatoes.

Relishes.
Radishes.   Lettuce.   Olives.
Canned Bartlett Pears.
    "   Peaches.
Dundee Marmalade.
Boston Crackers, Gruyère Cheese.
Coffee, Chocolate and Tea.
Cake à la Curtis.

[Wine list on the other side.]

The above shows that with a little forethought before starting, and a little pains in camp, the angler's *menu* may be very creditable to him, although, as in the present instance, the nearest settlement was not far from twenty miles distant. One good thing about camp-life is that we have no *dead dinners*, for the river breezes take away every odor of cooking even before the meal is over.

On Thursday we received from our friend Reynolds a kind invitation to occupy the York River for a week. Curtis and I accepted, Douglass going off by steamer to take a fortnight upon the Matapedia. We packed luggage in long rubber army bags and slung them across the back of an apology for a horse sent up from Gaspé, and went directly over the mountains to House No. 1, where we found canoes and extra men awaiting us, and then pushed directly for the Narrows.*

In lifting one of our canoes over a slight fall, we swung her around and half filled her with water, soaking our blankets, boxes of bread and crackers, as well as sweetening the men's black tea with brown sugar *en masse.*

Just below the Narrows canoes cannot be used, but the fishing must be done while standing and wading in from one to two and a half feet of water. Rubber wading-stockings are worn, with very large canvas shoes over them, the soles being studded with soft metal nails to prevent slipping upon the rocks. In a moment of excitement, while following a fish, one frequently gets in over the tops of his stockings, and the subsequent carrying of a few gallons of water in these for-the-time rubber-bottles is neither comfortable nor easy. Curtis improves upon the stockings by a pair of boots and trousers, such as are used by the Baptist clergy, and which permit wading, if need be, above the waist. Another of his improvements is a vertically adjustable piano-stool arrangement in his canoe, which, while voyaging, lets one down near the bottom to keep the

HOW FISH ARE LOST.

center of gravity low and prevent capsizing, and which when casting can be turned up for

a high seat. This, of course, is only to be used as last indicated when one is lame or very much inclined to laziness.

At the pools, some distance below the Narrows, are found numbers of fallen trees, projecting nearly at right angles to the low river-banks. These trees are the occasion, to nearly all anglers, of the loss of a few fish. Poling rapidly under them, while intent upon a running fish, they find their elevated rod within a few inches of the obstruction. On the instant, the rod is thrown forward, and this gives slack line to the fish and enables him to free himself. A second and too late thought tells him what every one of course knows, that a line from a given point before him on the water to the top of his rod, when held upright, is precisely the same as from the same given point to the top of his rod when it is dropped horizontally in the same vertical plane. Nine times out of ten an inexperienced angler forgets this, and does not quickly throw his rod to the center of the river, as shown in the sketch, and thus preserve his rod and keep a uniform strain upon his fish.

The old log-house at the Narrows is replete with pleasant reminiscences. On the pine doors, cupboards, and window-casings are *scores of scores* and sketches illustrating amusing incidents of life upon a salmon-stream. Sadly we note the names of one or two who, alas! can never gladden us again with their presence.

Higgs's well-known copy of Bagster's first edition of Izaak Walton is bound in wood from the door of Cotton's fishing-house, "*taken off by Mr. Higgs, near the lock, where he was sure Old Izaak must have touched it.*" Following our somewhat this conceit, we made our sketches and notes upon the soft bark of some of the old birches that overlooked our quarters.

In closing these "Notes," necessarily rambling as they follow the salmon, we may add that there are benefits to be derived from salmon angling other than those of pleasure and health; for the angler is constantly at school, and nowhere can one so readily and surely learn self-control, coolness

* While upon the river, I neglected to make a rough sketch of the Narrows Falls, and am greatly indebted to the kindness of J. D. Sargent, Esq., of Philadelphia, skilled in photography as well as in angling, for a photograph of a very similar Fall upon the Nipissighuit River in New Brunswick. With this photograph as a guide, we were able to give a pretty faithful representation of the Upper Falls of the York.

at all times, and the quickest possible adaptation in emergencies of means to an end, as in the contest with the wily salmon.

—The writer of this article is greatly indebted to his young friends Turner and Miller—artists of Washington—who, from his rough sketches and dictation, prepared the original drawings of the illustrations.

The picture of "The Rise" is from a photograph sent to the writer by the genial Prouty (firm of Bradford & Anthony), and copied by kind permission of the artist, Walter M. Brackett, Esq., of Boston. The original forms one of a series of four pictures, entitled respectively, "The Rise," "The Leap," "The Struggle," and "Landed." They were sold at a round figure in gold to an English amateur, who permitted Mr. Brackett to duplicate them and exhibit them at the Centennial. They are received by artists and competent critics as the best pictures ever painted to illustrate the taking of a salmon. Mr. Brackett reserved the right to photograph and copyright the same.

"THE RISE"—ADAPTED FROM BRACKETT'S PICTURE.

14
A
Matter of
Mascalonge
(1902)

A MATTER OF MASCALONGE

By EDWYN SANDYS

MUCH-NAMED, not infrequently much overrated, and not seldom much-abused, this fish occupies a rather ambiguous position among those species which by virtue of certain fighting qualities have earned recognition as game-fish. Greatest of our pike, and a veritable freebooter of fresh water, he has his full share of that strength, speed, and voracity which have earned for his tribe the rather doubtful notoriety they enjoy. The term " wolf of fresh water " is not so far amiss as at first glance it might appear. Scientific authorities have decided that the mascalonge and its near relative, the great northern pickerel, shall be respectively known as *Lucius masquinongy* and *Lucius lucius.*

The 'lunge is found in the Great Lakes, their tributaries, the waters of the St. Lawrence basin, and the Wisconsin lakes. Wherever its habitat, it is the same old lusty pike, the savage of unsalted seas, and a holy terror to any other fish small enough to fit inside of it. Just how large the 'lunge grows probably is an open question —eighty-odd pounds would be about the limit. I have seen one which scaled a trifle over fifty pounds.

The sportsmanlike methods of taking this fish are trolling with the rod and the long handline, and both frequently afford the liveliest of lively sport. Occasionally a medium-sized specimen surprises some angler who is using live minnow bait for bass, but such an event would be somewhat in the nature of an accident.

The variations of the name are rather curious, but they may be at least partially explained by the uncertainty whether the original name was Chippewa, French, or a mongrel blend of the two tongues. The Indians call it " maskinonje," the French " masque allonge," and these throughout the extensive range of the fish are varied into mascalonge, muscalonge, muskellunge, muskallonge, maskinonge, and masquinongy. For convenience, anglers use the abbreviation " 'lunge."

The fish is subject to much variation in color, but this is a matter of locality and by no means to be depended upon should one be asked to decide if some big captive is a 'lunge or a specimen of the closely allied great northern pickerel. The membrane of the lower margin of the gill cover is more reliable. In the 'lunge, it is furnished on either side with seventeen to nineteen bony rays to facilitate closing and opening the gills. These bony rays, termed branchiostegals, spread and furl the membranes at the fish's pleasure, somewhat as the ribs of an umbrella or the sticks of a fan perform their function. The great northern pickerel has from fourteen to sixteen of them, while the eastern pickerel *(L. reticulatus)*, and the western, or grass pickerel *(L. vermiculatus)*, have twelve or thirteen.

An easier identification mark, however, is found on the cheeks and gill cover. In the mascalonge the upper half of cheek and gill cover is scaled, while the lower half of both is naked. The pike has a gill cover scaled like the 'lunge's, but the entire cheek is scaled. The eastern and grass pickerel have cheek and gill covers scaled all over. Hence, if only the upper half of the fish's cheek is scaled, it is a 'lunge; if the entire cheek and half the gill cover show scales, the specimen is a great northern pike. Young mascalonge are distinctly spotted with blackish on a greenish or grayish ground. The mature fish shows less distinct markings, although they usually are discernible in the region of the tail. I have, however, seen big, old fish upon which the eye could detect no spot, the general color being grayish green with a few dim reflections. Again, I have seen fine fish of a nondescript tint, as like that of an old, dry rubber boot as anything I can think of. The young and old of the great northern pike have the sides marked with oval whitish or yellowish spots, several shades lighter than the ground color—hence, a fish with spots darker than the ground color is a 'lunge; with lighter spots, a northern pike. I have dwelt upon these distinctive marks

157

in the hope that what has been said may aid in clearing away a bit of the misunderstanding covering these two fine fish. If the inexperienced angler will remember about the scales of the cheeks and gill covers and the color of the spots, he should make no error in his identification.

The 'lunge and his nearest kin are remorseless destroyers of other fish. Like so many oldtime robbers of the Rhine, they have their strongholds from which to dash forth and raise havoc with the unfortunate wayfarer that may chance within view. The piscivorous habit is strongly suggested by a startling array of teeth, long and sharp, of various sizes, and so arranged that any fish fairly seized can see his finish without half looking.

There is something tigerish about the method of this grim destroyer. Is there a big nest of water weeds, or a handy clump of rushes, such as might readily conceal a few feet of huge rubber hose? Then swim wide of that spot ye fat, lazy, fool fishes, for this particular brand of rubber hose is only open at one end, and that end carries a contrivance that grippeth like a bear trap with freshly filled teeth, and moreover, the trap seems to be always set.

The crafty 'lunge knows how well his long body blends with all water growths; that one sweep of his always-ready, mighty caudal will send him speeding forth as though shot from a mortar, and that nothing upon which his wide jaws can make good their deadly grip is too big for him to tackle. Silent, motionless as a set spring, he waits in his ambush until a sizable victim drifts within range. The cruel eyes glow like wee incandescent lamps, but the careless prey sees them not, or if he does, mistakes them for two sparks of sunlight filtering through the tangled greenery. It is wondrous pleasant there in the velvet shade cast by the whispering rushes forever writing at the grand blue scroll above. From this same well-found shade, too, he can peer far out through the sunlit water and maybe make a small raid on yonder fairy fleet, where the silver galleons of the shiners drift on their lazy course. "I will tarry a while" thinks the visitor fish.

Indeed he will! Whish! Zip! The startled rushes sway and twist as the big, bent tail sweeps through its marvelous stroke; a swift hollow forms upon the oily surface, the sleepy, vertical shadows suddenly wake

and dance in frenzy; there is a thrill of action for yards about, above; below, there is bloody murder! A tiny silvery bubble rises to the surface, bursts, and leaves an iridescent patch. That much slipped out between the gripping jaws. A few feet under, a dim greenish form drifts back from outer shades and lazily noses its way through the cover until it is again headed toward the open. Then silently, like the shadow marking the sun's decline, it rises among the yielding stems till at a certain point all motion ceases. The trap is reset!

Perhaps again and again will the drama be repeated, for the 'lunge is a gluttonous feeder. While it, of course, is impossible to figure out the destruction with anything like accuracy, it must be no trifle. And the worst part of it is that the bulk of the victims are good-sized fish, old enough to reproduce their kind, hence of infinitely greater value than mere fry.

The unsportsmanlike methods of taking the 'lunge are shooting and spearing. The shooting usually is not so murderous as it might appear; in fact it is none too easy when the work is done with a rifle. A slowly moving, or even a motionless fish is a very deceptive mark owing to the fact that it almost invariably appears to be about four inches above its actual position. The refractive power of water has caused many a good shot to miss what should have been an easy mark, and, of course, the greater the distance and the sharper the angle, the more difficulty about driving lead into the water. In point of fact, a green hand will earn no glory shooting 'lunge, for, unless he can get almost directly above his fish, he will be very apt to blunder.

Nor will a keen and experienced man accomplish any serious destruction, for a single good fish would be a notable result of a day's skirmishing along the stream. Big 'lunge are only occasionally seen, and a glimpse of one is no guarantee of a sure chance to follow. The man with a rifle wants only big fish, and he may watch a stream all day and nearly every day for a month and not get one fair chance. When the 'lunge are running up stream the position of a heavy fish usually is betrayed by a steadily advancing furrow on the surface With his eye upon this telltale, the man with the rifle skirmishes along the bank, keeping well concealed and always endeavoring to gain some commanding point from which he may look, and, should circumstances warrant, shoot down.

Such points may be few and far apart, and the 'lunge may take a notion to swim deeper, or hug the farther side of the stream while passing, which demands that the man shall shift ground and endeavor to plan another ambush farther up. This sort of thing may be continued during an entire morning and no chance be offered; in fact, the odds are always in favor of the fish. A missed fish seldom gives a second chance. As it is quite possible to follow the wake of a fish for miles, to see the intended victim in the wrong place perhaps a dozen times, and eventually to lose him because you feared the risk of one or two doubtful chances, the shooting of the 'lunge is a feat seldom performed.

Spearing during the same season is well-nigh as uncertain. Some old hands at the game take very long-shafted spears and go sit at some handy spot from about dawn till as long as they can stand it. Others take chances with the short throwing spear, and, needless to say, seldom take much more than the chances.

The spearing through the ice inside a dark shanty is another method of the market fisher. He sits there smoking and playing the decoy and praying for "night or Blucher," and Blucher may be afar off and hotly engaged in some unknown corner of what is doomed to be a sure enough Waterloo. Meantime the watcher peers steadfastly down into a mystery of green vagueness, through which extend ghostly growths like the wraiths of tropic forests. Flashes of silvery light wink like aquatic fireflies and tell where burnished fry are playing, and possibly a yellow perch lances across the view and instructs the young idea that rod, pole, or perch are measures of deadly accuracy when used in finny schools. And after the fisher has grown to feel like the brown man of old, upon whose original invention his method is a glaring infringement, there comes a change.

The small fry disappear in some mysterious manner best known to themselves. There is a sort of glow in the water and from under the ice slowly slides a mysterious something. If the man with the spear be wise and ironed instead of nerved, he will play the decoy between his feet and coax the fish six inches further. Right where his neck, if he had one, would be, is the spot, and one must not be afraid of hitting him *too hard!* I've heard—of course 'tis mere hearsay and perhaps untrue—there's a way of putting a bit too much strength to it, missing the fish, and following head first after the spear. I cannot recommend this. There's a lack of ventilation and a prevalence of cold and damp down under there which are undesirable, if not positively dangerous. Getting wet up to his ankles may be a trifling matter to a robust man, but I suspect a good deal depends upon which end of him he measures from. A man may wet two of his soles with impunity, but the third never requires water unless—but maybe that's getting too far ahead?

In trolling for 'lunge the old-fashioned handline and spoon hook may be depended upon, but the method lacks the science which the use of a trolling rod demands. I have done a lot of it, and I prefer to go alone and do my own paddling, or rowing. A turn of the line around the thigh enables you to feel all attacks on the lure, while leaving both hands for the paddle or oars; and at the same time the line is where your hand can find it without loss of time. This is important, for the resistance of a heavy fish, aided by the forward motion of the craft, will tauten a line to the danger point before you have time for many motions of your hand. When paddling I make fast the paddle by a short cord, so it can safely be dropped at any point of the stroke. When once fast to a good fish I seldom bother about the paddle for turning, as there is a way of swinging a light craft head on to a taut line which is understood by all familiar with canoes and skiffs. An old pair of gloves is no bad protection, for a line sometimes cuts bare hands.

It is impossible to give anything like detailed instructions regarding the playing of a fish on a handline. A small fellow may be unceremoniously hauled in hand over hand; a big one must be humored. I believe in keeping at a fish all the time, taking no too pronounced liberties and allowing him none. So long as a firm, even hold be maintained on him, he is doomed, if the hooks are planted where they should be. Anything like jerking should not be allowed at either end of the string, for one stiff jerk may play havoc. Only overexcitement or rotten tackle are responsible for the loss of a well-hooked fish. On a hand-

After Mascalonge with the Short Throwing Spear.

line a big fish might demand ten or fifteen minutes of play—I should say an allowance of about one-half minute per pound would be about his limit. I know many men tell of much longer struggles, but I never have seen them. The fact is a man fast to a big 'lunge is apt to be mighty poor indeed as a judge of time. It's like the answer of the benedict to the bachelor who asked if statistics showed that married men lived longer than single men—" Mebbe it only *seems* longer."

A good rod for 'lunge is a high grade split bamboo, or an ash and lancewood, nine feet long and weighing twelve ounces. This, with a multiplying reel of good make and about seventy-five yards of plaited " No. 3," or " E " silk line, and a No. 3-0 Sproat, tied on gimp, will do the business. A large minnow, or a frog, makes a deadly bait, but many prefer a large trolling spoon having a single hook. Triple hooks for 'lunge are a nuisance. All baits for 'lunge should be moved slowly; a common fault of trollers with the handline is sending the boat along too rapidly. An excellent rule is to make as little noise and fuss as possible. From a boat pulled silently about twenty-five yards outside the weeds the bait can be cast to their very edge and slowly drawn away; I prefer, however, to troll along the edge, and by this method cover the most water with the least disturbance. Because a fish does not strike is no guarantee that it is not there, and for this reason I return to a good-looking place after a reasonable interval.

As soon as possible after the 'lunge bites is the time to strike, and the moment the fish is hooked the rower should make for open water. If this be delayed there may be trouble, for the 'lunge is apt to play the deuce if he can get to cover. A good boatman will watch every move of the game and take full advantage of every chance to assist the angler. Too few men are reliable with the gaff. It should be cautiously passed under the fish—this cannot be done too slowly and carefully—and then sent home into the throat, with a smoothly swift, upward sweep. So soon as the fish has been boated it should be rapped on the head and a knife blade passed through the spine just back of the head. This most effectually will prevent any unexpected flopping about, for a fish so treated is dead —not merely stunned.

The best fish ever I killed was taken in Rondeau Harbor, on the Canadian side of Lake Erie. While from appearances the Eau should be an ideal water, comparatively few, but usually large fish are taken from it. Upon the day in question I had trolled with the handline around one end of the harbor, a distance of several miles. There was a broad border of marsh, and plenty of weeds in the water, but the great trouble was an overabundance of bass. These were fine fish, but I felt like Hiawatha, and craved the big fellow.

When I reached the entrance to the harbor, the lighthouse keeper hailed me, and after refusing some fish because he could catch more than he could use, he asked:

" Why don't you try at the inner end of the piers for a big fellow? Anybody could kill them things! " The *things* referred to being some very fair bass.

For a moment I fancied he was putting up a job, for the spot indicated was unpromising for 'lunge, but he was in earnest and I knew better than to dispute his knowledge. If you are going to do a thing at all you may as well do it thoroughly—so I did. For an hour I paddled back and forth, taking a couple of good bass, but receiving no word from the desired big fellow. At last, when I had about decided to give it up, the keeper hailed me.

" You go too fast," he said. " Work clear down past that big clump of rushes, turn it and come back here and see what you do. Go slow, now," he concluded.

It seemed a foolish task, but I went as directed, slipped round the rushes and headed back. Somebody must have applied for a stay of proceedings, for on a sudden everything was brought up standing. " Strange there should be a snag out here," was the first thought; for the line had tautened like a harp string. But just then the snag got busy, and I grabbed the string and hung on to everything but a yell which broke away and ripped the sun-kissed silence plumb to the distant woods. Had I not known that horses didn't graze so deep, I might have imagined that I had hooked up somebody's three-minute stepper.

There was no mistaking the nature of the captive, for the way he fought for the weeds betrayed him, while nothing in that water save a sturgeon or a 'lunge could pull as he did. Headed off in his rush for

A Greenhorn and a Mascalonge.

cover, he presently steamed for open water, and the way the canoe followed was a caution to behold. For minute after minute he pulled and I hung on, getting a foot or so of line now and then. Eventually he appeared to abandon all hope of getting to the weeds, and made for the end of the piers. I knew there were stones and snags in that vicinity, and so handled him as roughly as I dared, but he had almost entered the danger zone before he gave any sign of weakening. Finally his efforts became erratic, then feeble, and he drew, loglike, close alongside, though still refusing to keel over and expose that white badge of surrender which I was mighty keen to spy.

"Gaff him, man! Quick!" shouted the keeper; but I had no gaff.

The 'lunge was so big he almost scared me. His bristling teeth were too horrible to contemplate in connection with fingers through his gills, and for a moment I hesitated. Then, grasping the paddle, I lifted steadily with one hand, while the paddle went slowly over my shoulder. It was risky, but it had to be.

"Don't! Don't! You-condemned-fool-you'll-lose——!" howled the keeper, but his protest was unheeded.

In all probability the strain I was under somehow got into my arm, for the only fish that possibly could endure such a clip must surely be a fossil and one of the toughest propositions in its line. As it was, the thin-edged paddle bit clear through the spine several inches back of the head instead of where I aimed, but I cared little about that. It wasn't *my* spine, but it was my paddle and my fish, and when a man can't paddle his own fish the way he has a mind to, things have got out of stroke.

The light keeper didn't like it. He said that nobody but several sorts of blank fools ever landed fish that way. When I assured him I'd have landed harder if I could have got more of a swing, it didn't improve matters.

"Why didn't you grab his gills? Them there teeth look sassy, but they can't actooally hurt nothin'!" he continued as he poked his fingers into the big mouth which I was holding open for a better view.

I always claimed the fish slipped in my hands, but he swore—quite a lot too—that I clapped the jaws shut.

15
A Fight
with A
Muskallonge
(1902)

15
A Fight
with A
Muskallonge
(1902)

A FIGHT WITH A MUSKALLONGE

By John R. Rathom

ILLUSTRATION BY A. B. FROST

THE dictionaries give twenty-three ways of spelling the word "muskallonge," but there's only one way to fight him and only one particular, peculiar kind of heart-palpitation that he gives the fisherman who catches him napping. For what the leaping tuna is to the Pacific Coast and the tarpon to Florida, is the muskallonge to the lakes of the great Northwest.

To begin with, call him by the familiar term with which sportsmen have come to know and revere him—the "musky." The very word tells of his standing as the greatest game fish in American waters, for he is the only one of them that has had his name so affectionately abbreviated. You can hear a devotee of the sport talk about the pugnacious bass, the trout, or the pike in matter-of-fact manner; but, if he knows the game and loves it, his voice takes on a different tone when he speaks of the musky.

Fishing trips are very much like love-affairs in one way: they say a man can only have one grand affair of the heart; to catch one's twentieth or thirtieth big musky is sport, sublime and bracing sport, too, but to catch one's first—well, I'll make a feeble effort to put the thing into words.

You have cut loose from all the reminders of a base and barren workaday world, and are being rowed over your chosen fishing-ground by a trusty and well-recommended guide. This human product of the city man's desire for sport generally sits ahead with one eye closed. The other is focussed perpetually on the back of your head in the attempt to hypnotize you into the belief that he carries on a private correspondence daily with every big musky in the lake, and knows the exact spots where they are waiting for you. He has already modestly informed you that "those waters" or "them waters" or "those places yonder acrost" are to him an open book, and that the only guide in North America worthy of the name "ain't no thousand miles out of this boat, sir, if I do say it meself."

He takes you at a moderate speed round the lake, skirting the edges of the weed-beds near shore, and circling others that spring up like islands in the middle of the beautiful sheet of water. Out between fifty and eighty feet behind you stretches your line, and back of it runs a fast twirling spoon with a bare gang of hooks or a minnow attached. The vibrations of the brilliant piece of revolving metal send a steady shiver down through your steel rod and into the very tips of your fingers, not only signalling "all clear below," but sounding a perpetual warning to you to be ready and on your guard. If you happen to be a stock-broker back in town you'll probably liken it to the sensation of standing with a ticker tape in your hand and waiting for the next move at the other end of the machine.

Steady! A swift tug at the line. If you are experienced at the game you simply smother an exclamation with a cough and begin to reel in slowly like a man who has a painful duty to perform, for you know that your hooks have picked up a sizable string of water vegetation. But if you're a novice your heart goes into your mouth, you frantically shove your rod up to set the points, and begin to take in line at a mile-a-minute pace, fully believing that the record fish of the season has fallen a victim to your cunning.

The omniscient guide, however, knows better before you have been at it a second. He glances at the hang of the silken thread as it runs down over the stern, and says, in a patronizing way (it takes him about a minute after you get into the boat to find out whether you are an expert or a beginner): "Take yer time. It's weeds."

"Holy Jehoshaphat! How can you tell it's weeds without the rod in your hands?" gasps the wondering novice.

"Enstinct," he answers, with a pitying smile. "Enstinct, I guess. Why, mister, if I didn't know them things like A, B, C I'd give up this business to-morrer. It's born in us fellers."

Two minutes, five minutes, ten, and fifteen minutes go by and you are still stooping motionless. You couldn't stay in the same position so long under other circumstances, even if it meant the winning of a heavy wager. The guide's quiet and continuous chatter only filters through your subconsciousness, for most of your thoughts lie with that whirling spoon. You note in the same half-unheeding manner that another day has broken. The morning sun begins to peep over the horizon and sends a glorious rosy light across the great pine forests that cluster down to the edge of the lake. The blue-black water changes its shade here and there, lit up by golden beams and little tints of gray. The drops that hang like dew from the swishing silken cord——

Stop! A savage tug, a twist, a sudden slackening of the line, and then sixty feet away a glistening, beautiful thing shoots straight as an arrow up from below into the air, twists himself frantically in his effort to throw his body off the hooks, and plunges again like a flash into the depths of the lake.

They might as well tell you not to breathe as not to get excited at such a moment. But keep your senses as clear as you may. With a sweep of the oars the guide brings you broadside on to the battle, and keeps you in that position as closely as he can all through the fight.

"Take in your slack." This is the warning that rings in your ears. Unless you heed it you might as well give up all hope of victory, for once let him get enough loose play for a successful jerk and he will spit the hooks out of his mouth as if they were straws. Down at an angle of nearly forty-five degrees stands your line, as taut as a bar of iron, and the depth tells you that he is as big as he is game. The top sections of the rod in your hand bend gracefully like a whip, and sway so rapidly with every motion of the fish that they seem to have become part of his own body.

For a moment or two all is strangely still. Then, as the musky deliberately runs up the line to steal the slack he cannot get in any other way, you watch the top of the rod jump back into place, and your heart sinks as you see what appears to be certain evidence that he is off and away. " I've lost him," you say to the guide in a pathetic tone. Almost before the words are out of your mouth the oarsman, half way as excited as yourself, but trying hard to appear indifferent, shouts :

" Pick up your slack, quick ; fer the love of me wild oats, pick up yer slack. He's there yet."

In confirmation comes another swift dash for liberty that almost throws the rod out of your trembling hands, and once again the steel tip bends till it almost touches the water. Tug, dive, spurt, rush ; this way, that way, up and down he plunges. Inch by inch, between every gallant effort he makes, you turn your reel, bringing in the dripping line and holding on like grim death to every foot as it comes over.

Suddenly there is that strange, silent easing up once more, but this time you remember your lesson and take advantage of it. Then you begin to breathe again in the belief that the fight is almost over and your cramped wrists and fingers are about to get a well-earned respite. Over? The ridiculous idea is knocked out of your head with another smashing leap that takes him a foot out of the lake and shows him

to you in the flooding sunshine only thirty feet away. Provided you don't drop the rod out of your hands in admiration at the sight, you have a fighting chance. So has he.

" Careful," says the guide, in a trembling whisper. " If that feller's a ounce he's a twenty-pounder. Hold him there a minute. Keep stiddy. I'll head into deep water."

Once, twice, three times your rod dips into the lake, and still the strain never eases, still that swift running creature below keeps up his plucky struggle. You feel the drops of sweat on your forehead, though the early morning air is as cool as the breath from some snow-clad mountain. Gradually he weakens, and you know that, barring accidents, you have won. Up, closer and closer, you draw him along till at last he floats there within a foot of your boat.

No eyes so wicked as a musky's. They glare up at you like an angry dog's, seeming to watch every motion you make. Be careful. Here it comes—his final despairing leap for liberty. As he makes it his powerful tail sweeps against the stern and deluges you with water. But the hooks hold, and once more, for the last time, you draw him again to where the guide waits with a revolver in his hand. A shot back of those glittering eyes, a shiver down the whole length of him, a swift jerk into the bottom of the boat with the gaff-hook—and you lie back in an ecstasy of exhaustion.

Then the guide, in order to impress you with the idea that he is about ninety-eight per cent. responsible for the victory, says, in a dreamy tone :

" I knew we'd get that feller if we went over a certain spot."

Drawn by A. B. Frost.

Another smashing leap that takes him a foot out of the lake, —

16
My
First
Trout
(1887)

"MY UNCLE AND I."

MY FIRST TROUT.

BY CAPTAIN THOMAS S. BLACKWELL.

"THERE's nothing in the world like it! Nothing at all to come near it in the way of sport, you may depend upon it!"

"Only fancy hooking a good big fellow who will take out your line like a sky-rocket; then his getting a fit of the sulks, and your anguish of mind as you feel he is trying to nuzzle off the hook against a root or a stone."

"Then whir-r-r! he is away again like a small steam-engine; and so the game goes on until at last he breaks your tackle and

173

escapes, only to make you doubly eager to hook another, or else you have him lying on the grass at your feet flashing with all the colors of the rainbow. And yet they put this rubbishy lawn-tennis trash in comparison with a sport like this! Faugh!" and in his disgust the old gentleman gave a kick at an imaginary tennis net, and in so doing got a twitch of the enemy which was at present laying siege to his left leg; the consequence was a volley of very sanguinary adjectives which are better left unrepeated, and sundry rare and novel wishes, which, if gratified, would be anything but conducive to the future welfare and comfort of the originator of the aforesaid game.

I was home on sick leave, having been brought to death's door by an attack of jungle fever caught while serving with my regiment in Bengal.

I had only arrived at my uncle's place in Devonshire a few days previously, but already the balmy May air was making a new man of me.

My uncle, Colonel Peppard, was a thorough specimen of the old East India Company's Service—the H. E. I. C. was as unmistakable as if branded on his forehead. He was a little, red-faced man, with short, stubby, white moustache and whiskers; a temper shorter and more porcupineish than his hirsute appendages; an indelible impression of the superiority of the "John Company's" administration to that of the "Brummagen Empress of India times" was one of his weaknesses, and fishing was the other.

A nice trout stream ran through the lawn of "Bangalore Lodge" (as the Colonel called his place), and here you might be pretty certain to find my uncle during the fishing season, except when, as at present, the gout had laid an embargo on him.

I had never desired to become a disciple of Izaak Walton's, but ever since my arrival the old gentleman had been drumming into my head the pleasures of "the gentle art."

The weather was all that the most fastidious angler could desire, and my poor uncle was writhing with vexation to see such a glorious "green drake" season drift past without his being able to make a single cast. Certainly, in my case, he behaved after a most scriptural fashion in "not sparing the rod," for morn, noon and night it was nothing but fish and fishing.

He was constantly trying to work me up into enthusiasm for the sport he loved so well, but I fear with only poor success.

I listened with praiseworthy patience, but my thoughts were all fixed on a lovely, fresh English face that I had seen in one of my rambles a couple of days after my arrival in Devon.

I was sauntering lazily along one of those avenues of flowers—a Devonshire road in May. It was a glorious feeling, after being kiln-dried in India for half a dozen years, and then cooped up in a crowded "trooper" for as many weeks,

"SO I DETERMINED TO TRY AND STOP HIM."

to snuff again the pure, balmy, perfume-laden breeze of an English spring morning.

I was strolling along in a dreamy way, drinking in the soul-stirring song of the lark, and the delicious fresh scent from the primrose-starred banks, when suddenly I was wakened up by a clattering behind me, and turning quickly I saw a pretty pony and a basket phaeton, with a young lady for its only occupant, coming careering down the long steep hill which I had just descended.

I saw at once that something had frightened the pony, and that he was running away, so I determined to try and stop him, as I knew there was a very sharp, ugly turn a little further down the road.

I drew to one side, but as the little gentleman flew past me, I made a snatch at the reins, and after running a few yards with him, succeeded in bringing him to a standstill.

I found that part of the harness had broken at the top of the hill, and that the carriage running against the pony's hind legs had made him set off in spite of all the efforts of his fair driver. The young lady was very pale and frightened, but after having assisted her out, and calmed down the fears of the miniature steed, she came to herself, and began to shower out a profusion of thanks.

"Indeed, I am *so* thankful to you, sir, for your courage and kindness. I don't know what I should have done only for you. We would surely have been capsized at the turn below there, for I had lost all control over the little rascal. Ah! Button! you naughty little fellow! What made you forget yourself to act in such a way?"

The callous Button, now that he found the world was *not* coming to an end, was behaving himself in a most cool, impertinent manner, cropping the primroses and what little grass had room to grow between the flowers in a most nonchalant way, as if he was in no way to blame for the whole business.

"Oh! pray don't mention it," said I, as I began settling up the dilapidated harness as I best could.

The sweetly pretty face, the witching smile and the silvery voice quite took me by storm, and all I could grunt out was, "Pray don't mention it!"

I don't know how it is, but we always find that whenever we wish to be particularly agreeable and polite, we generally fail most ignominiously.

I can remember after she drove off how savage I felt with myself.

"I START TO FISH MY UNCLE'S POOLS."

I, Harry Richmond! the first "ladies' man" of the "Royal Flintshire Fallbacks," to behave like a common lout!

What a glorious opportunity to say all sorts of pretty things! and to such a lovely, fascinating girl, too!

When she had regularly swamped me with thanks, and I had assisted her into the phaeton, she gave me her hand, and with the sweetest of smiles said:

"Well, good bye! and I am sure that when papa sees you he will be most grateful for the service you have rendered me to-day, and for which I feel I have most inadequately thanked you."

I raised my hat in a mechanical sort of way, and stood in the middle of the road, staring like a fool at the corner round which she disappeared.

It then began to dawn on me what an uncouth fellow she must have thought me.

But then she said her father would see me and thank me. Her father! Who was he? That was a question that had never entered my muddled brain to ask, and I now remember, too, that my fair enchantress had forgotten to inquire the name of her gallant deliverer!

Well, Harry Richmond, you have made a nice mess of it. You, who plume yourself so highly on your ease and self-possession with the fair sex!

*   *   *

My uncle's importunity, and the desire to have a quiet think over the divinity who presided o'er Button—and my heart— at last made me accept the oft-pressed-upon-me fishing-rod, and the old gentleman was in the greatest glee at having made a convert of me. I was given his own old pet rod, and a book of flies, which, if animated, would have created a nice little second edition of the Egyptian plague. I am afraid I paid very indifferent attention to his directions of how to fish certain particular pools of the river.

I only recollect one part of my instructions, which was, on no account to trespass on old Mr. Witherington's part of the stream. It seems that my uncle had inadvertently trespassed on this gentleman's demesne one day, and that Mr. Witherington, who was himself an enthusiastic angler, and, as a matter of course, extremely jealous of his riparian rights, had made a descent on the colonel just as he landed a splendid fish.

Very hot words ensued, and the lord of the soil ended by calling my uncle "a confounded old poacher," an appellation which was too much for the choleric old Indian, whose blood was by this time at *curry*-point.

He "went for" Witherington, catching him by the collar, and would have swung him into his precious trout stream, but for the timely interference of a man-servant.

As may be imagined, a deadly feud existed between the two veteran piscators,

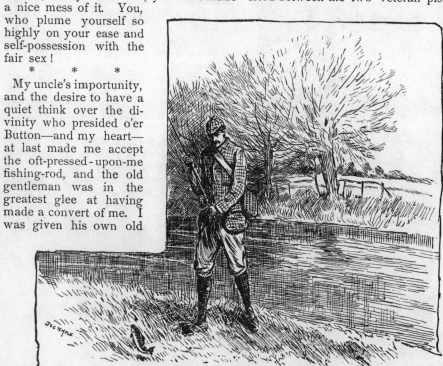

"I WAS GLOATING ON MY SPECKLED PRIZE."

and it was not to be wondered at that my uncle should caution me so particularly against straying into the enemy's country.

I started off on my way down the river, and began to think that "old Izaak" was not such a fool as I thought, after all.

It is a glorious thing to stroll along the banks of one of those lovely Devon streams. Here it dashes over the shingle, and leaps madly amongst the rocks, as if bent on seeking self-destruction in the mighty, insatiable ocean as quickly as possible; there it rounds that turn, and as the beauteous scene unfolds before it seems to change its mind, and come to the conclusion that life is too sweet to rush through it like this. Silently, solemnly, stilly, it glides between the mossy, flower-decked banks, swirling the foam-flecks (the only tell-tale of the late impetuous scurry) lazily round the deep, dark pools, and in and out amongst the gnarled roots. Here we find the lazy, aldermanic trout, the fat, well-conditioned fellow, who drones away his day at the foot of yon willow, a gentleman quite indifferent to the most inviting fly in the angler's vocabulary, and perfectly content "to bear the ills he has than fly to others that he knows not of." Here the

silence and serene peace seems to influence all nature.

"Bunny" sits up quite close to one, and hardly thinks it worth his while to retire to his burrow; the usually shy water-hen trots leisurely down the bank, jerking a sort of defiance with her tail; the thrush, perched on a hawthorn bush, with its canopy of snowy, delicately-scented blossoms, pours forth his rich wild notes to cheer his patient consort through her weary, monotonous nesting.

Here was a fit place to rest, and dream of that sweet, lovely face which had been my only thought since the first day I saw it.

I threw myself down on the bank and was soon lost to all sight and sound.

I know not how long I may have been in dreamland, when I was suddenly aroused by the hitherto neglected rod being nearly twitched out of my hand.

I had unconsciously let the top slip into the river, and the flies sinking to the bottom had, I suppose, tickled the fancy of one of the lethargic trout aforesaid, who, getting a tid-bit on such easy terms, had condescended to partake of it.

It proved quite a stimulant to him, and

"HERE, GILES! KICK THE POACHING RUFFIAN OFF."

the result was the jerk which wakened me up also.

I cannot say that I had been much benefited by all my uncle's instructions as to how to play a fish—my sole thought was to hold on to him like grim death, and thanks to the superior material of my rod and tackle, I managed to pitch him on to the bank in a most un-Waltonian style.

Must I confess that in my excitement I was vandal enough to forget everything—that fairest of faces included—in my triumph at having one fish at least to show my uncle.

I was gloating over my speckled prize as he flopped about on the grass, when I was startled by a shrill, angry shout of—

"Halloa! you, sir! what do you mean by trespassing on my preserves?"

A little, weaselish-looking man, his face purple with rage, was standing just a few yards behind me.

"What do you mean, sir, by coming in here?" he repeated, in a louder and more angry tone.

"I beg your pardon, sir," I said, "but I was not aware I was trespassing."

"Not aware you were trespassing, indeed! A very likely cock-and-a-bull story!" screamed my volcanic little friend, bursting into a violent eruption.

"Couldn't you read the notice at the bridge where you crossed the road? But, maybe, like the rest of your confounded, idle, poaching brethren, you can't read."

"Come, sir," said I, getting "volcanic" also, "this is rather too much. I'd have you know that I'm an officer in Her Majesty's service."

"The more shame to you," was his answer, "not to know better than go poaching on any man's preserves."

"I again repeat that I did not know I was trespassing," I said. "I never made a single cast all day, and it was only by the merest chance I caught that trout, as I was lying on the bank of the river."

"Humbug!" he screeched; "you're *lying* on the bank of the river still—as if I'd believe that *chance* brought you to the very best pool I have! I suppose you often enough carried away a good one from here before."

"I tell you I know nothing about your confounded pools; I am quite a stranger here, and have only been stopping with my uncle, Colonel Peppard"—

"Oh! ho! that's it, is it? The old poaching scoundrel can't get out himself, and so he sends you. You're a pretty pack up there!"

"Look here, now," said I, "you have insulted me most grossly, and I have let it pass, but I won't stand your insulting my uncle, when he is not here to defend himself. You may thank your age, and nothing else, that you are not at present cooling yourself in your pet pool."

"You would—would you?" he yelled, foaming with passion; "I dare you to lay your hand on me. Here, Giles! Giles!"

A big, strapping, young fellow—like a game-keeper, by the cut of his "velveteens"—came running down from a fine large house, which up to the present I had not noticed, as it was hidden by a clump of laurels.

"Here, Giles!" the old gentleman managed to pant out, "kick this fellow out on the road—the poaching ruffian!"

I saw there was nothing to be gained by arguing with the irate old party, or coming to loggerheads with the herculean Giles; so turning on my heel, I walked toward the house, closely followed by master and man—the latter keeping up a brisk fire of anything but complimentary remarks. But there is a limit even to abuse, and from sheer want of breath he had to stop, and left Giles to escort me on to the road.

As we were passing the end of the house I saw a young lady busily engaged at some flower-beds, and as she happened to turn her head slightly, what was my astonishment and delight to see my fair charmer of "Button" memory!

I gave a start of surprise, but as she was busy over her plants, she did not notice me, and I came to the conclusion that the present would be rather an inauspicious occasion to renew my acquaintance.

"What's your master's name, my good fellow?" I asked of Giles as we got to the road gate.

"Squire Witherington, sir," said he, touching his hat; "he's mair cross, sir, if anybody trespasses on him—but bless ye, he don't think o' it five minutes arter."

"And who's the young lady that is at those flower-beds yonder?" I inquired, in as unconcerned a tone as I could manage.

"Who's she? Why, that's Miss Lucy, of course," he answered, in a tone of wonder, as if that had been quite a needless question to ask.

"Oh! that's Miss Lucy, is it?" I said; "well, here, my man, get yourself a drink for your trouble," and I slipped a sovereign into his hand.

His face of astonishment was well worth the money, as he would look at it on his palm and then after me as I walked up the road.

I suppose he thought a bright, golden sovereign a very respectable guerdon for "kicking me out on the road," and would be happy to have a similar job often.

* * * * *

I felt a perfectly different man walking home—at least, I had discovered the object of all my thoughts since the day of my runaway scene.

Certainly, the prospect of renewing our acquaintance did not look particularly rosy at the present, but I trusted to chance to turn out the silver lining of what appeared to be rather a murky cloud.

I was bored to death when I got home to dinner by the multitudinous questions as to whether I had tried this pool or that rapid, till I was fit to wish all the fish in the world anywhere but where they were.

I managed at last to insert a wedge in the shape of old Witherington, to try and break up the mass of fishing lore which was being hurled upon me.

I just mentioned his name casually, as having seen his house.

That was quite sufficient to draw a tirade from my uncle.

Between the squalls I was able to make out that there were no sons and only one daughter, so I knew that "Miss Lucy," of "runaway" and "flower-bed" memory, was Mr. Witherington's only child.

Dinner over, I escaped to my room and destroyed about a ream of note-paper in trying to compose a suitable letter of apology to the old gentleman.

After many attempts I sent off the following short epistle, in preference to some which were much longer and more elaborate—

"DEAR SIR—I am exceedingly sorry that I inadvertently trespassed on your preserves this morning, and that in the heat of the moment I made use of language to you that I am most heartily grieved and ashamed of.

I had the pleasure and good fortune to be of some little service to Miss Witherington a few days ago. I sincerely trust she has quite recovered her fright.

Hoping you will forgive what was quite unintentional on my part, and also words uttered in passion.

I am, dear sir,
Yours, faithfully,
HARRY HEMSWORTH RICHMOND."

I sent this off by a messenger at once, and in a short time I got a note from Mr. Witherington saying he would never forgive himself for his rudeness, nor his unpardonable conduct to one who had behaved so gallantly in rescuing his dear child from the position of great danger in which she was placed.

He went on to say that he had been looking high and low to find out the gentleman who had been of such service, but owing to my being a stranger he had not succeeded till "the unfortunate—but fortunate—occurrence of to-day luckily put me in possession of what I so wished to find out."

"I am," he wrote "most anxious to see you and thank you, and also to ask you some questions about your name, which is one I feel a deep interest in. Come and dine in a quiet way with me to-morrow."

He finished up with, "And I am sure we will forget and forgive each other better than we can do with pen and ink." The P. S. was the part of the letter which interested me most: "Lucy is positively dying to see you, and thank you."

* * * * *

I need scarcely say that I accepted the invitation, making some plausible excuse to my uncle for my absence, as I well knew it would be almost the death of him, the bare idea of my entering the house of his sworn foe.

The old squire I found to be a most jovial host, and the best of company; Lucy—well, I am afraid I am too prejudiced a party to enter into a minute description; suffice it to say, that she was a most innocent, unaffected girl, and if possible exceeded in loveliness the ideal being that had haunted me for the last few days.

Both she and her father quite overpowered me with their thanks for the slight service I had rendered on the morning of the "Button" escapade.

"As to the disagreeable occurrence of yesterday morning, I think the least said, the better," said the old gentleman. "I know you will forgive me, and I have nothing to forgive you for. But there is one thing I am most anxious to know from you, and that is the name of your father. There is something in the way you sign your name that brings back to me a flood of sweet and bitter memories. The "R" in your signature reminds me so of a dear, dear friend of mine who bore the same surname as you do—poor George Richmond!"

"George Richmond!" I exclaimed. "Why, that was my father's name!"

"Your father! You don't mean to tell me that you are the son of George Richmond, who was rector of Hazlewood?" Mr. Witherington excitedly asked.

"Yes, sir; I am," I replied, "but I was but an infant when he died, and except what friends have told me of him, I may say he is a stranger to me."

"*His* son! *His* son!" he repeated again and again, as if in a stupor. "Oh! God! thy ways are wonderful," and he buried his face in his hands for some minutes. Suddenly starting up he said, "Boy, I must tell you my story. Your father and I were at school together; we both went to Harrow the same 'half,' and from the first day were firm friends. Our friendship ripened into a love more than brotherly, and we both felt the time bitterly when our course at Oxford was finished, and we had to separate on our respective paths in life. I had to come home here to take up the management of the estate from my father, who was getting into the 'sere and yellow leaf;' while George started in that vocation for which, from his gentle, kind disposition, he was so eminently adapted—the Church.

"We did not meet for some time, till at last he was able to get a few weeks' rest from the arduous duties which the curacy he held at Newminster entailed.

"It seemed like old times to have him again with me; but, alas! our friendship was not to be of long duration. Mr. Oswald, the rector of this parish at that time, had one daughter, Alice Oswald—a sweet, amiable, lovely girl.

"I loved her devotedly—passionately— but somehow she was always cold and reserved to me.

"Your father was, of course, soon introduced to her, as our families were on the most intimate terms, and I was not long in noticing the difference of her manner with him. My blood used to boil with jealous hate, as I would see the bright smile of welcome for George Richmond, and the cold indifference for me. I could not stand it, so used generally make some excuse and absent myself whenever our

family were going to the rectory, or theirs coming here. Your father became a daily visitor at the Oswalds', and one evening I was sitting in my own room reading, when he burst in, his face radiant with joy. 'Ned, old fellow! I have something very particular to tell you, that I'm sure you will be delighted to hear.' 'Well,' said I, very calmly, though a cold indescribable feeling of dread came over me, nearly choking me, 'what's the wonderful news? Have they made you the Archbishop of Canterbury? or are you parsons going to cut the somber attire, and take to the wearing of reasonable clothes?'

"'No humbug, Ned! I'm as happy as if I had just been appointed to a bishopric —Alice Oswald has promised to be my wife!'

"A perfect hell seemed to take possession of me in a moment. My brain seemed on fire, and the sight left my eyes. My look startled him, for he asked in a voice of surprise, 'Why, what's the matter with you, dear Ned?'

"'Aye! your dear Ned! you mean, sneaking interloper! with your twaddling cant, coming to rob me of the girl I love, and then glorying over it to me,' I screamed, as a hundred devils seemed to enter into me.

"'Ned!' he exclaimed, in amazement at the perfect tornado of rage I had given vent to.

"'Don't speak to me,' I yelled, as my fury increased, 'with your soft, hypocritical talk.'

"'Ned, are you mad?' he said. 'I forgive your harsh, undeserved words, and I am very sorry from my heart if——'

"'I want neither your forgiveness nor your pity, you snivelling hound! You are mean enough to forgive anything, but perhaps your groveling spirit would resent that—or that!' and I dashed my clinched fists into his face.

"This must have been the climax of my mad passion, for the instant I struck him, a horror of what I had done seized me.

"Never can I forget his noble face— white as marble—nor the look he gave me as he wiped away the blood and tears, and said, 'May God forgive you, Ned, as I do from the bottom of my heart.'

*   *   *   *   *

"This was the last time I ever saw him. The morning saw me on my way to London, and from there I went to the continent, where I traveled about for over a year till my father's death obliged me to return home. I found that your father and Alice had been married about two months after I left, but what was my sorrow and remorse to learn that he had died in a little over a year after his marriage, from a fever brought on by over-fatigue while engaged in his labor of love among the pest-stricken population of one of the slums of his district.

"Poor George! how the old love welled back to my heart when I knew he was no more! How the black, fiendish words of hate seemed blacker still under the bright-shining words of forgiveness!

"But those blows—what could wipe the remembrance of them away!

"I sought out his grave, and many a bitter tear I shed over his resting-place, but nothing could wash away the feeling of the bitter wrong I had done him. It was not long after that I heard of the death of poor Alice—your mother—but I was not aware a child survived her. How strange are the ways of Providence that *his* son should meet with me in such a way!

"Can you forgive me, my dear boy, for my treatment of your noble-hearted father?"

"My dear sir," I replied, "yours is indeed, a strange, sad story. I can only repeat my poor father's words, and feel assured that the bitter remorse you have felt has made ample amends for the wrong you did him."

*   *   *   *   *

I became so constant a visitor at the Grange, that I had at last to confess to my uncle, where I spent my time. At first he was furious and said he would not have me go there any more; but at last he cooled down, and a *carte blanche* from the squire to fish the Grange River finished the business, and the two old gentlemen were soon the greatest of cronies.

Lucy and I were left to amuse each other, and we succeeded so admirably that we thought it as well to make it a permanency.

*   *   *   *   *

The pool is a favorite spot with us on the fine summer evenings, and as our little boy and girl play about us, now decking up the original "Button"—a staid, sensible old fellow grown—with garlands of wild flowers, then darting off in the vain hope of capturing some inquisitive bird that has hopped down to inspect the work, we watch the circling eddies that the fish make in the still, dark water, as they rise at some unsuspecting fly. Though "nothing would ever make an angler of me," my uncle says, yet, as I look into my Lucy's sweet, sunlit face, I press her closer to me, and bless *my first trout.*

17
With the
Sierra Club
in the Kern Canon
(1909)

WITH THE SIERRA CLUB IN THE KERN CAÑON.

By Marion Randall Parsons.

One of the tenderfeet had fallen behind on the trail. A two o'clock arising and a long morning of staging, followed by a walk of seven hot, steep, dusty miles, had proved too much for urban muscles and wind and she had lagged behind. Nearing camp in the early dusk she saw brightly burning fires and a cheerful animation about the commissary department, denoting, she supposed, a dinner hour postponed to meet the needs of weary stragglers like herself. What was her horror, then, to hear roared in tones of authority:

"Last call for lunch! Get your lunches for to-morrow! You'll have to hurry!"

"Gracious!" thought the tenderfoot with mounting uneasiness, "I've missed dinner and breakfast and nearly lost lunch! If they are as forehanded as that with all the meals I'll starve."

It was therefore something of a relief to find that Charley Tuck, with a soft spot in his lazy old heart for laggards, had kept the soup and other comforting things piping hot for the last comers, and to observe his assistant slicing bacon for the morrow's breakfast; but many days had elapsed before that first impression of strenuous camp life was wiped from her mind.

Indeed, the first days of a Sierra Club outing, when the big party is on the march from civilization to camp, have in them little leisure for man or beast. The morning of July 1st, the second day of the outing, but the first of real camp life, dawned very early for us. At 4 o'clock a sleepy Chinaman banged a dishpan with a spoon, yelling a Mongolian version of "Everybody get up!" The cry was taken up by each Sierran as he awoke, until the whole camp was chanting it in unison. A short lull suc-

ceeded this pandemonium, while fingers were busy with
shoe laces and the bewildering intricacies of packing.
Before the last novice had crammed his belongings into
his dunnage bag most of us had finished breakfast and
started on the trail.

Wishing to avoid the high passes of Farewell Gap and
Coyote Pass, which wrought such havoc among pack-
mules and tenderfeet five years ago, we this year chose
the trail to the Kern leading from the Springville road
past Nelson's and over the ridge to Fish Creek and the
little Kern.

Our first night's camp was situated a couple of miles
below Nelson's in a grassy cañon wooded with oaks and
a few pines. Passing the little settlement with its neat
orchards and brown hay-fields, we were soon among the
conifers, giant yellow and sugar pines, cedars, and even
a group of fine sequoia.

It was all climbing that morning—from oak and chap-
arral to pines and bear clover; to forests of silver fir
and red fir, whose carpet of brown needles was brightened here and there by the flash of a red snow plant; to
clear streams bordered with mimulus and columbine running through green meadows where the cyclamen bloom-
ed; and higher still to the silent tamarack country with
its marvelously blue sky and its trail of white granite
sand. Here we had done with climbing and could swing
along a comfortably level trail with an occasional outlook
up the cañon of the Little Kern to the high mountains at
its upper end bounding the well-remembered pass of
Farewell Gap. Then it was down, down, down to the
valley of Fish Creek, where camp was made for the
night.

An amusing incident of the next day's travel was the
fording of the Little Kern, the more cautious members
laboriously removing high boots and stockings and picking their painful way across the rocky bottom barefoot,
while a few of the more enterprising made almost as
amusing a picture hopping across on the rocks below

the ford. A short climb out of the Little Kern brought us to the lower end of Trout Meadows, whenceforward it was easy traveling, up the meadows and the long defile that led us to the brink of the Kern Cañon cliffs.

The first permanent camp was established on the neck of land lying between Kern River and the lower Kern Lake. This is the smaller of the two lakes the cañon boasts and is admirable for swimming, the water being quite warm. The upper lake, separated from the lower by one of the kernbuts that are characteristic of this cañon, is a comparatively recent addition to the landscape, having been formed less than a half century ago, either by a landslip, or by debris brought down from a small side stream during a flood, which dammed the river at the mouth of its narrow passage between the east wall and the kernbut. The stumps of trees killed by immersion in the lake thus formed are still standing in great abundance, some of them eight or ten feet out of water; others, lying concealed beneath it, make boating, especially in the canvas canoes that enthusiastic fishermen like to use, a rather dangerous pastime.

The fishing in this lake and in the river, both above and below it, is a well-known attraction of the Kern, and our fishermen found it a paradise for them this year. Even the inexperienced anglers had a share of the good luck. Dark stories are told of the unsportsmanlike deeds of one of the fair fishermaidens, who was observed to drop her rod with a whoop of delight, splash ankle-deep into the river and haul in a two-and-a-half-pound trout hand-over-hand. And when a pained bystander offered a few hints on the advisability of playing a fish, she remarked tranquilly:

"Well, I got him, didn't I?"

But it must be said of our fishermen, that they were most temperate in their enjoyment of the unusually fine sport, and that by common consent all fishing would cease for a day or two lest the fish appetite fail and the victims of the rod be wasted.

Fishing, swimming, and a two-days' trip to the volcanic region in the vicinity of Golden Trout Creek occupied the first week of the outing, at the end of which camp was moved ten miles up the cañon to the junction of the Big Arroyo with the Kern.

An interesting feature of the side trip to the volcanoes was an experiment in stocking a lake with golden trout.

There has been a close season on golden trout for several years and the only fish of that variety caught by our party were the hundred that were transplanted.

Up in the camp at Long Meadow the word went forth from the Deputy Fish Commissioner that for a short half hour the ban would be lifted and those desirous of catching the far-famed trout would be given the opportunity to aid in this, our first fish-stocking experiment. A dozen fishermen lined up on the banks of Golden Trout Creek with half as many agile assistants in attendance, each armed with a pail of water. The successful angler, crying peremptorily for "Pail!" much as the distracted shop girl summons "Cash!" on a bargain day, dropped his gleaming captive into the pail. Thence it was transferred to the large fish cans, shaped like milk cans, but with ventilated stoppers, which, strapped to a pack mule, served to carry the fish on the trail.

The golden trout were not only wonderfully abundant, but kept biting so fast that the assistants were taxed to their utmost to respond to the calls. In a very short time the cans were filled to the requisite number, when the ardent anglers reluctantly ceased fishing. The mules were in waiting and the unwilling emigrants were at once started over the rough, steep trail to their new home, a lake beautifully situated on the high plateau between the Kern Cañon and the rugged gray peaks of the summit crest. A curious contrast was observed in the actions of the golden trout when released to those of the rainbow trout transplanted in a subsequent experiment at Moraine Lake. The golden trout leaped from the can and sped at once far out into the lake, while their less gamey

FISH PLANTING ON GOLDEN TROUT CREEK, FORMERLY VOLCANO CREEK,
KERN RIVER REGION.
From photograph by Glenn Allen, 1908.

FISH PLANTING IN MORAINE LAKE, KERN RIVER REGION.
From photograph by Glenn Allen, 1908.

KAWEAH PEAKS FROM MORAINE LAKE.
From photograph by C. W. Pohlmann, 1908.

FISHING SCENE ON KERN LAKE.
From photograph by James Rennie, 1908.

brethren, the rainbow trout, went timidly, and as long as
we watched them kept near the bank, swimming close
together in a school.

From the camp on the Big Arroyo a party of forty-six
started for the climb of the South, or Red Kaweah Peak.
About a mile north of camp the trail led up the cañon
wall to the high country to the west known as the Cha-
goopa Plateau. The sky was overcast when we started
and we had not been long on the trail before the rain
overtook us, light, grateful showers that hung sparkling
drops in the firs and washed the dust of the trail from
the delicate pink pentstemon and purple daisies that
brushed against us as we passed. Now the clouds would
part, showing a distant snow-capped peak or a patch of
brilliant sky; or again a downpour of heavy drops would
drive us to the shelter of a friendly yellow pine or a
canopy of tamaracks.

Our trail, after leading us across the wooded plateau
for several miles, all at once emerged from the shadow
into the wide, level stretch of country named the Upper
Funston Meadow. It was as if the gate to the High
Sierra had suddenly been thrown open, for beyond the
green meadow with its little meandering stream and its
gay carpet of flowers rose the nearby western peaks
which the trees had hitherto concealed from us, the Red
Kaweah, gray Needham with its steep eastern precipice, and the square-topped, unnamed ridge to the south.

At the ranger's cabin near the southern end of the
meadow (a spot endeared by the memory of a fruitful
strawberry bed) the trail became quite indistinct. We
passed from one flower-studded meadow to another and
beyond the third one climbed the rocky moraine that
gives its name to Moraine Lake. As this was our ren-
dezvous with the pack train, and as the weather was still
inhospitable, we built a great camp fire on the lake shore
where, contentedly enough, we turned now a wet side
to the fire and now a dry side to the rain until we reached
a condition of moist steaminess rather suggestive of
Turkish baths.

Towards 1 o'clock the pack train reached us. The mule bearing the fish cans was brought to the lake shore and the rainbow trout, caught that morning in the Kern, were with due precautions deposited in the lake. They seemed a little dazed after their rough journey, or perhaps they were confused at being the center of interest for so large a group of people, for they had not ventured to swim into the depths of the lake when we left.

Our plan was to head in a northeasterly direction and camp as high as possible on the slope of the Kaweah. An attractively situated lake (on the map!) was our provisional destination.

We formed a picturesque procession, trailing through the woods, women in scarlet sweaters and short skirts; men, khaki colored, both as to clothing and complexion; and the sedate, slow-moving pack animals. Crossing wee, flower-decked meadows we followed a little soft-voiced stream whose merry chatter was lost once in a while in a burst of thunder or rush of rain which sent us scurrying to shelter. The lake was found at last, a pretty little sheet of water, but so meagerly furnished with the elements of comfort that we turned our backs on its rocky shore and scanty timber and descended half a mile to the edge of a meadow where we made camp. Even there the trees were mostly "all high and no wide," as the disgusted Jap cook expressed it, and as light showers continued to fall throughout the night more than one aspiring mountaineer awoke next morning to find one extremity or another resting in a puddle of water.

After breakfasting by firelight, we quickly formed in line and were ready to start by dawn. Following an easy contour we soon reached timber line, where the more difficult climbing began.

The South Kaweah, bearing the reputation of being an easy peak to climb from any point of attack, had been chosen by the committee as a try-out for Whitney. It was, therefore, a most startling surprise to our leaders to find the climb almost from the first beset with difficulties and dangers far greater than any to be found on Whitney. Our approach was from the south, where a rocky spur seemingly afforded easy access to the main body of the mountain. Almost at once, however, we found ourselves in a short but very treacherous chimney where every moment we were menaced with that gravest of dangers to a large party, falling rocks. In mountain-climbing many places which may be surmounted with ease and safety by two or three climbers may become veritable death traps where thirty or forty people are concerned; and so, though probably not many of the novices appreciated it, the few minutes in that chimney were much more hazardous than the dramatic climbing we encountered on the knife-edge connecting our spur with the mountain proper.

I think few of us will ever forget the first glimpse of that wicked, crumbling knife-edge that we caught from the high pile of rocks above the chimney—half a mile, or more, of it, sapped right and left by the snows that, gathering in the vast cirques at its base, insidiously loosen and undermine the great boulders, leaving them, after the thaw, so lightly poised that a touch might set them loose. Its great advantage, however, lay in the fact that our line of progress led along its crest, where a loosened rock might crash its harmless way down the precipice without danger to the climbers who were now behind instead of beneath its course—always providing that it did not carry a climber with it. This last danger, indeed, and the necessity for carefully testing the stability of each rock before venturing its support for hand or foot, wrought in some of us such excess of caution that we could scarcely induce our reluctant limbs to move at all. It seemed the wildest of follies to stir a hairbreadth from the hand- or foot-hold which had proved firm toward the untried possibilities that the next step held. Slowly, and with the greatest care, we crept, crawled, and clambered along that knife-edge, some of us grimly silent, some amazingly voluble, while far below us the voice of Stub, the packer's dog, who had obstinately and trustfully persisted in following us that morning, could be heard in violent protest against the folly of mankind and mountaineers.

Of the forty-six climbers who started forty-one reached the summit before noon. The few who failed to register had made the worst part of the climb, but were prevented by mountain sickness from attempting the final thousand feet of safe but difficult work that lay between the end of the knife-edge and the summit. So they were guided down one of the intersecting ridges to the south.

Those of us who reached the goal will long remember the panorama which greeted our eyes. Northward, close at hand, loomed the deeply dentated crest of the North Kaweahs, their rugged flanks descending in sharp knife-edges towards the treeless upper reaches of the Big Arroyo; the Great Western Divide lay beyond, lofty, boldly carved peaks and giant cirques in whose barren waste of rocks and snow scores of little glacial lakes shone and glittered like jewels; to the south and east the series of high plateaus were merged into one vast plain cut deeply by the Big Arroyo and the Kern; and facing east and towards the north again we looked across the basin of the Kern to Williamson and Whitney, their mighty forms half veiled in storm clouds.

The western slope, which we chose for the descent, proved to be composed of loose shale, easy on the downward path, but of so tedious and uninspiring a nature for an ascent that, forgetting the tremors of the morning, we were soon congratulating ourselves on having missed its drudgery and having enjoyed the most interesting climb the Kaweah could have afforded. While we had been climbing the packers had moved camp to the shores of Moraine Lake. There, at the close of the day, we found them, with fires cheerfully burning and supper under way, and Stub, weary and footsore, but with unchastened spirit, ready to greet each returning mountaineer with wild yaps of delight.

ON KNIFE EDGE OF SOUTH KAWEAH.

From photograph by Eva Channing, 1908.

CREST LINE OF SOUTH KAWEAH.

From photograph by Eva Channing, 1908.

OVERLOOKING OWENS VALLEY FROM MT. WHITNEY.
From photograph by James Rennie, 1908.

Following a climb of so many varied emotions, the ascent of Whitney came to many almost as an anticlimax. Whitney is easily accessible to all whose heart and lungs can stand its rarified atmosphere, and probably no other mountain in the world unascended by a railway can boast such an enrollment of visitors. Five years ago 150 members of the Sierra Club registered there; this year fully 100 added their names to its list.

Starting from the main camp on the morning of July 14th, we journeyed up the Kern as far as Junction Meadows, the first night's camp. It was a perfect day. Exquisite little meadows, full of flowers, here and there invaded the groves of tall pines, of firs, and of libocedrus that filled the floor of the cañon in its more fertile reaches; sandy flats, forested by junipers, ragged, bent, twisted, incredibly old, contrasted strangely with the verdant meadows; lofty cliffs of wonderful sculpture and coloring towered above us close on either hand; and always our course lay near the shining river which now leapt and flashed over a rocky bed in the sunlight, now swept in wide curves under the green gloom of the cottonwoods.

A steep climb up the cañon wall next morning made a short cut to Crabtree Meadows, the base-camp for the Whitney climb. This short cut was only discovered after considerable exploration by one member of our party and should be definitely marked for the use of pedestrians, as it is five or six miles shorter than the horse trail.

The Whitney climb, while uneventful, was very successful; and those who enjoyed the unrivalled view from the summit, the endless chain of peaks and the wonderful sight of the Inyo Desert lying over ten thousand feet below returned full of enthusiasm.

A few days later we broke camp at the Big Arroyo to start on the homeward trail. The story of the knapsack parties which cut across country to the Giant Forest is told elsewhere; the main party journeyed with the packtrain by way of Coyote Creek and Farewell Gap. Bullion Flat, remembered by those of us who visited it five years ago as the bleakest, most desolate and uncomfortable camp the Sierra Club ever made, was this year a part of a wonderful flower garden whose masses of color stretched in almost unbroken splendor from Coyote Pass to Farewell Gap. From Mineral King the party crossed Timber Gap and made a short day's trip to Redwood Meadows, giving a few energetic members the opportunity to climb Sawtooth Peak.

The last day on the trail was one of many beautiful pictures—a brilliant dawn flying rosy banners far above the majestic crowns of the sequoias; a golden sunrise gleaming upon the wild, serrated skyline of the Great Western Divide, which rises high above the cañon of the Kaweah; an ever-widening panorama as we gained the heights of the Seven-Mile Hill; a camp among the firs, and a rocky point from which we glimpsed the sunset land.

And another last picture we remember, the campfire in the Giant Forest—the dark circle of trees; the inner circle of faces, dimly illumined, receding into shadow at the edges; and the firelight strong upon the central figure, our chief, John Muir, who, making his life one with the mountain world, has learned through its beauty and its wonder to read its soul.

18
Bass
and
Bass-Fishing
(1897)

18
Bass
and
Bass-Fishing
(1897)

BASS AND BASS-FISHING.

By Ed. W. Sandys.

IT is all very fine for expert anglers to claim that fishing without flies is not fishing at all; but in my humble opinion that is going altogether too far. I am quite willing to admit that the art of properly casting a fly is both difficult to attain and very satisfactory when thoroughly m a s t e r e d : further, it is conceded that the skillful playing of a strong, hard-fighting fish upon the lightest of tackle is a very pretty and engrossing performance ; yet it is not necessarily all, or, for that matter, one-half, of fishing.

In judging the merits of a game fish, beauty and fighting qualities are not all the points to be considered. For instance, in trout-fishing the angler mainly depends upon his skill in casting and playing, while in bass-fishing the capricious temperament of the fish affords a broader opportunity to the angler who is also a wily tactician.

Anglers are apt to be almost as narrow in their views as they are enthusiastic over their favorite sport. One man must needs be at the butt of a two-handed rod and fast to a mighty, fresh-run salmon before he can experience the *real* excitement of angling. Another is ready to claim that the protracted battle at the salmon-pool is rather a question of tackle and endurance than of the finer points of fishing. Delicacy of action and subtle resource constitute his standard of skill ; and, of course, in his opinion, only the beautiful trout is worthy of the master-craftsman. A third man recalls a mental picture of roaring waters and writhing suds of foam, and is ready to make affidavit that nothing but the acrobatic ouananiche can satisfy the true angler. And so they praise what they are inclined to, and damn what they have no mind to ; and each is a deuce of a fellow, while those who do not agree are deserving only of contemptuous pity.

They are partly right and partly wrong. Lordly salmon, gamy trout and buckjumping ouananiche are fit for any man to play, but they are not the only game fish of our Northern waters. Do I remember right, or was it only a dream born of the drowsy July day ? Methinks it was real, that experience at the mouth of the storied salmon river, above which only dollars or invitations passed. Those things which came in with the swirl of the tide and fought with the freedom of the *untied*—they were real, too !

rent, and the air resounded with more than the whine of mosquitoes. It had rained a few drops on the distant hills, or some fool up-river had spit in the water, or some pebble had rolled in, or some old thing like that, and King Salmon lay at the bottom of his pool and refused to have fun.

We, common members of the fishing seven hundred thousand, had no big rods and didn't care a hang if the salmon rotted in his pool—in fact we had a sneaking notion of gaffing him, or shooting him with a revolver, but this was frowned down. So we went mud-larking about the river's mouth after sea-trout, and by sacrificing the airy trifle which represented our dignity, we had more fun and lively sport in one hour for nothing, than all the big rods had in a week, in spite of their outlay of pistareens and profanity. If any man had dared to say that those sea-trout were not good game fish, he'd have run a chance of getting chucked overboard. They rose well, they fought well and they broiled well—what more could be desired?

There is another fish, and I love him, for he always does his best, which is as much as the most aristocratic fin can do. He is no swell, he scorns all frippery in the line of spangles, ruby fins, silver mail, and what not ; he is a rum 'un to look at, but a rare good 'un to go,—he is the black bass, as good on tackle or board, as game as the best. In the South he is commonly called "trout."

They call him *black* bass, presumably

HEAD OF LARGE-MOUTH BLACK BASS,
SHOWING EXTENSION OF ANGLE
OF MOUTH BEHIND EYE.

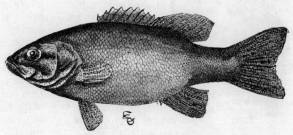

SMALL-MOUTH BLACK BASS.

It is true that they were only beggars of sea-trout ; but they bit and fought like Kilkenny cats, and they got away with some tackle now and then. For three days the big rods never arched to anything more than the pull of the cur-

because he is usually *green*, or anything but black ; yet call him what you will, only look to it that you never "call" him unless you have a pretty good hand yourself. You may ask "Is he really a game fish in the proper sense ?" I will make the Yankee answer—" Did you ever catch one?"

Pound for pound, the black bass of cold rapid waters is as game, strong and altogether satisfying as a fish need be. Extremely large bass may play logy and lack the speed to make a contest really exciting ; so do very large trout. Hook a "small-mouth" weighing anywhere between one and three pounds, and I fancy that he will prove quite lively enough. I have taken many trout and bass, large and small, from the best waters of this continent, and I have not yet made up my mind which is the better fish.

For the table, if the choice lay between a four-pounder of each species, I should choose the bass. If the fish weighed less than one-half pound apiece, and there were enough of them, the choice would be for trout. On the hook, it would be a bit of a puzzler—put either on and let it go at that. In the matter of beauty there can be no comparison : the trout and the grayling are the most lovely of fresh-water fish, they can beat the honest old bass playing spots alone, with face-cards barred ; the bass's face-card is a very poor card to play.

In habitat, and certain habits too, the trout has something the better of it. One's environments while trout-fishing are, as a rule, wondrous pleasant. Picturesque rocks, tangled greenery, foamy currents and shadowed pools are always present. The flash and music of hurrying waters, the stirring voice of milky cascades, the life and sparkle—the *tinsel* (if I may so express it) of water-pictures, appeal to the trout-fisher. Perhaps these are responsible for some of the fame of the fish ? A picture cunningly framed, a gem in a masterly setting may appear to be better than it is, and it must be remembered that many of our trout-streams are surrounded by the fairest fragments of the great Footstool.

In its repeated risings and almost playfulness the trout is more apt to impress the spectator than does the swart gladiator who lurks in his gloomy shades and comes forth only to fight. The habitat of the bass, lakes and the larger streams, seldom offers such delightful "bits" as mark every bend of the trout-water ; in fact, when the bass has the center of the stage he must make his own impression without depending upon

scenery. How well he can do this the bass-fisher knows.

There are two varieties of the black bass : the small-mouth (*Micropterus dolomieu*) and the large-mouth (*M. salmoides*). Both are so widely distributed throughout Canada, and the Northern, Eastern and some of the Southern States, that no attempt is made to give a complete list of the good bass-waters. Wisconsin and Minnesota have many waters which annually attract hosts of anglers. Illinois, too, offers excellent opportunities. New Yorkers know the resources of Lake George, Glen Lake and others. Maine has Belgrave, Highland, Maranacooke and other good waters. New Hampshire's well-known Winnipiseogee, Sunapee and Smith's Pond ; Massachusetts' and Jersey's lakes and ponds have well-earned laurels. In fact a page of OUTING might be filled with the bare names of haunts of the bass.

Up Canada way the dusky fighters make themselves very much at home. Every important lake and stream in Ontario, from Amherstburg to distant Port Arthur, and several lakes and streams in Quebec, richly repay the bass-fisher. I have killed grand fish at St. Clair Flats, in the Thames, Rondeau Harbor, the Trent, the Niagara, Muskoka waters, Rideau waters, the St. Lawrence, Ottawa, Sharbot Lake, Lac du Talon, Nipissing, Trout Lake, and so on to Loon and Silver lakes near the northern end of Lake Superior. A two-pound bass and a one-pound trout once rose together in Loon Lake, and so electrified a certain angler that he laid down his rod, put his foot on it and let the fish fight it out. They worried each other in excellent style. Eventually both were landed, perhaps to establish a record for fly-fishing.

Considering the multitude of waters in which the bass abounds, it is not difficult to account for his popularity. He is indeed, *the* fish for the host of anglers who seldom find an opportunity to visit the best, which means the remote, trout-streams. No fish has better qualifications than he to please all tastes. When he decides to notice fly, bait, or lure, there is no nonsense about his methods. He just *grabs* the supposed dainty, promptly discovers his blunder, and at once begins a hurricane fight for life and freedom. Very frequently his efforts are successful, for he is exactly the chap to thoroughly try an expert or to rattle a novice. He scorns the give and take policy— only *take* finds favor in his methods— take forcibly, hook, with or without line, or rod and all if he can. Hook him fairly and you have roused a small devil who will yield only when nearly killed. The first touch of the steel starts him rushing matters. A few savage jerks, a zigzag resistance, as a puppy worries at an object held in the hand, a sullen, downward boring, light- ning rushes from side to side, a swift, upward shoot which carries him well into the air—these are a few of his favorite tactics. If you are fishing from a boat, he will bore under and foul the line unless most judiciously handled. Right well does he know the possibilities of an anchor-tackle or a con- venient root! A moment's carelessness may enable him to reach one or the other, and if he ever gets to where he aims, one defiant tug will almost cer- tainly free him. No wonder the inex- perienced angler smashes tips and tackle in trying to play such a fish.

I have seen a bass of about three pounds, after a brief struggle to reach some favorite hole, leap inches above the water three times in rapid succes- sion, each time shaking himself, appar- ently in a direct attempt to dislodge the hook. His third leap landed him, free of the hook, fairly upon the middle seat of my skiff, which he had barely touched before another wild flop car- ried him over the low wale. A plump in the water was the last heard of him.

Some writers have disputed the shak- ing at the hook by a leaping bass, but I have seen it so often that I cannot help believing the fish does it intentionally, with the idea that the objectionable thing in its mouth may thus be got rid of. The height to which a lively bass can leap from the water is another dis- puted point. Men who write as though they meant what they said speak of leaps three and four feet high. I have said *inches* when, perhaps, at least one and one-half feet might have been nearer the mark. I do not dispute the three-foot limit, first, because there is no good reason for doubting the fish's ability to do the thing, and, second, be- cause I never had a chance to accurately measure a bass performance.

In one instance, which is distinctly remembered, a fish of about two and one-half pounds, cleared the stern of my Peterboro canoe. The stern of that model is narrow, and when one man is in about the center of the craft, the wales are a considerable distance above water. This particular bass left the water at least a foot from the canoe, and struck water again fully that dis- tance from the further side. The leap must have been a yard long, and the fish appeared to pass a foot above the canoe ; but I was so busy attending to my end of the game that I forgot to notice whether I was at the center thwart or astern of it. In the latter event the stern would have been a good deal lower than the true trim, and the fish's leap not so high as it appeared.

I have seen bass leap higher when playing, feeding or frightened than any of my hooked fish have done. I have an idea that some of this leaping is an attempt to get rid of a troublesome par- asite, and sometimes it seems to be a sort of final struggle by a diseased fish. An instance illustrative of this was when a very large bass leaped over a huge log upon which I had just stepped. This fish seemed to rise fully four feet in air, and when it struck water it circled about, belly upward, meanwhile convulsively strug- gling and working its fins as though in direst extremity. No marks were visible upon it, and it drifted away, still belly upward.

Another instance will give an idea of how high an unhooked bass can leap when frightened. One moonlight night two of us were working down river in a skiff. We had been sailing until a dead calm fell, and for lack of room the sail was left up, while I poled our craft from the stern. Between the boat and the bank was a belt of grass in wa- ter three feet deep. My friend lay with his head against the mast and one hand holding the sail clear of his face. Our stealing advance startled a bass in the grass, and the fish leaped for deep water. It struck the sail well above the lounger, fell against his face, knocked his pipe out in the first round, and scared him so badly that he yelled like an Indian and came near dumping the whole outfit. This was a great leap, and the fish had no deep water for any preliminary rush.

Writers differ concerning the relative merits of the large and the small mouth varieties as game-fish. Much has been written on this subject, the trouble being that too great enthusiasm has caused pens to trace what unprejudiced judgment will not support. Those who thoroughly know the bass appear to find little or no difference in the gameness and fighting qualities of the two varieties. My own opinion is that either fish is quite good enough for me, yet the small-mouth is my favorite. He appears to fight a trifle faster and to be a bit better as a stayer than his open-faced cousin. He, too, is the *leaper*, for I cannot recall an instance of a large-mouth leaving the water when hooked. I do not pretend to say that the latter fish does not leap, but I never saw one do more than flop over on the surface.

The resemblance between the two is sufficiently close to deceive any but practiced eyes. Specimens of each, lying side by side, would show differences which a novice might detect, yet there are many anglers who cannot decide offhand upon the variety without having the comparative test. The small-mouth is a slightly neater model, and it has smaller scales upon body and cheeks. This, again, is comparative. There is, however, one simple and reliable test which will identify the variety. I will endeavor to avoid confusing scientific lingo in explaining it. In the small-mouth, the maxillary does not extend beyond the hinder border of the pupil, while in the large-mouth it extends considerably beyond the posterior margin of the orbit. In good old plain fish talk, both varieties have infernally large mouths; but the inner angle of the mouth of the small-mouth (?) does not extend behind the fish's eye, while in the large-mouth the angle of the jaws will be found to extend, perhaps, one quarter of an inch to the rear of the eye. So, if you happen to be asked to decide a dispute as to the variety, examine the fish's head. If its mouth extends behind its eyes, say "Large-mouth;" if the mouth does not extend behind the orbit of the eye, say "Small-mouth," and offer to bet on it. The winner will surely treat you and call you blessed.

The small-mouth bass prefers clear or running water and a gravel or rock bottom; but these are not imperative. The large-mouth delights in weedy waters, such as ponds, small lakes and sluggish streams. Such waters have, as a rule, muddy bottoms, which appear to suit the large-mouth. The color of the two varieties is a bronzy green, darker at the back and paling to a yellowish white upon the lower parts. As a general rule, the large-mouth shows the lighter tint, but it must be remembered that the coloration of both varies considerably in different waters. Both are voracious feeders, and take the bait greedily when in the proper humor. But they (especially the small-mouth) are capricious, and frequently will refuse anything the angler can offer.

Both will rise to the fly upon a favorable day, the large-mouth being, perhaps, the freer riser and more decided in the attack upon the fly. The large-mouth attains the greater size. A five-pound small-mouth is as large a specimen as the ordinary angler may hope to see. Two fishes, weighing respectively eight and one quarter pounds and eight pounds ten ounces, are credited to Glen Lake, New York. Regular old "whalers" of the large-mouth variety, are on record. That expert on the bass, Doctor James A. Henshall, has killed Florida large-mouths weighing well up in the "teens." For the table, of the two, I prefer the small-mouth, not that I am prepared to state that the large-mouth is *always* inferior, but because the latter's penchant for mud and weedy waters appears to spoil his flavor.

The favorite haunts of the bass are about reefs, mats of weeds, submerged and floating logs, cavities in rocks, old wharves and piling, under trees overhanging the water, and wherever a permanent shadow affords a darkened lair. Here the strong fellows lie in wait ready to dart forth upon whatever may appeal to their fancy. Very frequently, excellent fishing is to be had in open waters far from any visible shelter for the bass. But, as a rule, in these cases sunken reefs, timber, or other shelter, or some particularly good feeding-ground lies below where many fish are taken.

The appetite of the bass is comprehensive, yet at the same time fastidious. Their natural food mainly consists of crawfish, minnows and frogs, though they also devour insects, larvæ of various kinds, worms, young fish, mice, etc., etc. The most reliable baits, according to my experience, are crawfish, minnows, small frogs, larvæ of the bee and the cockchafer, grasshoppers, worms, metal and pearl spoons, artificial minnows and insects, and the standard bass flies. For regular use upon *all* waters, I should be very much inclined to rate the effectiveness of these baits in order as named. He who finds the nest of the short-tailed field-mouse will do well to remember that a pink, juicy young mouse and a sturdy bass require no introduction; and there is a plump white grub, with a copper-colored head, to be found in rotten logs and stumps, which a bass will seldom refuse.

Such a list of baits will give the angler plenty of variety, and bass must be in a queer humor when one or another will not coax a fish. I have started with a can of worms and a bucket of the best of minnows, and though bass were plentiful at the points fished, these baits would not find favor. Then I'd turn over pebbles and bits of sunken stuff near the bank until a few crawfish had been captured. Sometimes, though rarely, these too would prove useless. Then for a live frog, or a plump grasshopper. Should these fail, tear up a few sods where the turf overhangs the edge of the bank. Break up the sods and you may chance upon one or more big white grubs. These should do the trick, as will young bees and wasps if a nest can safely be harried. If all these fail, and you can get no young mouse, why—er—that is—O! just tell the bass to go to thunder for the time. *Don't* do what I once saw a chap do—thrust an arm into a sand-martin's hole and draw forth a day-old fledgling, put it on the hook and catch the biggest bass taken that day!

The successful methods of bass-fishing are with bait-rod or fly-rod, using the baits mentioned, or standard flies; skittering with a spoon-bait, and trolling from a boat, using either the rod or the long hand-line and spoon or artificial minnow. The hand-line is one of the surest, and, at the same time, the least worthy methods for a true fisherman to employ. There is little sport in hauling in fish by main strength, when compared to the scientific handling of a good rod. But in trolling with the rod one may enjoy all the play he wants, if care is taken to keep sufficient line on the reel. It is not good business to allow too much silk to run out when the said silk is attached to a rod one is desirous of keeping intact.

Fly-fishing for bass is not to be successfully performed by any duffer who can flick a fly for a few yards on a trout-stream. Longer casts are the rule, and the work must be artistically done to be at all successful. The large, gaudy flies may appear almost clumsy to the trout-fisher, but they must be placed at the proper spot and in a workmanlike manner, or the bass will seldom notice them. Upon those rare days, however, when the fish are really rising freely, the flies will richly repay whoever knows the mysteries of rightly using them. The best rod is the bass fly-rod as turned out by reliable makers. I have no axe to grind in this direction, so leave the reader to make his own selection. Rods of split bamboo, bethabara, greenheart, steel, or lancewood, are all excellent. The weight of the best will be between seven and one-half and nine ounces. Bait-rods, as made by leading manufacturers, require no improvement. The choice is one of material, and may be made according to taste. Very cheap rods are apt to disappoint their purchasers.

In fishing with minnow, or crawfish, or in skittering with a spoon, some of the fly-fisher's skill, and sometimes *more* than the fly-fisher's skill comes into play. It is not every fly-caster who can properly manipulate a live or dead minnow, a crawfish, or a spoon. There is a knack born of experience in picking out the opening among reeds where a big bass should lie; there is an art, peculiar to experts in this sort of work, in placing minnow, crawfish, or spoon just so, and unfortunately these cannot be taught upon paper.

One point about baiting may be referred to. When using a dead minnow (which I have found to be, if fresh, about as good as a live one), I pass the hook through the mouth of the fish, then out through the opening of the gill and finally through the tail. This simply *strings* the bait upon the gut or gimp. I've had lots of people tell me that this was a fool way to do; that it wasn't according to the books, and so on — but for all that, *it catches bass*, which is about all the books teach. Furthermore, when a fish is hooked, the minnow is almost certain to work up the gut, or gimp, and so escape destruction and be good for another bass. This is quite an important matter when minnows are scarce. The dead bait is made to imitate the motions of a live minnow by the play of the rod.

In baiting with crawfish I believe that the "proper caper," as told in books, is again ignored. As a large hook is used for bass, and as a crawfish when going to cover, moves backward with a rapid, wavering action, caused by the jerky motion of its curved tail playing under its body, it occurred to me that this might be successfully imitated. So, instead of removing the large nippers and hooking the crawfish crosswise of its body as many anglers do, I insert the barb into the crawfish's mouth and then force the barb lengthwise through the body and out through the tail. This, of course, kills the bait, but that makes no difference in its effectiveness.

A crawfish thus placed upon a hook of suitable size, is in exactly the attitude assumed by the creature when swimming. Now, if it be sent down, tail first, past apertures in rocks, or other bass shelters, the big claws will dispose themselves naturally, while a slight shaking of the rod will cause a beautiful imitation of the crawfish's natural wavering dart. When bass are taking crawfish they will never refuse this bait unless the angler makes himself altogether too noisy or conspicuous. This method has also another good feature in its tendency to save the bait. Very frequently, when a bass is hooked the crawfish is forced far above the hook and so preserved to do another turn. When we consider that the best crawfish, *i. e.*, the medium sized ones, are both difficult to capture and very fragile when hooked crosswise, anything tending to make one bait good for two or more fish is well worth attention.

The crawfish are taken from bushponds and ditches, from their burrows (capped by curious little mud-towers), and from under stones and sunken rubbish near the banks of streams. The best thing for catching them is a quick, sure hand. Their big claws look very formidable, but the actual nip is a trifling matter, not worth bothering about. No matter how the crawfish may be placed upon the hook, it should be carefully handled and any unnecessary upward jerking avoided, as the upward pull is liable to break the bait. If the bass does not promptly strike, raise the bait gently and send it down in another spot.

When using flies, spoons, or other artificial baits, if the fish are rising, cast where the eye locates them. If the fish are quiet, one must depend upon his knowledge of their habits. An opening in a mat of weeds, a shadowed nook at the edge of rushes, beside snags or reefs, where a tree overhangs the water, into which insects may drop—these are very "bassy" spots. One who knows the fish soon learns to locate the probable lurking-place of a big one. This mastery of the situation is the result of experience and observation, and is never acquired from a course of reading.

The time of year when one should fish for bass is apt to be regulated by the time one is able to get his holiday. Those fortunates who can fish whenever they feel inclined know that the first and last weeks of the open season, before and after the heated term, are much the best. In some waters the fishing is at its best during April and September; in others, further north, June and September are the months; but any good water will yield some fish all through the season. A bright day, with just enough breeze to raise a merry ripple, is about right, especially for flies.

In regard to the best hours of the day for fishing, views differ. The argument that a bass, being a predaceous fish, feeds mostly at night, and so should be more disposed to take the bait at earliest morning and latest evening, sounds reasonable. Unquestionably, the best time for the fly-fisher is during the evening hours, but I have my doubts about the early morning work. From eight A.M. to about eleven o'clock, and from four P.M. till dark are the times I should select. In the old days we boys fished a river famous for bass, and we had a sort of generally understood rule that it was no use "tryin' for 'em" till the morning was well advanced. Boys, too, are apt to thoroughly understand the *practical* side of such matters and not to bother about what books have to say.

I knew one old darkey (his kind are apt to be posted, too) who used to begin fishing about gray dawn, but inside his black hide was an undying love for channel cats. Anyway, I used to start in sight of him, about nine o'clock A.M., and at points where he had fished hours before, I'd kill bass that would make his mouth water. Be the truth what it may, I never did much with bass before the sun had got pretty high.

The strike of the black bass is unmistakable. No other of our fishes takes hold with such vigorous decision. A relative, the rock-bass, is a lively biter, but even he lacks the power of the black fellow's reckless grab. The latter takes the bait with a rush which fairly jars the chap holding the rod, and at once moves toward the favorite retreat. The time to strike is as soon as possible after the first warning. The bass may generally be said to hook himself. Quite frequently, bait, hook and inches of tackle are swallowed; and fish so hooked are apt to do some high and lofty tumbling. The fish's habit of bolting the bait makes a disgorger a very useful implement.

I have stated that an average hand with the trout-rod need not necessarily be successful in fly-fishing for bass, and an important reason is found in the manipulation of the flies. Trout methods are not bass methods. In fact, bass-fishers may be said to almost *troll* with their flies. Experience teaches the proper spot for the flies to fall, the next thing being to closely imitate the movements of an insect which has fallen into the water. For this reason the flies are skittered against the current, or breeze, suffered to sink and drift for yards at a time, and brought to the surface by a continuous, jerky motion—all this to simulate the struggles of a drowning insect. Do not fear that the bass may fail to see the lures, to appreciate fine work by the rod. The strike may be delayed until the flies are being raised for another cast, but when it comes there is small chance of the fish being missed. A list of useful flies might include Furgerson, whitewing, Henshall, Seth Green, polka, grizzly king, Rube Wood, Lord Baltimore, Montreal, coachman, silver doctor, magpie, Cheney, Chubb, oriole, Parmachene Belle, professor, Gov. Alvord, the hackles, bucktail, and some few others.

The question of what to do with the fish when caught deserves a few words. In the old days I used to string them through the gills, and fasten the string to a root, or tow it behind the boat. Later I learned that a fine, strong chain, having a cross-pin at one end and a bodkin-like arrangement at the other, made the best of fish-strings. On this the fish was strung through the lower jaw in preference to through the gills. Later still, I began to figure upon just how much pain a fish was capable of feeling, and the result was not altogether satisfactory. Now, while I do not believe a fish to be so sensitive to pain as is a warm-blooded creature, yet the old-fashioned stringing savors of unnecessary cruelty. Hence, I deem it better to kill all fish promptly when removed from the hook. A smart rap from a small stick at the junction of head and body will stun a fish, and the blade of a pocket-knife pushed down till it cuts the spine just behind the head, will forever prevent that fish from experiencing any sensation whatever.

It is claimed by some that fish so killed are better for the table, but that point I am not prepared to decide. I favor the speedy immolation, and certainly a number of fish so killed and wrapped in grass or fern, so that they cannot touch each other, should be in prime condition when home is reached. "But," some novice may ask, "suppose I kill fifty big bass; have I got to wrap 'em all up separately and make a bale of green stuff out of 'em?"

My only reply is, you will seldom find yourself so situated that you have any right, under the true angler's code, to kill fifty big bass. Ten *big* bass are plenty for any decent angler to kill in a day's fishing. If the reader is one of that band of butchers who fish for count, I care not for what becomes of his fish or of him. If he could get fifty big bass on a string and then get tangled up with the lot till the bass had dragged him to the nethermost whence, a number of decent people would cheerfully send flowers!

And now for a glance at one of many delightful days spent with this sturdy fish. The surface of the lazy river is wrinkled by the soft July breeze. Three hours ago the sun climbed above the forested hills, and the shadows along the eastern bank are still cool and darkly defined. The old dog sits sedately in the bow of the canoe and ponders upon many things. Little of actual sport for him to-day, yet he loves to go where he can poke about among the rice and rushes and see how the young wood-duck and coot are thriving. Possibly, he may find an odd cock or a young muskrat in the wet cover, and in any event he can keep cool and assist now and then at the landing of a prize.

The canoe glides up river; there is no need for hurry, so the paddler puffs at his pipe and slowly swings his blade, feeling at peace with all the world. For half an hour the performance is such a thoroughly lazy one that the prospective angler's content is immeasurable. He believes in being as indolent as circumstances will allow, and he also believes that if more people understood the sweet, wholesome joys of such a cruise, the world would be a better place to live in. But he is not forgetting his fishing. He knows every foot of the water, and when the canoe nears a certain bend it is quietly run ashore.

Off this point lie some sunken trees in fifteen feet of water, and here the first trial is made. The baited hook looks like a knot of worms when it is ready to go down. It has been in the water about two minutes when the rod suddenly arches and the checked line vibrates in response to a series of short jerks. Soon a struggling fish appears at the surface, where it promptly turns over, gapes wildly and gives up the fight. Its jaws and under-parts are velvet black, and its reddish goggle-eye stares inanely. It is gently removed from the hook, and suffered to go wiggle-waggling back to its green retreats. Even a rock-bass a foot long is unworthy quarry.

A second trial raises a flat fish, which gleams with pale blue and gold. Upon either side of its head are dark tabs edged with scarlet, which add to its beautiful coloration. It, too, is loosed to bide the coming of the small boy, for sunfish don't count.

A minnow is substituted for the worms, and lightly cast far out above the outer edge of the snags. Soon there comes a vicious surge at the line, the rod arches and the reel mutters a surprised protest. A lithe, bronzy shape is fighting hard at the end of the silk. Its splashing struggle attracts the dog's attention, and he leaves his investigations along the water's edge, and sits with cocked ears to watch the unequal tussle. Nearer and nearer the fish is drawn, but its eel-like suppleness and strength battle for every inch of tether. At last the long, rounded, olive-green body floats idly on the surface. The peculiar caudal and scales,

the small snaky eyes and suggestive mouth proclaim a hard fighter but useless prize—the dogfish. This captive is not suffered to depart in peace; he is slammed good and hard against a tree, after his quick effort to bite the fingers working at the hook.

No use wasting further time here, so the canoe is pushed off and sent gliding upon its way.

Here is the site of an ancient mill, the few broken piles showing where the ice had wrecked the crazy wharf. A minnow is cast into the shadow; and can it be that it falls into a pair of waiting jaws? Whiz-zip! Now we have it! Hi! Up he comes, to miss by a hair the bristly end of a pile. Hi! Up he comes again, and the rod bows its acknowledgment of a foeman worthy of an all-greenheart. Firmly hooked, and a mill to a finish. Nothing asked, nothing given; black bass versus greenheart, silk and skill. The odds are too great, and at last he yields, conquered, but never disgraced.

Another trial with minnow fails. Then a crawfish from under a scrap of sodden bark is offered and at once accepted. Another leaping, swirling battle ends with the death of a four-pounder. After that all baits appear to lose their attractiveness, so the canoe moves on.

It is needless to particularize. Below the deserted brick-yard, under the low-hanging basswood, where the three trees stand in the water, at the edge of the lily-pads, etc., fish were killed or lost, as the case happened to be.

Nine beauties were packed in grass when the shadows began to creep across from the western bank, and nearly as many lesser fish had been released on account of lack of inches.

The old dog had fun, too, and he learned much. His duck and coot were doing finely; he found two cock and caught one young muskrat, which he released, not because its fur was not prime, but owing to an indifference manifested by his master concerning the important capture.

During the cruise homeward he sat nodding gravely with every paddle-stroke, and when he had reached the landing he sniffed at the bass and glanced up, as much as to say "I see it all now; it's a very restful, pleasant style of thing, quite good enough for filling in time during the close season."

THE OLD DOG HAD FUN, TOO!

19
King Tarpon,
The High
Leaper of Sea
(1909)

KING TARPON, THE HIGH LEAPER OF THE SEA

BY A. W. DIMOCK

ILLUSTRATED FROM PHOTOGRAPHS TAKEN BY JULIAN A. DIMOCK

IN VIRTUE of royal qualities, majestic mien, coruscating courage and the knightly abandon of his battling, the tarpon is not merely the "Silver King," but *the King*. He accepts the sportsman's challenge by leaping into the arena in full, flashing armor, and so joyously meeting his challenger in his own element as to place tarpon fishing forever in a class by itself.

The game is great. It thrills the most stolid of human participants to the tips of his toes, and to compare with it any kindred sport is a tiresome travesty. The tarpon is the most beautiful of big fish, the most spectacular of finny fighters, a swift swimmer of dauntless courage, the one all around game fish at every age and without a streak of yellow in his makeup.

I have wasted photograph plates and time on bass, trout, lady-fish, ravallia and other fish that pretend to jump, and, compared with exposures on the King of Fish, the result has been about as interesting as so many flyspecks on the film. The average leap of the hooked salmon could be beaten by a sick tarpon in his sleep.

The photographs herewith fairly present this royal fish as he appears when playing the game with his human adversary. They were taken by the camera-man during two summer months spent by him and the scribe on the Gulf coast of Florida, two months that gave daily evidence that of sports that thrill there are few on earth like fishing for tarpon.

We followed and fished for them with fly-rods, with heavy tarpon rods and with hand lines. We were fast to three hundred and thirty-four, of which sixty-three were on an eight-ounce fly-rod. Excepting a two-pound specimen, taken for the table, we killed none, although a few were eaten by sharks while being played.

In fishing for pleasure, the average sportsman spends from thirty to ninety minutes over each fish, keeping within twenty to one hundred yards of the tarpon as he plays him. As we were fishing for the camera, a long range contest was useless, and we fought the fish fiercely from the time they struck, regardless of the risk of their breaking loose. We smashed five heavy tarpon rods, broke several lines that would each sustain over sixty pounds and broke or straightened at least a dozen tarpon hooks. We held the canoe from which we fished as near the tarpon as possible, and as soon as he seemed tired pulled it beside him and took the hook from his mouth. Frequently we found this exciting.

From Charlotte Harbor to Cape Sable we exploited the tarpon fishing ground with thoroughness. The avoirdupois of the fish caught varied from one and one-half pounds each to more than one hundred times that weight, while their length ranged from eighteen inches to over six and one-half feet. We captured them in the Gulf of Mexico, while white-capped waves spilled water over us, and we were towed by them through narrow overgrown creeks, where sometimes our quarry escaped by leaping into the bushes above our heads. We caught as many as twenty-five in a single day, and then, as on many other

"Frequently we found this exciting."

days, stopped fishing because the plates of the camera-man had given out.

The tarpon can be played gently and easily, with a light strain from a smooth running reel, with an effort that wouldn't tire a robust child, for one, two, or three hours, until he rolls over on his back, exhausted and ready for the hook to be taken from his mouth. Or he can be fought furiously from the start, the boat dragged near him and little line yielded, while the fish leaps wildly and frequently, around, beside, over and even into the boat of the fisherman. This method calls for strength of muscle, tackle and nerves, but there is little in the line of sport that returns bigger dividends in excitement. I was never harmed in the game, but tarpon landed on my head, caromed on my shoulder, swamped my canoe and one even dropped his big, slippery form squarely in my arms. The camera-man smiled at my coating of slime, but when a tarpon jumped in, and Joe jumped out of the motor boat, he forgot to laugh—until later. Often a leaping tarpon struck his boat, sometimes landing on the gunwale and nearly falling inside, and many times he had to wheel

quickly around to save his camera from the deluge of water thrown by a leaping, frantic fish.

To catch tarpon one must go to the right place at the right time. Small specimens, of from two to fifteen pounds, are usually found in fresh water, in creeks and pools near the head of rivers. Larger fish, of from twenty to sixty pounds, seem to prefer the brackish water of streams nearer the Gulf, while the really big fish, weighing from eighty to two hundred pounds, are more frequently caught in the big passes or near the mouths of large rivers like the Caloosahatchee. The small fish near the heads of the rivers can be found at any season, but in general it is hardly worth while to fish for tarpon before April, and it is much better to wait until July and thus escape heat and mosquitoes. In May, South Florida weather becomes warm in the shade and hot in the sun, while mosquitoes on the shore are sometimes almost unendurable to folks who have never fished in a salmon stream. The rains of June cool the air and seem to drive away the mosquitoes, for the temperature of July and August is not unpleasant, breezes are

214

almost constant and mosquitoes are so few that we often slept on deck beside the shore without a mosquito bar. Then, too, such luscious fruits as sugar apples, pine apples, mangoes and guavas are in their prime, while there is always food for sentiment in gorgeous masses of clouds, wind-driven and sun-painted, and such feathered flocks and other wild creatures as the women and tourists of Vanity Fair have permitted to live.

We began our work in Captiva Pass, beside which we anchored the *Irene*. A little motor boat with a reversing propeller, and Joe, our young skipper, to run it, held the camera-man and his tools. I sat with Frank, my boatman, in a canoe which he paddled while I trolled for tarpon. The motor boat backed, filled and hovered on the sunward side of us, while the camera-man kept his seventeen pound weapon trained upon us and his hand on the focussing screw. Sometimes both boatman and camera-man got tired. Then the motor boat towed the canoe, from which both Frank and I fished, and the camera

rested on a seat. When one of us had a strike the other took in his line and seized a paddle, the painter of the canoe was cast off, the motor boat maneuvered for position, the paddler labored to keep the canoe on a plane with and near the fish, while the fisherman coddled or worried the tarpon, to keep him quiet or make him perform, as camera conditions called for.

There are deep holes in Captiva Pass, above which the water swirls when the tide is swift. From these holes tarpon rise continually, but it is quite useless to fish for them. They will even knock a bait aside as they come to the surface to blow. It is better to troll just inside the Pass, near the channels which lead to it, or wherever the tarpon can be seen rising. The fish bite best on a falling tide. We had no fresh bait on our first day and used spoons and trolling lines. Our only returns were in cavalli, Spanish mackerel, and sharks. I was hopeful for a moment, when after a strong pull on my line a fish shot into the air. But it was with the twisting, low leap of the mackerel shark, the only one of his

"A tarpon dashed under the canoe, and before I could dip the rod enough to clear the craft it was smashed."

species that jumps. It is unwise to pull a shark against the side of a light canoe, so we landed and dragged the brute up on the beach and pounded his head with a club, to punish him for being a shark. That night Joe went out with his cast net and we had plenty of fresh mullet for bait in the morning, when the fish proved greedy and we collected seven.

The outgoing tide was so strong that the first tarpon struck carried us out into the Gulf a mile and squandered two hours of

a moment I feared he was going out to sea, but he tamely surrendered the line and scrambled back to shore. We then anchored the canoe and the first tarpon struck brought up the anchor line as he jumped beside us. Day by day the tarpon in the Pass became fewer and more finical. Often a wave rolling behind my trailing slice of mullet showed that a tarpon was following it. I wiggled the bait seductively, settled it back confidingly and withdrew it coyly. Sometimes I succeeded, more

"Of sports that thrill there are few on earth like tarpon fishing."

time. Sometimes he swam smoothly, with occasional graceful leaps, then in furious mood threw his supple body, convulsed with passion, above the surface of the water. We fought the others so hard that we broke two lines and straightened three hooks. As the tide and a tarpon were carrying us swiftly along the beach out of the pass, I sheered the canoe to the shore and Frank sprang out, carrying his trolling line. A sudden dash of the fish tore the line from his hand, and as its tangled mass struck the water he sprang after it. For

often I failed. Finally, out of twenty rises in one day I only struck three fish. Something was needed to make the lure more tempting. We tried various small fish with indifferent success. At last I chanced to put a needle-fish on the hook, and it was seized as it touched the water, then another and another were taken. Thereafter, when the tide was high, Frank patrolled the beach with a fowling piece and shot needle-fish as they wandered along the water's edge. Few tarpon could resist the new bait. If ever they did resist its supple attractiveness, it was quite useless to fish any more on that tide with any lure whatever. When the bubbles of a tarpon rose to the surface, or he came up to blow, we paddled within fifty feet, threw the bait at the disturbed water and often captured the fish.

Captiva is a little pass and the fish needed a rest, so we moved six miles up the coast to Boca Grande, the big pass, a mile wide with a ten fathom channel, the home of great sea-creatures, from dolphins to turtles, from sharks to devil-fish. The pass was

they drifted nearer. Soon the spray was flying over the canoe, while from the crest of the waves solid water spilled into the low-sided motor boat, which was quickly cut loose from the canoe, since it barely had power to carry itself out of the turmoil. A canoe is at home among big waves and the hour we spent in that tossing water was delightful, even though the work of the camera was not advanced. When the tired tarpon had received his freedom we paddled to the beach, and, keep-

"We fought the fish fiercely from the time they struck."

wind-swept when we arrived and its turbulent water alive with fish of many kinds. Flocks of gulls, terns and pelicans above, and splashings of jackfish and tarpon below, marked the presence of great schools of minnows. Nothing was easier than to strike a tarpon, but then the trouble began. Tide and the tarpon were carrying us out to the near-by, foam-crested rollers, while the motor boat vainly struggled against them. We were rushing through the water away from the breakers, yet minute by minute, as in an uncanny dream,

ing near the shore, made our way back into the harbor, which we reached at dark, with nothing but pleasant memories to show for the work of a strenuous day.

Thereafter, when the wind was high and the tide strong, we either fished from an anchorage, or cast anchor from the canoe whenever a tarpon was struck. Sometimes, but seldom, the line on the reel got low, the fish having carried off five hundred feet and we had to take in the anchor and follow him. It is rarely that a fish weighing less than two hundred pounds

"In virtue of royal qualities and the knightly abandon of his battling the tarpon is not merely the 'Silver King,' but THE KING."

"As we were fishing for the camera a long range contest was useless."

will swim a hundred yards against a forty-pound pull, and after the first few strenuous minutes it was usually possible to reel in the line until the excited tarpon was leaping beside the canoe. Often he struck it, sometimes half capsized it, and more than once leaped over it. Funny things happened, as when a big tarpon, which I was playing with shortened line, rose beside and against the canoe, shaking his great open mouth so near my face that I put up my hand to push him away and an instant later was struck in the back by the hook which the tarpon succeeded in ejecting as he leaped high and again on the other side of the canoe; or as when Frank was taking the hook from the mouth of an exhausted tarpon which he was holding, the fish broke away, dove under the canoe and rising on the other side threw body and tail against the back and head of his antagonist in a resounding spank that nearly knocked the breath out of his tormentor's body.

In all our rough play with the tarpon alone, there was never a thought of danger, but of a certain occasion I think seriously even to-day. A tarpon which had just jumped near the canoe was rising beside it for another leap when he was struck by a great shark and bitten in two. A blow from the tail of the monster nearly swamped the canoe and the water that fell over it was mingled with the blood of the tarpon. Although I believe that, contrary to public opinion, no shark in this country ever attacked a living human being in the water, yet I don't know the consideration that would have sent me overboard voluntarily in the vicinity of that tragedy. It was the day of the shark, and I lost a second tarpon similarly a few hours later. Some days afterward I had played a tarpon until, from his feeble leaps, I fancied him ripe for the removal of the hook, when he suddenly darted away with renewed vigor. I was quite unable to restrain him, and as we neared the end of the two hundred yard line the anchor was taken in and I turned the rod over to Frank. He suggested that a shark had swallowed our tarpon, a surmise which proved to be correct. I paddled the canoe to the beach where, after much toil, we succeeded in stranding the brute, and the camera-man who had photographed the earlier leaps of the tarpon now pictured him at rest in the stomach of his slayer.

When fishing in the big pass we often found it well to fasten to the line a sinker of from one to four ounces in weight, with a bit of twine that was not too strong. If fastened too firmly it would have torn loose the hook or snapped the strongest line, when the fish shook his head in real earnest. Fishing with a sinker added to our trouble with sharks but gave us plenty of grouper for chowder, as surface trolling filled our larder with king fish and Spanish mackerel, as by-products. The leap of the tarpon is usually an effort to get rid of the hook, which he often succeeds in sending, with the bait, hurtling through the air, as shown in many of the photographs. It is to be regretted that no picture was obtained of a needlefish which was thus thrown high by a tarpon and caught before it could reach the water by a man-o'-war hawk, which was wisely soaring above us.

There were days and tides when the tarpon seemed crazy and would rise to salted bait as freely as to fresh. One day we took twelve tarpon which rose to salted baits almost the instant they were cast, and we then stopped fishing because the plateholders of the camera-man were empty. That night he complained that he was tired of the camera and proposed to try some moonlight fishing with a rod. He caught two tarpon with two baits, and thereafter, using a handkerchief as a lure, captured three more. These were taken in Boca Grande Pass, about two hundred yards from the railroad wharf, a point which I look upon as mighty near the center of the tarpon industry of the country.

For several weeks we vibrated between Boca Grande and Captiva Passes, as conditions of wind and tide indicated. Then, when twenty-nine days had given us one hundred and fifty tarpon, we remembered the rest of our programme and sailed for the Caloosahatchee River. At the favorite pools a few miles above Fort Myers we chanced to draw blanks, while five days at Nigger Head, eight miles below the town, gave us thirty-five tarpon, all of goodly size.

Marco lies on the Florida coast forty miles below Punta Rassa and the Caloosahatchee River. I had enjoyed for years a personal acquaintance with most of the tarpon in that country and felt humiliated that only fourteen responded to my advances during three days.

A strong wind from the north carried us down the coast, and on the day we lifted our anchor at Marco we dropped it in the Shark River bight, a few miles north of Cape Sable. There are tarpon in the many mouths of Shark River at all seasons, but two hours cruising in the motor boat disclosed so few that we sailed north four miles and entered Harney River, where I had arranged to donate two eight-ounce fly rods, with sundry extra tips and second joints to the baby tarpon that I knew lived in a nursery near its head.

The head of Harney River lies among the lilies of the 'Glades and is the only open path from the coast to that mysterious region, but not every pilot can follow the labyrinthic ways of that beautiful river. From the tangle of oyster bars at its mouth we sailed seven miles to its junction with a branch of Shark River at Tussock Bay. Two miles of an E.N.E. course brought to light an old Indian camp on a tiny pal-

metto key. From this key six miles of a crooked course averaging N.E. led through twisting, grass-grown channels, narrow straits, broad sluggish rivers and swift, winding creeks, until the bowsprit of the *Irene* rested above the grass of the 'Glades. The possessor of craft of the woods may find near here an old, well-hidden Indian camp, where he can gather lemons and limes by the bushel, to the tuneful jarring of rattles.

From the head of Harney River to Tussock Bay the pools and creeks are filled with tarpon weighing, each, from twenty ounces to twenty pounds. In five days I captured twenty-five on an eight-ounce fly rod. The lure was a tiny strip of mullet, sometimes cast, but commonly trolled, since it was necessary to strike nearly straight from the reel to fasten the hook in the hard mouth of the quarry, the weak spring of the rod being insufficient. There is no fish more gamy than a young tarpon, and one of about five pounds weight led my canoe a mile through a crooked creek, jumping at short intervals and finally

"We caught as many as twenty-five in a single day and then stopped fishing because the plates of the camera-man had given out."

escaping by leaping over my head into a clump of bushes where the line caught and held the fish suspended until broken by his struggles. Other small tarpon tangled the line in the bushes after a much shorter chase, and one five-foot tarpon which had strayed into a wider portion of the stream showed his contempt for our snares by making his first—and last—leap high up in the branches of a tree that overhung the river's bank. Photographing in these narrow creeks got on the nerves of the camera-man. There was seldom a chance to get the motor boat in position, and the few negatives exposed in the twilight of the overhung streams developed into something like flashlights in Africa.

Three miles north of the mouth of Harney River, Broad and Rodgers Rivers enter the Gulf by a common outlet. In the latter stream not a tarpon was to be seen, while Broad River was full of them. They were all big fellows, and the fly rod was laid on the shelf. The anchor was dropped near a bunch of the fish, and as Frank and I were launching the canoe, Joe picked up

my rod and was quickly fast to a tarpon which promptly broke both rod and reel. I rigged up a rod from a stick of bamboo, while Frank used one of heavy, orthodox make and both of us fished from the canoe. My first strike was before the bait was three feet from the canoe, and for some hours one of us was always fighting a tarpon, while the other paddled and the camera-man circled about in the motor boat, either stuffing slides in his camera or holding the seventeen-pound weapon aimed at us. We were in full swing, and had already captured ten of the creatures, when a tarpon which I was playing with a short line dashed under the canoe, and before I could dip the rod enough to clear the craft it was smashed. The fish was so tired that we managed to secure him and lift the hook from his mouth. This is accomplished by placing the thumb in the corner of the tarpon's mouth, clamping the fingers around a bone that projects from the side of the jaw, and holding firmly while the free hand removes the hook. The thumb in the tarpon's mouth is quite safe, as he always

"From the head of Harney River to Tussock Bay the pools and creeks are filled with tarpon weighing, each, from twenty ounces to twenty pounds."

"We smashed five heavy tarpon rods and broke several lines that could each lift over sixty pounds."

"Then in furious mood threw his supple body, contorted with passion, above the water."

"The first tarpon we struck carried us out into the Gulf."

"The first tarpon struck brought up the anchor line as he jumped beside us."

"Several times the tarpon leaped in the air and swam around with renewed vigor."

throws open his jaws when he struggles. The next fish employed the same ruse of dodging beneath the canoe, and as Frank tried to hold him by main strength our last rod was smashed. Not to let such fishing get away, we sailed that night to Everglade and improvised rods, one of which, made from a hickory hoe handle, seemed unbreakable—but wasn't. We returned to Broad River at once, only to find it barren of tarpon.

Six miles up the coast we picked our way through the labyrinth of oyster-bars at the mouth of Lossmans River, and explored that stream for a day, quite in vain.

Next above Lossmans and ten miles north of it lies Hueston River, in Chatham Bend, where in three days we caught thirty tarpon, after which we sailed to Chokoloskee Bay and exploited Turners River which empties into the southern end of the bay.

The fish caught in Turners River ran generally from fifteen to thirty pounds, although I took one on the fly-rod measuring over five and another about six and one-half feet, the latter requiring about three hours to bring to terms. This fish was struck half a mile from the mouth of the river, and his first rush nearly emptied my little reel, that held less than a hundred yards of line. Frank thought I was excited when I was only cross because he didn't paddle faster when the fish was running away and slower when the line was coming in faster than I could get it on the reel. As the fish leaped above the surface or darted away my fingers were burned by the friction of the line, which must never be slack nor ever allowed to overrun. Often the tarpon shot high in the air, snapping his head, while I shivered lest the hook tear loose. Sometimes the canoe was beside him and once he darted under it. With a quick turn of the wrist I slapped the rod down on the water, parallel with the canoe, and thrust it elbow-deep under the surface. The fish drew it crosswise of the canoe and I held it, with a finger pressing the reel until Frank could turn the craft around. I have often had to resort to this dodge, but have not always been as lucky as on this occasion. The tarpon carried us down the river, out into the bay, and back and forth until my arms were aching, my fingers numb and I was glad to change places with the camera-man for a full hour.

When the fish seemed weak I led the line to where Frank could reach it and gently draw the creature near enough to seize his jaw. Several times the tarpon leaped in the air and swam away with renewed vigor, but finally he was seized, held, dragged over the gunwale of the canoe and—his liberty restored. Our big rod was broken in this stream by the first rush of a tarpon, which we think was the largest we saw during the trip. In three days we caught in this river fifty-six tarpon, thirty-two of which were on an eight-ounce rod.

We finished our fishing at Allen's River, where the tarpon, with a few exceptions, weighed from three to ten pounds each, and where in two days we caught eleven, six of which were taken on the fly-rod.

To summarize, our catch was as follows:

15 days Boca Grande Pass	84	tarpon
14 " Captiva Pass	66	"
5 " Caloosahatchee River	35	"
3 " Marco	14	"
5 " Harney River (fly-rod)	25	"
2 " Broad River	13	"
3 " Hueston River	30	"
3 " Turners River (32 fly-rod)	56	"
2 " Allens River (6 fly-rod)	11	"
52	334	

Never twice, perhaps, would the relative abundance of tarpon in the places named be similar, but in gross, in the same season, they would doubtless tot up about the same. Excepting in Boca Grande, continuous fishing would quickly reduce the daily average, from diminished supply of fish and their increased sophistication.

Between these passes and streams are others in which tarpon, at times, abound. They can be found scattered through the broad, shallow waters and deeper channels of the whole, great Ten Thousand Islands. I have found them far out in the Everglades, in lagoons in the Big Cypress Swamp and even in a deep little lake, a hundred yards in diameter and ten miles from any other body of water.

I am principled against elaborate equipments, but, if you fish with a tarpon rod, you've got to pay three or four dollars for a line that you would dare show to a cultivated tarpon, and you really must have an automatic brake in the handle of your reel. Even then your knuckles will be knocked off if you don't fit to it some sort of stop— a simple loop of string will do. I hate to advise it, but if you can spare the twenty, thirty or forty dollar tax for a powerful reel of fine workmanship, containing the automatic handle brake with stop, you will find it for your soul's welfare. Then, unless your reel seat locks securely, lash the reel to the rod all you know how, and in any event lash the rear pillar of your reel to the rod, that a sixty-pound pull on the line may not fall with multiplied leverage on the weakest part of the reel. Most fishermen don't do this, but all fishermen will wish they had—if they fish for tarpon long

posed between the hook and the swivel, and with the tarpon rod as many feet. No. 13 piano wire can be bought for seventy cents a pound in New York, or seven dollars a pound paid for it in Fort Myers.

Don't carry that criminal weapon, the gaff hook. Don't murder your game. To object to taking a tarpon for mounting, or other rational purpose, would seem fanatical, but to wantonly sacrifice these beautiful and harmless creatures, after they have added so greatly to your pleasure, is causeless cruelty. They can be

"The game is great—it thrills the most stolid of human participants to the tips of his toes."

enough. A light trout rod feels mushy and looks out of focus whenever the smallest tarpon is at the other end of it. Tarpon will rise to a fly, but the fly-rod must be very stiff or the fish, will seldom be hooked. A good bass rod, and trolling, are more appropriate for this fish which rises readily to a spoon. The hook should be short in the shank, for the mouth of the tarpon is hard and the leverage of a long shank breaks the imbedded hook with reasonable certainty. With the light rod, three or four inches of piano wire should be inter-

measured without harming them and the cube of their length in feet, divided by two, gives their weight in pounds as nearly as needful. You can even take them aboard, as proof of your prowess. Of course a gaff hook would simplify this, as shooting them at first would make it easier to play them, and landing a tired tarpon by hand is almost as exciting as playing a fresh one.

No trust controls tarpon fishing. No sport on earth offers greater legitimate excitement. And half the glory of the game is in its humanity.

20
Game
Qualities of
Game Fish
(1910)

"POUND FOR POUND AND INCH FOR INCH THE BLACK BASS IS THE GAMEST FISH THAT SWIMS."

GAME QUALITIES OF GAME FISH

BY SAMUEL G. CAMP

Photographs by the Author

EXACTLY what constitutes the "sport" of angling is difficult to define. It is, essentially, a case of many men of many minds. Anglers, the world over, are kittle cattle. The personal equation figures largely. When a man merely says he is "going fishing" his destination and purpose remain beautifully indefinite. To one individual fishing means derricking bullheads from a mill pond by moonlight; to another it spells fly-casting for salmon on some classic Canadian river; and between these extremes there are almost numberless ways and means of fishing, each having its enthusiastic adherents.

Possibly, in point of fact, there is less difference in the sporting qualities of really game fishes than in the like qualities of men who go fishing. In the final analysis the question practically simmers down to the methods and tackle adopted. The man who kills brook trout on shark tackle naturally develops a small opinion of the game qualities of *Salvelinus fontinalis*. Obviously to obtain sport in angling you must use sportsmanlike tackle. What that is depends upon circumstances.

Environment plays no inconsiderable part. It is questionable—or, rather, it is not—whether one would derive much amusement from catching trout, on even the most approved tackle, from an arti-

THE BROWN TROUT LIKES THE SWIFT WATER.

GOOD RAINBOW WATER.

ficial pool in civilized surroundings. At a certain trout hatchery in the Commonwealth of Massachusetts the custom prevails of allowing anglers (?) to cast over one of the ponds—at fifty cents the cast. At times parties who have been unsuccessful in whipping the nearby streams patronize the wise hatchery man with—if they happen to be at all expert with the fly-rod—reasonably weighty results. This, of course, is strictly a question of "meat"—not sport. That, from one point of view, this sort of fishing is in the nature of a sporting proposition can hardly be controverted. However, it has nothing to do with the normal sport of angling.

Environment is most intimately connected with the continued appeal of fly-fishing for brook trout. The fly-caster fishes for sport as well as for fish; and half the sport of trout fishing is in "getting away from things," wading secluded forest streams and camping where the steam whistle, the honk of the motor car, and the exhaust of the motor boat are things unheard. It is evident, then, that to consider rightly the sporting qualities of the various species of game fishes one must eliminate the angler's personal equation and also the question of environment; it is necessary to consider the brook trout, the black bass, and others strictly on their own merits, and

THE BAIT-CASTER.

also on reasonably light tackle, quite apart from individual preferences or surrounding conditions.

With many anglers the first and foremost quality in a game fish is that of rising freely to the artificial fly under reasonably favorable conditions. And since, undoubtedly, fly-fishing is the finest art of angling, it would seem not unreasonable to require this quality in a candidate for rank in the first flight of game fishes. Fly-fishing is not a matter of pretence or affectation; and that fly-fishing is the best of all the varied forms of angling is a proved condition and not a more or less true theory.

So, with malice toward none and charity for all, we must rank first among the game fishes those which rise to the artificial fly—the Atlantic salmon, the brook, brown, rainbow, and other species of trout, both the black basses, the ouananiche, and the land-locked salmon. Formerly it would have been necessary and proper to include the grayling, but this fish is now so rare as to be practically non-existent to the American angler, although, with the brown trout, it shares the attention of the English fly-fisherman.

Of the three best known species of trout, the Eastern brook trout, the brown, and rainbow trout, it may be said that each possesses marked differ-

FISHING FINE AND FAR OFF.

ences in the mode of resistance when hooked. Possibly the thing wherein the brook trout, *fontinalis,* differs most radically from the brown and rainbow trout is in the rarity of its leaps from the water unless practically dragged out by the rod. You will find that, with occasional exceptions, the general axiom that the brook trout does not leap on a slack line holds true.

To digress for a moment, anglers should always bear in mind the fact that certain individual fish will sometimes develop and exercise traits quite opposite to those ascribed to the class to which the individual belongs. Thus a small-mouthed bass will quite frequently fail to leap when being played on the rod; or, contrarywise, the common pickerel, as a class certainly not over-active or apt to take the air when hooked, will sometimes emulate its gamer relative, the mascalonge, by one or more very strenuous leaps. To appraise rightly the sporting qualities and the average character of resistance of any particular game fish it is necessary to have taken a good number of specimens of that certain species under normal conditions.

A good many years ago the writer read the statement of William C. Harris that "the brook trout does not leap on a slack line"; since then, in all my trout fishing, I have taken particular pains to verify this. The speckled brook trout does not leap on a slack line, but when hooked in fast water and held hard it will quite often do so with usually disastrous effect upon the hopes of the angler, unless the hook is very firmly fastened. While, then, as a rule, the brook trout is not a chronic leaper such as the rainbow or the small-mouthed black bass, it is always well not to count your trout until he is in the creel; for while he will not leap on a slack line, the chances are he may do so when the resistance of the rod grows very appreciable; and, as a usual thing, when a trout is hooked in fast water, it is necessary sooner or later to practically give him the butt.

That the habit of leaping from the water when hooked is distinctly a sporting quality in a game fish goes without saying. The possession of this faculty or characteristic, the instinctive rush of the fish up through the water and into the air, with usually, a savage shaking of the entire body—a fish does not "shake its head" for anatomical reasons—doubles its chances of getting away, always puts the angler on his muscle when he knows that he is dealing with a "jumper," and lends a spectacular interest to the occasion quite unknown when playing a deep-water fighter.

Of our common fresh-water game fishes the small-mouthed black bass and the rainbow trout, *Salmo irideus,* are the most prone to take the air; in fact, it may be said that it is the exceptional small-mouth or rainbow which does not leap at least once at some period of the play. Either of these game fishes, in contradistinction to the speckled brook trout, will often leap at the first feel of the hook. A small-mouthed black bass when hooked in even fifteen or more feet of water will often at once shoot up to the surface and out into the air, shaking its entire body viciously, the height of the leap depending upon the momentum acquired in the upward rush and the size and muscular development or condition of the fish.

When the Black Bass Leaps

Rather curiously, considering the fact that the average angler's love of fishing for the small-mouthed black bass is largely founded upon its leaping abilities, almost every veteran black-bass fisherman does his utmost to defeat the intention of the fish to leap by "tripping" it with the rod. This is done by lowering the rod-tip to the water, sometimes even submerging it, and putting a strong sidewise pull on the fish when it is just below the surface and about to break water. Sometimes this procedure is successful, sometimes not.

In any case, it is open to debate whether it is not about as well to allow the fish to leap, always observing the well-founded rule of lowering the tip to a leaping fish. Personally, I have, with malice aforethought, tried both ways in alternation when fishing for the small-mouthed bass and other leaping game fishes, with practically equal resultant losses. But obviously there is more sport and probably in the final analysis more sportsmanship in allowing the fish to leap at will.

The brown trout, *Salmo fario,* a fine game fish and the chosen quarry of the English fly-caster, undeservedly condemned by some American anglers for reasons which I have detailed in a former article, classes easily with the leapers. It does not, however, leap as readily and instinctively as the rainbow trout or the small-mouthed black bass; but, nevertheless, it will usually break water under much less restraint from the rod than the speckled brook trout, and, on occasions, will even leap at the first feel of the hook.

In June, 1909, when casting the flies over a large, deep pool below a falls, I hooked a two-pound brown trout. At the time the fish rose and was fastened I was casting something more than fifty feet of line and the trout was hooked at the outlet of the pool where there was considerable current. Consequently it was some time before the trout was brought within reach of the landing net —it fought deep-down and with bulldog persistence. An attempt by my companion to net the fish only resulted in scaring it out into the center of the pool again. Once more I nursed it in to the net, and again, at the first movement of the official netter, it ran away seemingly no more tired than at the outset. At no time had the fish shown any inclination to leap.

I then settled down to kill the fish on the rod before making another try at netting it, and—here is the point—when the trout was again, and finally, drawn within reach of the net, to all intents and purposes thoroughly played to a finish, it jumped a good two-and-a-half feet from the water—and landed square in the net. That is a pretty good sample of the kind of fight a brown trout will sometimes put up; and it also shows that you never can tell whether or when a brown trout will leap.

As a rule the brown trout will most often leap when hooked in fast water. Occasionally it will leap more than once. I once saw a three-pound "brownie" jump three times just about as fast as it could get back into the water for a fresh hold. This fish, by the way, when finally landed (I handled the net myself) was held only by a noose in the leader wound around its gills. Its frantic efforts to shake out the fly had succeeded, but, at the same time, it had "roped" itself in true Western fashion.

The large-mouthed black bass is not as chronic and instinctive a leaper as his small-mouthed brother; possibly the rarity of its leaps, as compared with the customary tactics of the small-mouth, may be explained by the fact that it is most often taken in quiet water. The large-mouthed black bass distinctly favors the still waters bottomed or margined with weeds and rushes, and it has been truly said that "light tackle and running water are four-fifths of the game qualities of any fish." However, anyone who has taken a considerable number of large-mouthed black bass will hardly deny the fact that rather more than occasionally the large-mouth jumps —and does so with telling effect upon tackle and the nerves of the angler.

The sea salmon of the Atlantic coast, the ouananiche and land-locked salmon, the mascalonge, and certain other varieties of trout not above mentioned are also to be classed with the leapers. Of all game fishes the ouananiche is the most active and persistent in its aërial tactics. Taken in running water, "on the fly" in more senses than one, it will usually leap twice at least and sometimes a half-dozen times.

Little Choice Among the Trout

There is little comparison among the Eastern brook trout, the rainbow, and the brown trout as to the readiness with which they rise to the fly. Under reasonably favorable fly-fishing conditions, and presuming that the angler uses some degree of discretion in the selection of the flies and the requisite nicety and skill in casting and fishing them, any of these trout will rise to the artificials quite frequently enough to satisfy the demands of the fly-caster—the man who fishes for sport.

Anglers who carefully nurse a prejudice against the brown trout, founded upon hearsay evidence and not upon first-hand and exact knowledge of this fish—for it seems to the writer that anyone who has had much experience with the brown trout in a typically good trout stream must be willing to admit it to an honorable place among our game fishes —hold the opinion that the "brownie" is a reluctant and infrequent riser to the flies. On the contrary, at least in the streams where the writer has taken this fish, and, I believe, the world over, where the fishing conditions are normally favorable—the brown trout rises to the flies with no less frequency or readiness than either the speckled brook trout or the rainbow.

On occasions, when fishing a stream inhabited by all three of these trout, one will take more brown trout than "brooks" or rainbows; and, on other occasions, the brook trout or the rainbow will lead the score, presuming that the stream is well stocked with the three varieties. There is little to choose as to the sporting qualities of our best-known species of trout in the matter of rising to the flies.

The opinion has been expressed by competent authorities that the large-mouthed black bass rises more freely to the flies than the small-mouth. Dr. James A. Henshall has said that, in his opinion, the small-mouthed black bass and the large-mouth are on a par as to game qualities when taken on the same tackle in the same waters. Personally the writer, in common with many other anglers, believes the small-mouth to be the better game fish. To me it has always seemed that the fight of a small-mouthed black bass is faster and far more brilliant than that of the large-mouth; that the small-mouth is more inclined to break water; and that, while possibly weight for weight it requires no longer time to bring a small-mouth to the net than a large-mouth, the small-mouth is rather more apt to make things interesting for the angler.

One reason for a well-founded preference for the small-mouth over the large-mouth is the cleaner habitat and living of the former; as in the case of the brook trout, the small-mouthed black bass instinctively seeks pure, running water and the rocky or sandy bars or bottom of lake and river, while the large-mouth prefers the still and weedy waters. However, comparisons are always odious, and in the case of *Micropterus dolomiei vs. Micropterus salmoides,* as in other similar matters, "much may be said on both sides."

The phrase "light tackle and running water are four-fifths of the game qualities of any fish," while a rather sweeping statement, approximates closely the truth of the whole matter. As an instance, one might cite the case of the ouananiche and land-locked salmon; these game fishes are essentially the same so far as anglers and the sport of angling are concerned, and yet the reputation of the ouananiche as a sporting fish is far in advance of that of the land-locked salmon simply because the former is usually taken on fly-tackle in swift water, while the latter with few exceptions, as in Grand Lake Stream in Maine, is taken by trolling in the still waters of lakes and on necessarily heavier tackle.

Any fish, no matter how game, if taken on tackle of such strength that its every chance of escape is eliminated and its every resistant leap or rush simply smothered by the weight of rod and strength of line, will naturally not only afford no sort of sport but fail entirely in showing the game qualities it really possesses. So it would appear that, in point of fact, the sporting qualities of game fishes depend to no little extent upon the game qualities of the angler himself as evidenced in his choice of tackle.

Suit your tackle to the occasion and the quarry, on the basis of giving the fish at the very least an equal chance of winning, and you will soon discover the fact that a half-pound brook trout possesses all the sporting qualities of a twenty-pound salmon. If, however, you elect to use salmon tackle on trout, you will not find the sport over thrilling—although you may kill more fish.

21
Among the Trout and Grayling
(1888)

OUTING.

VOL. XII.   MAY, 1888.   NO. 2.

AMONG THE TROUT AND GRAYLING.

BY D. D. BANTA.

"WHOA!" cried the Preacher, and Henry's horses came to a stop. "Indeed," said the good man, "I can't endure this any longer," and he slid down to the ground, leaving the driver and me to stand the bumping and jolting as best we could.

The time was in the last summer and the place a dense wood some ten or twelve miles southward from those two copper-industrial towns, Houghton and Hancock, of the Michigan Upper Peninsula.

More than three years before I had heard a rumor of grayling being found in the Otter Creek waters — a stream having its source in the forest-covered highlands southward from those towns, — but I did not at that time, nor for some time after, give the rumor credence. Why should I ? Had I not read in journals, in books, nay, in that truly great and authoritative work on "The Fisheries and Fishing Industries of the United States," published under the auspices of the United States Fish Commission, that the Michigan Big Fin was confined to a few streams in the Lower Peninsula ? "Only in this limited locality, short of the Yellowstone region, is found the already famous Michigan grayling," was the emphatic language of the author in that publication, and, of course, I could not, in the face of all the authorities, credit the rumor.

It would be needless to explain how it came about, but there came a time when my faith in the authorities gave way, and now, not to verify rumors are we bound for the Otter waters, but rather as those who go to take possession of a land already mapped out and to taste of the sweets we already knew it had in store for us.

We left Houghton at an early hour with our boat and outfit in a two-horse wagon, and after a gay trot of eight miles in the cool air of the morning, over a smooth road running parallel with, and often in sight of, Portage River and then Portage Lake, down to Pike Bay, we turned off to the right and made a journey of five and a half miles by surveyor's line over a "corduroy" road to La Chapelle's Camp, on the banks of the Otter, where we embarked. By surveyor's line it is five and a half miles, mind you, but by "corduroy" it is anywhere from eight to eighteen. The first time I went over it I found it eight miles from bay to camp ; the second time it was fourteen, and at the third trip (for I have been over it that many) my driver swore a

241

mighty oath that it was eighteen, and I did not controvert with him.

No blame could attach to the Preacher that day for refusing to ride longer. I, who sat by the side of Henry on the one spring-seat, felt as if it were doubtful whether I could keep my spinal column intact or not, and how much worse it must boat?" asked the Preacher in anxious tones, as Henry passed out of sight on his return journey.

"Can we? We've got to do it," I answered; but nevertheless I did not just then see how it was to be done.

Had we not made diligent inquiry as to the capacity of the stream and been

THE BANK ON WHICH OUR TENT WAS PITCHED.

have been for the Preacher, perched as he was on top of the springless boat. At any rate he rebelled and slid down, as I have already said, and walked every blessed step of the way thence on.

At about noon Henry dumped me and boat and outfit on the banks of the Otter, amid the ruins of La Chapelle's lumber camp, where a thousand rancid smells and stinks and several porcupines awaited our coming. As we looked at the narrow, shallow stream of crystal water and listened to its music as it rippled over the stones, our hearts misgave us. What a promise of navigation was held out to us to be sure! There we were with a canoe sixteen feet long and quite 150 lbs. of *impedimenta*. "Can we go down that stream in that

warned only against its rapids, its quicksands and its sweepers? How hard it is to get the truth concerning places hidden away in the forests!

That afternoon we spent in arranging our load in convenient packages for carrying, and encamped for the night on the La Chapelle ground. We refreshed our knowledge of the geography of the stream at the map, and took notice of its courses and distances. Through ten sections of land it meandered southward from our starting-point, and thence eastward through two other sections, where it took the back track, north-easterly, through four sections, and then widening into Otter Lake two more miles were consumed, soon after which it was swallowed up in the larger

Sturgeon River, which, after crossing one congressional township, debouched into the Pike Bay we so lately left on our journey to La Chapelle's camp. A wire six miles long would connect the beginning and ending points of our proposed voyage — a voyage that, as the section lines go, measures twenty-four miles, but with the thread of the stream—ah! who can tell how far it is around that loop of running water?

But distances, nor prospective rapids, nor logs, nor sweepers disturbed our slumbers that night. Had we not been told that after five miles the grayling fishing began, and that it waxed better and better clear on down to the Big Rapids, wherever they were? Aye, and we had been told better than that—a great deal better! —that both grayling and speckled trout were there, and that both grew larger and larger till good honest three and three-quarter pounders would kick the beam ere we reached the Big Rapids. Ah! It is so easy to believe in big fish! What a rosy

the northern lights, quivering and dancing under the pole-star, nor for that matter the porcupines that alternately gnawed and squeaked at an ancient beef-barrel not far from our tent, kept us from dreaming dreams of wives and homes that night. How sweet our slumbers under the stars on our feathery and odoriferous balsam beds!

" Oh, peaceful and sweet are forest slumbers,
    On a fragrant couch with the stars above,
As the free soul marches to dulcet numbers
    Through dreamland valleys of light and love."

It was with aching bones we made our camp the evening of the first day down, though I must say we did not find that first day's journey as hard a one as we feared it would be when first we saw the Otter. For the first mile or so it was everything we had expected. The stream was shallow; ripple succeeded ripple, and every few rods was a log which had to be cut out or the boat jumped over. With a rope at the bow and one at the stern, one

"THERE! THERE! I'VE GOT HIM!"

sky ours was, to be sure! As we lay prone upon our balsam bed that night and rehearsed the glorious possibilities awaiting us, the Preacher kicked the blankets off in his enthusiasm and insisted on an early start the following morning. Not even

of us went before, pulling like a canal horse, while the other brought up the rear no less laboriously.

In due time we came to the worst obstruction we had encountered, where we had to unload and lift our boat over a large pine log against which much drift-wood had lodged, but immediately below that an important affluent swelled the Otter to a third larger stream, and thence on there was no lack of water.

On the door-posts of the La Chapelle camps and on bits of barrel-heads and

staves tacked here and there to the walls, former vainglorious fishermen had left records of their sport. One fellow had written that on a certain July day, which he declared was the "hottest day of the year," he had scored 200 fish, and his companion 150. Of course that was a fish lie, and a clumsy one at that. His even numbers, not to mention his "hottest day," proved that. Here beneath the shadows of the plumey balsams, with the waters fresh from the springs in the hills plashing over the stones and running in silver ripples over the white sands, the "hottest days" never come.

But this was not the only fellow who had taken the pains to post himself a liar on the walls of the old camps. More than half a dozen others had done like-wise, one claiming a score of eighty, one of sixty, one of fifty, and so on, all even

numbers. One original had caught "forty speckled beauties;" another, whose number I have forgotten, had cooked and eaten his catch, after which he had "washed it down." Had I looked far enough, doubtless, I would have found a record made by the man who "pumped lead," for the fools, like empty tin cans, are found everywhere.

Of all the historians who had left their stories on the old camp walls, there was but one who held my credence. His was an unambitious record, but I could read between the lines that it was the unvarnished truth. "I caught," so ran his

ONE DEER WE SAW.

history, "about thirty-five fish to-day, and had lots of fun. My wife fell in the creek."

But falsehood, even, will sometimes gender the truth. After all the lying records the truth came that there were speckled trout in the Otter; that they were fairly numerous, and that there had been a good deal of fishing for them at one time or other;

and so it was no surprise to us, when, during an hour's fishing late in the afternoon of our first day, the Preacher captured a panful of as beautiful specimens of nature's handiwork as the lover of the gentle art ever sees.

Every stream I happen to navigate is the crookedest till I try the next one, but really, the Otter excels them all in this particular. It is a crooked stream that doubles the distance, but the Otter triples it at the very least. It has already been shown that in straight lines it is not over sixteen miles from the place where we entered the stream to Otter Lake, but a gentleman who had been over the ground and had taken the sense of lumbermen who had driven logs over it, told me that by the thread of the stream it was not less than fifty-two miles between the two points, and I cannot think he was wide of the mark.

But is not the winding stream the beautiful stream the world over? The Otter's waters well up from icy springs more than 600 feet above the Great Lake's level, and are as clear as crystal. They run the greater part of their race through narrow valleys filled with bushes and saplings, while hills, covered with lofty pines, with balsams, maples, beeches and birches mainly, rise, dark and sombre, on either side. Here the white pine, *Pinus strobus*, looks down in gloomy grandeur on the rank green of an alien wood. The pine of this region is a doomed tree—doomed by both nature and man. Only the monarchs of this species one sees, not the saplings and the thrifty young trees. The time of the succession of the hardwoods has come, and the monarchs are the sport of the storm and the prey of the axe.

As we descend the stream we find its valley widening, till, as we approach the lake, it passes into wide stretches of reed-covered lagoons. Over this valley, all the way from its beginning in the hills down to the lake itself, of cool August mornings rise in fleecy folds clouds of gray mist, but, as the day advances, the clouds disappear, and the sun shines in, giving color and beauty to a luxuriant vegetation. Of all the vegetable growths, the fisherman would, perhaps, first see the *Alnus incana*, or hoary alder, as in this northland he soon learns to associate its presence with that of the speckled trout. Here the wild clematis makes a vine-tangle that tries the legs of the stoutest, and coarse-fibred ferns grow rank in the waste spots.

One flowering plant, the *Eupatorium purpureum*, or "Joe Pye-weed," engaged our attention, off and on, for more than half the way down. Early of mornings the bumble bees would flock to the Joe Pye patches, and, alighting upon the flowers, begin the exploration of the flower-cups in that active, fussy sort of way so characteristic of the honey-gathering "busy bee." After a time, however, they ceased to play the part of busy bees, but became heavy and dull, as if under the influence of a stupefying drug. While one never seemed to yield to the influence so far as to be unable to whip out his weapon on occasion, yet they all lost the power of using it in that adroit and skilful manner so characteristic of the bee tribe. It was an easy thing to pick one off the flowers between the thumb and finger and impale it on a hook. Of course the insect would resent this ill-treatment, thrusting out a formidable enough looking sting, but it lacked the power of squirming and twisting around so as to stab its enemy whether or not. Occasionally I would let one fall to the ground, but, instead of showing

anger and flying away as a common bee would have done, it would slowly scrabble to its legs and then remain quiet. Hit the weed a slight blow, and all the occupants of its blossoms would tumble helplessly to the earth. There came a moment to each one, however, when it appeared to have had enough of dallying

life hiding in the shadows. Even the birds are songless, and when surprised, as they often are, flit noiselessly out of view. But along the valleys of the streams, where the sunshine comes in and all the conditions are favorable to the sustaining of animal life, one may expect to find it abounding. It was so along the valley of the Otter.

"This green and sun-streaked glade was rife
With sights and sounds of forest life."

What a covert for the wild beasts the brushy thickets next the stream and the dark woods beyond did present! Side by side in the moist places were to be seen the tracks of the deer

WE LIFT THE BOAT OVER A LARGE PINE LOG.

at nature's distillery, and had thoughts of home. When that time came, the boozy bee would steady himself and try his wings, and, seemingly after satisfying himself that he could do it, he would fly heavily, slowly, and droningly away.

What was the matter with the bumblebees? One scientific friend ventures to say, "Possibly it came of the cathartic principle known to permeate the boneset tribe." Another suggests that the bumblebee, having no regard for the Joe Pye blossom, savagely tears it open to get at the sweets within, and that the weed has learned to distil a poison for its own protection. I am sure I do not know.

The visitor from a lower latitude will be impressed with the silence he finds reigning amid the deep woods of the North. Doubtless he will see abundant evidences of the presence of animal life, but it is a

and of their mortal enemies — the gray wolves. Twice we heard the "long-drawn howl" of the night prowlers, and one day as I stooped to drink at a spring, while wandering in the forest, I noticed in the soft earth beneath me the footprint of Lupus. He had lapped there not many hours before. Two or three places we saw where bruin had left the print of his moccasin, but neither wolf nor bear gladdened our sight the voyage through. One deer, and only one, we saw, and that was one evening as the shadows were dropping down, when one carelessly ran bang up against our camping-ground, to the Preacher's great disquietude. The young man carried a little rifle, and I verily believe would have shot that deer, law or no law, had it not run like the wind into the bush.

But if the kings and princes of the North woods kept in the background the birds came to the fore. Ducks flew, quacking at every mile or so, and how often we surprised flocks of the ruffed grouse that had come down to the margin of the stream to drink or feed off the choke-cherries and red raspberries that here and there grew.

Probably the bird that most engaged our attention was that pugnacious feathered knight of the woods, the kingbird, or bee-martin (*Tyrannus Carolinensus*). Seldom does one see so many members of this family in so limited an area, and we could account for it only from the great plenty of insect life here to be found. I have mentioned the bumble-bees, but the yellow-jackets were far more numerous than they. The region abounded in these peppery little miscreants. I seldom made a foray into the woods on the hills that I did not find one or more nests occupied by the most intrepid of the race of yellow-jackets I ever saw. On five several occasions I stumbled into these nests and got stung every time, and so I know.

In the region lying between Lakes Superior and Michigan, myriads of blue-bottles and green flies are ever ready to pounce on fish or flesh and deposit their eggs. On the Otter these flies are remarkably scarce, but the yellow-jackets are not in numbers much behind the flies between the lakes, and eat as persistently at fish or flesh cooked or uncooked as the flies blow. This scarcity of flies on the Otter was a curious circumstance, and I wondered if the great plenty of yellow-jackets had not something to do with it. The fly is the yellow-jacket's lawful game, and many a time have I amused myself in camp watching the jackets (and hornets) catch flies, which they do with great dexterity, after which they carry them off bodily to their nests. And so the bee-martins in turn catch the yellow-jackets, and may it not be that the great abundance of these insects accounts for the absence of the flies and the presence of the birds?

" Hallo-o-o ! "

Did you ever, while in the midst of a great wilderness, miles and miles away from the nearest cabin, call for a companion who had wandered off to fish or shoot and had overstayed his time by an hour? How the sound of your voice, after winding in and out among the trees, seems to come back to you and mock you.

" Hallo-o-o ! "

That Preacher and I reached this new camp-ground by two o'clock of this third day of our journey down, and after erecting our tent and eating a hasty dinner we went fishing, I up stream and he down, first making a solemn compact that we would return at the least by an hour of the sun. I have had my sport. I waded up the Otter a mile, and as I whipped the deep places, now and then securing beautiful specimens of the speckled trout, the swamp sparrows, from the moist thickets, twittered in their excess of joy. On my return two wretched porcupines turn up in the boat, gnawing away as if their life leases depended on it. What caricatures in animal life these quill-covered beasts are, to be sure! With all the things edible in that boat, the two animals were gnawing, the one at a bit of plank, and the other at an ax-helve. I whip them into the bush, scattering their quills like leaves, and then I cut the balsam browse for our bed and make ready my creel of fish for the frying-pan, and, while listening anxiously for the return of my comrade, note the nearly-setting sun.

" Hallo-o-o ! "

And still there is no answer. Surely the Preacher is not lost. No man can get lost whose camp is on the stream in which he is fishing. And yet I am uneasy. I have had one or two lost fellows on my hands in my time, and do not care to have the like again. There were the quicksands! That very day I sank to my waist as we came down, and but for the boat, to which I clung, did not see how I could have pulled out. In spite of all reasoning to the contrary, I am apprehensive, and the plaintive note of a wood pewee, piping from the dead limbs of a maple hard by, somehow adds to the feeling.

" Hallo-o-o ! "

" Whoo-pe ! "

" Ah! There he is, the rascal. If I don't give him a piece of my mind ! "

And against the strong current of the Otter " the rascal " came, slump, slump, slump! A little precatory cough smites my ear, but I am not to be placated by a little cough. No, indeed. I'm going to lecture that young man, and so I must make him feel that I am displeased at the very outset.

" Well ! " exclaimed the young man, as he reached the top of the bank on which our tent was pitched. But I made no reply. I was busy just then assorting the browse for our bed, and besides it is not an easy thing to begin a lecture to a young man for overstaying his time when he is the only young man within fifteen miles of you.

"What do you say to this?" the young man smilingly asked, as he held up the prettiest catch of fish I had seen for many a day. Merciful fathers! If that Preacher didn't have a pound grayling — a for-sure *Thymallus tricolor*, and no mistake! And you ought to have seen his eyes and heard his story! Such fishing he had had, and such vaporing in the telling of it! And what a comely, shapely fish that big fin was to be sure. I put it apart from the others; I turned it over and over; I pulled up its magnificent dorsal; I stroked its silvery sides and counted its markings, and declared it the handsomest fish I had ever seen. And then I made a pot of tea and fried a pan of my own trout, while my comrade dressed his, and, after the supper was over and the dishes put away, we went to bed, when each told (mayhap magnifying a little) the story of his own afternoon's adventures; and the lecture was indefinitely postponed.

That night, about midnight, as nearly as I can tell, the Preacher aroused me, exclaiming:

"There! There! I've got him! I've got him!"

"Got what?" I asked.

"That big trout! Don't you see him there in that hole?"

"No! In what hole?"

"M–m–m–m–m–m!"

The bottom had dropped out, but I knew the Preacher was a confirmed angler. Hitherto I had doubted. His rifle and his shotgun had been the themes of his best sporting exploits, but I knew that henceforth his day-dreams, as had been this of the night, would be of flies, and fins, and rippling streams. And I let him sleep on.

Four or five miles below the place of our starting we passed the last of the upper rapids into a current flowing deep and strong, over bottoms mainly of sand and gravel. After twelve miles by the stream from the last of the first rapids, the first of the second appear, and these, after a few miles, culminate in the Big Rapids.

In this region of smooth water, many conditions combine to insure a goodly fish population. The exceeding crookedness of the stream, its many deep holes, its numerous hiding-places for fish, under submerged logs and depending brush, not to mention the blankets of a confervoid alga—of which more anon—all invite those wariest of the denizens of the wilderness waters to come and stay. Then there is a fair distribution of sunshine and shadow, and *such* water! From the sources of the Otter clear down to the Big Rapids scarcely a drop of swamp water contaminates the crystal tide. All the way down, from springs and spring brooks, not to mention larger streams made up wholly of spring water, the volume of the Otter is not only continually enlarging, but its temperature is kept down to an icy coolness, while a never-failing fish food supply is all the time being carried in.

What a delightful angling experience it was, to take both trout and grayling out of the same pools, and sometimes both at the same cast! What an opportunity to decide which was the gamier fish, the speckled trout or the grayling, and yet how hard to make the decision when the opportunity came! I have ever treasured the memory of some former seasons spent among the grayling of the Lower Peninsula as the pleasantest of my sportsman life, and had come to the point of awarding the palm of gaminess to the grayling. But since I have fished the Otter I am constrained to a change of opinion. The Lower Peninsula grayling is a gamier fish than are the trout in many of the streams of this upper region, because they are in better water, but when all the conditions are the same as in the Otter, where both fish were at their best and fairly equal in size, I was inclined to shift over to the side of the trout. Yet there are points wherein it seemed that the grayling excelled the trout. When it leaves the deep pools on a foraging expedition, and is fairly in the biting mood, I think it is a better biter than the trout, and a more persistent. At such times it will rise to the fly with a fierceness and *abandon* that is truly marvelous; and if in its furious strike it fails to secure the coveted prize, it will strike again and again—up sometimes to the fifth or sixth time, and is therein a more excellent fellow than his neighbor, though I must do that neighbor justice by saying that he frequently surprised me by making two or three rushes at a fly ere he took it or fled for good to his place of hiding—a performance so often repeated by the Otter Creek trout as to lead me to reflect that possibly he had been taking lessons from his grayling neighbor.

While a grayling always "fought a good fight," the trout could fight a more desperate one. The grayling had as many resources as a trout, but it seemed to me he gave up the contest a little sooner. The

Preacher describing the difference in this particular one day, said : "A hooked trout acts like it is *bound* to get off at all hazards ; a hooked grayling like it *wanted* to get off very much."

And after all, this is what the fisherman might expect, for the grayling is a finer fibred and bluer blooded fish than the trout. He is the aristocrat of our Northern waters. Look at the two fish side by side, and note the shapely, arrowy outline of the one, with its thin lips and comely mouth, its tapering body and deeply notched tail, and its superlatively beautiful dorsal. Behold the perfect taste displayed in dress and decoration ! Why, if you will but note his bearing in yonder pool toward the other fish, you must see that if he thinks at all, he must think as I do in regard to his lineage. One day I sat in the screen of some bushes, right by the edge of a strong current sweeping into the blue depths of a wide pool, watching the play of the fish therein. Forming the segment of a circle were half a dozen trout and two or three small grayling, lying head up stream, awaiting such chance food as might come floating down. Presently another grayling, one of lordly size, came swimming lazily that way, with his banner waving high over him, and at once the trout dropped abashed out of view, leaving the field clear to him and his kind. How grandly and majestically he moved back and forth across the current of insweeping waters, his waving dorsal reflecting even to me the brilliancy of its colors. Every bit of flotsam that went dancing down the swift waters he must needs first inspect, and the thought came to me that his lordship might never be in a better mood for a brown hackle than at that very time. But in vain I offered the choicest treasures of my book. I let them float down to him, but after duly inspecting them at a safe distance, he seemed to turn up his royal nose at them. I dropped them lightly on the water close beside him, and then at a greater distance from him, hoping that in his eagerness he would rashly snap them up to inspect afterwards. Not he. A trout not much under his size, seeing the cast, came from his hiding-place, but my lord with a flirt of his tail, warned the would-be intruder away. Then I impaled a stupid bumble-bee from a "Joe Pye" blossom on my hook, and let it float down. The bait he saw, and was evidently interested in ; at last he stuck his blue-blooded nose close up to it, while his elegant tail

was turned towards me. It was his mistake and my opportunity. I gave a quick jerk, and, as luck would have it, drove the sharp steel into his aristocratic nose, and in spite of his best endeavors he soon lay on the white sand at my feet.

Still it must be confessed that the scale is not far from equilibrio. Another fisherman might award the prize for gaminess to the grayling. But let this be as it may, as a race, *Salvelinus fontinalis* is the hardier. There was a time, doubtless, when the grayling kingdom extended to all suitable waters from Lake Huron to the Mississippi. Its presence in this Otter Creek, three hundred miles from any other grayling stream, tends to prove that ; and so does that other fact which observation seems to teach, that whenever the trout find their way into a grayling stream a war of races is at once inaugurated which in the long run proves disastrous to the grayling.

The largest Michigan grayling I ever saw was one taken from the Au Sable River several years ago, and which weighed 28 ounces. We had been led to expect we would do much better than that in the Otter, but did not. The largest I caught weighed 17 ounces, and was 14 inches long, and my comrade did no better. I went down the creek one afternoon late, my cast being made up of a white miller for a stretcher, and a brown and gray hackle for droppers. The fish were not rising freely, and of those that came to my creel the largest did not exceed half a pound. I had reached the top of a long and shallow-looking stretch of water, lying in the shadow of a steep bank, and was debating whether I had not better return at once to camp. Not a sound was heard save the

" .   .   . wavelets lazy slaps
On log and stone around."

At a venture I made a long cast down stream, and was electrified at the bold but ineffective rush made by a grayling. A second cast was made with a similar result, when again recovering my line, I made a third one, and this time the white miller hook went home. My! what a splendid fight followed. Thrice he leaped clear of the water, and ultimately came ashore revolving like a vertical wheel with the hook as a centre, a feat that no other fish performs, as far as I have noticed, and a very pretty feat it is. He was indeed a beautiful fish, and had a dorsal fin four and a half inches high by the rule.

The Otter is utilized every spring at

the melting of the winter snows by the lumbermen who float their logs down its current to the lake, a use of the stream which must tend to the extirpation of the fish, but which at the same time causes the fishing, in most respects, to be an easy pastime. The logging does not, of course, affect the quicksands nor the kaolin beds that one comes across, now and then, in his descent of the stream, and neither of which is it desirable to set one's foot in while wading, but one soon learns to steer clear of both quicksands and kaolin beds.

There is a hindrance to easy fishing, however, that I never saw elsewhere abounding as in the Otter, which is caused by a confervoid alga of some sort, and which the fisherman would generally characterize as a "green moss." It is certainly the most trying, to the fisherman's patience, of anything I ever met with. It is a green-colored, slimy, gelatinous-feeling growth, that hangs in long, ropy festoons or in broad sheets, hitched to the snags, brush, logs and rocks lying in the creek. By reason of its readiness to attach itself to the fisherman's flies and to wrap in mucous folds around his line, not to mention the easy escape it offers to a hooked fish, it comes nearer turning the contemplative angler into a powder magazine than anything else I ever saw. Logs, and rocks, and rapids, and quicksands, and overhanging brush, and brush all criss-cross with twigs, and brush all covered with serrated leaves, and weeds, and rushes, and grass, and all other ordinary and extraordinary agencies, moral and immoral, that, now and then, the fisherman runs across, have I been able to hold my own against and maintain an even temper. But that confervoid staggered me. I watched the Preacher, to hear what he would say, but in silence he vengefully clutched at the slimy tormentor and yanked it off his flies and line, and went on with his fishing. But I could not keep silent. I tried all the mild words I could think of — the very mildest first, bear in mind, such as "Oh my!" "Shocking!" "Dear me!" "Don't it beat all!" After which I advanced to "Great Cæsar!" "*Jemima!*" "*Jerusalem!*" (prolonging the *je* in both cases). "Consarn it!" "*Con*found it!" (prolonging the con, unnecessarily, perhaps); after which, with the unparalleled provocation at hand, it was a short step to "Darn it!" and then, probably, though I am not quite

sure, came "Dang it!" and if so, I am sure the *dang* came quick and sharp, like the sting of a yellow-jacket. *Facilis descensus!* I wonder if I did take the next step. I am not certain, and, owing to the nature of the case, never can be. But let me offer a word of advice to the fisherman who contemplates a trip to Otter Creek, but who would "swear not at all:" Do not go, or else take a good hand along.

What the alga was to the waters, the porcupine was to the land. These solemn-looking varlets met us at every camping ground. They are stupidly fearless and impudently meddlesome. At any hour of the day, and especially if the day be a cloudy one, a hedgehog may be met with, but towards sundown, be it cloudy or clear, the entire population is on foot. If one, in its wanderings, happens to spy a camp, it ambles right up and takes possession, unless the rightful occupant is at home, in which event it will retreat slowly to the bush and patiently wait for him to leave. Anything tasting of grease and salt it will gnaw. All the night long, after I had whipped the two out of the boat, the beasts prowled around our camp, and, in spite of the fact that our boat was anchored off the bank, one managed to climb in about midnight, and such another disturbance as it did create with its *gnaw*, *gnaw*, *gnaw* at a greasy plank, is seldom heard in the wilderness. By the moonlight, at the risk of staving in the boat, I shied a club at the disturber, which, missing it, nevertheless knocked our two innocent landing-nets overboard, one of which we never found.

How many of the animals came around our tent that night we never knew. All night long, when awake, we could hear them prowling, in that furtive, sneaking manner so characteristic of the hedgehog, and not infrequently, within a few inches of our heads (outside the tent, of course), would one stop and make that muffled, chattering noise which is peculiar to most of the rodent tribe. The Preacher hung his hat up "on the ground," that night, where one of the rogues found it and proceeded to ornament it by cutting a deep notch in the rim. Another mounted to a stationary seat at our bark-topped table, and, while we slumbered, it stripped it of all the oilcloth table-cover within reach. Probably it had not struck so toothsome a morsel in many a day as was that bit of oilcloth; unless, indeed, it was our dishcloth, which that hog, or some other, chewed into shreds the same night.

We were not surprised, on looking around the next morning, to find that a hedgehog den was hard by our camp. Numerous holes, smooth with frequent use, leading under the roots of a giant birch, testified to this. It had been our purpose to spend another day and night here, but we had had enough of Porcupine Camp, and during the morning set out for a more hospitable region. Two miles below we came to a spot where the prospect was most pleasing, and once more we reared our canvas house. But hardly had the evening dews begun to fall, when not far off, and in the heart of a dense thicket of underbrush, a porcupine began to bark at us. An effort, with the shotgun in hand, to find it, proved unavailing, for whenever we came within a few rods of it it would shut up, and so further search was useless. This animal's bark was suggestive of the bark of a puppy and the half squeal and grunt of a pig, and it kept it up that night till we both went to sleep.

About midnight I awakened, to hear the barking still going on, but before morning it ceased. I have heard their noise quite often, but never knew one to keep at it half the night before.

Shortly before landing at this new camping-place we ran upon a beaver. The surprise was mutual. Our furry friend did not stop to make our acquaintance, but dived like a loon and then swam a little sidewise, the left fore-foot reaching farther forward than the right one, and with great swiftness, a distance of thirty yards or more, to a place of safety in the deep water above his dam. We camped no great distance below that dam, and had to break it down a little in order to get our boat over. This dam showed much skill in its construction. Indeed, it was not apparent to me how man, without the aid of tools, could have made the dam with the material used and in that strong current of water. A submerged log, lying across the stream, served as a sort of bulwark, against which a great mass of sticks, brush, weeds and leaves had been matted and woven into such a compact body as to dam the water to a height of not less than fifteen inches above.

Two finished dams we crossed over during our voyage, and I know not how many unfinished ones. All along the creek beaver signs were abundant, not only in the dams, finished and unfinished, but in the freshly-cut green brush of the birch and also of the *Populus* family, the bark of which the beaver feeds upon. Their "slide-ways" down the steep clay banks remind one of youthful diversions. Indeed, I have heard hunters and trappers say that beavers love to slide down hill the same as do boys. This may be true, and especially of the young fellows, but the old ones, on whom rest the responsibilities of life, use the slide-ways in the very serious business of bringing down to the waters the green wood from which they strip their daily food.

We saw but the one beaver during our journey. It is a wary animal, and seldom allows itself to be caught napping.

Our days on the Otter, like all red-letter days, passed all too swiftly away. On the eighth we ran the Big Rapids, and the trout and grayling were behind us. Thence on back to civilization the descent was easy. Through groves of evergreen and hardwoods commingled, and on down to the treeless lagoons, and thence into Otter Lake we sped as fast as the strong current and the pushing-pole could drive us.

How delightful is this river navigation! What a shifting of scenes at every bend of the stream! Expectation is always on tiptoe for the new. Imagine, if you can, O reader, our boat gliding smoothly beneath the sylvan shadows or over the sunny water, where sound of human voice seldom comes and noise of grinding wheels and whistle of engine is never heard; where the wild deer steals down at midday to drink, and strange birds sing fearlessly in the twilight of thickets, and you may imagine something of the felicity that now and then comes to the summer outer who seeks the out-of-the-way places. Even the last obstruction to our progress, where once more we were compelled to unload and lift our boat over a tangle of fallen elms, did not moderate our enjoyment.

Two days we spent in a cozy camp under the shadow of the hills on Otter Lake—two days of idleness and rest. We had been told, and we saw, of the abundance of the pike (*Esox lucius*) and pike-perch (*Stizostedium vitreum*) swimming in this beautiful water, and we had anticipated sport with them, but it was not to be. We could find no pleasure capturing pike and pike-perch after having so lately had our choice among the trout and grayling.

22
Trouting
Over the
Old Hockett Trail
(1898)

THE CAMP AT TUOHEY'S.

TROUTING OVER THE OLD HOCKETT TRAIL.

(CALIFORNIA.)

BY J. R. MOORE.

THE Mount Whitney region of the southern Sierras, with the district lying directly north, including the Yosemite Valley, is perhaps the roughest of the whole of that exceedingly rough range of mountains. It was the favored home of the grizzly bear, now almost exterminated thereabouts. The very roughness of the country makes it surpassingly beautiful; its variety of aspect, its ruggedness of form and ever-changing color, together with its great forests, in which are found the famous California big trees (*Sequoia gigantea*), the great sugar pine, most distinguished of its kind the yellow pine, with firs and cedars of enormous proportions, and adding to them a valley like the Yosemite at its head and the highest peak in the United States at its feet, all unite to render it a spot almost unique.

Numerous rivers head in these mountains. To the northward are the Merced and the King, flowing into the San Joaquin, and to the south the Kaweah and the Kern, flowing into Tulare Lake; all following the western trend of the watershed.

In the rivers and lakes of the Sierras there are seven kinds of trout to be found. These embrace four varieties of the rainbow species: the two of the upper Sacramento and McCloud Rivers, one called *Salmo irideus shasta*, the rainbow of the fish culturist, and another, *S. irideus stonei*, or No Shee trout. In these waters is also found the only char of the Pacific Slope, known as *Salvelinus malma*, the Dolly Varden trout.

As you go further south, the rainbow is found in all the numerous streams running through the range until you reach the neighborhood of the Truckee River and the lakes in that region, including Tahoe, Independence, Webber, Donner and others, where, besides the rainbow, which is plentiful in the Truckee, the *Salmo mykiss*, or cutthroat or black-spotted trout, abounds. A number of the streams in this vicinity have also been stocked with *Salvelinus fontinalis*, the brook-trout of our Eastern seaboard.

This makes five varieties, and, going still further south, to the Mount Whitney country, two others are found, the *S. irideus gilberti* or Kern River trout, and *S. irideus agua bonita* or golden trout of Whitney Creek. It is of these two beautiful fishes, of which little has as yet been written, that some account will be given.

Should one enter this country from the Nevada side, following the railway down as far as Owens Lake, the trail into the cañon of the Big Kern would doubtless prove the easiest mode of approach. The usual method, however, is to start from Visalia, in Tulare County, California, and go eastward by wagon road as far as Mineral King, some sixty miles, and then by pack-horses over Farewell Gap to Trout Meadows, say, twenty-five miles, and from there into the cañon of the Kern, another day's ride.

We left Visalia on the 21st of June, and, as the snow in the Gap was not to be trusted so early in the season, were obliged to take the old Hockett Trail up the south fork of the Kaweah River, regulating our marches by the feeding grounds where pasturage was available for our animals. Our route, therefore, led us by Tuohey Meadows, Soda Springs and Trout Meadows, thence into the Kern, a much longer and far more difficult journey. Seven pack animals (six of them bronco mules, three-year-olds) and eight riding horses, with John Broder as guide, philosopher and friend, "Uncle Bob," the indispensable, a packer and a cook, completed our outfit.

If one happens to be roughing it on a trail, the companionship of John Broder is a liberal education, while from the view of the vaquero, "Uncle Bob" will furnish the points and the history thereof. Then if it be your misfortune to fall in with such a Mexican as the "Barrel Organ," a name he earned early in the march, a cook that didn't cook, and adding to this a packer who had to look to the "boss" to throw every diamond hitch; with six beautiful bronco mules which bucked their packs off every now and then, and had to be blindfolded, and lariatted both fore and aft, in order to replace them, you would be in the way, if an observing person, of seeing lots of fun.

The writer started from Visalia with "Uncle Bob" on a buckboard over the Mineral King road, expecting to overtake John with the pack-train before going many miles. After reaching the foothills we began to think that John must have had some differences to settle with those mules, for he was not within sight. We pushed on to Dave Carter's, about thirty miles out, where we called a halt.

Dave Carter is from Virginia, and his welcome was warm as he bade us come in. Although the house was filled to overflowing with Dave's family, and could therefore offer us no shelter, it is entirely surrounded by magnificent fig and mulberry trees, which make as good a roof as any camper could wish for, so, after getting something to eat, we adjusted our beds beneath the foliage and turned in for the night.

John and the pack-train arrived next morning. He had had several differences with those mules. The whole outfit on reaching us was in such a demoralized condition that it was deemed prudent to move on but five or six miles further, to the south fork of Kaweah River, and go into camp.

Getting off the dusty road and striking south by the trail was a great relief. We were soon among the hills, in beautiful timber skirting the river, where everything was green and wild flowers were growing in profusion, nodding their white, blue, yellow and purple heads to the gentle southern breeze.

After arranging camp we put our rods together and went to the river for a mess of trout, strictly for the pot. Now, the Kaweah is much resorted to by the sportsmen of Visalia, and is pretty well fished out; for few of these anglers have got beyond the ken of worms and grasshoppers, and they go for fish.

We did not find the trout over-numerous nor of any great size, but they rose to our flies in sufficient numbers to furnish an abundant meal. Pretty little rainbows they were, though quite unlike the variety found across the divide.

Reveille sounded at three A. M., and came in loud notes from the "Barrel Organ." With the prospect of work ahead the Mexican suddenly discovered pains in his interior that could be expressed only in heart-aching groans. He could not get breakfast, nor pull a pack-rope. Utterly impossible. We were truly concerned for him and believed him to be in dire extremities. A large dose of chlorodyne was administered. He then mixed up about a quart of sweetened flour paste, which he heated over the fire, and swallowed the whole mess, after which he sat down by a tree and groaned as loudly as ever. We had to turn in and get breakfast without him, and pack the animals as well. It was a circus, and we all played clown to the six trick mules. Betimes the outfit was started, the Mexican having saddled his horse and dropped in behind.

The weather was delightful. The forest - covered hills in their richest green of early summer, the ground carpeted with masses of wild flowers, the distant peaks glistening in the sunshine, and the fresh morning air united to bring a sense of enjoyment to the faces of all save the "Barrel Organ" and the mules.

The Hockett Trail was built by a man of that name, under a grant by the Legislature of the State, in order to supply the mining camps in the neighborhood of Lone Pine, some one hundred and seventy miles from Visalia. During his ownership a toll was collected for its use, until the State finally regained possession by purchase. In the early days the trail was kept in good condition. Easier means of access have long since been found to reach Lone Pine, and the old trail has fallen into disuse. The mountains of the Big Horn are almost like pampas to it, and the trails of the Yosemite, kept in admirable condition, seem in comparison like veritable boulevards.

"Uncle Bob" twice led us off the trail, and once with almost disastrous results. A halt was called, but the mules, not understanding our language, crowded up, and one, getting a push on his pack, went ears over tail down the mountain. In his revolutions we saw a wheel going round, showing at rapid intervals, four legs, a pack, two ears and a tail. Why he did not go down three thousand feet into eternity will always remain a mystery, but he brought up with his forefeet against some obstruction about one hundred and fifty feet below, and we finally got him out--the pack still on his back, no bones broken, cut and bruised somewhat, but quite ready to follow on when we turned and picked up the trail again.

For many hours we had been rapidly ascending. The giant sugar and yellow pines, the huge cedars, became fewer in number, being replaced by firs and tamaracks. The mountain peaks quite near at hand were entirely covered with a mantle of snow sending down great white stripes where it filled the rocky ravines on their sides, while patches of considerable size lay still unmelted by the side of the trail. At intervals one saw the wonderful snow-plant, transparent in vermilion, and almost crystalline in appearance, looking far more like a creation in candy than a vegetable form.

The severity of the climb had been hard on the animals. Packs had to be re-adjusted frequently, and no one was sorry, when with the sun well below the western hills, the divide at Tuohey's Meadows was reached. The day had also proved a mule tamer. The business end of those animals had lost its aggressiveness, and one could approach them in comparative safety.

The Mexican had ridden this tough march and was not long in arriving, but the saddle had scarcely left his horse before the groans were resumed. A good dose of cholera mixture followed the chlorodyne; he mixed himself another quart of sweetened paste, partook quite liberally of other food, wrapped himself up in blankets, and was still groaning when sleep overtook us.

The horses were rounded up before daylight in the morning. In the wet places considerable ice had formed overnight, and the cool morning air, suggestive of early December, greeted our awakening. With a bit of breakfast aboard, we headed the outfit down the incline for Soda Springs. After passing beyond the flat of the meadows, the trail again assumed its old ruggedness. In the steep descents we most frequently led our horses, and did about as much walking as riding.

The previous day had tried our animals so severely that we determined to make a shorter march of this. Reaching the camping place about 2 P. M., we selected a beautiful spot where a small stream ran dancing down into the Little Kern River, which flowed within a quarter of a mile southward of us.

We were now on the other watershed, and I was curious to see the trout. Moreover, we wanted fish to eat. The size of the stream as well as its character, forbade the possibility of any finny monsters, so a 5¼-oz. Leonard rod was soon rigged and quickly shot the flies over the rippling waters. Commencing with the brook by the camp, perhaps a dozen quarter-pounders were landed before reaching the Little Kern, out of which a sufficient addition was made to furnish the requisite "pot." Nothing over a half-pound fish was killed, but their eating quality was so far superior to those of the Kaweah as to command instant recognition. Their other peculiarities will be referred to later. Throughout our whole day we had been traversing a country of surpassing loveliness. Every turn of the trail brought forth changing views of snow-capped mountains, rocky peaks, dark and sinister-looking defiles, with forest-laden valleys and sparkling brooks and waterfalls. But the wild flowers had almost disappeared, and grass was nowhere to be seen. We had reached the country into which, in early spring, vast herds of sheep had been driven for pasture. The flowers had gone; where the grass should have been, nothing was to be seen but the gray soil.

In the flat country immediately surrounding the southern end of the Sierras, a large number of French immigrants, mostly from the Basque provinces of the Pyrenees, have settled. They own little or no land, few even have citizenship, but they raise sheep and drive their herds over the country, especially in the mountains, in search of

ON THE MC CLOUD RIVER.

free grazing for their support. As soon as the grass crops out in the spring they leave the plains for the foothills, and before summer is over have consumed all the grass to be found in the meadows or on the most difficult pleateaux of this mountainous region. In fact, they are a band of grazing tramps. One man, three or four sheep-dogs, a small burro packed with provisions, and about fifteen hundred sheep usually make up the outfit. In bands of about this size, it is said, some three hundred thousand sheep are driven into this locality annually. A considerable portion of this region, more especially the northern section of it, is held by the Government as a forest reserve, and within it is situated the Sequoia National Park, instituted for the preservation of the big trees, of which there are something over two hundred thousand on the reservation. A troop of cavalry is maintained for the protection of the forests, as well as to keep the herders off, but the soldiers reach the mountains about the Fourth of July, going in from the north, while the herders entering the mountains from the south have occupied the country since April, and little remains in the way of fodder for those who come after them. Fortunately, an enterprising Frenchman has rented Trout Meadows, where he has saved the grazing, and charges a small amount per head for animals stopping there. Mr. Funston, who owns the meadows in the Kern River Cañon, has preserved them as well, but he is a lover of his kind, and you are welcome to feed there as long as you please for nothing. Were it not for these two oases in this desert of fodder, animals could not be maintained on the Kern, without packing in grain.

We had descended to a lower altitude. All the snow had disappeared, and, though the air was fresh and bracing, it had reached a comfortable temperature. After spending a refreshing night at Soda Springs, an early start was made for Trout Meadows. Our course took us down the watershed of the Little Kern, though rarely in sight of the stream. While the country is not so rough, neither is it so picturesque as that of the previous day, and we reached our destination early in the afternoon.

The route into the Kern River Cañon from Trout Meadows was a much more difficult journey than I had imagined. Its early stages were fairly easy, but when we reached the divide the old rugged characteristics appeared, and the legs of our horses were "all of a tremble" after reaching the top of some of those many rocky climbs, where we halted that they might regain their wind. Through this winding trail every moment was enjoyable, for at every turn some new and entrancing scene was discovered, and when the great river came into view, flowing with rapid pace through a cañon that vies with Yosemite in loveliness, we could but stop and gaze. This, however, did not get us to camp, so on we went, struggling up the rough ascents and down the loose and treacherous rocks, crossing shady brooks in sheltered defiles, tak-

NEVADA AND VERNAL FALLS FROM GLACIER POINT

ing a peep here and there at phantom-like waterfalls issuing from the sides of mountains miles away, until we reached a spot on the river most commonly used as a camp. After looking over the ground, the conclusion was reached that the grazing was not sufficiently good to hold our animals in safety.

Leaving the Hockett Trail at this point, where it crosses the river by a ford and leads to the southeast, we pushed on to Funston's Meadows, some six miles further up-stream. On the route we passed two beautiful lakes, made by a big landslide which fell into the river and blocked up sufficient space to form them. Dead trees still stood out of the water in many places, and the huge boulders with broken timber carried down marked a scene of wild confusion in that mighty tumble. Toward the end of our journey the sides of the cañon rise to splendid heights in rough, treeless crags, but the bottom through which the river flows widens out for perhaps a mile along its course, and here one finds Funston's Meadows, with grass in plenty, and as charming a spot as one could wish for a permanent camp. Down by the riverside, in a grove of tamaracks, where a rapid made music, we pitched our tents.

There was still plenty of daylight left in which to go a-fishing. Rods, reels and fly-books came from the packs, and up-stream we went. The Kern for a river in the mountains is a large one, though partaking of all the characteristics of mountain streams, with rapids and pools in profusion. It is fairly high at this season of the year, and carries an immense volume of water considering its altitude. It is without those peculiarities, however, which lead to the growth of exceedingly large trout, by which is meant fish of five to fifteen pounds in weight, a feature which has made the Williamson River of Oregon and the Walker River of Nevada so famous. It carries, however, large numbers of two-pound fish, with an occasional three, four or even five pounder. Quite good enough this for anyone. Then the fish are most beautiful in appearance, far handsomer than the rainbows of the Williamson, which, though yielding to no trout of the Pacific in their rising and fighting qualities, are the plainest of their species.

We had not gone two hundred yards from camp before we commenced taking fish. First, one weighing about a pound, then a little chap of half the size, next a greedy two-pounder rose, and presently another of the same weight. So on we went, until our creels began to pull a bit at the shoulder, when we sat down to have an inspection.

The most interesting feature of the trout of Kern River rests in the fact that it is said to furnish the connecting link between the cutthroat and the rainbow species. Consequently, the first thing to look for was the cutthroat mark, which is a deep scarlet blotch on the half-concealed membrane between the two branches of the lower jaw. In the specimens we caught it was not strikingly developed, though discoverable in all of them. Unfortunately, at this early season the fish were not in high condition. They were dark in color, and over their entire length and breadth profusely covered with spots, much more so than any true trout we had ever before observed. The fish had not as yet recovered from the effect of spawning, which evidently occurs very late in these waters, and their lack of activity upon the rod was a disappointment to the spirit of the angler. Their reputation as fighters, however, is high, and no doubt, later in the year, when they have recovered their full vigor, they will make as merry a struggle for life as any of their kin.

The individuals under observation offered as great a variety of tints as can be found in our Eastern char, and their coloring is certainly beautiful.

Were it not for the faint streak of red down their sides they have little resemblance to any of the other rainbows.

The small scales of the Kern River trout and an indication of the cutthroat mark give him a claim of relationship to the *Salmo mykiss*, while the red streak on the side and the color and profusion of spots connect him with the *Salmo irideus*, and serve to produce a most interesting individuality.

We made our way up-stream, climbing many difficult wind-falls to reach the various pools, and by nightfall had a goodly catch of fish. From their varied appearance and great diversity of color one might imagine they were of a dozen different varieties, but color in trout is often as fantastic as the taste of gentle womankind. We whipped the stream for several days, both above and below our camp, with varied success, taking fish from one-half to three and a half pounds in weight. This largest specimen was a spent male, twenty-two inches long, which in good condition would certainly have tipped the scale at five pounds.

The great curiosity of the region is the golden trout of Whitney Creek, *Salmo irideus agua bonita*, and this we had yet to see. Some four miles below our camp at Funston's, Whitney Creek flows down through a little cañon of its own into the Big Kern, on the opposite side of the stream, and in order to reach it the river must be forded.

Riding down-stream about two miles, a place in the river came in sight which looked favorable to crossing, at least it did to John, and we took to the water. The footing on the bottom proved the correctness of his judgment, and though the current swept us down a considerable distance and the water at times nearly reached the backs of our horses, we landed safely on the other bank. I confess I was glad to get there. A climb of about three thousand feet out of the cañon of the Kern, brought us up again on the old Hockett Trail, which, crossing the river at a ford some distance below, makes its way through the watershed of Whitney Creek to the flatter country around the southern base of Mount Whitney, where Lone Pine is situated. A moderate ride brought us to the top of Whitney Creek Cañon, where we tied up our horses and proceeded to climb down.

Though the cañon is small when compared with the immensities of the region, it has an individuality as well as a beauty quite its own. Its rocky sides are of volcanic formation, generally of a reddish-brown color, in striking contrast with the granite and limestone of the locality, while the timber within it is plentiful and greatly varied. Looking up the stream one sees a succession of waterfalls of various heights, the one which breaks the sky-line at the top making perhaps seventy feet in its descent.

That it is one of the most beautiful spots in this surpassingly attractive country no one would question. But, how any fish can live in this succession of falls, with water surging and flying over rocks everywhere in its precipitous descent, where scarcely a spot larger than an ordinary table-top approaches throughout its entire length anything like stillness, seems a mystery to the beholder. Yet, here is the home of the golden trout.

It was a stiff climb down to the bottom, where we put our rods together, and out of the little eddies soon commenced to lift those golden beauties, in appearance the most remarkable of the *Salmonidæ.*

In color the golden carp, commonly known as gold-fish, is about as ten-carat metal compared with these, their color reaching the deep orange of old and

CAÑON OF WHITNEY CREEK.

pure gold. Their bodies are so smooth as to give the impression they are scaleless. All have the finger-marks so universally shown in young rainbows, and it would seem, if this be the sign, they have discovered the fountain of eternal youth. Scarcely any spots are observable save upon the head, tail, and fins, while even there they are not numerous. In this respect these trout are as immaculate as the sea-river forms or those inhabiting alkali lakes.

This extraordinary appearance led us to an examination of the water in which they live. While the water of the Kern and the brooks flowing into it was as clear as crystal, and excellent for drinking and domestic uses, that of Whitney Creek was of an altogether different character. It was of a milky appearance, with a decidedly hard feeling and alkaline taste. There was nothing in the weather to rile this or other contiguous streams, and the inference is, there must be something within its own bed to produce this notable characteristic. The alkaline water would account for the scarcity of spots upon the fish; and there may be some chemical property in the volcanic rocks through which the stream flows, to produce the extraordinary color they exhibit. In a few instances this golden hue was observed in the trout taken from the Little Kern, but it was confined to a streak upon the belly, and slight indications back of the gills; otherwise the fish were the same as those of the Big Kern.

After fishing a few days more for the sturdier trout of the big river, where they were gaining in strength and rising with far more avidity, we regretfully took our rods apart, stowed away our angling paraphernalia, and prepared to turn our backs upon the improving sport.

The packer was dispatched to round up the animals in the meadows above the camp, and soon we heard their footfalls in a gallop, resounding from up the cañon. Leading the band came the six bronco mules, with ears pricked high and ominous switching of tails. Their long rest and food in plenty had restored to them their amusing little ways.

It required the active exertions of all to catch them and we were obliged to blindfold and lariat, as in the early days, before the packs were adjusted, but, eventually, the cavalcade was in readiness; and as the sun came peeping over the craggy peaks at the head of the cañon, we bade farewell to Funston's and the Big Kern, which had furnished us with so many days of pleasure and of sport.

23
A High Sierra
Circuit on Headwaters
of King's River
(1910)

A HIGH SIERRA CIRCUIT ON HEADWATERS OF KING'S RIVER

By Wm. Conger Morgan.

The stages had rolled away one by one, leaving in their wake a trail of dust not so tenuous but far more persistent than the trail of a meteor. Our little party stood alone in the shadows of Giant Forest, as we were to prolong out outing another fortnight by tramping through the High Sierra at the headwaters of King's River.

In the cool of the morning the descent of the Marble Fork and even the ascent of the other side in the bright sunshine was most invigorating and delightful. We paused to look down the valley to where the cañon walls rose steep, and to note also the gathering storm-clouds which later in the day sprinkled us with fitful showers. Up and across Silliman Creek our trail lay, past Willow and Cahoon Meadows, whose flower-dotted surfaces had been badly ruffled by the packtrain returning from its summer outing with the Sierra Club. Near East Fork we noted a new trail built out to Twin Lakes, which empty into Sugar Loaf Creek, one of the tributaries of Roaring River. Pausing for lunch at J. O. Pass, we met a party coming out from King's River whose members assured us that Glenn Pass, over which we hoped soon to travel, was unquestionably impassable for animals since there was no snow to cover the talus.

The divide between the Kaweah and the King's rivers makes interesting travel. At Profile View the late afternoon shadows had settled in the depths of the distant cañon, but the heights were yet splendidly illuminated. To the right loomed Brewer and its two stalwart guards, King, Gardner, and those other peaks that make the upper King's River unsurpassed in the Sierra. Down the slopes and through Marvin Pass we hurried to Horse Corral on whose broad acres, knee-deep in grass, were grazing a score or two of animals. A cup of hot tea was Mr. Kanawyer's welcome as we dropped into the grass for a few moments' rest, and a camp-fire big as the biggest lighted up the little grove in which we slept that evening.

The next day's journey led us through Summit Meadow and then down on to the floor of the King's. The day was hot. A glaring sun beat against the lofty walls of rock and its reflected heat gave to the gorge the character of a Turkish bath. Scarcely a breath stirred and the river seemed to keep the air at the maximum humidity. Walking was oppressive; everything seemed uninteresting; and the writer recalled vividly his first entrance into Yosemite Valley when, on a similar day he toiled ankle deep through the granite sand below El Capitan and would not have given a copper to have had Bridal Veil Falls in his back-yard forever. But such days pass! The six miles from Cedar Grove to Kanawyer's seemed twenty, but were finally over; and a plunge in the snow-fed water washed away the dust from our faces and the fret from our minds.

We laid over a day to outfit for our round trip into Paradise Valley, up Wood's Creek, over Glenn Pass and down Bubb's Creek. Our first day consisted of a pleasant stroll up the South Fork through the timber and shrubbery that covers the river bottom. We watched the rainbow trout in the crystal water and picked cool, luscious berries from bushes drenched with dew. At Mist Falls we watched for a long lunch-hour the cataract of jewels pouring over the rocks and forming rainbows which framed-in the exquisite picture of Gardner Falls on the opposite wall of the cañon. Then came a scramble for a couple of miles of bad trail over very wicked talus, followed by a leisurely saunter through the wooded meadows of Paradise Valley.

Knowing that the Sierra Club had stocked the creeks of Paradise Valley with Eastern brook trout, we were anticipating the pleasure of beholding these dainty fish within the rim of our frying-pan, so while passing up the valley we kept a sharp look-out for them. But, though the water seemed ideal, we saw no trace of a fish. Snakes there were in this as in the other Paradise, but not a trout of any kind; and although it seemed useless to "go a fishin'" when no fish were to be seen, we dropped our flies into most of the promising water, but neither from riffle nor pool did we get a rise. What has become of the fifteen thousand fish planted here in 1906? Have they worked their way up the stream to the headwaters? We saw nothing of Eastern brook trout up Wood's Creek. Or have they gone down over Mist Falls? Some certainly have, for more than a dozen have been caught about Kanawyer's during 1907 and 1908. It is much to be hoped that most of them may yet be found in the waters of the upper basin.

We made camp that night at the foot of the spur which so conveniently runs out on the floor of the valley, affording a magnificent view of the three cañons radiating from this point: to the north the gorge beneath Muro Blanco, to the east the valley of Wood's Creek looking to Mt. Baxter and Sawmill Pass, to the south at our feet the beautiful Paradise. Our sunset reveries from this bluff were interrupted by the bringing in of a fine buck which furnished us with venison for several days to come.

The ardor of the next day's tramp up Wood's Creek was dampened somewhat by showers and the fear of showers. Our views were confined to the immediate valley, for a pall of cloud rested on the shoulders of the titan peaks—King, Gardner, Rixford, Black, Diamond and Baxter—which guard Rae Lake. We made camp in the rain, but by night-fall a few stars and a faint moon appeared. As we sat about the camp-fire, drying out and enjoying the warmth which worked its way into the marrow of our bones, the flickering shadows brought to our minds thoughts of one who was "sleepin' out an' far" that night somewhere beneath the crests of the same peaks that loomed above us.

A VIEW ALONG THE RIVER, PARADISE VALLEY.

From photograph by W. L. Huber, 1908.

PLATE LI.

RAE LAKE, WITH MOUNT RIXFORD IN THE CENTER OF THE SKYLINE.

From photograph by W. L. Huber, 1908.

The succeeding day was given up to an investigation of the region. Here glaciers have cut down into the solid rock for more than a thousand feet, scooping out a broad basin between the ofttimes steep and well-polished sides. Above the lake rise the ragged remnants of rock which mark the original levels when the ice-king began his carving. The whole spirit of the region is wild, untamed, untameable. The smooth and rounded surfaces of Fin Dome serve by contrast to emphasize the sharp and rugged lines of other peaks. Breathing in the air from an elevation two miles above sea-level, one feels the boldness and strength of the mountains in each bone and muscle and longs to climb each peak and gaze out far and wide from this crest-ridge of the continent. But for another day the climbs; to-day the limited look-out and such as may be gained while circling the lake with fishing rod in hand.

And such fishing! From the rocks we could see them, the hungry monsters that inhabit the depths of Rae Lake, coming up to the surface occasionally for the sun-loving insects. A cast of the fly, a swirl of water, a tightening of the line as the angered fish feels the sting of the barb, a mad rush and then—well, we didn't lose either rod or reel, but all else went in the first experience of more than one of our party. When later, new leaders and tested lines had been reinforced by greater care and caution, several beauties were successfully landed and record catches established by all.

It is a well-known fact that when newly planted in waters furnishing an abundant food supply, trout grow to enormous size. After a dozen or twenty years, when offspring "compounded annually" cause a struggle for existence, the size of the fish diminish and all grow to about one weight. In many lakes of the Sierra the second stage has been reached, notably so in Bullfrog Lake, where the fish run remarkably even and about ten inches long. In 1901 fish were first planted in Rae Lake. They are now plentiful and very large. The heaviest caught by any of us was something under four pounds. A "six-pounder" was reported taken by a man whom we met coming down Wood's Creek.

In "Our National Parks," John Muir speaks of the headwaters of King's River as being particularly liable to mid-summer thunder showers. If any of us, as the result of experience elsewhere in the mountains, felt disposed to question this statement, our doubts were entirely set at rest; for during ten days every afternoon brought rain in larger or smaller quantities. While at Rae Lake we were treated to a Class A thunder storm. For more than two hours rain fell in torrents, lightning flashed and thunder rolled through those mountain wilds until it seemed as though the foundations of the earth must be giving way beneath our feet and we might expect the crags to topple above our heads any moment.

Our experience would suggest the advisability of being provided with some rain-proof garment when starting for a trip into this region. A jacket of waterproof silk, reaching below the hips or even to the knees, would be light, could be rolled tightly into a small bundle and would be very serviceable as a protection against cold as well as water.

On the following morning we set out early to conquer Glenn Pass. The trail indicated on the government maps crosses Rae Lake where the long neck of land runs out into the water so suggestively. Our examination of this route on the previous day suggested a possible soaking for men and animals, an indication which we have since learned was fully borne out by the experience of another party* which did cross at this place. We crossed the lake at the narrows, half a mile further to the north, and found it a much better ford.

Turning south we picked our way along the lake shore, gaining elevation as opportunity offered, until we struck the Glenn Pass trail running west. This leads over rough talus lying at a sharp angle. After crossing the chain of lakes lying in the basin of a little cirque, the trail starts

*Sierra Club Bulletin, Vol. VII, No. 1, p. 22.

right up a steep talus pile of large rock for the 12,000-foot level. This rise of 800 feet can be made easily by foot-folk, but it looks difficult for laden animals, and the trail is very bad. In order to avoid any danger from falling rocks, most of the party made the ascent before the packtrain started. Imagine our surprise, then, to see them appear on the sky line in less than an hour after leaving the lakes!

From the pass the government maps indicate a trail running westward to Charlotte Creek. Five hundred feet below the pass to the south side lies a little lake, or rather two lakes, which empty into Lake Charlotte two miles below. One of these lakes is not shown on the government map and doubtless was well muffled in ice and snow when the survey was made. Between the pass and the lakes an enormous fan extends. Forsaking the trail, we plunged straight down hill to the lake and followed down its outlet without difficulty, saving half the distance and all of the "very bad going"* which we have since learned is to be experienced in attempting to follow the indicated trail.

We did not stop at Lake Charlotte, although it is one of the most beautiful mountain lakes and is filled with fish, but enjoyed it only while skirting its shores on our way to Bullfrog Lake, where we camped. Pictures of this region usually consist of white snow and white sky, separated by a very ragged line of black rock. The exceptionally light snowfall of the year 1908 showed us the true Bullfrog without its mantle of white. On the one hand the rounded, comparatively gentle slopes of Rixford, on the other the perpendicular ramparts of the Kearsarge Pinnacles; before us the lake, skirted by the trail leading over Kearsarge Pass, probably the oldest gateway across the Sierra Nevada. We laid over here for a day, and while some of us spent the time fishing and idling among the beautiful Kearsarge lakes, others climbed up to look over the brim of the cup in which we found ourselves.

Starting from the level of the lake, about 10,500 feet, we ascended the peak to the northwest of Bullfrog which,,

---

*Sierra Club Bulletin. loc. cit.

rising something over 12,000 feet, looks down upon the little lakes toward which we had plunged on the day before. Following along the ragged rock of the ridge we scaled the pinnacle above and to the east of Glenn Pass, then scrambled to the top of Rixford, crossed over to Gould and rested upon its fantastic summit. From here we descended on the eastern side of the divide to linger for a few moments about Heart Lake, then crossed back over Kearsarge Pass on the old trail.

Much of the sky was overcast with black storm-clouds and sunshine alternated with rain, producing most weird and beautiful cloud effects. Though by no means as high as many another peak, Rixford, set in the center of what is one of the most ragged sections of the country, offers to the mountaineer an unsurpassed spectacle. Half a mile below our feet lay Rae Lake appareled most exquisitely in purple and green. Above the glacier-swept valley, the mountains lift their heads in defiance to the storms. To the east lies the long sweep of Owens Valley. To the south are Bullfrog and the Kearsarge lakes. Above them is the sharp arête of the Kearsarge Pinnacles and University Peak, the white patches of snow emphasizing by contrast the extreme blackness of the storm-drenched rocks. On the horizon, piercing the sky-line with their sharp and angular crowns, stands that unsurpassed cluster of peaks which, radiating from Central Peak, includes Bradley, Keith, Junction, Stanford, Deerhorn and the spurs of the two Videttes. To the west, the gentler valleys of Bubb's Creek and Charlotte Lake. To the northwest, between Mt. Gardner and Fin Dome, the Sixty Lake Basin, thickly studded with emerald tarns. In five hours we traveled as many miles and never set foot below 12,000 feet. Nameless peaks by the score loomed about us on every side. The most vivid impressions of the whole outing came from this day in the clouds in the region of Rixford and Gould.

Next day we moved down Bubb's Creek to Junction Meadow, about a mile below East Creek, where we

LITTLE LAKE, BELOW GLENN PASS.
From photograph by W. L. Huber, 1908.

PLATE LIII.

LOOKING UP EAST CREEK TOWARD MOUNT BREWER.

From photograph by W. L. Huber, 1908.

camped in a beautiful cluster of huge pines. Passing through the poplars that grow in profusion along the bed of the stream, we noted the work of avalanches which occurred in this region in 1906. The trees were broken and twisted and torn in an amazing way. Whole sections were laid as flat as wheat in the swathe. Many trees had been broken half off and laid prostrate. Some of these had received sufficient sap from the shreds of bark connecting the stump with the top, to remain alive, and now, accustomed to short rations, were green again, turning their heads once more to the sky. So badly was the timber down that for considerable stretches a trail had to be cut out with axes.

A side-trip up to East Lake and Lake Reflection occupied the next day. The air was so clear that the summit of Brewer seemed within a short hour's walk, yet five hours would probably have been much nearer the truth.

In the morning we returned to Kanawyer's and the next day started on the trip out of the cañon, spending a night at Cedar Grove and another at Bearskin Meadow. The dash and zest for the trail were laid aside at the Grant Grove of Big Trees, and resting in the shadow of a giant sequoia, for an hour or two we allowed the peace and quiet of the Sabbath morn to steal into our hearts. Two nights and the intervening day we rested at Sequoia Lake, near Millwood, enjoying most thoroughly our long swims in the warm water.

And although the embers of the last camp-fire are dead, the glow in the heart kindles anew as the twilight hour creeps over us with its subtle spell calling forth the spirit of reminiscence. Again we feel the bracing air of the mountain-side laden with the fragrance of balsam and fir. Once more the song of birds mingles with the whispering of the pines and the murmur of the brook. We start afresh on the dewy trail; we climb the heights; we seek the noon-day shade; and then, as purple shadows gather on the western slopes, return to camp and friends and—fall asleep.

24
Sea
Fishing Off
San Clemente
(1897)

24
Sea
Fishing Off
San Clemente
(1897)

SEA-FISHING OFF SAN CLEMENTE.

By Stuart-Menteth Beard.

LOWLY the constant, steady whirr and clank of the engine had sent me off to sleep while the stars had been shining, and my comfortable bed in the deck-lashed boat on the bow of the yacht had been rising and falling with the rhythm of the long Pacific swell. But now sleep had become a crime. The stars had faded ; night had left us ; and as I looked over the gunwale of my boat-bed, I saw the disk of the sun looming gloriously above the horizon. The ocean was calm and the air clear, with every promise of a beautiful day ; and the stanch little *Fleet Wing*, her tapering topmasts far above my head all a-quiver from the jar of the screw, was going like a race-horse, while our wake unwound, ribbon-like, for hundreds of yards toward Santa Catalina far astern.

The captain had the tiller. Grouped around him stood the doctor, Beau Brummel, and the captain's friend ; and their animated gestures, but more especially such interjected fragments as, "Took a forty-pound yellowtail there," "Mesquite Harbor," and the like, plainly indicated to me the subject of discussion, our destination. And thus reminded, I rolled over on my elbow and took a long look at our promised land.

As I lay admiring the rugged, cañon-scarred sides of San Clemente, the Cabrillo's island of 1542, a shout of "There she blows !" brought me to a sitting posture. The captain pointed toward a huge, dark object, possibly a thousand feet away, above which there floated something resembling a tiny cloud of steam. "A sulphur-bottom," replied the captain's friend. "Look; he's got company, too." And as whale number one disappeared with a gentle flourish of caudal and a great oily roll of his broad back, four more big fellows broke the surface and greeted our ears with their peculiar and characteristic "puff." It was a grand sight.

"Albacore!" The word burst from me. There they were, hundreds of them; the water alive with the jumping school, dead ahead. "Out with the handlines. We've got to have bait." We had been disappointed that morning at starting, our promised liberal supply of fresh sardines or smelts from the Avalon seine fishermen having completely failed us. Some bait we had, but it was salt; here was the chance for an unlimited quantity, at any rate for "chumming."

While one of the others steered, the captain speedily uncoiled his handlines. These were white, the size of an ordinary lead-pencil, and some two hundred and fifty feet in length. To the eyes of the man of light tackle, they did indeed look formidable—but they have their uses.

"Harry," cried the captain as he paid out a few yards, "look at those new jigs you made for me. They are beauties." He was speaking to Harry Elms, the best and surest guide in Avalon, who seated in the stern-sheets of his boat, the *Otter*, was towing behind the yacht. Harry nodded, and leaned over to watch critically the action of the bone jigs, as they played in the water alongside the boat. They darted from side to side without whirling, thus closely imitating a wounded fish. They seemed perfection. And yet, "Wait a minute before you let out," he called; "I can better that one." Saying this he rolled up his sleeves, seized one of the jigs, and after giving its brass wire a swift, sure turn, threw it overboard once more. "It'll act better now, and you'll have one on there in not over a minute; see if you don't." "The time is too short, Harry," interrupted the doctor, just to plague him; "I bet on the other one, anyhow." "I never bet, doctor, but you are wrong. Look at 'em!" and he pointed ahead at the approaching school.

The captain lost no time in paying out his lines, and arranging a two-foot slack-knot in each, to give warning of a strike. The albacore were feeding at the surface, as is their custom, and their long winglike fins flashed in the sunlight as they repeatedly threw themselves completely out of water in pursuit of the tiny kingfish, their prey. On we went at full speed, right into the midst of the school. The doctor took out his watch, and standing near Harry's pet line, provokingly called out the waning seconds of that prophet's minute. "Forty," said he; "forty-five," and he glanced with a smile at the still dangling loop of the slack-knot; "fifty, fifty-five, fifty-eight—you are going to"— "Win!" shouted Harry. And the loop vanished, the line rose with a jerk, tense as a fiddle-string, and six voices yelled as one, "Slow up, Shorty!"

That abbreviated ruler of oil and dynamo was all ready; he knew his business. The engine dropped to half-speed instantly; the yacht's way slackened; the tightly drawn line cut downward through the water as the strong fish made his first deep dive; and then began a steady, slow strain, force against speed, courage and swiftness, as he was brought unwillingly in. Up and down, right and left he dashed, like all his kind bleeding profusely and staining the water a deep crimson, and with now and then a showing of powerful side-fins as the pressure forced him to the surface. Closer and closer he was dragged, fighting constantly, until he lay splashing helplessly, with fins in air, just astern of the *Otter*.

"All ready; take him in now, Harry." Not quite yet, however; for at that moment both long fins caught the water together, and in spite of his loss of blood and the speed with which he was being towed along, his last gallant rush carried him well under the yacht's counter. "Look out for the screw!" "Put her ahead, Shorty!" several of us exclaimed. The yacht sprang forward for fifty feet or so at a quicker rate; the now exhausted fish, safely out of danger, once more dropped astern and this time came to the surface within reach of the ready gaff. "Applecore!" triumphantly from Harry; and one lightning movement transferred our capture from ocean to the *Otter's* bottom-board, against which his tail immediately began the curious "albacore tattoo."

So much for one, a thirty-pounder; and a minute later we had another on the opposite line. Thus in quick succession we continued to catch them, until at length, with our stock of bait assured, we drew in toward the island; whereupon, the school abandoned us. Clemente's frowning walls now towered far above our heads; and avoiding the great kelp rafts, home of myriad fish, which extended for many rods off shore, we coasted southeast for several miles, and finally dropped anchor at Mesquite Harbor, our objective point. We lost no time in getting the camp outfit ashore and pitching the tent; and within an hour, six of the party were ready for fishing. So the captain took his boat, and accompanied by Beau Brummel and the captain's friend, started for a favorite and somewhat distant ground. The doctor and myself, with Harry Elms to chum for us, elected to try a spot of pleasant recollection near the yacht, where on a former visit three of us in six hours, using fresh sardines, had taken nearly one thousand and eighty pounds of fish, especially yellowtail.

If one stands looking seaward from the beach of this tiniest of bights, Mesquite Harbor, its safety as an anchorage as well as its insignificance is manifest. The ocean has here eaten its way into the bluff and formed an almost landlocked, crescent-shaped basin, considerably less than a hundred yards across. To the left is a rocky point, and in direct line therewith and sharply defined, there extends for many hundreds of feet out to sea a huge kelp bed, which serves as an efficient breakwater.

The *Fleet Wing*, protected by this and by the sheer walls of rock to the right, rode safely at anchor in the center of the harbor and within a short distance of the shore. Just outside of her, but nearer to the body of kelp on the left, we took up our position, Harry securing the *Otter* by means of a "float-anchor," from which we could let go readily when it became necessary. His object now was to chum or draw the fish around us, especially from the neighborhood of the kelp. This Pacific seaweed is peculiar. Yellow as gold, and apparently possessing the characteristic attraction thereof, it is the terror of the angler. For it rises from a huge parent stalk, often nineteen fathoms beneath the surface, spreads itself out on every side, a dense and tenacious mass, and affords a sure retreat for which the hook-troubled fish invariably flees.

While the doctor and I were busy getting our tackle in order, Harry took an albacore, and deftly cutting it up, threw the small pieces of greasy flesh overboard in every direction. They sank slowly through that marvelously clear water, the oil spreading itself abroad, and soon the fish began to gather in numbers to the feast. First the trim, swift little smelts, a great school, came dashing out from the protecting kelp and eagerly seized morsels of the bait. And as the smelts vanished like a puff of smoke before the vanguard of the bass, also from the kelp, we struck together and quickly boated a brace of three-pounders. Then indeed the fun grew fast and furious.

Every cast was rewarded; a novice would have caught fish in this charmed spot. If a bait succeeded in sinking through that waiting stratum of rockbass, a short, sharp jerk on the line and a strike in return invariably initiated "trouble" with a whitefish. These brave fighters deceived us once or twice, for our nerves were tingling; and when the reel gave an unusually pronounced cry, and the rod doubled up under the strain of a ten-pounder, it was hard not to disregard still-fishing etiquette by crying out unnecessarily, "Cast off, Harry. Yellowtail!"

Harry had been alternately chumming and stowing away fish as they came aboard. His pleasure in our success was manifest, and when there came a sudden lull in the sport, I saw him look over the side as he muttered half to himself, "There must be a jewfish around." At this moment the doctor hooked an unmistakable yellowtail; for we had seen him as he bit. Away he went for the kelp. Harry cast off immediately from the anchor-float, seized the oars, and admonishing the doctor, "Stop him or you'll lose him," rowed gently toward clear water. The fish, a possible eighteen-pounder, was game, but the doctor brought him out of danger cleverly and had him killed in about nine minutes, while we were still near our anchorage. And now occurred a singular thing.

The yellowtail had begun to "circle," sure sign that the fight was almost over. Ten feet away he swam, his side toward us, and his great crescent tail, late so full of power, now feeble and moving faintly, as it just served to keep him beyond the gaff. I had my scales in my hand,

GAFFING A JEWFISH.

ready to weigh him; and I was just on the point of saying, "Well done, doctor," when Harry, who had been looking intently over the side, shouted with startling earnestness, "Look out! Reel, reel! Bring him in!" And well might he shout. The doctor gave the butt to the yellowtail unhesitatingly, reeling rapidly; the fish yielded to the strain and came toward us; Harry rose eagerly, kneeled on the gunwale, and stretched out his gaff to receive him—but all too late. Something vast, something of gigantic strength it seemed, resembling nothing so much as a great fresh-water black-bass, rose shadowlike from the bottom far below. Then, with fins erect, eyes gleaming, and with huge mouth all agape, he rushed at the weary yellowtail, engulfed him as a bass does a minnow, deluged Harry with a single parting sweep of his mighty tail, and was gone ere we had had time to twice draw breath. "So much for a Piscatorial Israelite," said I, as the doctor sadly drew in his now empty hook, while Harry laughingly wiped the salt water out of his eyes and looked curiously at his gaff. "I came near losing this also," remarked that foolish fellow, "or, at any rate, taking a sudden swim." As he spoke he raised the steel point. Trans-

fixed thereon we saw a single black-bordered, big scale. *He had tried to gaff a live jewfish!*

That was practically the end of our morning's sport. Had we been provided with fresh smelts or sardines we should have done better. But, as it was, when we picked up our float again, we found that the tide had turned, and either that or the unseen presence of the jewfish—for which, being ambitious, we tried industriously—had caused an unfavorable change in the fishing. We caught a few more whitefish and bass, and saw numbers of large yellowtail, but they refused our albacore baits. So, finally, when the captain drew alongside and we learned that the three hand-lines had dismally beaten the rods, we were more than ready to go aboard the yacht for dinner.

The afternoon was spent in much the same way, with a fair run of luck in the shape of several yellowtail and plenty of bass; but it was not until after supper that the real adventure of the trip took place. This was as follows:

Harry had rowed Beau Brummel and myself out to the anchorage of the morning, and in company with the rest of the party, who were near by, we had begun the final fishing for the day. We were all late, having been slow in going in for supper; but we hoped for at least a few good yellowtails during this favorable last hour before dark. The place had been so thoroughly chummed that fish must be there, we reasoned; and so we worked accordingly. So lavish had we been with the chum that bait was beginning to run short; but when Beau Brummel got a savage strike and Harry quickly let go to avoid the two anchor-ropes, we felt encouraged, thinking it had not been wasted. We did not need to go far, however. That skilled boatman gave one keen and suspicious glance at the peculiarly acting hand-line—of which he is a past master—as he seated himself again; then drawing in his oars as though he scented trouble in the near future, he said one word resignedly, "Shark." That told the story. Thereupon Beau Brummel did not waste time; he drew the beauty in by main strength.

Up he came, lashing the water, rolling himself in the line, snapping right and left— as ugly a seventy pounds of sandpaper hide, long fins and cruel teeth as one could find. Harry hates sharks and he took chances with this one, in that he did not wait to have him tired out. And how he did slaughter him. He grabbed a long-handled knife and the gaff, jerked the

THE "FLEET WING" GOING LIKE A RACEHORSE.

brute's head out of water and upside down against the boat's gunwale, and dodging a furious snap aimed at his thigh, he stabbed right and left until the water was red and the shark had ceased to struggle.

The other boat greeted our prize with shouts of derision, especially the doctor, but his enjoyment was short-lived. He had one himself in less than a minute. The captain closely followed suit, and then began a regular shark carnival. Every body caught sharks and hooked sharks, and expensive yellowtail hooks were bitten off at an amazing rate. I had lost four; the sun had set; the bait was all gone, and I was thoroughly disgusted.

"Toss me that albacore head, Harry; I want the eye. Here's for one more," I said, "my last, and without any wire on my hook either." I took the great eye, larger than that of an ox, and passing the hook's point through the cushion of fat at the back, I brought it out in the center of the cornea and dropped it overboard. It sank out of sight into the now darkening water, and as I paid out the necessary forty feet of line, I waited, expecting to see my hook nipped off as usual.

The light was rapidly failing; we could barely see our rods. Suddenly my tip began to bend; then it straightened once more. "They havn't gone yet. Look," and as I spoke, the line tightened, the rod curved, and I struck firm and strong. The fight was on.

The rod-angler becomes accustomed to certain methods in landing large fish, such as yellowtail, from a boat. I was sitting between the other two, facing the stern, in my accustomed seat, a tarpaulin-covered box of tackle belonging to Harry. Consequently, as soon as I had thus hooked the fish, from force of habit and without having to think at all, my rod dropped into my favorite position when meeting a rush:

butt under right thigh, right thumb on spool of reel, left thumb in leather brake-strap, and left knee supporting rod ; I was ready.

The fish started like a shark, heavy and lifeless. As Harry cast off I gave the butt sharply ; I was convinced that that was what I had, and I wanted to bring him up immediately before he could cut the light fifteen-thread Cutty-hunk line and get my hook. But for all that I accomplished, I might just as well have tried to lift a house with my rod. It did wake him up somewhat, it is true ; for the click gave a sharp snarl, and the rod curved for the moment, until the tip was almost under water.

"What have you got there, anyhow?" called the captain. "A big shark, I think," replied Harry. "And he'll cut the line in less than a minute," I added. But I was wrong ; the line continued to hold, much to our surprise, and, of course, I was going to fight him just as long as it did.

"Play him gently," suggested Harry. "We must get him away from here." The harbor was much too small for anything like this ; the yacht's anchor-chain too dangerously near ; the kelp too easy of access. We wanted open water, even if we could not have light. For indeed, by now, the darkness was upon us ; I was managing the fish simply by knowing my rod and by "feel." We therefore began coaxing him out toward the open, and he seemed not unwilling to go. I was beginning to understand, too, that if this were a shark, it was most emphatically a large one, and foul-hooked probably, or the line certainly would have gone long since.

"Now give it to him," cried Harry at length, when we were well out of the harbor ; "let's see what he is ; wake him up!" And I did.

On my reel, finest and most powerful of multipliers, I carried a thousand feet of line ; my striped-bass rod was a marvel of pliant strength ; in a word, my tackle was of the best, and yet I needed every one of these advantages in the contest which now ensued. There is as much difference in individual fish as there is in men ; they do not all fight equally well. But this fellow, a professional pugilist without doubt, easily outclassed all the members of his tribe that I myself have conquered, or that I have seen others conquer ; he was terrific.

Thus far he had been more or less passive, merely swimming slowly out to sea as we desired him to do. But when I brought the pressure to bear on him— Heavens, what next! The reel gave a loud, pulsating scream, shrill and continuous ; the good rod buckled until the very varnish must have cracked as I gave him the full power of the arc ; and the line melted from under my thumbs as if it were never going to stop. I had awakened him. From that time on, it was a continual give and take. He seemed to have the strength of a bull and the disposition of a demon. If by nice management we succeeded in retrieving a hundred feet of line, the reel shrieked immediately, he was off like a shot, and that and three hundred feet more probably had to be patiently gathered in. And how dark it was, too. Yet Harry was readiness itself at the oars. The boat seemed instinct with life, and turned, or went ahead, or backed as the case demanded ; how he did it I don't know, for I myself could see little or nothing.

Beau Brummel, vastly interested and very patient, had cheered me with kindly words of encouragement from time to time ; and now he raised his voice in a loud shout, "A lantern! Bring us a lantern!" From somewhere, a long way off in the darkness, came a faint reply, "All right. We are coming."

This was good news. Since the line had held so well thus far, I began to have some faint hopes of killing this strong creature, whatever he might prove to be. Therefore, when that "bright spark of hope" drew nearer, and the two boats began to exchange greetings, I felt decidedly encouraged. They ran alongside of us for an instant and Harry stood up and passed back the lantern—truly a dim affair but nevertheless *a light*—to Beau Brummel. My eyes were completely dazzled, as is always the result under such circumstances, and for a little the lantern's rays confused me beyond measure.

In that same short interval, my game antagonist hastened to make one of his peculiarly erratic rushes. Away like lightning he went for a few yards on the port side, then stopped, turned, shot toward the surface, and going with equal speed, passed under us to starboard. By a great effort I kept a tight line throughout ; but therein lay the danger. Harry had not yet regained his oars; therefore the boat was not under control. In a second the powerful fish had my rod at a perilous angle. "Down with your head!" I shouted. Almost before I knew it, I was on my feet, my right thumb controlling the spool of the reel, the rod-point deep in the water, and the butt pointing up; I had taken a step forward, kneeled on the vacant seat— for Beau Brummel with ready promptness had anticipated my movement and was out of the way—the rod had been passed around the stern, and the reel was singing merrily as the brave fighter began another hundred yard run.

And so the battle went on without pause. Tireless as ever, that great fish took us farther and farther up the coast and more and more out to sea. The nearly full moon rose from behind a stormy bank of clouds and, thanks to her, but more especially to my comrade in the stern—who shall forever have my gratitude—I could now manage the fish better than formerly. The lantern, held behind a large straw hat, showed me my rod-tip without blinding my eyes, and this, too, during the remainder of that long fight.

Presently a rapid change in our surroundings began to threaten us. Heretofore the ocean had been calm, and the gentle, long swells had caused us neither discomfort nor anxiety. But now a quick puff of air fanned our cheeks and set the lantern-flame to quivering. Again it came, and in a momentary lull when the reel was silent, we heard the far-off murmur of water as the rushing wind swept over it.

"I don't like this," said Harry. "We're going to have a 'woolly,' sure. They usually blow from that direction."

These winds, sudden and strong, beat the water into wool-white foam; hence their name. In this instance the waves rose like magic. In five minutes we were in a bad plight. The *Otter*, most seaworthy of boats, would ordinarily have ridden easily. But she was now well laden, and more than that, we were fighting a large fish. Consequently, as we turned this way and that in our endeavors to follow the brute, we were more or less at the mercy of the waves. The water came in by the bucketful; we began to be in danger.

"Harry" I said at length, and I think my voice broke a little, for this seemed bitterly hard after all our long struggle, "it's no use. We've got to cut him."

"Not yet. I can keep her going a little while longer. The wind will help us, too, if you can *only* turn him. *Fight him!*" And at him I went anew, while the waves splashed over my knees and the boat pitched and rolled. It required the nicest handling of the rod not to get a dead strain somewhere and part the tackle. But by the most careful management, by keeping my left foot like a ready spring to raise or depress the knee that supported the rod, I averted disaster frequently and even forced the fighting somewhat. More than that, the creature was turned at last; and now he began to swim more slowly, with occasional furious, short rushes, in the direction in which we supposed the yacht to lie.

We gladly followed, far more at our ease, since we were not running before the wind; but not for a moment did I cease to worry and tire our game. And thus for a mile and a half he went, traveling quickly, the moon illuminating the tumbling wave-crests, and faintly outlining the cliffs ashore, by which we marked our progress.

"The harbor is our only chance," said Harry, after a long silence. "We've got to have still water to gaff that fellow. I don't know what you've got, anyhow. It's not a shark, that is certain."

"Does he give up any?" inquired Beau Brummel.

We had arrived opposite the entrance to the harbor; that was indicated by the yacht's lantern, more than a quarter of a mile away. Could we make it? "Yes, he is nearly dead," I answered. "Turn, Harry; let's try to make the harbor." The boat swung round; immediately we were broadside to the waves once more. We were in trouble again.

The fish had lately become an almost lifeless weight, and his strength seemed just sufficient to keep him a few feet beneath the surface and out of sight of our straining eyes. Now it became doubly a matter of patience and skill to bring him along. The rod, tested, could, at the outside, pull only four pounds and a quarter; this I knew. Therefore, the effort necessary to steadily draw him through that rough water, while the waves rolled and tossed us from side to side, was trying in the extreme to both nerve and muscle.

Many times Harry had to pause, or even back up, so that I could recover the line which the mere inertia of that heavy body and the lurching of the boat had caused to be jerked from the reel. Those were twenty very long minutes. But, finally, a welcoming hail from the other boat—which had left us because of the storm—told us that we were drawing near to the great kelp raft protecting the anchorage.

I was glad beyond expression. A few minutes later, too, they cheered us heartily as we left the rough water behind and entered the harbor. Thereupon, a kindly impulse turned them into efficient pilots. They located the possible danger on every side of us. It was, "Keep to the left, Harry; here's a bunch of floating kelp;" or, "Look out for the yacht's anchor-chain over there;" and a dozen more suggestions, with queries as to what we thought we had. Harry said little; he was anxious. He was keeping mid-channel, between the yacht on one side and the kelp on the other, and slowly directing our course toward the very heart of the little bight. Here was a fine sand bottom, well removed from any kelp—an ideal place in which to boat a big fish.

All seemed to be going well. The two lanterns—the one steady and half hidden behind the hat, the other restlessly swinging now here, now there, as the doctor alternately tried to help us find our way, or sought to satisfy his curiosity—filled the little inclosure with the weird shadows of men, of boats, and of the yacht. Here nature was at peace; without sounded the roar of the wind and the dashing of the waves which we had so recently endured and which we had now escaped. Nearer and nearer we came. The water began to grow shallower. The excitement became intense. Now our curiosity was to be satisfied.

For three hours and thirty-four minutes had we given battle to this creature that we had never seen. During all that time the line, cutting down into that black water to meet the mystery there, had constantly kept the rod in a beautiful arc. At last he appeared to be exhausted. Momentarily, we expected to see him rise to the top. Harry, with spear at hand, watched for an opportunity, ready to drop his oars and strike. The lanterns searched the waters to find him.

Suddenly he appeared to awaken, to realize his danger. It was a final effort, truly, but we could not know it. Part of his old-time viciousness returned to him. Straight for the kelp he dashed, and my heart was in my mouth as by an extreme effort I finally checked him, not ten feet from his goal. He paused, swung round, and this time he was away toward the yacht. I felt disheartened. I was desperate. How long was this to continue? Were we going to lose him here at the very last? Was all this work to count for nothing?

In a flash came a mental picture of the anchor-chain and its fatal possibilities. I was nearly worn out myself, nearly fainting with the fatigue of a long day and an exhausting fight; every nerve was trembling. In a last effort I pressed down hard on the sole-leather brake, stopping the reel entirely, surged back on the rod, and gave him the butt. For a fraction of a second he went on; then paused, wavered, turned, and as the grayish-white oval of a broad belly suddenly rolled above the surface, together we all exclaimed, "Why, it's a jewfish!" The fight was over.

"And he's the gamest jewfish, too, I have ever heard of, and I've seen a lot of them," cried the captain a moment later from the deck of the yacht, as Harry made certain of the now dying gladiator by using his spear. "Get a rope through his gills and we'll hoist him right aboard. How far did he take you, anyhow, Harry?" "Four miles and over." "A great fighter, truly." "Look," said Harry, taking my hook from a well-worn hole in the jaw of the fish, "he couldn't reach the line to fray it through in that position."

And then, congratulation and kindly comment from everyone. As for myself, I had little to say. It was past midnight; my rod had become a weariness to sorely aching fingers; I was too tired to even pull off my completely worn-out thumb-stall—but I was happy. I had taken, in fair fight, a very game if moderate-sized jewfish—he weighed two hundred pounds twenty-four hours later; I had had magnificent sport; and, best of all, I had earned honestly and fairly the record of the Pacific coast for the largest rod-killed fish.

Painted for OUTING by Henry B. Snell.

THE END OF A THREE-HOUR'S FIGHT.

25
Bluefishing
Off
Fire Island
(1897)

25
Bluefishing
Off
Fire Island
(1897)

BLUEFISHING OFF FIRE ISLAND.

By Frederic De Garis.

"THE blues are here! They ketched some big fish outside, yesterday—an' they're bitin' like savages," the captain added, stirred for the moment from his usual taciturnity. "Shall we try it ag'in?"

The captain and I have trolled and chummed for bluefish, with results that have fluctuated on our angler's scales from "fisherman's luck," to very fair catches—but with all our fishing we never had experienced one of those starred days so often told about; those rosy periods when the fisherman runs into such schools of fish that he becomes exhausted in handling them.

Now, for me, one of the beauties of bluefishing has been the everlasting hope that some day, *when everything was just right,* one, just one day of such phenomenal luck might be mine. With each succeeding summer, when the roving hordes of blues come up the coast, leaving detachments in the Great South Bay and Fire Island waters, the fingers itch to battle with these fighters. With every season there lurks the idea that the day we want has surely arrived. It always ends the same way—the captain and I "try it ag'in."

With a sixteen-mile sail to Fire Island, in the face of an adverse wind, we decided to start that same morning, anchor for the night near the "Surf Hotel" and be ready to run outside before daylight the next morning. Provisions, ice, and the various articles that go toward insuring a comfortable trip, were stowed on board, with dispatch. Our guns and some snipe-stool were not forgotten—because, should the annual flight of shore-birds take place while we were on the bay, there were numerous fine shooting-points where we were going.

Trips with the captain always have a peculiar charm. In the first place, the captain is all right. Next, his "yacht" is a good-sized, steady working-boat—a sloop-rigged sharpie, with speed. Again, the winter cabin, with bunks and stove, guarantees restful sleep and hot meals. It is a cozy sort of a place in a stiff sou'-west breeze, even on a summer's night.

The captain and I constituted the officers and crew, cooks and roustabouts of our craft. When everything was shipshape and snug the crew was ordered to trim up the fishing-tackle, and the crew did so.

291

Painted for OUTING by J. L. Weston.

OFF TO THE FISHING GROUNDS.

We use lines of heavy, braided linen —two hundred and fifty yards in each line. On the end we bend a leader of piano-wire, two or three feet long; to this the squid—of lead, pine, pearl or bone — with its ferocious hook, is attached.

"Wind's veerin'," exclaimed the captain, while I was busy with the lines. "Yes—yes. We'll hit her up soon—and no durn long tacks neither."

So it proved. We drove along so fast that five o'clock found us close to the inlet. Several boats had passed us on their way home—all reporting fish. The captain was quietly reading the signs.

"Way them gulls is actin' — think there's goin' to be fun out there. S'pose we keep right on goin'? We c'n hustle back without sayin' a word, if we don't like it."

I agreed to this, although it was rather unusual for a boat to go out for blues at that late hour. But it was tempting. From all quarters the sea-gulls were flying toward one spot on the ocean, where numbers of them were hovering about, making the shrillest cries. They were more excited than I had ever seen them. This could have only one meaning. Some smaller fish, menhaden, young mackerel or other prey were being slaughtered by a big school of blues in such quantities that there was an abundance of food for the hungry gulls.

Down the channel we sped—through the inlet and over the bar. A very respectable sea tossed us a little as we worked our way out—but that is part of the game sometimes.

Soon we pass the leaning spar-buoy that marks the reef.

The blues and the gulls are making a great commotion in sea and air, further inshore. They are covering waters too shallow for our sloop to venture into, so, chafing under the restraint, we are compelled to wait and watch the rolling breakers where the massacre is being enacted. In places, the waters boil and seethe with the lightning-like movements of the fish. Shining menhaden, pursued by remorseless blues, make wild leaps into the air; the shore is fringed with a line of glistening, sparkling fish that have leaped out upon the land in their despair.

With lines overboard, we cruise around, hoping that the next whim of the school will take it into decent depths.

"There they go, out beyond the bell-buoy!" The captain brings the sloop about and heads for the free water.

Bar! Shoal bar! the incessant bell warns us as we approach. *Bar! Bar near!* it tolls as we slip by, with a clang from its very soul that seems a protest against its monotonous duty.

The screeching gulls resent our coming and are loath to give up the field. The captain takes his ranges with shore objects and buoys, and we pay out line until the squids are far astern. Ours is the only boat on the ground. The sun will soon dip below the horizon. In the tumbling seas that brush us aside with their increasing force, we shall have lively work.

Suddenly, the line is nearly dragged out of my hands—it would have been if past experience had not taught me what to expect when the bluefish strike. Give him a little line in his first rush— you cannot budge him until the first tug is eased. Ah! there he breaks—a grand chap! Now keep the line coming— keep it coming—don't let him get a foot of slack if you can prevent it. Don't let him try the tricks of his tribe—he will either shake the hook out of his mouth, or, turning back on the line, if he can, above the wire, will by accident or design, cut it in a jiffy with his shark-like teeth. How he fights and shakes himself—and what a splendid battle it is with that long line out! You fairly hear the water hiss behind him as he cleaves it in those mighty side-rushes; but my legs are braced apart to meet the pitching of the sloop, while my hands gather in the singing line as fast as I can haul and drop it between my feet. Don't jerk, or you'll tear the hook out of his mouth! Keep ahead of him!

Oh, but this is glorious sport! There he is—his silvery sides scintillating in the green depths. Now, look out; lift him clear of the boat, or you may lose him if he once gets a purchase against the side with that powerful tail.

A good throw and a lucky one—just in time—the hook pulled out as he struck the fish-tub. Rat-a-plat-plat, he beats a merry tattoo as he flops around trying to jump out of the tub.

"An eight-pounder, I'll bet," is the captain's verdict. "We'll just fish that hole for fair."

We barely have the lines straightened after coming about, when the captain yells : "Hold on ! Take the wheel ! I've struck suthin' big ! Keep a straight-away course !"

I spring astride the wheel-box, with my line trailing out over my shoulder, and bring the sloop up in the wind.

"Jee-rusalem !" the captain shouts. "Luff her ! luff her a little ! We're goin' so fast I can't manage him. Spanish mack'rel, by cracky——"

" Hurry up, cap'n ; I've got another," I respond, as I feel the line sagging down on my shoulder.

"Comin'—so's this fish." He swings in a smashing big mackerel, a prize, and grasps the wheel.

My fish is yet hooked, but before I can get to work the line slacks ; there is a feeling of goneness in it as it tautens—the fish has broken loose. Never mind, there are others.

We make short runs back and forth over that charmed space, and just as surely as we get abreast of the bell-buoy we strike fish. Every minute is full of excitement—every nerve tingles under the intense strain ! Often we each hook a blue at the same moment ; then it is turn and turn about at the wheel, kicking and plunging as the heavy cross-seas hammer our bows to windward.

"We'd better make tracks for inside waters," said the captain, at last, and he almost sighed. The fish were as plentiful as ever, but it was fast growing dark. There are safer places at night than the shoals and sand-bars off Fire Island. The skipper of the big steamer thrashing out to the southeast evidently had the same thoughts, judging from the columns of smoke pouring out of the funnels.

Big combers were curling up over the bar. When we were in the middle of it, the grandfather of all waves rushed in, seemed to suck up the shoal water, and, if the giant had not given us a tremendous push, the sloop would have crashed down upon the gleaming white sand. As it was, we scraped the outer edge of the bar, but no damage was done our strong hull.

"Gettin' purty dusty out here. Yes—yes. Time we was mosein'," commented the captain.

Safely inside, the count showed twenty-three blues and the Spanish mackerel ; all notably big fish. We had not loaded the sloop, but we had done remarkably well, and had been on the jump every second of our limited time. My long-wished-for day *had* arrived, and, as the captain prophesied, there had been "fun out there."

We anchored near one of the islands in the upper channel, and iced the fish —all save one ; at ten o'clock we were eating that one with a relish which comes only with a broiled bluefish right out of the water, after a longish fast and a fair share of hard work.

26
The Best
of the
Bass
(1902)

26
The Best
of the
Bass
(1902)

THE BEST OF THE BASS

By EDWYN SANDYS

I GOT home about midnight—or some-where in that latitude. Grounds and house alike were one black mystery, but where the gate was supposed to be a dull white spot showed. I knew it would be there. Others of the family might pass in and out; they might leave early and return late, yet see nothing, but when I came home it was different. Just as sure as I neared that gate, no matter how long after midnight, just so sure was I to see that whitish-looking spot. Cold and damp made no difference—it would be there.

"Your wretched, neglected wife!" says my lady reader.

No'm, not the same. My wife hasn't got ribs like a spiral spring, nor four legs. I am referring to a D-o-g! D'ye s'pose I'd want my wife out there keepin'-tabs-and-gettin'-cold-feet and—but I digress. Not until I was within a step of him did the grand fellow move; then he slowly rose upon his hind feet and placed two dappled paws upon my breast, while his shapely muzzle sought my lowered face. For a moment my hand played with the silky softness of his thin ear, then as he regret-fully slid down I asked, "Want to go, old fellow; want to go?"

Did he want to go! Such caperings, fool pranks, and fancy steps! Did he actually understand? Aye, right well. In his strange dog wisdom he knew that within four hours something would be doing, **and** just so sure as I went up for that much sleep, just so sure would he sleep on the door mat instead of in his kennel, and be lying there quivering and shuddering, pointer fashion, in an ecstasy of anticipation when I stole down 'twixt the dawn and the day.

How could he know? Don't ask me. I cannot explain, though I have my theories. Good dogs know much more than most people imagine. Educated dogs, that are made close comrades, especially those which have been owned, trained, and handled from puppyhood to their prime by only one man, get to know that man, his moods, and methods as few people know each other. This dog could read my face and interpret every shading of the voice. I could make his ears drop with one glance of mock severity, or set him bounding with a mirthful chuckle.

As usual, I was sitting up and rubbing my eyes before the clock gave its first warning skir-r! It's funny about that clock. If I didn't wind and set it, I'd oversleep till any old time; but after solemnly fixing the infernal machine, the appointed hour will find me staring at it, face to face, with exactly spare seconds enough for me to grab the thing, stuff it under the bedclothes, and sit on it to smother its tirade, lest others be needlessly disturbed.

It was a perfect morning. Through the wide open window crept the rare breath of summer, a-tremble with bird music and rich with the sweetness of garden, orchard, and pine below. One glance at the flaming east told the story, then a plunge into cold water, a scramble into flannel shirt and knickers, a fumble with the other things, and I stole downstairs. I say stole down advisedly. This getting down was ticklish business. On my feet were lacrosse shoes —partly for comfort and silence, but chiefly for the sake of the canoe they would shortly be in. One door was hard to pass. One hundred times had I essayed to do it, and exactly one hundred times had I failed. But the rubber soles would fool her—I was almost past.

"That you, my son?"

"Yep."

"Going to dig that bed for me—so good of you."

"Yep; goin'-to-dig-out-right-now."

"Did you say dig out, or out-to-dig?"

Then I skipped.

Did I dig garden? Sure! I dug about four yards square, where the worms were good and plenty. Then I snatched a breakfast, gave the dog a bite, packed a snack— and fled from the wrath to come! Not until the good canoe had slid well around the first bend did the wicked cease from paddling. Then the pipe was set going and Don and I straightened up and looked at each other. He knew—the villain! But she couldn't get either one of us till night —and she never could hold anything against a fellow for more than three minutes and a half.

For miles the land was level, and the stream lazy. In such a country there could be no swift water, and this one dawdled along with almost no perceptible current. Yet it was no mere trickle of moisture, but a river full eighty yards broad and twenty feet deep. A few miles lower down its banks dwindled to nothingness and the broadening waters drowsed through marshy wastes suggestive of Lincolnshire fens in olden days. But above my starting point the land gradually rose higher and higher till it formed cliffs of rich clay, twenty feet and more high. The windings of the stream were so erratic that in one stretch of sixty miles by an air line the actual distance by water was one hundred and twenty odd miles. Nearly every mile of water was good fishing, but to a lazy canoer the upper reaches, being more wooded, were more attractive. Every one of the innumerable bends presented a picture of a steep, tree-covered bank upon the one hand and opposite a brushy flat of greater or less extent. This was caused by ages of the cutting away of the bank toward which the current happened to set, and a corresponding deposit of silt and rubbish by the slack water opposite. Such an apparent mystery on a lazy stream was naturally explained by the spring freshets. Then the water rose twelve, fifteen, or twenty feet and went raging lakeward; jamming miles of ice which uprooted hundreds of trees and plowed like a glacier into every opposing bank. After the frost was out, the soft, undermined bank slipped here and there, and pitched grand trees, top first, into the stream. And where they fell they lay, perhaps for several seasons, until an unusually heavy flood tore them from their anchorages and flung them, battered and whitening, against some projection lower down, there to await the fiercer mood of an angrier torrent.

Such wrecks occurred at short intervals, and he who knew the river knew what to do at such points. With one tree already wellnigh submerged, and its fellow bending far over it and only awaiting a wind from the proper quarter, or another flood, to complete its fall, the bass found ideal quarters. The submerged tree was a fortress from which dusky freebooters might raid at will. The overhanging tree cast a shadow of velvet darkness, fit screen for piratical deeds, and—well! you know some grubs and larvæ are ridiculously fat and careless and bound to slip from the smooth twig now and then. And young birds, too! It's simply awful the pace infants go these days. A young naked thing with its eyes barely open actually trying to fly! and it comes down through the leaves with a spat-spat—its silly pinkmeaty abortions of wings spread and its wretched little bare legs kicking, and it lands—in the water? Occasionally. Sometimes it lands directly in a bass—and again the bass has to make a rush of a yard or so to save the bird from drowning.

And then again a few feet of overhanging sod break away. Those mice are so silly. They will nest in the eave, as it were, and then they must bore up so as to let down the surface water when the rain is busy. And then the whole affair tumbles in, and they wonder why. The sod makes a splash which no fish could help but hear. Then the earth melts away and leaves a big ball of dry grass which floats and floats and rocks about till some kind-hearted bass takes a bunt at it to find if it needs any assistance. And it loosens up, and a half dozen or more little pink things fall out and go wavering, twisting, and shuddering toward the bottom. And kind Mr. Bass sees how it is—he has babies of his own—and he gathers them in where neither the nasty wet river nor the horrid black mud will ever touch them again.

And then there are the frogs, grasshoppers, and crickets. Let a man, or even an old cow, but move along the bank above and all these three must needs start a-jumping. Nobody's going to touch them, but they will jump, and they never look where they are going. Over the bank—then, of course, plop into ten feet or more of water. And the bass, trying to enjoy a little peace and quiet under his log, has to hustle out and save life. Things, even very foolish things, cannot be suffered to drown right at one's door. And the crayfish! Perfectly safe under the sunken stuff, if they only would stop there. But no! Out they go, backward at that! never looking where they are going—flip-flip-flip—in a crazy rush; actually jostling decent well-mannered bass; even striking them in the face in their vulgar impetuosity. What can a poor bass do with folk like these? No rest for him! His life is one long struggle to teach his neighbors sense. But through all his toil and patient, uncomplaining effort he at least has some satisfaction—his missionary work is strangely effective. Devil a one of them all—be it bird, beast, or bug, ever requires a second course of his potent pedagogy. The man who knows his craft as he should thoroughly understands all these minor points. He knows what the large and small-mouth black bass will take, and why, and when. He knows that the fish seldom, if ever, feed freely before the sun has got well above the trees and that from about seven o'clock till eleven is the best of the morning. Why then the early start, do you say? Oh! well, it enables one to dodge all work around the place, to enjoy the best part of the day on the water, and to secure certain requisite baits. Some half mile from the starting point the canoe halts where a small stream flows into the river. Here is a tiny bay already golden with sunlight, and a trifle up the stream is much waterlogged rubbish. A can and minnow tackle are produced, and while the old dog goes prowling after a possible woodcock I take a dozen plump shiners. The next move is for crayfish. These are found beneath the sunken stuff, but the taking of them is an art known only to the experienced. Fragment after fragment of rotten wood is cautiously raised, and every now and then a "nipper" is exposed. The hand steals toward a victim, which is deftly secured. These lobsters of fresh water bite a bit, or nip, or whatever their pinching process may be termed, but they do no serious damage. Now and then one takes hold along the soft side of a finger, but rarely is the skin broken. A dozen are soon secured, and then the trip proper is resumed.

I now have these baits—worms, minnows, and crayfish, and all are good at their proper time. Bass are very capricious feeders. Some days they will greedily take what they may have refused the previous day. A knowledge of this, and of what baits may prove tempting, is invaluable. One of the deadliest of baits is a big white grub found in rotten logs and sod. The larvæ of the humble bee and wasp, very young mice, grasshoppers, and small frogs are all tempting upon occasions. The fry of the catfish, too, is in some waters a reliable bait. Upon the stream in question I preferred crayfish, white grubs, minnows, and worms, in order as mentioned, and I always endeavored to have at least three of these. Now and then the fly tackle was called into play, but it was always unreliable.

The places where bass are sure to be include all types of submerged trees and snags, well shaded spots under overhanging trees and banks, and mats of watergrasses and lily pads. In the stream in question a fish is seldom taken from open water above a clean bottom. In swift streams having rocky bottoms the conditions would be entirely different, but I am speaking of one stream, not of bass fishing in general. The advantage of a thorough knowledge of the water is of the greatest importance. For instance, a mile up stream a big stump just shows above the surface. The current sets in there, and the spot is good for one fish, or two, if one doesn't make too much row over the first. Two bends above, on the opposite side, a big basswood hangs over—two or three fish there. A half mile farther right in midstream, and apparently open water, is a fine spot. Not a visible vestige of a snag or shelter of any sort, but twenty feet below an old tree lies on the bottom. Above that again is a small bed of weeds, At first glance it is no good, but there used to be a brickyard above, and the stumps of two piles broken off below water yet remain. About these is a lot of broken brick, all unseen, and it is a good place. And so it goes from point to point for fully ten miles. Almost invariably the fish lie on that side to which the current sets. The veteran knows this and changes from side to side of the stream as its course changes. A novice probably would select a pleasantly shaded, baylike spot on the

wrong side and fish there for hours, taking drum, catfish, dogfish, mullet, or sunfish, but at the most, only an occasional, wandering bass. The black fellows lie in the current, with noses upstream, because they are strong pirates and they know the running water will bring prizes their way. When a bass is taken at some unlikely looking spot, that spot should be kept in mind. There probably is some unsuspected shelter below which even the tackle may not find. In any event, a good lair for one bass is apt to prove equally good for another later on.

But to return to the canoe. A clay cliff throws a shadow upon deep water which might repay a trial. The cliff is bored with rows of black holes, and a cloud of sandmartens wheels on tireless wings. The soft muttering of dainty throats fills the air as the gentle little communists weave to and fro. The rod is shipped up and a plump shiner selected. The point of the hook is passed in at the mouth, out behind the gill-cover, and under a strap of skin behind the back fin. I use the bait so, because I have found it works well. Of course a bass swallows a minnow head first, but I don't want him to swallow it. That means a mangled bait and more or less trouble to recover the hook. The number of minnows is limited, therefore I want, if possible, to make one minnow kill two fish. When a bass grabs my minnow, I strike smartly and take chances. A fish so hooked forces the minnow up the gimp and out of the way, and so may preserve it for another turn. The third cast provokes a faint strike, not at all like the aggressive dash of the bass. A turn of the wrist makes a swift commotion of waters, followed by a peculiar steady strain. At the first purr of the reel the dog cocks his ears and eyes the wavering silk with keen interest. The rod goes steadily backward and foot after foot of silk rises from the water. Then the gimp, and then a long, olive green form, trim as a torpedo boat. Two long, snipy jaws, a lean bony head, a glowing eye, and—flick! The mangled minnow follows the slack line into the sunlight as the fish vanishes with a marvelous sweep. A gar, and where two or three of this kind are gathered together is no place for a decent fisherman with only a dozen minnows. The gar is a curious but utterly useless fellow, a loafer and a provoker of scaly language withal. Seldom will a hook hold in his bony jaw, and should it hold he affords but brief play. When recovering your hook his mouth feels like a barb wire fence with a cat-brier hanging to it, so wise folk only shoot, spear, or heave rocks at him. The dog is disgusted—he knows all about gars and the "talk" which they incite. He also has a shrewd idea of what is coming.

The paddle strokes are firmer and a purl of music whispers from the bow. We are nearing, hey! old dog, and never have we rounded this bend without a thrill of genuine pleasure. Look at it and say can this be the North? For once, and for nearly a mile the river runs straight, a giant corridor of green, high-roofed with flawless turquoise. The liquid floor narrows away like a mighty lancehead pointing to a glory of dazzling sunshine, and the soft-draped walls receding in perspective true, lower and soften to a golden haze of the distant open. Huge velvet shadows hang like windless banners; each tree seems rooted to a tree inverted, and over all is flung a living mesh of vine and creeper, bloom and bud and burnished leaf. It must be fairyland! From tents of green, sound silver pipings and tinkles of tiny revels. A pause, and the flutter of foliage surely is the clapping of wee hands. It is fairyland! Yon sun-dried pebble by the water's rim takes flight and curves away on trembling pinions which shake sweet music from them as they go. A sandpiper? Nonsense! Hark!—Tick-turr!-tick-tick-turr! A fairy clock hid midst those leaves, its ruby pendulum swinging in plain view? Absurd! The clock has stopped, and yonder the pendulum, a dart of fire winged with ebon smoke. 'Twas the tanager swinging on a living cord. That rattle a snare drum? See where the quick ring broadens. 'Twas Alcyon striking the silver galleons of the dreamy sea of this our land of Spain. Can grief be here? A sobbing, sweet and low, a hopeless misery floating from a tender breast too rudely torn; a widowed mother peering through the pane, racked by raw memories and the joys of others which she may not share. O! actor dove, we know thy sweet deceit. Thou sham of arms bereft; thou widow of one dry eye, with t'other roving for a comforter; thou male with female voice and gentle wile. Aye! pat thy fat side with a crafty wing and

bow thy shapely head in mock humility—all's fair in love. But that same wing can whistle to arrow flight, and strike full lustily should swearing trooper squirrel thrust his bold nose above the twig-wove platform where two white eggs lie. A rasping jar—a cymbal lightly clashed; a form of steel and bronze o'erlaid on jet, a heavy flight, a gleam of an eye like a diamond flashing from its kindred coal; a tail awry which seems to drag like an idle oar—the grackle. From an unseen meadow above floats a sound as though some sprite had stolen a string of gold and silver bells and was madly racing hither and thither from keen pursuit. But let us leave the bobolinks, their neighbors the larks and sparrows; the orioles, thrushes, catbirds, warblers, finches, climbers, and what not. The air is vibrant with their voices, but we are not a-birding to-day. Here is the spot, it is the hour, and Don and I are the people.

A log—
Half sunk in the slimy wave,
 Rots slowly away in its living grave,
And the green moss creeps o'er its dull decay
 Hiding the moldering dust away
Like the hand that plants o'er the tomb a
  flower
 Or the ivy that mantles the fallen tower.

Don is all silent expectancy as the canoe is drawn up and the tackle adjusted. Next to actual shooting he loves fishing, and he sits with wrinkled forehead in such patience as he can muster. I decide to try minnow first, and while I am arranging the bait there comes a sudden splash as though from somewhere a brick had fallen. Out of the tail of one eye I see a shiner skip over the surface from the immediate vicinity of a heavy swirl. Good enough! It's minnow he's after, so the bait is right anyhow. In a moment my minnow is out far beyond the ripple and coming in with a wavering motion produced by slightly shaking the rod. But the cast is a blank. Another, too, fails, so I study for a moment. That fish is under that log is the decision; so the minnow is cast perilously near the shelter. Another failure. At this moment I notice something. Looking from the dense shadow toward the sunlit outer water, I mark an unsuspected snag some yards to one side. Mebbe he's there, I think, as the minnow again goes out. Still no result. Now comes the advantage of a variety of baits. A crayfish is impaled, and at once there's a sharp strike and the rod

"A gleam of bronzy mail, a bristle of angry fins."

Drawing by Martin Justice.

arches. A moment's feel of things proves that whatever is on the hook it is no black bass. A brief struggle, and a squarebuilt rock bass comes to the surface. Don is dancing with excitement, but a word sends him down. His time is not yet. The big-eyed captive is promptly killed, then the pipe is lit, the water meanwhile getting a few moment's rest—always a wise plan. As I hook a crayfish by passing the barb through the mouth and out through the tail (which gives the natural curve and insures the bait going downward tail first; as it should) the same bait serves twice, it having slipped up the gimp out of the way. But it fails. Another bait is wanted, so I climb the bank and find a half-rotten log. To heave this over is the work of a moment, and as the fragments fall apart three or four fat white grubs are revealed. I impale one of these and cast it to the edge of the shadowed water. Whether the bait is actually pitched into a bass' mouth is problematical. It certainly looks that way. A strike so savage as to make me fairly jump, and the fight is on. This is the best of the bass! With a rush he goes for his lair, and with a twitch I plant the steel and feel it take hold. A second's breathless pause, and then the royal fellow realizes what has happened. Whiz! and he is away like an arrow, while the silk hums through the guides, and the reel voices a startled shriek. Well I know there is no fray anywhere, so gradually the check is put on. Tense as wire stands the silken tether, while the rod arches till it seems as if something surely must give way. Five anxious seconds—then whish! up he comes fairly into the sunshine. A gleam of bronzy mail, a bristle of angry fins, a patter of falling drops, and plunk!—he has gone. But not far. Wise man never yanked at fish like this, so instinctively I have eased him down and away upon his second run. A fierce zigzagging, a worrying, backward pulling, a vain effort to bore to the log below, another dash, then up he comes again.

Have you seen him—the length and the breadth and the *mad* of him—and *is* this business, or is it not better than pawing coin or thumbing bills? The dog is a picture. He stands trembling with excitement, his blazing eyes following every movement. As the fish leaps he stiffens in every fibre; as it falls back his muscles slacken to the fear that the prize is lost. Heart and soul he is with his master in a game he cannot fathom, and he can barely contain himself. A leap and a grab might

help, but he has not been called upon, so he suffers and whimpers and dances in an agony of uncertainty. But the headlong scrimmage slackens to an obstinate resistance. "You've asked for it, you beauty; now you'll get it," I mutter as I shake him up. One minute of doubt, and slowly, proudly, like the king he is, he yields, and a white ray flashes from his snowy belly.

A low cluck electrifies the dog—'tis a well understood signal. With a visible effort he restrains his impulse to rush, and steadily marches to the water and in up to his shoulders. Cautiously the fish is towed within his reach, and wise from a previous experience with fins, he grips it by the belly and carefully bears it ashore. Is he proud? Does he understand? Look at him! He has waited long for this, the crowning moment, and as the released victim flip-flaps in the grass, he dances an accompaniment of quadrupedal joy unmeasured. Then he shakes himself, takes a roll, and comes twisting and mincing, with deep, gusty breaths which say as plainly as words, "We caught that bass!"

There were other battles and other triumphs—five more in all—but let the one suffice. Great fish they were, too; as they tugged their cord which bound them in a shadowed nook. But only a half dozen? Aye! Why more? Two for friends, three for home, and room for one inside. A tiny fire mid the green, a lounge and a' smoke on a scented couch, a search of a thicket for information of interest to man and dog, then hey, for the chase of the paling west into the evening land. Let the fragrant shadows creep, who cares? The bow is singing a foamy lullaby, the craft is skimming o'er liquid gold, the white puffs swiftly float astern; 'tis well, my lords.

But your feet are wet!—who cares? Your breeches are all green from grass and moss! What of it—it's what they're for—who cares? But you haven't done a stroke of work to-day! Who cares? But there's the garden patch not dug yet! Who cares? That big fantailed bass weighs plump five pounds—goldfish wouldn't buy forgiveness like that fellow! Do you understand?

27
On and
In the
Ottowa
(1895)

ON AND IN THE OTTAWA.

By W. Thomson.

THE Ottawa river, at Point Fortune, is some five hundred yards wide, and for the most part very deep. Immediately above the village is the great Carillon dam, near which are many great rocks, some wholly submerged and some rising above the surface. In the eddies among these rocks numbers of pike, black bass, pike-perch, eels, gar-pike, and various other kinds of fishes, including the lordly muskallonge, find congenial haunts. *Esox nobilior*, however, is rarely taken here, he, as a rule, preferring the more placid, weed-fringed waters further down stream and the quiet lagoons and bays. Nevertheless, after spawning time is well past, an occasional monster will make his lair in the lee of one of the huge boulders below the dam; and woe betide the unwary sucker, mullet, big chub or wriggling eel which ventures to invade his domain!

The local angler casts anchor in any selected spot, and still fishes with worms, minnows, frogs, crayfish or any favorite line bait from his boat, using either a rod or handline, as his fancy may dictate.

At one part of the river the water is fifty feet deep, and in it is the most delicious little fish that I know of. It is silvery white in color, formed somewhat like a bass, and runs up to about one pound in weight. I do not know its proper name, but the French *habitans* here call it *poissons blanc* (white fish). It undoubtedly belongs to the herring family, and yet is no more a herring than a bass, being infinitely superior as a pan-fish to either. I know of no other water in Canada where it is taken.

Very early one morning my friend Ned and I caught a pailful of minnows; then took a small flatboat and paddled out to a broad rock which rose several feet above the surface, about one hundred yards from shore. We climbed to the top of the rock and, creeping across it, peered cautiously over its streamward edge. For some little space on that side of the rock the water was smooth as a mirror, singularly clear and about twelve feet deep. Ned drew a piece of dark colored cotton over our heads, and we lay, cheek by jowl, with only foreheads and eyes projecting beyond the angle of the rock. After a moment we could see quite distinctly over a considerable area of the river's bottom—and a most interesting sight it was. Numbers of fishes, of various kinds and sizes, occupied the quiet pool. Some lay motionless among the stones at the bottom; some, with slightly quivering fins, hung at irregular depths, and others swam unceasingly to and fro, as if on patrol. From an adjacent miniature maelstrom erratic visitors flashed ever in and out.

By-and-by a monstrous sturgeon sailed slowly in without exciting the least alarm, and after a turn or two sank to the rocky floor and lay still as a log. But the next moment we observed a frantic skurry among a shoal of well-grown fry. A long, dark streak dashed into their crowded ranks, and a great pike seized one of the luckless youngsters and retreated behind a boulder to gorge the prey at his leisure.

And now occurred a curious thing. A little school of large suckers, or mullets, emerged from the outer depths and swam peacefully along the bottom, feeding as they went on such slugs and snails as lay in their way, when this same pike darted out from cover, and, closing his jaws upon the head of the leading fish—which was probably eighteen inches long and about three pounds in weight, attempted to regain his hiding-place, while three-fourths of the body of the struggling captive still protruded from his mouth. He was not, however, to bear off the prize so easily, for, even as he strained to gulp it down, another and much larger pike shot into the arena and seizing it crosswise, in the middle, savagely tried to wrench it from the hold of the lawful owner. The latter, even if he would, could not relax the grip of his backward-pointing teeth so long as there was a strain in front, and the enraged combatants tugged and tore with furious jerks until, finally, they actually separated the unfortunate sucker into two parts and each of the water-tigers retired with his portion.

During this battle royal, the other fish had darted away, and at its conclusion only the unexcitable sturgeon was to be seen. But as we knew they would soon return, we stepped well back from the edge, put our rods together, bent on salmon gut leaders baited with large minnows, and, keeping always out of sight ourselves, began to fish. When we went in to breakfast at eight o'clock we were almost ashamed to exhibit our catch, for we had seven pike, twelve black bass and nine large pike-perch. However, as we found plenty of people in the village glad to take the surplus off our hands, there was no waste.

That same evening, about an hour before sundown, I went out to the rock again, this time alone, and putting the bait tip on a ten-ounce split bamboo, I tied a spoon and a flight of swivels to the line and began to cast about, keeping the lure at least three feet beneath the surface.

I caught two nice bass and one chunky pike-perch, and then sat down, and in mere idle play kept sinking my spoon to the bottom and letting the automatic reel retrieve it, for a number of times in succession. I was drawing the spoon rapidly toward the surface, when it was taken midway with a heavy surging rush, and then, after a momentary pause, borne straight away into the seething caldron beyond the placid pool.

Now, although this adjacent rough water whirled about in many a mad gyration, the actual current was not so very strong, and I knew that, barring the fouling of some sharp rock, I could, in due time tire out my quarry. Meantime the reel was flying around at a furious rate and nearly forty yards of line had run out before I dared to check my customer at all; then I put on the pressure and in less than thirty feet further turned him about and began to bring him slowly back.

At this moment my host strolled down to the shore and called out: "Hello, T——, what luck?" "Ah, Ned, you're just in time," I replied. "Jump into your skiff and bring the long-handled gaff. It's going to be a job to get this fellow in."

In two minutes my friend was on the rock beside me, and by this time the fish, despite many a sidelong sweep and boring plunge, had been brought within twenty feet of where we stood.

"Look out! Ned, I'm going to make him show up," I cried—and I did so. "By George! it's the great-grand-daddy of all muskallonge," excitedly shouted Ned, as a long, glistening form, with steel-gray back, silvery, black-dotted sides and enormous wide open jaws, floundered slowly to the surface and lay, for a second, quite still.

"It will never do," he continued, "to gaff this fish. I'll paddle around to the other side and knock him properly on the head when you bring him up to me."

I had no time to answer, for just then the fish dashed off into rough water, and my hands were full of business. But the old giant's course was nearly run. I forced the fighting and in less than ten minutes he lay within reach of Ned's hickory club, one heavy blow from which, delivered far back on his monstrous head, completely stunned him. He was lifted into the skiff, and his spine was at once severed. He was in prime condition, and at the house the tape line and scales gave the following record: Length from tip of snout to end of tail, fifty-six and a quarter inches; greatest girth, thirty-two inches; weight, forty pounds five ounces—the largest "musky" taken in the Ottawa that season; one of thirty-eight pounds, captured below St. Andrews by Prof. Robertson, of Montreal, ranking next in size.

One morning, some weeks after the capture of the big fish, I took the scow, and a box of worms, and went to the deep hole to catch a mess of "*poissons blanc.*"

My boat had no regular anchor, but carried, as a substitute, a large stone, tied to a common clothes line. It was no easy task to handle this hundred-pound clumsy makeshift. I had never tried to do it alone, but thought I could

Painted for OUTING by Marc Lucas.

TOO BIG FOR THE GAFF. (*p. 432.*)

manage it: so, when I arrived at the proper place, I took a half-turn of the rope, close to the stone, around my right hand and lifted the ponderous weight high enough to clear the gunwale, intending to lower it slowly to the bottom as the line should pay out gradually. But, unfortunately, in making my half-hitch, that part of the rope nearest the stone overlapped what should have been the upper part of the loop, and when I sought to swing the anchor off, its weight, and my own, caused the boat to careen at a sharp angle, the cord jammed tight on my hand, and I was dragged unceremoniously overboard and down, down, down, down, for what seemed to me about fifteen minutes!

I had presence of mind enough to keep my mouth shut, so that when I finally touched bed-rock, after a journey of, apparently, several miles, I still retained perfect consciousness, and, though suffering horribly from the effort of holding my breath, easily freed myself, and, with a few vigorous kicks, rose to the surface. I had been immersed about a minute, and ten seconds more would have finished me.

Luckily the anchor-rope was not tied to the scow, this being always done after we had payed out sufficient length of it. If it had been so secured, the straining pull of the flat-sided craft would have kept the cord taut, and I should not have been able to disengage my hand. As it was I soon swam to the boat and paddled off homeward—a wiser and very much wetter man.

28
Fall Fishing
for
Lake Trout
(1910)

FALL FISHING FOR LAKE TROUT

by Samuel G. Camp

Illustrated with Photographs by the Author

THE angler for bass or brook trout or, for that matter, anyone, angler, canoeist, or hunter, who elects the fall months for his outing, would do well to include among the possibilities of his trip a try for lake trout. The additions to the general outfit necessary for trolling for "lakers" are not at all bulky or numerous, and where good fishing for lake trout obtains—and this is the case in numerous localities, particularly in Maine, Canada, the Adirondacks, the Berkshires, and many other places identified with the sports of fishing and hunting—the results are such as to render the trouble of selecting and packing the requisite tackle quite inconsiderable; moreover, while of a very special sort, the tackle for lakers is a matter of little expense.

The Great Lake trout, or namaycush trout, *Cristivomer namaycush,* and the muskellunge, *Esox masquinongy,* are the "big game" fishes of the sweet-water angler. Of the two the muskellunge is undoubtedly the better game fish but, unfortunately, far less widely distributed than the lake trout. The muskellunge, also, as a surface fish, that is, for the most part inhabiting the shallow water along shore in the vicinity of the weed beds, may be fished for with more sportsmanlike tackle and methods than are practicable in the case of the namaycush, the latter being essentially a deep-water fish.

Fishing for lakers when done rightly, is far from being poor sport, but the angler to get any appreciable results must know his fish and the way to fish for them. Lake trout fishing is quite unlike any other form of fresh-water angling. Many lakes and ponds containing lake trout in abundance have been fished for years by anglers for bass, pike, or pickerel, without so much as a strike from a laker.

The range of the Great Lake trout

—the name having reference to the Great Lakes and not, as some anglers and angling writers seem to understand it, to the size of the fish—is given by Jordan and Evermann as follows: "The namaycush trout is found in most large lakes from New Brunswick and Maine westward throughout the Great Lakes region and to Vancouver Island, thence northward to Northern Alaska, Hudson Bay, and Labrador. It is known from Henry Lake in Idaho and elsewhere in the headwaters of the Columbia. It is known also from the Fraser River basin, from Vancouver Island, and various places in Alaska."

The lake trout is so highly—and justly—appreciated as a food and game fish that it is now artificially propagated by both Federal and State hatcheries, and the range has accordingly increased far beyond its original limits. Stocking waters with lake trout is usually very successful and few, if any, failures to obtain results are reported. In every case where the stocking is carefully and intelligently done success is almost a matter of course. The lake trout is a hardy fish and its growth is rapid, especially so when planted in lakes not previously having it, since in such waters the food is very abundant.

It is a noteworthy fact that many of the "big trout" stories industriously circulated every year, particularly fish tales from Maine and Canada, are founded upon the more or less authentic and skilful catching of a good-sized namaycush on trolling tackle and not upon the taking of a brook trout, *fontinalis,* on the fly. Of course, in Canadian waters and also down in Maine some very large brook trout are taken by fly fishermen quite frequently, trout running from three to six pounds and—far less frequently—heavier than that.

Anglers who specialize on lake-trout fishing consider a six-pound fish a small one. Anglers who specialize on fly fishing for brook trout do not, it goes without saying, so regard a six-pounder. Consequently if you are a worthy and

READY TO START.   THE NECESSARY TACKLE IS NEITHER COMPLICATED NOR
CUMBERSOME.

hard-working fly-caster with, as yet, a two-pound trout as your record fish, do not be unduly shocked and downhearted when a friend not overskilful in angling affairs writes you from the North Woods that he has captured an "eight-pound trout." In every case where the catch is merely hazily reported as "a trout" it is well to examine the facts before bestowing possibly unearned laurels. In some localities the lake trout is called "togue," and in others it is variously known as "lunge"—very easy to confuse with the muskellunge, "tulade," "laker," "Mackinaw," and "salmon trout." The lake trout should certainly never be called a "salmon trout" for reasons stated in the following paragraph.

What the Lake Trout Is

The lake trout is a charr, not a salmon trout, having the characteristic lack of teeth on the front of the bone in the roof of the mouth, this being the most striking difference in formation between the charr trout and the salmon trout. The lake trout is a charr—a large and coarse one, to be sure, when compared with the more familiar and finer-grained speckled brook trout, but, nevertheless, a charr. If your trout has teeth on both the front and rear of the bone in the roof of the mouth it is a salmon trout; if only on the rear of the roof of the mouth it is a charr.

Occasionally the namaycush attains a very large size, sometimes over one hundred pounds, but thirty pounds may be safely stated as the heaviest fish the angler may hope for. Lake trout weighing between twelve and twenty-five pounds are taken quite commonly where the fishing is ordinarily good, but the average weight of fish taken by anglers is somewhere in the vicinity of eight pounds.

The head and mouth of the lake trout are quite large proportionally, and the head is depressed. To the writer it has always seemed that the rainbow trout, *Salmo irideus,* is the most finely formed in these respects of any of the so-called trout, including both the salmon and charr trout. The tail of the namaycush is deeply forked. The coloration is ordinarily a rather dark gray marked profusely with spots of a lighter shade. The head is marbled, or vermiculated, like the back of the brook trout. Generally speaking, the lake trout is a handsome and well-formed game fish, the larger specimens, as a rule, having length in proportion to depth. A fifteen or sixteen-pound fish will measure thirty-one or thirty-two inches.

It is said that early in the spring the lake trout comes into the shallows for a period of a few days when it may be taken on ordinary light tackle. However this may be—and the writer is inclined to believe that this period must be very short indeed and that in some lakes it does not occur at all—angling for lakers is done almost entirely by deep trolling. Also it is a fact that the early season excursion of the namaycush to the surface waters is quite apt to take place before fishing for them may be done legally.

In lakes where early fishing for lakers on the surface and in the shallows is a condition and not a theory they may be taken on the fly as well as by trolling. Successful surface fishing for lake trout is, however, a pretty rare thing, and it does not seem advisable to discuss it here to any extent. For trolling heavy bass tackle will answer the purpose, and for fly-fishing a fly-rod suited to large stream and bass fly-fishing, say a ten-foot, seven-ounce rod, will be right. On this rod you should use forty yards of size E enameled line on a single-action reel. Flies dressed on Sproat hooks numbers six and eight will be large enough, and good patterns for lake trout are: royal coachman, Parmachene belle, Montreal, and silver doctor.

As above stated, the lake trout is essentially a deep-water fish, habitually seeking the very deepest portions of its habitat. It should be trolled for, therefore, in the deepest parts of the lake, in water from fifty to one hundred feet or over in depth, preferably where the bottom is rocky, and off rocky reefs extending down into deep water. This being the case, it is not difficult to understand why anglers for bass and other fish never strike a namaycush, and also

OFF ROCKY REEFS RUNNING DOWN INTO DEEP WATER ARE LIKELY PLACES
FOR THE "BIG ONES."

why tackle of a very specialized sort must be used in lake-trout fishing.

In mid-summer another good place to "work" for lakers is in the vicinity of spring holes. Almost every lake has its resident fisherman or fishermen—gentlemen of infinite leisure and obscure habits who "live off the lake" by guiding and fishing—and who, for a suitable stipend, will reveal to you the geography of the lake bottom as regards the bars, reefs, spring holes, etc., matters of the utmost importance, for many reasons, to the angler for lake trout.

As for the practical side of deep trolling for lake trout, the matter of tackle, there are two methods in general use. You can use either a hand line with a heavy sinker, or you can employ a copper line—which sinks sufficiently deep by its own weight—on a fairly heavy trolling rod. The former method is distinctly the less sportsmanlike and desirable, the latter method, only recently introduced, makes a much better sport of lake-trout fishing than it has ever

been before. In detail the tackle for these two ways of deep trolling is as follows:

For trolling with the hand line, in which manner it is to be regretted the greater share of lake-trout fishing is still done, you will need a linen line of twenty-one or twenty-four threads at least one hundred and fifty feet in length. The line, it should be stated, must be of rather large caliber in order to prevent its cutting the hands when in use. Cut off eighteen or twenty feet of the line at the end and tie in a triple-action or "three-way" swivel at the point of cutting. To the third swivel tie about twelve feet of line weaker than the main line; this is for the sinker line and it should be weaker than the main line so that if the sinker is fouled when trolling the sinker line will break rather than the main line.

Use a swiveled dipsey sinker of four to eight ounces, according to the depth of the water. The bait and arrangement of hook or hooks will be the same as for use with a metal line and will be discussed in a later paragraph. It is a good plan to tie the sinker to the line in such a manner that when the trout has been led in close to the boat the sinker line may be taken into the boat and the sinker instantly removed from the line by a single pull. Any simple jam-knot will make this possible.

The better method of deep trolling consists in using fifty to one hundred yards of braided copper-wire line on a trolling rod of suitable weight and dimensions. In this way you avoid using the heavy sinker—a thorough spoil-sport —as the weight of the copper line sinks it sufficiently deep, and also the use of the rod, of course, makes the fishing better sport. This line is made of a number of fine strands of copper wire braided over a silk core and should not be confused with the inferior solid copper wire line.

The braided copper line spools well on the reel, does not easily kink, and even if it does, the line is not apt to break at the kink—no one of which things may be said for the ordinary line of solid copper wire. Braided copper line may be had in fifty-yard spools and in two sizes, E and F, of which the smaller, size F, is the best to use in lakes of moderate depth. Size E should be used in very deep waters.

The Right Kind of Reel

A reel is made and sold generally by the tackle dealers particularly adapted to deep trolling with braided copper lines. It is single-action and supplied with a strong and easily manipulated drag; it is made of metal and is of large diameter in order that each revolution of the spindle may take up a good quantity of line. With solid-copper lines large wooden reels, the same as used in the commoner forms of salt-water fishing, are generally used. The metal reel described in this paragraph is far superior to the wooden reel and should by all means be employed for the sort of angling under discussion.

Of course, any reel of large size, either double or quadruple multiplying, may be used. These last, however, if large enough to handle the metal line and of good quality are rather expensive. The single-action metal reel recommended herein is quite inexpensive and also quite good enough for the purpose, as it is taken for granted that deep trolling, in all probability, will be tried only occasionally as a foil to your fly or bait casting.

In the matter of the rod any good trolling rod with a stiff backbone will answer the purpose. Its length may be from seven to eight and a quarter feet, and its material bethabara, noibwood, split bamboo, or steel. The lancewood rod is excepted because this material is apt to be too whippy. The reel seat should be above the handgrasp. The guides of the rod should be fairly large to allow the line to run freely. German silver trumpet guides are the best.

The rod should weigh from eight to nine ounces and, as noted, should have considerable backbone in order to handle without strain the heavy metal line. A "Henshall" casting rod in bethabara or split bamboo will be a very good one for the purpose. If you do not care to make much of an outlay for your lake-trout tackle use a steel rod. A very short bait-casting rod should not be used.

The leader and arrangement of hooks and bait are the same in both methods of deep trolling with either linen or copper lines. Leaders of fine steel wire are used to some extent but it would seem, are hardly necessary. A leader of either double or triple-twisted gut is quite strong enough and is preferable in a good many ways to one of metal. To each end of the leader should be attached a clew-spring swivel for connection with the line and the trolling gang or artificial bait. One or two extra leaders should be carried in a soak box.

For use with the natural minnow regular lake-trout trolling "gangs" are sold by the tackle dealers consisting generally of three burrs or treble hooks and a lip hook on gut. This number of hooks is neither imperative nor sportsmanlike and, at most, it is best to use not more than the lip hook and one treble. The gang should be tied on double gut.

The natural minnow is the very best bait for lake trout, and the minnows should be large, from five to seven inches in length. Brook "shiners," variously known as carp, chub, dace, etc., are the most effective. Sometimes when it is difficult to obtain shiners large enough small suckers are used, but these are not ordinarily very successful. I have even known small brook trout to adapted to lake-trout fishing; the best of these are the ones which do not revolve in the manner of the orthodox spoon but play from side to side when drawn through the water. When deep trolling it is often impracticable to keep the boat moving fast enough to get sufficient spin on the ordinary trolling spoon. The wooden bait-casting minnows and phantoms may also be used with mod-

A REST AT MIDDAY. TROLLING FOR LAKE TROUT IS HARD WORK.

be sacrificed for the purpose of trolling for lakers. It seems hardly necessary to condemn this.

In some localities it is difficult or even impossible to obtain minnows and in that case resort may be had to various artificial baits. These are not as successful with the lake trout as the natural minnow, but, nevertheless, many good fish are taken on them. One of the best artificials for lake trout is known as the Silver Soldier. This is a minnow made of German silver, simply a flat, curved piece of metal cut in minnow shape and fitted with a single hook.

A number of trolling spoons are erate success. The spoons used should be fairly large.

A very necessary item in the kit of the angler for lake trout is a good gaff. The smaller trout, from four to eight pounds, may safely and preferably be landed in a large landing net, but for the larger fish a gaff is practically imperative. The landing net should have a handle at least four feet in length and must be strong throughout. On one lake where the writer trolled for lakers the local anglers used a frog spear (!) in place of a gaff—a four-pronged affair something like a small pitchfork. It was somewhat amusing and rather ex-

THE AVERAGE WEIGHT OF LAKE TROUT TAKEN BY ANGLERS IS IN THE
VICINITY OF EIGHT POUNDS.

citing to listen to the ensuing conversation in case a poorly hooked trout was knocked off the hooks when the fisherman jabbed it with the "grains" and the weapon failed to hold.

If it is desired to mount the fish as a trophy the gaff should not be used. The best alternative in case neither gaff nor net is at hand is to shoot the fish with a .22 pistol or rifle. Another good way to land a large fish without net or gaff is to "beach" it; play the fish until it is exhausted, then row slowly ashore and draw the fish out where the water is quiet and where the beach slopes gradually to the water.

Deep trolling requires one man at the oars or paddle and another to handle the rod. The boat should move slowly in order that the line may run sufficiently deep and its progress should at all times be at an even pace. From time to time, when using the hand line, the angler should "feel bottom" with the sinker to be certain that he is fishing in the proper depth of water.

When a fish is struck it should never be hurried into the boat but played in gradually and carefully. As a usual thing, particularly when a hand line is used, the lake trout will do most of its fighting after being brought within sight of the boat. It will then make swift rushes from side to side or, again, bore steadily down into deep water. At such times line should be freely given, not reeling in again until the fish stops running or sounding.

The namaycush should never be landed until it is thoroughly played to a finish—a lake trout of good size, if prematurely taken into the boat, will make things exceedingly interesting and most unpleasant for the occupants of the craft. The method of deep trolling with wire lines, with certain obvious variations of tackle to suit the occasion, may be used for other game fishes than the namaycush in the summer months when the hot weather has driven them to the deep waters—and used with marked success.

29
Fishing Along the Pecos, New Mexico
(1891)

29
Fishing Along the Pecos, New Mexico (1891)

FISHING ALONG THE PECOS, NEW MEXICO.

BY JOHN CARNIFEX.

NDER the improved conditions of travel the number of persons who go to the Rocky Mountains for trout fishing is constantly increasing. The means of transportation are now so complete, the time and cost of the journey have been reduced to so comparatively low a figure, and the pleasures of the trip are so many and varied that many a man makes an annual excursion to the great white peaks in preference to any other part of the country.

After all, trout fishing means more than merely trout catching. If it were only a matter of obtaining so many to-day and as many more to-morrow, and of eating them meal after meal as a sort of medicinal change of diet, the object certainly would not justify the expenditure of time and money which anglers are willing to put upon it. Fish, even trout, can be got nearer home than New Mexico, and, regarded as a delicacy, can certainly be bought in the market cheaper than they can be caught by the city man.

But trout fishing is an art—who can deny it?—and all art is largely a matter of sentiment. The mere utility of an artistic thing becomes secondary. A small gourd or a match box or any other plain little receptacle will do to hold snuff, but will any snuff taker deny that the indulgence would not be sweeter if his pinch could come from the delicately wrought hollow

of a box made by Benvenuto Cellini?
We can get information from the rough
type work of a newspaper, but how much
more pleasure to read from a large white
page, with clear and graceful type, bound
in the dainty taste of the workmen for
Louis Quatorze? Sings the old hymn:

It is not all of life to live;

and it is not all of fishing to fish.

There is the joy of anticipation, and
for this you must have confidence in the
place you propose to go to. Then there
is the sense of really taking an outing,
and this will not come unless you exchange your accustomed scenes for those
quite new or at least different. There is
the exultation arising from skillful victory
over a worthy antagonist, an exultation
to be felt only where the fish are truly
game. Finally these pleasures must not
cost too much in toil, weariness or discomfort or else they will disappear under
the shadow of these ills. Nothing is
worth more than its value, so that it be-
hooves one to choose in pleasure taking
of every sort, fishing included, the means
which shall bring results within their
proper price. The game should be worth
the candle.

Now, one cannot find anywhere or
everywhere in the Rockies all these conditions. There are hundreds of streams
which contain what young writers are so
fond of calling the speckled beauties; but
those that contain the most trout are almost inaccessible. In the rivers where
they grow largest they are likely to be
dull spirited, tamely submitting to be
dragged out like a varlet sucker, and in
others, where the fish are good, the region is so comfortless or the banks and
bottom are so bad that the angler must
take infinite and vexatious trouble, paying out in toil and patience more than
his creelful is worth after he has obtained it.

One river exists in the Rockies, however, where the angler can go with an assurance of catching plenty of trout, and
gamy ones, and can carry on the fight
without exhausting either his body, his
patience or his purse, and where he will
find his vocation yield a return in health
and amusement and improvement of mind
and muscle quite beyond the pleasure of
successful angling, which itself is enough
to satisfy a reasonable man.

This river is the Pecos, where in its
upper part it escapes from the mountains
of eastern New Mexico and starts on its
course toward the Rio Grande.

South of Pike's Peak the front or
easternmost range of the Rocky Mountains bends somewhat westward and continues southward in that most picturesque
of Colorado's ranges, the Sangre de
Cristo. This again breaks at the border
of New Mexico into several lines of south-
ward-reaching summits—frays out, as it
were, into a fringe of mountains which
gradually sink into the plains of the
lower Rio Grande.

Loftiest of these terminal ranges is
the Glorietta, whose foothills and ter-
races fill northeastern New Mexico and
abound in brooks fed by the snows that
lie all summer upon the central peaks;
springs and rivulets and snow-bank
meltings, escaping through the mossy
bogs and coursing along the cañons,
gathering into torrents that find their
way ever downward and eastward into
a central valley, where they unite to form
one powerful stream. This is the Pecos
River, which takes its name—the Spanish
word for sheep — from the vast pastures
which lie along its lower courses, where
thousands of flocks are herded night and
day by sleepy Mexicans, as they have
been for three centuries past.

Hither, just 350 years ago, came the
armed explorers and traders sent by the
Spanish conquerors of New Mexico to
find what lay in the unknown spaces northward. They discovered valley after valley
filled with a quiet, simple-hearted, indus-
trious people, cultivating extensive and
varied crops, irrigating their fields by an
ingenious system of small canals, and
dwelling in large community houses, serviceable for defense against the nomadic
savages of the plains and governed by
rulers who believed themselves viceroy of
the sun. With these soldiers came Catholic friars, as eager to win souls and lay
up treasures in heaven as their captains
were to accumulate wealth upon earth.
Rejoiced at the discovery of this great
harvest ripe for the church, they first fell
upon their knees; then they fell upon the
people.

Upon this river here, just where it escaped from the green foothills, stood one
of the fortress settlements of these Toltec
frontiersmen, a *pueblo* or "town," as the
Spaniards justly styled it. Others were
back in the hills. It was a point of van-
tage and the Spaniards took possession.
Years passed. Soldiers and priests came

and went. Battles were lost and won. The pueblo was destroyed or fell into ruins, of which only the shapeless heaps remain, but the clergy had built a church out of the enduring adobe, and that queer result of the Spanish domination, the mixed breed Mexican peasant, took possession, raised his scanty, neglected crops, attended his numberless sheep and goats and herded his ponies and long-horned cattle. Life was as calm as the long summer days on these rolling uplands ; the people as bovine and unprogressive as their herds.

Then came the Yankee. As the Spaniard had swept through and over the aborigines three centuries before, so did the American explorers and frontiersmen, reckless and energetic, crowd out of the way the inactive Mexican. He saw with stupid wonder the rule and customs of his ancestors replaced by the politics and enterprise of the North. Mines were opened, great ranches fenced in, cities established, railways hurried athwart his pastures and hotels and trading posts arose beside him, but he only looked and wondered and went on his way. Now the traveler lounging in that acme of civilization, the Pullman car, glides swiftly through his country and sees to-day substantially the same herdsmen and puebloan whom the priests " converted " so long, long ago.

The point of approach to this fishing in the upper Pecos is Rowe, a station on the Atchison, Topeka and Santa Fé Railroad, about half way between Las Vegas and Santa Fé. The train leaving Chicago each evening lands you at Rowe the second afternoon, without change of cars. The season opens June 1.

At Rowe itself there is nothing except a few rude houses, but the station agent, or someone else there, can always supply a carriage and driver to take the visitor over to the Ellis ranch, seven miles distant, which is the stopping place for fishermen ; or, if notice be given them by mail, the people at the Ellis ranch will send a team to meet you.

The road is excellent, allowing the horses to trot nearly all the way, so that the drive seems a short one and gets you to the ranch in good time for supper. It passes close to the old church and pueblo already spoken of, both of which are falling slowly into ruins, yet are regarded by the village Indians of the Rio Grande valley with peculiar veneration. Here, tradition says, Montezuma, the hero-god—

not that earthly Montezuma whom Cortez conquered in Mexico—last reviewed the battalions of his followers before he miraculously disappeared, and it is here he will some day reappear with conquering power. A perpetual fire was kept burning in the pueblo when the Spaniards first went there, and mingling their paganism with the Christianity taught them by the friars this fire was transferred to the church and acquired a sacred significance. It is only a few years since it was allowed to go out, and then only because the Indians who had attended it moved away.

Ellis ranch is prepared to entertain very comfortably parties of fishermen, including their women folk, and its charges are moderate. It stands close to the river and is at the centre of the best section, a length of some ten miles of ideal trout water.

The river comes dashing down cool and clear, between low hills sparsely overgrown with cedars, among which rise many great yellow pines looking as if planted by some ancient landscape gardener. Close along the bank grow thickets of trees and bushes which cast their shade far out, but do not interfere in the slightest with the use of the rod. The bottom is everywhere rocky or gravelly, and the depth is not usually over one's boot tops, though there are deeper places here and there which would require wading trousers if one proposed to walk through them without getting wet.

In the lower part of the ten-mile stretch above Old Pecos the river is so wide that in wading up one naturally makes casts on each hand, right and left. Higher up the torrent grows more narrow and rapid, until finally it becomes too tortuous and overgrown with brush to admit of proper casting ; but even then it may be fished successfully by other methods.

As to the trout, there is no end to them, all the way up to the patriarchal five pounders which are more often heard of than seen. They are locally considered of two varieties, distinguished as "silver" and "salmon," the latter having more red upon their bellies and generally richer in color all over ; they run somewhat larger than the grayer ones, but do not make so good a fight. All, however, are gamy in a high degree—a quality in which the trout of Colorado and Wyoming are deficient. Whether this is due to some special characteristic in the Pecos, or whether, as has been suggested, it is a matter of education, the reader may speculate upon for himself. The "interesting fact remains," as they sing in "Patience," that when you hook a Pecos River trout you have got to play him very nicely if you mean to bring him ashore.

Herein lies the special glory of this river over most Western streams. To haul a trout in hand over hand by main strength, or toss him over your head into the grass, as a girl would a perch, is insulting to the prince of brook fishes. He should be treated like a gentleman, given a fair chance in the tourney, allowed to show his prowess and craft against your skill. This done, when at last you have defeated his most insidious cunning and baffled his fiercest rushing, you would bring him to life and let him go again if you could, for you are not only proud of yourself but proud of him.

The flies recommended for this river, after an experience of several seasons, are these : Royal coachman, cowdung, brown hackle, cock-a-bondhu, Seth Green and professor ; also the English flies hare's ear and yellow, blue-bodied black hackle and orange - bodied red hackle. No. 9 is the proper size of hook.

While anyone may live comfortably at the ranch, the banks of this river afford the most delightful of camping places. The ground is warm and dry, shade and fuel are abundant and the cleanest and purest of water is ever at hand. The tent should be placed well above high water mark, however, for now and then in midsummer terrific thunderstorms burst upon the mountains. An amount of water falls in half an hour that is almost incredible, and it comes pouring down the dry gulches and concentrates into the river with amazing quickness. Only a few moments suffice to turn the limpid cascades into a boiling turmoil of deep, muddy water, which rages and booms in a way you would have thought impossible a few moments before. An hour or two later the supplies of rain have ceased, the flood rapidly subsides, and perhaps before the day is done—certainly by the next morning—the water is pure again and the trout biting as usual.

This valley is 7,000 feet above the sea, but in the latitude of Norfolk. The air therefore has not the chill which would belong to it in a northern region at that height ; yet it is rare and bracing and full of the spirit of life. This is one great advantage in going to the far West, that you find yourself not only amid new scenes and amid grand scenes (for the tall old summits, hoary with never-melting snow, tower up beyond the green hills all along the horizon), but in an atmosphere and climate quite different from what you have been breathing at home. "The high glens and valleys of the Southwest," reports one enthusiastic angler who had been tramping along the Pecos, "are surrounded by a charm peculiarly their own. There is a bright crispness in the air, an intense blueness in the sky, a contrast of colors caused by the mixture of the dark foliage of the pine, the tender green of the cottonwood and the delicate silver of the aspen, which together clothe hill and vale, that belongs to these alone."

For a camping party this region is perfect, and you can move about and explore the numberless tributaries and headwaters of the Pecos, all of which are full of trout, without incumbrance or a wearying distance to walk homeward at night.

The catch varies in New Mexico as in New York according to the expertness of the angler. I recall one man, who knew well both the river and his rod, who told me that on the best day he ever had he caught 125, averaging nearly half a pound each, the largest weighing slightly over two pounds, and in his opinion at present less than seventy-five a day would be considered a poor tally by a scientific angler. This doesn't count the little ones, which one throws back again with an angler's blessing and advice to grow bigger before they let their appetite get the better of them again. A friend of mine from Chicago caught in three successive mornings forty-five, sixty-three and fifty-seven fish, all over half a pound in weight.

This is not the only place in New Mexico or Arizona where one can get trout, but it is probably the best place. There are brooks coming out of these same mountains within a few miles of Santa Fé and of the Las Vegas Hot Springs to which tourists will be able to find their way. The mountains of the mining region in the southwestern part of New Mexico have many tempting streams, but they are rather difficult to get at for the ordinary traveler ; the man going into that region on business or for the fall hunting, which is good down there, is certainly advised to take his rod along. The Atlantic and Pacific line across Northern Arizona passes in the neighborhood of the San Francisco peaks through an excellent fishing district, and a most beautiful country withal for camping and general enjoyment.

There, too, the tourist has the advantage makes an excellent headquarters for fishing and shooting trips. Another convenient and profitable centre in the same region is Williams Station, where the rail-

MY FIRST TWO POUNDER.

of some civilization. The considerable town of Flagstaff, standing in the midst of a picturesque wooded hill country at the foot of the San Francisco range, way company sustains an eating house, which is in effect a hotel capable of taking care of any small party or outfitting them for travel or camping.

30
The Greatest
Trout-Fishing Town
in the World
(1910)

THE OUTING MAGAZINE

VOLUME LVI   JULY, 1910   NUMBER 4

"THE GREATEST TROUT-FISHING TOWN IN THE WORLD"

by C. E. Van Loan

Illustrated with Photographs

SARATOGA—east of the Mississippi the name stands for medicinal springs, roulette wheels, and horse racing. West of the Missouri it means trout. The first time I ever heard anything about Saratoga, Wyoming, was in the smoking compartment of a Pullman on the line of the Union Pacific. The ragged landscape of the "backbone of the Rockies" went sliding by the window and the five men beguiled the time with stories of the old cattle days, the case of Tom Horn, and kindred subjects.

Some tall stories were told, quite evidently for the benefit of the one lone Easterner in the compartment who paid for his drinks with paper money and wore nose glasses. One Wyoming man looked over at another Wyoming man and said:

"Quite a blowout they had over at Saratoga, wasn't it?"

"Yes, indeedy!" said the other. "I hear they had about four thousand pounds of trout for the visitors. Took some of the boys two days to catch that mess."

"I beg your pardon," said the Eastern man. "I *beg* your pardon, but . . . four thousand pounds of . . . *what* did you say?"

"Trout!" said the Wyoming man, heartily. "Fish! Natives! Rainbow! Eastern brook! Greatest trout fishing in the world!"

The Easterner gulped once or twice and fell out of the conversation. It was plain that he regarded the statement as a lie and resented it. It seemed like crowding the truth to me and later in the day I chided the Wyoming man for gilding the lily and thus destroying the market for his pleasant fictions, for the Easterner went back into the observation car and read a newspaper for the rest of the afternoon. The Wyoming man was reproachful.

"But that was *true!*" he said. "Didn't you ever hear about the trout fishing in the North Platte around Saratoga?"

IT'S A COLD DAY WHEN THE TROUT WON'T RISE IN THE NORTH PLATTE.

At Rawlins I met Colonel Anderson, who is a truthful man and a division superintendent. I asked him about the four-thousand-pound catch and he said it was quite true.

"They do it every year," said he.

A few months later I heard more about this Wyoming paradise for the angler. It was at the "Frontier Days" Carnival in Cheyenne, a great out-of-door show which every American should see at least once while it lasts. When the present generation passes away there will be no more Frontier Days, and electric cars are already humming through the streets of Cheyenne. The old West is dead, but its ghost gets out of its grave and steps a few fast heats on Frontier Days.

I was working my way through a crowd in front of the old Interocean Hotel to get a look at Chief Soup Bone in all his warpaint, when a man took me by the lapel of the coat and murmuring "Allow me!" snagged me with a bright yellow streamer about ten inches long and two inches wide on which was inscribed in large black letters "Let's Go Fishing!" At the bottom it said "Saratoga, Wyoming."

"BALDY" LIFTING A BIG ONE OUT OF THE WATER JUST TO SHOW
HE CAN DO IT.

I did not care to advertise the town and I would have removed the sign but for one thing. The Saratoga "booster" had used a trout fly in place of a pin and he had passed the barb of the hook through the lapel. There was no use in saying anything. The man who decorated me was once the manager of a winter hotel in Southern California. They do not make any language which can reach a man in that class.

Then in order to prove to me that the cause was worthy, this abandoned citizen dipped into his inside pocket and brought to light the most amazing collection of photographs, principally of gentlemen in khakis completely surrounded by trout, and it had not been necessary to hold the fish close to the camera either.

"The greatest trout-fishing town in the world!" said this man. "You can catch two-pounders right off the bridge in the middle of the town. No trouble at all. And if you want to go a few miles up or down stream where it isn't fished to any great extent, you can . . ."

Well, you wouldn't believe what he said, and neither did I, but there was no getting away from the photographs. And outside of the fact that the man used to run a hotel for tourists, there really wasn't a thing to be said against him.

I began to think about Saratoga, to dream about it. I cannot pose as an expert fisherman or an authority on fly casting. I know several of these authorities and they are in their glory once a year at Madison Square Garden. When I go fishing, I am for a material rather than an artistic success. I want to *get* something. The idea of a country where two-pound trout hung hungry in every riffle appealed to me.

A few weeks later a Chicago friend wired me at Denver asking about the fishing in the Rocky Mountain region. I wired him the route to Saratoga and three nights later I met him in Cheyenne. It was midnight and he was leaning over the brass fence on the end of the observation car, trying, from this poor position, to see what it was that had once made Cheyenne wild. He was the kind of a man who carries three different toothbrushes, a nail file, and other miscellaneous junk in a pigskin case which is bought in London, and he was and is one of the best fellows that ever looked a manicure lady in the face.

A Town Full of Fishermen

The Saratoga reception committee met us as we stepped off the train. That was a leisurely train. It took the whole morning to make the forty miles and it hesitated every few miles as if alarmed at the coveys of sage chickens which it put up along the track. Saratoga makes a specialty of saying "Welcome to our city," and there is one man in the town who puts on a frock coat every time the sacred duty of hospitality calls him to the depot.

The California hotel man was among those present, fearfully and wonderfully gotten up to resemble the cowpuncher pictures which are made in Metuchen, New Jersey. As the Chicago man stepped ponderously to the platform, California advanced and presented him with a two-pound trout, still limp and sparkling. Chicago was flabbergasted. He stood there for a few seconds, looking down at the fish which he held in his gloved hands—chamois gloves at that, and he never wore them again.

"Why . . . why . . . it's *fresh!*" stuttered Chicago.

"Certainly!" said California, without the quiver of a muscle. "I just stopped on the bridge over there on my way down and dropped a fly on the water for a few seconds and this one came along. . . . Of course, you understand I didn't have time to pick a real good one! Had to take the first fish that showed up."

"Right in the middle of the town!" murmured Chicago.

We were next presented to a tall man, hairless as an ostrich egg and lacking only the eyeglasses to make him the living, breathing reincarnation of that other famous Wyoming citizen, now among the immortals, Bill Nye. The likeness was startling. Chicago and I started to tell the man about it, but he stopped us at once.

"Cheese it!" said he. "I've been trying to live it down for these many years. Why, I saw Nye once on a passenger train down near Laramie and I'm darned if I could see any likeness. I've got the makings of a handsome man, I have!"

This was "Baldy" Sisson. Baldy does not claim the distinction, but I rise to remark that he is the world's champion trout fisherman, give or take fifty pounds. Commie, the tourist hotel man, has reduced trout fishing to a science, but with Baldy it is a fine art.

Saratoga is a town full of trout fishermen and some of them could put Ike Walton in the infant's class, but not one of them can wet a fly with the Hon. Baldy. Talk about Bob Davis and all the other flycasting authorities! Baldy would have them carrying his fish baskets! If the good Izaak had lived in Baldy's time, he would have held the inkwell and Baldy would have written the book.

Give this Wyoming wizard any old kind of a rod at all—he isn't a bit particular whose rod he uses—a dependable reel, and a battered old Jock Scott fly and turn him loose along the reaches of the North Platte and I will back him against the world. He can get more

Photograph by J. E. Stimson, Cheyenne, Wyo.

PLAYING A GOOD ONE WHERE THE WYOMING BUTTES CUT OFF THE VIEW.

fish on one old fly than most men could get with a wagon load of dynamite.

Baldy is the fisherman's chaperon. He is always ready to hook up the bays and go out on a trip up or down the river. He has a wagon in which there is an ice chest and he takes the field equipped like a bartender.

Baldy left us at the hotel.

"I'll be around here in about two hours with a rig," said he.

Chicago, still carrying the two-pound trout, moaned over this great waste of time. Then he went to his room to unpack his kit. I didn't have any kit worth mentioning and so I went for a walk down the business street of the town. Every window contained trout flies. The jeweler told me they had been taking the Silver Doctor to beat the band, while the grocer said that the big imported Royal Coachman was the real Rocquefort, and the undertaker put in a few enthusiastic words for the Jungle Cock.

"Hell!" said the eminent Baldy afterward. "It ain't the fly so much as the way you skitter him along the water!"

Up in the room at the hotel I found Chicago knee deep in imported flies, spinners, silk line, spring reels, rods, waders, and other things. The pride of his bursting heart was an imported rod which must have cost him a small fortune, and it took him almost as much time to get ready for the field as it takes Barnum and Bailey's show to get off the lot with their twenty acres of canvas. Among other things he had a revolver with a nine-inch blue barrel, a light rifle, a camera, and a pair of scales.

As we rolled out of town, Commie regaled us with the history of Saratoga. According to that great man, Saratoga was the original "Medicine Bow" of Wyoming. There is another Medicine Bow now; Owen Wister wrote about it. It is a small town with a big league graveyard, but Commie says that the present Medicine Bow is an impostor.

The Indians called Saratoga "Medicine Bow" because of the great bend which the Platte makes and the hot springs which lie in the angle of that curve. Out of the rocks the hot water bubbles up and flows away to join the icy flood of the Platte. These hot springs are said to be good for rheumatism, chilblains, toothache, sciatica, erysipelas, gout, and housemaid's knee. Commie says so and he owns them.

"Y'see," remarked Commie, "in the old times this used to be a great stamping ground for the plains Injuns. It wasn't so very long ago that they were massacreeing people all up and down this river and over at Fort Steele they wiped out a few companies of regular infantry. When the Injuns got bunged up by staying on the warpath too long, they used to come over here and go up against the springs.

"They built their medicine tepees right over the springs themselves and got up a noble sweat. Only bath they ever took, y'see, and of course they used to feel better . . . and lighter. All right. Then the forty-niners came through this part of the country and they brought a little smallpox along with 'em. That was new stuff for the Injuns and the first thing they knew, they had a fine hospital list, and they didn't know what was the matter.

Too Much " Good Medicine "

"The medicine men went out and telephoned the great spirit and got orders to hike for Medicine Bow and the healing springs. They came in here by the hundreds with their sick and the medicine men built the tepees over the springs and herded the sick bucks into 'em and parboiled 'em for about two or three days. Then one of the Comanche medicine men got a new message from the great spirit. The sick bucks weren't doing very well under the old treatment and this medicine man thought it would be a grand idea to take the patients out and heave 'em into the river and try cold water for a change. Nothing but running ice water around here in the spring, you know.

"There were more good Indians around here that spring than ever before or since. Die? Say, they went bulging into the great hereafter ten abreast! First they were going to kill the medicine men, but one of them got another wireless from the great spirit and sent out a signed statement that a curse had been put on the springs. Just the same as giving out word that the operation and treatment were highly successful, but the patient died. Since then the Injuns haven't come within forty miles of this place. Ain't that so, Baldy?"

"I dunno," said Baldy. "*You* own the springs; I don't."

For an hour we rolled swiftly along the flat country and from time to time wandering bands of sage hens rose almost in front of the horses' feet and went flapping heavily away, Chicago speeding them on their leisurely way with some very fancy revolver practice. To the left the North Platte twisted away down the valley; to the right were the hills, their peaks more than eight thousand feet above the level of the sea. As Baldy remarked, there was no trouble in getting a lungful of air in that country and "it went to the head like dry wine."

"This'll do," said Baldy at last, pulling up in a meadow close to the bank of the river.

"A little four-bit pool for the biggest fish caught?" suggested Commie. *He* had a few minnows hidden away under the seat and regarded a pool as an endowment. Chicago cluttered up half an acre with his unpacking, oozed himself into his waders, and crashed through brush like a hippopotamus. He needed

A FOUR-POUNDER TAKEN FROM THE PLATTE.

nothing but a deep-sea diver's helmet to complete the picture.

Commie dropped down toward a promising looking riffle, flicked a fly once, twice, and then the tip of his rod bobbed and the reel began to whine. About the same time something took my fly and I was so busy losing my first customer that I failed to see Commie land the first fish of the expedition, but the cows two miles away on the hills heard him yell. Shortly afterward Baldy yelped twice and I saw him, a quarter of a mile away on a sandbar, working at his trade. Every time I saw Baldy that day he was either putting a fish into his basket or reeling one in where he could get at him.

Commie landed half a dozen in the first half hour; I got three and then we went to look for Chicago. We found him on the edge of a deep pool, casting with painful accuracy. He held up one finger in warning.

"There's trout in this hole!" he whispered. "They come up and look, but they don't seem hungry. What's the matter with 'em, do you suppose?"

Baldy arrived, serene and calm in his high white collar.

"Won't bite, hey?" said Baldy. "Well! Well!"

Then he swung his arm forward and dropped his disreputable old Jock Scott fly on the surface of the water and it

JUST GO DOWN TO THE WATER'S EDGE AND CAST YOUR FLY OR BAIT.

moved back toward him like a thing of life.

"You got to skitter him some," said Baldy, "or else they won't . . . hullo!"

There was a flash of tarnished silver and white and Baldy's line went taut in the middle of a series of ripples. Chicago groaned.

"Ain't hungry, hey?" said Baldy.

And then, to rub it in, he stood in the same spot and took four nice fish out of that pool, one after the other. The fourth one he hooked when the fly was not four feet from his shins. Chicago thought there might be something the matter with his fly and Baldy traded with him, catching just as many on a Coachman as he had taken on the Jock Scott.

We fished until we were tired bringing them in. The average weight was probably close to one pound and we took no fish which weighed more than a pound and a half. They were game fighters, every one. When the sun dropped behind the rim of the western hills we drove back to town in the long Wyoming twilight.

That night we had breast of young sage chicken, roast duck, and fried brook trout for dinner. I have seen Chicago argue with a head waiter for twenty minutes over the introduction of a single condiment into a salad; this night he ate like a plowman and went to sleep standing up in the hall, trying to unlock the door of his room.

The next day we went down the river, Baldy coming for us before daylight. Shortly after sunrise we "outspanned" in a clump of trees near a ramshackle bridge. Baldy always allowed us a time handicap. He stayed to make his horses comfortable and Commie, Chicago, and I went on down to the bridge. A deep hole had been worn about the piles on which the bridge had been built and there on the surface of the barely moving current were not less than one hundred trout, all of them well over a pound in weight, some of them evidently three-pounders.

SOMETIMES THEY COME THREE AT A TIME IN THE SAME POOL.

I believe Commie said they were feeding. From the silent contempt with which they treated my fly I am of the opinion that they were already fed. Chicago experimented with all sorts of flies, dragging the gayly colored bits of feathers and silk over the backs of the fish without a response. They simply would not bite. Commie bombarded them with the biggest flies in his book and hurled some pretty warm language after the flies. Not a thing doing.

Then Baldy came along, climbed down to the bank, and, wading fifty yards down stream, snatched a nice fish out of a riffle on his second cast. But even Baldy could not make those big fellows lying on the top of the water pay the least attention to a fly. They were neither hungry nor curious, and after Chicago had worked himself into a perspiration without the slightest response, he was ready to take his small rifle to those trout.

Baldy wandered down the river and I followed him for a couple of miles

trying to find out how he did it. He would amble up to a pool under the bank, flick his old Jock Scott fly a couple of times, and then reel in a fish. He never seemed to be in a hurry; he found fish everywhere.

Back at the bridge Commie was doing a land office business. He had managed to secure some minnows. Commie is another fisherman who goes out after results.

"The main idea," says Commie, "is to give the fish what he thinks he wants. If he doesn't want silk and feathers, me for what he does want. I give him credit for knowing his own mind."

Evidently the big fish by the bridge wanted minnows and Commie, aided by Chicago, was having a lovely little time with some two-pounders. Baldy wouldn't bait with a minnow. He said he had no conscientious scruples about it. A man who can juggle a fly like Baldy Sisson doesn't need to bait with minnows.

We wound up the campaign at Til-

339

"BALDY" AND "COMMIE" EXTENDING THE RIGHT HAND
OF FELLOWSHIP.

ton's Ranch, twenty miles up the river. Tilton's Ranch is the home of Mountain Charlie and other Wyoming citizens. Mountain Charlie's two brothers, long deceased, stuffed and mounted with great care, hang on the wall in Tilton's dining room—two twenty-pound trout taken out of the North Platte within gunshot of the ranch house.

Mountain Charlie is the old he-trout of Wyoming. He is old enough to vote and he lives in a deep hole at the foot of a bluff where the river makes a sharp bend. Tilton's boy swears that Mountain Charlie is a twenty-pounder at least, and Tilton's boy has seen him. Others

have felt him, but not for long. Unless he has some way of getting rid of them, he must wear in his wicked old jaw a fringe of trout flies of all sizes and colors. He is sinful and tough and worldly wise with the wisdom of years of experience with "dude" fishermen, and if he ever comes to an untimely end it will be at the hands of a small boy, fishing with a throw-out line and baiting with a chunk of raw meat.

"Oh, yes," said Tilton's kid, "they hooks him all right and then . . . *biff!*"

Mountain Charlie has carried away enough flies to stock a small store and line enough to reach from Tilton's to

340

Fort Steele and most of the stories about him degenerate into the appraising of the value of tackle he has carried away. The program never varies, a sudden splash, a deep strong tug at the line, a rush of boiling water . . . and the rest, the low, earnest profanity of the fisherman.

Of course Chicago heard about Mountain Charlie. He procured a few live minnows and a stiff rod—a telegraph pole, Baldy called it—and tramped down to the bend. Baldy was busy with his team, but Commie and I went along in the capacity of an advisory board.

Chicago splashed through the shallows until he came to the head of the long riffle which led down to the pool and there he hooked his minnow and sent it straight down with the current, while Commie, at heart a bait fisherman, reviled Chicago for his lack of sportsmanship.

"Oh, *all* right!" said that pestered individual. "I believe in giving a fish what he wants to *eat*. This old boy is a cannibal, that's what *he* is. Couldn't raise him with a fly in a million years. But a nice little minnow now, nice fat little minnow. . . . *Yea, boy, I've got him!*"

Beyond question, Chicago had something. He set himself, and over the water came the snarl of a driven reel. The line whipped straight out of the pool and across the river. The fish was breaking for shallow water. Close to the bank he leaped and doubled back again, and Commie and I raced up and down and howled encouragement. Chicago, yelling like a maniac, was striving to hold his fish without the loss of more line.

"Never let it be said that you quit!" yelled Commie. "Hang to him, old kid!"

"I ain't quittin', but I think *he* is!" panted Chicago. "These big fish can't put up much of a fight!"

"He *is* coming in rather easy," said Commie thoughtfully, watching Chicago handling his reel. "Can't be Mountain Charlie."

Chicago waded out on a sandbank, towing his prize after him.

"Mountain Charlie!" he croaked. "I guess Tilton'll have to get another whale around these parts! This one's all in!"

The fish came in with a few faint splashes. All the fight was gone out of him. When he was twenty feet away Chicago got his first real look at his prize and his chin sagged.

About that time Baldy came crashing through the brush, wild-eyed.

"I heard the hollering," he said. "What is it? Did he hook the big feller?"

Chicago reached down and thrust his finger through the gills and raised a three-pounder out of the water.

"*What?*" said Baldy. "All that yellin' for a minny like that?"

And he turned around and went crashing back through the brush. Chicago didn't care. He said that he had landed the best fish of the trip and he didn't care where Mountain Charlie spent the winter.

In order that there might be a flavor of everything in this remarkable trip, Chicago, swollen with pride, furnished us with a touch of the tragic. He stepped off a slippery rock on the edge of a pool and took a header into the icy water. The bib-waders, enclosing him from the armpits down in an air-tight casing, received the rush of water and the air was forced downward into the feet. Chicago's head went down and his feet came up, threshing wildly.

We finally got him out on the bank and rolled him, for he was full of very fine drinking water. When he recovered, he bequeathed his bib-waders to Baldy, who remarked privately that when he wanted life preservers, he'd get the kind that didn't go around the feet.

Baldy Sisson is still on the job. We hear from him about twice a year when he sends us trout-fishing pictures just to make life seem a little bleaker than usual. According to Commie, there are still several large trout in the North Platte and Mountain Charlie remains at large, the lord of Tilton's Ranch.

I do not own any hot springs at Saratoga, but I bear witness that the town and the river are all that Commie ever said they were and if you knew Commie, you would recognize this for a pretty stiff statement.

31
The Fishes
of Our
Boyhood
(1897)

THE FISHES OF OUR BOYHOOD.

By Ed. W. Sandys.

THERE was not a trout in our country. The region of rock ended miles to the eastward, and with it the laughing brooklets and tumbling falls, the ripples and shadowed pools beloved of the speckled fellows. We had waters a-plenty— deep, calm, slow-moving rivers and creeks, which took their own time in reaching the big lakes which half surrounded our territory. The country had few slopes, except the banks of its waterways. For miles one would not find a stone. The great levels of fat land bore alternate growths of ancient forest and bountiful crops. It was not a trout country.

Of all the old crowd of boys, who knew the ways of every beast, bird,

ROCK BASS.

(*Ambloplites rupestris.*)

and fish indigenous to their stamping-ground, possibly not one ever set eyes upon a trout, until after he had traveled considerably beyond the confines of his native district. What the eye does not see the heart does not crave after, so we troubled ourselves not at all about the trout.

Our waters teemed with other fish. We had fishing in plenty and good fishing at that, and, perhaps, after all we were better off without the trout. In a trout region, as a general rule, one fishes for trout and nothing else ; quite frequently the trout is the only fish available, hence the youth of that region, while they may know all about trout, remain in igno-

rance of a dozen other varieties of interesting fish.

In our country things were different. In order to be a successful angler and so to command the respect of one's associates, one had to know more or less about a dozen kinds of fish, at least as many kinds of baits, and also the methods by which the fish and baits might

YELLOW PERCH.

(*Perca Americana.*)

best be brought into close relationship. The old boys knew these things, and many other things not to be found in books. They could tell you when, where, and why to try at a certain place for a certain fish, and what bait to use. Then, if you did not catch the fish, they'd take the tackle and prove that their knowledge was correct.

Those were indeed glorious days : from sunrise to sunset, care-free ; at night, a dreamless sleep. We were for ever busy, on, in, or about the water. To rise, feed, and flee to the river ; back, feed, off to the river, was the daily programme. We knew every foot of bank and shallow, and most of the depths ; where the turtles buried their eggs, when the muskallonge might be expected, when the pike followed the

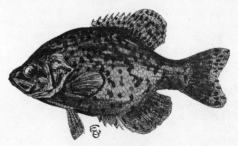

CALICO BASS.

(*Pomoxys sparoides.*)

345

overflows; in fact the waters had no secrets. When a new boy came into our midst, as he sometimes did, with tales of the trout and trout-fishing of distant parts, we hearkened not to him. Instead we took him fishing, and speedily convinced him that what he knew about trout was not a circumstance to what we knew about fish.

And such fish as they were, too! With the thought arise mental pictures of strings upon strings of captives, large and small; of happy, sun-browned, barefooted boys, forever wading, perching, prying along the banks; stealing marches upon each other, using every resource which practical knowledge and ready adaptability could command, in order to finish high hook at the close of the day. The boys were no minnowfishers, and few indeed were the blank days. Fine fish, up to five pounds in weight, rewarded those youthful toilers; indeed, a few plump bass sometimes stopped awkward questions concerning truancy and other trifling lapses from rectitude.

Let us glance at the fish which afforded such unbounded enjoyment, for many of them are worthy of an expert's attention.

As a course before the fish two forms of life may be discussed. Neither may be considered a fish, but both were very interesting to the boys—the one as a bait, and the other as an unfathomable mystery. Let us first take the bait.

It is the crawfish, the miniature lobsters of fresh water. These were very abundant in the shallow water at the river-banks, in the creeks, and in certain bush-ponds. At times crawfish are the best of baits for both varieties of black bass, and also for rock-bass. We always selected medium-sized crawfish, and instead of spitting them crosswise upon the hook, as is usually done, we forced the hook in at the mouth and out through the tail. So placed and allowed to sink freely, the bait gives an irresistible imitation of the crawfish's backward, wavering rush to shelter.

The best thing for securing such agile bait is a boy's deft brown paw; the nip of the large claws is only a trifling matter. The crawfish are found under stones and sunken rubbish in the streams, in the bush-ponds, under bits of sodden bark and sunken leaves. Their burrows, capped by curious little mud-towers, are familiar objects to those who go much afield. When not easily obtainable elsewhere, the crawfish may be taken from its burrow by overturning the mud-tower, lowering a bit of flesh fixed to a cord into the hole, and jerking the bait when a nibbling is felt. The boys had another method: "Fuzz it and churn for 'um," was a common expression, which meant to break a switch with a ragged end, and manipulate this into the hole until the outraged crawfish took a tight grip and was promptly jerked from its stronghold.

The creature referred to as a mystery is what is termed the "horsehair snake," in reality, a hairworm. It is found in all of our waters, and greatly resembles a hair from a horse's mane. The boys all swear that this hairworm really is a horsehair turned into a snake, and many grown persons will back up the claim. People have declared that they have taken a hair, placed it in a bottle of water, corked the bottle, and kept it so until the hair turned into a snake and swam about. Of course, science will accept no such testimony. The worm may be found in shallow water, perhaps lying upon the bottom like a snarl of black thread, or like a hair-spring of a watch, or closely twisted about a spear of grass. Where horses drink one may find genuine hairs and the hairworms in close proximity, which doubtless accounts for the hairsnake story. The hairworm is a gordioid nematode worm, which considering its structure and habit of snarling itself up is a good, if not very interesting description. The worm's first stage of life is as a parasite, the hairlike form representing the adult. It swims like a snake.

Now for the fish. Largest, most imposing and most difficult to take was that king of the pike family, the muskallonge. Just how large these chaps ran is an open question. About forty-five pounds might be the limit for trolling with the hand-line and spoon. Much heavier specimens were occasionally speared or shot. The largest fish were secured by spearing through the ice. The best I ever saw was one that had died from some unknown cause, and lay stranded upon a sand-bar. In prime condition this fish should have weighed fully sixty-five pounds.

During late May and early June the muskallonge made their way up the

larger streams, two fish, male and
female, usually traveling together.
The old Leatherstockings understood
the habit of the fish, and the boys soon
learned all about it. At such times
fishing-tackle proper was of little use,
though now and again a troll attached
to a very long line did tempt a strike.
Much more reliable were the very long-
handled spear and the rifle and shotgun.
From gray dawn till an hour or two
after sunrise was the best time for muskallonge, as the fish might be discovered
swimming near shore, or playing over
the bars. As a general thing the first
intimation of their proximity was the
sight of a strongly defined wake stretching far upon the placid water, as the
fish moved a trifle below the surface.
Then the important matter was to get
to a commanding point ahead of the
apex of that wake without alarming the
fish. This was rather a difficult thing
to accomplish, as it frequently demanded some lively skirmishing through the
brush and up and down wooded banks.
I have known gun and spear to chase
the watery sign, losing it and finding it
again and again for good two miles, and
then fail to obtain a fair chance.

Some of the old hands at this work
had favorite points where they would
post themselves like overgrown kingfishers and wait for fish to pass. This
method demanded much patience, and
it had a disadvantage in the fact that
fish might be playing just beyond the
bends above and below the stand, and
the watcher not know it. As a rule the
odds were in favor of the man who
cautiously stole along the bank and kept
a keen eye upon the water ahead. During the best part of a morning he could
cover several miles of stream and, perhaps, have as many as three or four
chances.

In practiced hands the long-handled
spear did excellent service, but woe was
the portion of the duffer who attempted
to use one. Badly scared fish and a
much surprised man were the almost
certain results of clumsy work, and fish
once scared seldom gave another chance
that day. Many of the country lads
used cheap rifles, which were all right
where the opposite bank was sufficiently high to stop glancing balls, but there
always was the undesirable chance of a
ball going somewhere upon a dangerous
errand. A reliable shot-gun was as

deadly to the fish, not dangerous in
other directions, and much handier for
quick work.

Our pike, small brother to the muskallonge, we did not hold in very great
esteem. They ran from a pound to
about fifteen pounds in weight, were
full of bones, and the flesh was rather
insipid. When the main streams over-
flowed their banks in the spring, the
pike sometimes occupied the lesser
tributaries and ditches in astonishing
numbers. Then the short spears and
guns were busy day and night, for the
fun was great, though the fish were not
prized. By the light of torches, lanterns and bonfires, many large pike
were shot and speared during the warm,
muggy nights when the run was at its
height. Later in the season pike were
taken by troll and hand-line, by whipping with rod and spoon, or other artificial lure, and by minnow-bait, the
"shiner" being the best of small live
bait, the frog ranking next.

What we termed "pickerel" (wall-
eyed pike) were better table-fish, but
could not be depended upon for a day's
sport. There was a heavy run of them
about spring freshet time, when tons of
them fell victims to the seines. At this
time, too, numbers were speared in the
discolored eddies, but later, during the
regular season for the rods, only one or
two would be found among a day's
catch of good fish. Specimens weighing five or six pounds were quite commonly taken, while the seines took
much heavier ones.

Three curious fish found in our waters
were taken solely for the fun of playing
them, for none of the boys would ever
carry one of them home. Most abundant of these was the "sheepshead"
(freshwater drum), a good-looking, silvery fish, somewhat like the lake shad.
They ran large, ranging from one to
ten pounds, took various sorts of baits
freely, and fought pretty well upon
light tackle. All of the upper parts
were of a pretty, silvery blue, which below shaded off to a dead white, like
white kid. In the head of this fish are
two enamel-like substances, roughly circular in shape, and about the size of a
nickel in the larger specimens. These
were termed "lucky stones," and the
boy's first business, after landing a
sheepshead, was to crush its head with
his heel, or something as convenient,

SUNFISH.
(*Lepomis gibbosus.*)

and extract these two precious affairs. One or more of them lurked in every boy's pockets, for were they not equal to the famed rabbit's foot of the South? No boy cared to hook and lose a sheepshead, and none would dream of casting away the dead fish without first "gettin' his luckies." The "stones" were marked upon one side with a design which suggested a pollard willow with a badly bent stem, the rough resemblance of this bent stem to a letter L, being, presumably, the cause of the luck theory.

I have caught scores of these fish, yet never tasted one; nor have I met a white man who had done so. I have heard that the flesh is astonishingly tough and flavorless, and that the sheepshead required a power of cooking before one could chew it at all. This may be so, yet the actual experimenter does not appear within my field of acquaintances. The negroes used to carry home a large sheepshead now and then, but the majority of the swart Waltonians voted the fish "pizen fo' shuah." At certain points we used to kill from a dozen to twenty sheepshead in a day, the fish freely taking worms and crawfish, so freely of the latter that many a

bait intended for a bass got into the wrong pew.

The second of our curious fish was the gar-pike, as a rule, very abundant. This fish was also voted "pizen," and none would touch it for food. To the boys they were "swordfish," and only good to have fun with. A big gar, with his round, tapering body, stiletto-like jaws, sharp teeth and wicked-looking eyes, was an unpromising customer who appeared to be full of bite. During warm weather gars floated for hours at the surface, and their trim lines someway suggested speed, power, and something of relationship to marine torpedoes and things like that. The bony structure of their long, lean jaws frequently baffled efforts at hooking them, and, if hooked, their teeth were apt to cut anything but gimp. I have, however, taken them with minnows, the play afforded by them being poor. A specimen a yard long would be deemed a large fish in those waters.

WALL-EYED PIKE.
(*Stizostedion vitreum.*)

While the adult gar is decidedly ugly, the young are very beautiful. The very small ones look like gold bodkins, while one of about the size of a lead-pencil, with his bronzy tinting, snow-white belly and gleaming gold eye, in modeling and coloration may well hold his own with the best. These smaller fish may be found floating among the bent water-grasses, and so closely do they match their surroundings that sharp eyes are required to locate them before they dart to shelter. One flick of the tail, which is always kept in a slightly curved position for instantaneous action, will cause the smooth, slim body to vanish in what is apparently a miraculous manner. We used to take the floating gars by stealthy work with a small landing-net made of mosquito-netting, the fish being interesting for aquariums.

The third of the freak fish was prized

WHITE BASS.
(*Roccus chrysops.*)

PIKE.
(Esox lucius.)

on account of his decided method of taking bait and his stubborn resistance when hooked. He was never eaten, everybody agreeing that he surely was "pizen." This fish, the bowfin (*Amia calva*), was always termed "dogfish," and he was an ugly-looking fellow. His greenish-yellow, snaky-looking body was not pleasant to contemplate, and there was an ugly expression about his big mouth and a glint in his lurid eye which suggested a disposition not sugary, to say the least. Careless fingers would get pinched when removing the hooks; indeed some of the boys cut him loose and sacrificed hooks rather than have anything further to do with him beyond clubbing him to death.

Early in the spring we speared and hooked many mullet, which were also taken in large quantities by the seines. The red-finned, olive-backed, foolish-looking fish were held in fair esteem for the table, especially the large ones. When the water was very muddy from the freshet, the red fins were about all one could distinguish, as the fish rolled in the eddies, or struggled against the rapid current. At such times one had need to be quick with his spear, and at the same time to instantly estimate where to strike. With the mullet came the pallid-looking suckers—bony, worthless creatures, which were not deemed fit to carry home.

After the clouded waters had run clear and had regained their normal level, came the cream of our fishing. Then the bass were on the feed, and the sport they afforded was something never to be forgotten. There were plenty of bass—large and small-mouth black fighters, weighing from one to six pounds; square-built rock-bass, sometimes over a pound in weight; shapely white bass, not much as fighters, even when a foot long, yet dainty for the pan; and lastly, the calico, or grass bass, a showy, mottled fellow, sometimes a foot long, and a quick, jerky fighter.

Upon many days a catch would include specimens of all of these varieties of bass, as they take the same baits and favor the same haunts. Most prized of the lot were the black bass, especially the small-mouth. His big-mouthed cousin ranked second, calico and silver were equally esteemed, while the rock-bass was by no means to be despised. Some of the boys had jointed rods and reels, but the majority favored a bamboo cane, or a springy pole, cut in the woods. For these the lines were made fast near the butt, then carried with a few turns round the pole to the tip, and there made fast, the free line being a trifle shorter than the pole. Floats were seldom used, the boys, as a rule, preferring to trust to their hands to determine when to strike.

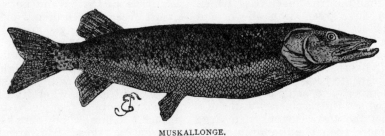

MUSKALLONGE.
(Lucius masquinongy.)

The bass were found in the greatest numbers about old piling, submerged trees, where trees hung far over deep water, and near lily-pads and dense grasses. The best baits were crawfish, minnows, white grubs, frogs, grasshoppers, larvæ of bees and wasps, and worms; and they were esteemed about in the order as named. If one bait did not promptly tempt a fish some other was substituted. The boys knew where and how to secure all in their season.

The fishing was never confined to one spot for any great length of time, nor did the boys believe that silence was either golden or necessary; in fact, they chaffed each other and joked at will. The rule they followed was that one place was good only so long as bites were not too far apart; and when the water within reach had been once thoroughly tested a move was the proper thing.

A small-mouth black bass was the prize first tried for, say about a submerged tree. For him minnow, crawfish, frog or grub, as the case happened to be, was deftly cast a few yards from and all about the supposed stronghold. If two or more of these baits failed to tempt the desired victim, the conclusion was that the black bass, if thereabouts, was not in a biting humor. Then a rock-bass was voted good enough, and the bait was sent down as close as possible to the submerged tree-trunk, and into all likely-looking dark holes. The rock-bass, all honor to him, was usually there and ready to make a fight. So one promising place after another would be tried, the sport for the day ending perhaps two or half a dozen miles from the starting point.

The rock-bass, for his size, was a good fighter, and also a very tasty morsel when properly cooked. He—also termed "goggle-eye" and "red-eye"—frequently turned up as black as one's boots, always blacker than the true black bass, which is of an olive-green tint above and lighter below. The boys called the rock-bass the "black bass," while large and small-mouth black bass were known as "green" bass. Now and then, great catches of white bass were made.

I remember once, after a heavy rain, taking (where the discolored water of a creek met the clear current of a large river) more than one hundred white bass within one and one-quarter hours.

I fished standing in a small shooting-skiff, and dropped the fish behind me as fast as they could be removed from the artificial baits. The rod used was short and stiff, and there was hardly any playing. This happened about the middle of a town, a few yards from a bridge from which a crowd eagerly watched the fun. I might have taken more bass, but the weight of the catch, all in the stern, brought the little skiff so low behind that, before I knew it, the water was pouring in. A yell from the crowd warned me, and I got ashore with only my feet wet. That catch is, or was until two years ago, the record for white bass in that water. Presumably, the muddy water of the creek brought down so much feed that all the fish in the neighborhood were attracted to the common point. They took my bait before it was two yards below the surface, and just as it passed the line between the muddy and clear water.

Another reliable fish for sport and fairly good for the pan was the yellow perch. These handsome fellows frequently traveled in large schools; and, when once a school had been struck, some lively work was certain to follow. The fish would range from half a pound to three times that weight. The best bait for them was the worm, although other baits frequently proved attractive. On a good perch day and at a good perch place, the catch might number from twenty to nearly one hundred fish.

A very beautiful fish, excellent for the pan and dearly loved by the small boy, was the sunfish or pumpkin-seed. A large one would weigh about three-quarters of a pound, but specimens of quarter that size are more commonly taken. They are greedy biters and game in their own way, but their mouths are too small for ordinary bass hooks and baits. A very small hook, bearing a portion of worm, will be at once taken by a sunfish, if he be there; and he *is* there in almost every stretch of our old waters. He delights in sunny shallows, in pools among the grasses, and he is also given to lying beside roots and rubbish near shore. It is a common sight to see these fish poised with wavering fins above their spawn, where the sand and gravel are only a foot or so below the surface. When a boy marks sunfish so engaged, those fish are as good as caught. They will not desert the spawn, and they will bite, in hunger or anger, at anything dropped too near their precious charge. This fish, with the shiner and young perch, ranks among the first victims of pin-hook wiles.

Among rarely taken specimens were the young whitefish and the herring. These were delicate-mouthed, yet most palatable dainties, but so small a part did they play in our sport that they are not properly included here. When they did take the hook the bait was a worm.

The catfish and bullheads, however, could always be depended upon—thirty, forty, or more of them during an evening. What the boys called "channel-cats" were taken from midstream by long hand-lines which had a sinker at the end and one or more hooks bent to short lengths of line above the sinker. Worms were deadly bait, and shortly after sunset was the best time. The catfish were of all sizes, from fingerlings with more horns than body, up to great whiskered varlets of twenty-odd pounds. With the exception of the head, repulsive with its huge mouth, small eyes and long appendages, the smaller channel-cat is a handsomely modeled fish. The body is clean-cut, the fins are well-proportioned, while the silvery, scaleless, slippery skin is not unattractive. Fish of about one pound in weight were excellent eating, though many people would not touch them. At home, I had them prepared, half-a-dozen together, in a manner most acceptable. The process I do not understand, but the fish reached me entombed within a solid mass of transparent jelly, in which were also a few slices of hard-boiled egg, some sprigs of parsley and a dash of vinegar—all ice-cold. Good? Say! The block of jelly would be as large as two brickbats, and I could get—but there! Those days have passed away.

These fish had to be very carefully removed from the hook! The long horns, or feelers, were perfectly harmless, but in the fins near the gills were awful serrated spikes which could inflict most painful wounds. If given a chance, the slippery fish would swing his head vigorously, whereupon his captor's hand or wrist was certain to suffer. The small "mud-cat," or bullhead, also had these weapons with a complete knowledge of their use. Quite frequently wounds from them caused a severe inflammation, which sometimes extended to the temper and the talk of the victim.

When fishing for channel-cats after dark, the boys often started a big bonfire. A lot of fun is mingled with the ashes of those old fires. A row of hand-lines stretched to the outer darkness, and the boys sat more or less patiently, each holding his cord. A whispered "Got a bite," would stop all conversation, and then would come the quick strike and the unerring snatch-snatch as dirty hands flew through their task of recovering the line. If the resistance told of a heavy prize, muttered grunts and inarticulate exclamations added tenseness to the situation, till the big fish threshed the surface within the fire's light. Then would go up such a yell of triumph, that our folks in nearby houses would not know whether we had merely caught a good one, or had all tumbled into the river. If we eventually turned up at home, they knew that everything was all right, and they were, or they pretended to be, greatly pleased to see us. Sometimes a boy *did* fall in and elicit nearly as many yells as greeted the fish, though the yells lacked the ring of true enthusiasm. We were such water-dogs that nobody bothered about a little thing like that.

At intervals it happened that a boy got a bite which puzzled him, though those hands could feel and recognize, through thirty or forty yards of line, any fish that touched the bait. Upon these occasions the excitement was keen. The last heave would surely reveal either a mud-turtle or a mud-puppy. Both of these are awkward customers to handle. The turtles could bite like fury, and fingers had no business near their cutting jaws. The shortest way was to cut the hook free, and allow the turtle to keep it as a souvenir.

The mud-puppy was different. No power on earth would induce a boy to touch that slate-colored, slimy, writhing shape. Its fate was ever the same. The cord was cut, and into the fire went the puppy. This creature, by the way, is a repulsive-looking water-lizard. His heavy body, four stumpy legs, apparent lack of eyes, and bunches of external gills, were neither understood nor appreciated by his captors. He was "pizen," and no respect was owing to those who might claim that he was harmless. He would bite, or at least he would try to do so, for never to my knowledge was he allowed an opportunity to illustrate what he was capable of in that direction. Peace be to his ashes, for he suffered much!

The lamprey, too, could cause quite a commotion. This creature, the boys could never understand, and they were more or less afraid of it. I do not remember ever taking one upon the hook, but at rare intervals one was seen attached to a fish—I think, invariably, to a bass. The lamprey, or lamper-eel, may once have been considered a delicacy, but the boys would have none of him. He was from a foot to a foot and a half long, eel-like in form, and possessing a round, sucking mouth, with a palate well supplied with small teeth. Behind the mouth, upon either side, were seven small openings, which greatly puzzled the boys.

I have more than once seen bass walloping about with one of these suckers firmly attached, and the fish's actions indicated that it was either in pain, or in deadly fear of its comrade. One bass which I shot, and from which I detached the lamprey, showed an ugly-looking raw spot where the sucker had been; I have also seen many bass that bore similar scars. Once, when some boys were wading in a pool, left by high water, a lamprey fastened upon a bare leg. That boy did more "stunts" in five minutes than he would attempt now for five thousand dollars! The thing finally let go, and only a slight mark remained.

So much for the fishes of boyhood and, incidentally, for the boys themselves. Of that happy party some have since learned about the fishes in the Shadow River. The others are scattered far and wide, some glad with human hopes, some gray with human griefs. Some have seen the great salmon-rivers and trout - pools of remotest wilds, and have learned the science of modern tools and perfected methods. Perchance their bare-foot training has ofttimes stood them in good stead. It may be that the survivors would gladly cast aside their modern improvements for the privilege of once again assembling about the old bonfire; to see the lines leading into the darkness, the floating captives upon their separate tethers, the mud-puppy roasting upon his pyre, and some boy carving his initials upon a hapless, hissing turtle.

Quien sabe?

32
Summer Days
on the
Mirimichi
(1902)

SUMMER DAYS ON THE MIRIMICHI

By TAPPAN ADNEY

N northern countries the transition from winter to summer is swift; hardly has the last patch of snow disappeared from the sheltered woodland ravines and the swollen torrent subsided when the tender green buds of the alders and birches burst into full leafage; the crow and robin are building their nests, and the denizens of the cool, sparkling brooks have begun to seek their summer homes.

Thus, although May had a few days more in which to run its course, the fields, the trees, the air had taken on the character of summer. The old mare, with her three passengers, was no doubt thoroughly leg weary from forty miles, up hill and down, since daybreak. For the past eight miles not even rude settlers' cabins had broken the loneliness of the narrow forest road. When, at last, there broke into view a field with gray buildings in the distance, illumined in the rays of the parting sun, the old mare, voluntarily quickening her pace, seemed hardly less than ourselves to feel that our journey was ended. The buildings soon became more distinct, and one by one the graceful elms, which in the primeval forest are inseparable from fertile valleys, marked before us the course of a stream toward which for many weeks we had been turning the eyes of fancy in pleasant anticipation. "Bryden's" at last, and beyond a region of forest, lake, and river that has been recently described as the largest untouched wilderness remaining east of the Rocky Mountains!

We soon found ourselves in what might have been either a dooryard or barnyard—or both; between a barn, which for size would be the pride of a Pennsylvania Dutchman, and a rambling assortment of low frame buildings, arranged in a row for the convenience of the provincial winter season. Both house and barn gave signs of age, and but for the presence of a solitary hen in the dooryard the wayfarers might easily have imagined an abandoned farm that, like many another in New Brunswick and Maine, should never have been taken from the moose and bear. Less easily might the travelers have imagined themselves at a hotel famous the length and breadth of the Mirimichi Road—perhaps not unknown beyond. Of course, the hotel of the city is one thing; the summer hotel is another; this was neither. I have called it a "hotel"; it was merely "Bryden's." Sixty teams of horses at once in the big, generous barn! A hundred men crowded, one knows not how, into those rooms, which are broader than they seem at first. Now and then a fisherman in summer, and some hunters in fall, keep the road from becoming entirely grass-grown; these stable their horses in the barn and hire boats on the river. It is not in summer, but when the ice king holds the land in his grasp and the winter snows mantle the leafless forests, that "Bryden's" awakes. The grass from the broad meadow lies in the barn; stores of bacon, beans, flour, and molasses are replenished and again replenished before spring. From "Bryden's," on roads leading eastward and northward, are dozens of lumber camps. So the road which now knows only the casual seeker after recreation resounds in spring and autumn with the shouts of rugged, uncouth men in coarse, bright woolens, oil tanned moccasins, and thick, warm caps; with the tinkle of bells upon great, shaggy horses, drawing bob-sleds piled high with oats, hay, flour, beans, pork, axes, and "peevies." All winter long come and go the teams of the "toters," hauling provisions for the men and feed for the horses. And, as must be when a man gets in from facing the cold and the snowdrift, each driver must stop and his horses must rest at the first, or the last, or the only house on the road. Then what nightly gayety; wild, but always good natured! Horses fed; supper (in relays, of course) at the long, pine table, with benches for chairs; and then—from deep pockets and other mysterious sources of apparently exhaustless supply — emerge "long necks" of whiskey, or "John de Kipers" (gin), which are passed from hand to hand. Nor is the stranger known. Whether or no, every man must drink—nor may any overstep the bounds of politeness by declining, however often the bottle comes. Crowded into the big, low ceiled room next the supper room, the doors closed to the frosty blasts without, the revelers clear a space and the "step dances" begin. Two at a time face each other, stepping off the time in unison to the rhythmic beats of the shouting on-lookers' hands and feet, or the strains of hornpipes and reels jerked out at marvelous speed by tireless fiddlers until, exhausted, one or both fall out amid approving shouts. The singing, shouting, laughing, dancing, drinking goes on the long night through.

The clock on the wall shows four; horses are fed, and, before the light of day has streaked the eastern sky, weary, sleepy men are again on the road, facing the drifting snow. There is much work and little play in the lumberman's life. And who would begrudge what is, after all, but an occasional night's respite from dull care and sorrow?

As for the proprietor of this highly interesting and probably altogether unique establishment, surely he has earned summer's comparative rest—an opportunity of which he is not reluctant to avail himself, if I might judge by the picture presented upon our arrival at the door.

Stretched at full length upon a bench at the back of the narrow porch which sheltered the public entrance was a man above fifty years, in shirt sleeves, his head supported by a pile of grain sacks. His eyes turned toward us, but he gave no other sign of recognition or of stirring. The picture of ease and contentment with all the world he presented there, with his ruddy countenance, needed not the warm glow of the evening sun to produce any illusion of tint or shade.

"Mr. Bryden?" spoke that one of my companions who by right of previous acquaintance might reasonably act as spokesman. A pink hand rose slowly toward the pipe, a curl of smoke, the pipe was slowly withdrawn, and a slight nod acknowledged our presence. Then, as with great reluctance he slowly stretched his arms, swung to an upright posture, stretched his arms again, knocked the ashes from his pipe, his blue eyes appeared slightly to twinkle as he arose to swing wide open the gates of backwoods hospitality.

"Fishing?"

"That was our purpose, mainly, in coming here."

"Put up your horse, boys; you know where the barn is, Sharp." Then adding, as apology: "I always lay down with my pipe after supper, and I never let anything bother me." Knowing the man I am sure that if the governor-general himself were to drive up he would stir neither hand nor foot until he had finished his pipe.

"Then you were not burning a smudge to keep off the mosquitoes?" said Sharp.

Our horse was crazy from the swarms which were attacking her; our own pipes served but feebly to protect us from the ravenous creatures for which "Bryden's" is famous.

"Mosquitoes?" with a look of injured surprise. "Mosquitoes?" (Here he drew his hand down the side of his neck). "There 're no mosquitoes here now." (Slap.) "There was *some* a week or two ago" (slap), "but they won't bother you now."

Our ancestors were savages. I can assign no other reason for a man's liking more or less to sleep with day clothes on, under a rough, hairy blanket, on ground rendered somewhat more resilient by fir boughs; drinking tea which is mingled with wood ashes and pine spills, and eating with no tool but a long bladed belt knife. Still, it needed no second call at daybreak next morning to rouse us off the unyielding

"The event of the trip was a double."

hemlock floor of the barn. As the sun came up behind the trees everything and everybody seemed cheerful. The very mosquitoes, shaking the night's dew from their wings, gave their bills a hasty whet, and were glad—that we had come.

We lugged to the brook everything a man (in health) would really require for a brief free and independent existence— axe, light shelter tent, water pail, tea kettle, a tin cup and plate for each, a gunnysack of potatoes; an old trunk holding bread, butter, corn, sugar, tea, salt, pepper, extra articles of apparel, rod cases, spare rods, tackle; everything which rain, or sunshine, or boat water might injure.

Our craft was a double ender, a yard wide over the top and twenty feet long, the bottom narrow for threading the boulder lined channels. It was nicely painted red and there were racks along each side to hold the rods. Could Sharp have had his way it would have been instead a "nice, light pirogue" (can one imagine a boat hewn from a solid pine log being light?). That is really better than the Indian's birch, which is very easily cut by the sharp, stony bottoms of the shallow streams. An Indian always "shoes" his boat with strips of cedar when going down such streams. Narrow, long, straight of side, a little wider at bow than stern, the bow rounded upward so as to rise over the contending current; such is the ideal "pirogue." The man who has set bone and muscle upon the stiff young spruce pole that drives the boat upward against the swiftest rapids learns in time the form that goes ahead with least resistance.

Abounding in rapids and shallows, as these northern woods streams are, the paddle is seldom touched. Except on lakes and streams of considerable size, progress, whether up or down, is by the pole alone. One person (or two, if skilful) may assist the steersman, who stands in the stern and who not only must be ready with supple knee for each sudden rocking of the canoe, but must know to a nicety the turn of the pole, after the forward push, that holds the canoe in the teeth of the current ready for the next. To a beginner the strain is like that of learning to ride a bicycle, with this advantage in favor of the former, that water makes softer falling than earth.

One notices a difference in the color of the water of different streams. Those which flow through hardwood lands are clear and colorless; those from bogs and evergreen forests are tinged with brownish, like the steepings of tea; nor is the water so pleasant to the taste. Mirimichi is one of the latter, but the rich red brown, bespeaking an origin in the great "barren" and spruce hills against the source-springs of Tobique, only enhances the beauty of the deep dark pools which abound in this river as in none other of my acquaintance. Its beauty is the beauty of clear wine. By contrast the tender leaves of the fringing alders, of the graceful overhanging birches and elms, seem more green; more white and snowlike the flecks of foam floating along on its bosom, in interminable procession seaward.

Fan shaped is Mirimichi; not one river but several, meeting at a common point. Ours, the "Main Southwest," stretching a hundred and fifty miles eastward and westward, and almost dividing the province, is the principal "rib." At the point where they meet, seagoing vessels enter from the Gulf of St. Lawrence. It is miles across, and no man yet has told where river ends and sea begins, except by the tide. Together these streams drain the greater part of the wilderness, which for a generation to come will be the wildest of "accessible" regions in the East. On the westward Tobique carries detritus from the same hills. On the north Restigouche and Upsalquitch, and on the east also is Nipisiguit—all inferior in volume to the Main Southwest Mirimichi. At no point from the settlements is this fish and game paradise reached more easily and quickly than here, a fact not commonly understood.

In quick succession pool follows pool; now broad, long, and deep; now so shallow the boat almost drags; winding, twisting, hurrying, resting, each only for a moment. Alders, birches, elms, and leaning spruce shade first one side and then the other, sometimes both; until the Forks, a famous pool for salmon, are reached, and there the waters from north and west meet in a beautiful pool, shaded by lofty evergreens. Now between widened banks, slowly at first, then faster, the stream flows gently on, a considerable and dignified river.

Salmon, Mr. Henry W. Wells says, are

the finest fish, pound for pound, that the fisherman can take. It does not behoove, therefore, that the gentry should lie in pools suitable for sea and brook trout, which need not space in which to run and leap and send the reel a-whizzing!

A cast or two in the pool, then the upward journey. Tedious, muscle-rending, exasperating in its slowness—there is nothing poetic about poling a heavy boat up a swift, shallow stream. It is "bone labor," permitting no rest, unless one whips the pools as he goes. Bucksawing wood, taking bad medicine, poling a boat against a swift stream, are the same to me. My friends, however, claim they like it. I believe they do. Larger, more varied in its banks, the river showed new beauties at every turn. The short view, the alluring bend, the picturesque bit of rapid, pool, or foliage discover themselves, rather than magnificence. The charms are those of detail following detail in varying and pleasing succession, the imagination supplying that isolation and wilderness which are here, but which the eye, from the river, does not survey. Its upper reaches are less like a river than a glorified brook. On the inside of each turn are pretty banks of sand and gravel, where one may step ashore, cast under the overhanging tree or bunch of driftwood at the far side, and then wade or take the boat to the next. The big trout prefer the larger pools, but no spot where the water rests, if only behind a submerged boulder in a rapid or under a tussock of waving shore grass, is too insignificant to hold its fish— when the water is right. Two miles from the Forks we boiled once more the kettle of tea, and ate a dozen trout which we had picked up on the fly. As we journeyed on tracks of moose were observed on the sandy beaches—some obviously as fresh as the morning. Hardly had we been gone an hour when, turning a bend in the river, we saw, head down stream in the edge of the water, a moose. Seventy-five yards away he stood gazing as curiously as a cow in a pasture. How odd, how awkward looking; the short, round body on the tall legs; the short neck, the long, ill-shapen head, with mulelike ears set stiffly toward us! Small spike antlers betrayed his sex and age. The clumsy, foolish youth! As tall as a horse now! What will he be a dozen years hence, with antlers that one might imag-

ine were some upturned pine root? He looked at us for some moments, then leisurely took a step or two shoreward, turned his head once more, and then stepped among the alders which closed around him. When opposite the spot we could see two ears waving to keep off the flies; still not alarmed.

Who shall tell the delights of days so auspiciously begun? The blue sky, the fair, warm days, the pools at their best; each day's work carrying us only just as far up stream, or down, as we wished, like bees from flower to flower. Then, at night, the open tent facing the stream, the fire of driftwood in front, the broad blanket spread softly over evergreen boughs, stockings on the ridgepole drying after the day's wading, the savory smell of frying potatoes, corn, and fish. If a shower fell by night the wide waterproof covered all snugly. And if it rained as it did that day, when the sky turned suddenly black, the wind snapped the frail fir trees, and the rain fell not, but was driven in sheets; or if, when rushing down stream in mad race to outstrip the current, the boat did strike a snag and one vaulted headlong into a deep, black pool—who was the worse after clothes were dried?

There was the "Alder Ground," so called because the high banks recede from sight each side for several miles, leaving only alders and a few elms to shade the pools; pools which abound in brook trout of any bigness one may wish, and sea trout, which come up from the gulf to spawn. Most beautiful of all is "Bruin Farm Pool," where the river, emerging from evergreen forest, skirts a broad, natural opening where bears come for berries, and, crescent-like, doubles on its course. Two miles above "Bruin Farm" and twelve from the Forks, Bedell Brook, with its dead water, attracts the sportsman. Here, amid forests of spruce, now dead from the water of beavers' dams, the trunks standing ghostlike along the banks, or prostrate in the water, are found the largest brook trout on Mirimichi. Seven and eight pound fish are said to have been taken here. Three and a half is the largest I have seen; while the event of the trip was a double, hooked at a single cast of a parmachenee belle and a squirrel-tail. The two weighed respectively two and three-quarters and two and a half pounds. One was landed in the net, the other by a quick grasp in the gills.

Fifteen miles above the Forks are the Falls, where the river in two leaps rushes through a gorge. "Fourteen-mile Brook," an insignificant stream, yielded to two alder poles and shortened lines a ten pound creel level full in an hour's fishing. Who would ask for better? Once a moose muddied the pool so we could not fish. It left a footprint, I swear, like a breakfast plate. Another ran crashing through the lines with loud "gruffs." Again, a mother caribou, with her pretty fawn, was drinking from the spring where we went for water. The flies, too, reminded us continually that the country was theirs, that we were theirs to feed and wax fat upon. Not alone mosquitoes, but blackflies and midgets ("bite-um no see-ums," as the Indian aptly calls them), which latter show themselves not by reason of exceeding smallness and burn like red hot irons as the fish begin to bite. And the moose-fly, clumsy, blundering, yellow and brown fellow, who stabs like an assassin. The salmon did not favor us with so much as a rise. The only one we saw had scars of battle from encounter with spears of poachers on the lower reaches of the river. Ten, twenty, thirty pounds is the weight of salmon which the Mirimichi gives to him who has in his favor season and humor, water and lure.

33
Toll
from the
Salmon Host
(1905)

TOLL FROM THE SALMON HOST

By W. S. PHILLIPS

PHOTOGRAPHS BY THE AUTHOR

THERE is a time on Puget Sound that breathes contentment into the souls of men—a time of soft pearl-gray days with an air from the north, just the right air, tempered to a fraction of a degree for the comfort of the body fabric. To-morrow perhaps the breeze shifts seaward and comes in, creeping, mysterious and heavy with the breath of the tropics, straight from the Kuro Siawah that washes the shores of old Japan. To those who know, these vagrant airs bring word of the coming landward of a countless host of armored warriors, each clean in a suit of burnished silver mail, each full muscled and prime—a fighter that has no equal, inch for inch, pound for pound.

There is that about this coming of the salmon schools from the silent mystery of the deep sea which stirs an angler as nothing else under the blue sky can do. The dainty, beautiful trout of the tumbling mountain rapids can be had in this westland for the taking any day, and he is well worth his kill. The bronze mailed bass lurks ready in the shadow of the sunken log in many lakes hereabouts, but, while both can furnish their limit of sport they lack the element that puts the salmon fisher on the rack and makes his blood surge with a longing to meet and try conclusions with the salmon hordes fresh from the deep water.

I have fished across many degrees of latitude and longitude and felt the savagery of the whole gamut of fighters, yet I cannot tell you just what the charm is that brings me to the waterfront of Puget Sound in the misty, pearl-gray days when the northerly trade wind dies and the southwest trades are born. There is a mystery, a compelling influence, about it that drives one to the lazy, heaving sea to watch, keen-eyed and expectant, for the first leap of gleaming silvery bodies that betray the incoming host.

When that first fish breaks water in September how quickly he conjures you! Your boat breasts the incoming tide on the in-stant. Your line, a thin, strong linen, pays out and loses the glare of moving, glinting copper and nickel as the spoon drops outward and downward into blue water, until it follows a hundred feet astern. A quiet measured pull away across the slow-moving tide that is clean, blue and transparent as the skies. Your rod, with reel dragged to hold the strain, yet free to sing when the fish strikes, rests at hand so that the oars may be dropped and the rod grasped instantly.

Perhaps you are early and only the advance guard of salmon is coming in. You row and row, sometimes for hours, always watching, always expecting the reel to suddenly scream madly as the savage strike carries the line out in smoking fathoms. Can you feel the strain?

Perhaps you are later in the season and the fish are running in uncounted thousands, so that, look where you may, you can always see the flashing silver curve of a leaping fish in the air and there is a steady splash, splash on all sides continuously, as they leap and fall back into the leaden sea. It is then only a question of minutes before your reel will scream—then you fight; each time you think it the best yet; you conquer or lose as the case may be, and back you go to do it all over again five minutes later.

How can I tell you about this royal sport so that you can understand? Suppose we go together; go out to the deep water that basks under the smoky mists yonder and see what we shall see.

The line is over and the three-inch spoon is telegraphing its under-water doings by a rhythmic pulsating throb as steady as a quiet heart-beat. Your line, out over the stern of your own boat, behaves the same and we row quietly across the stream of the tide.

Chug! A fish breaks water four points off the starboard bow and hurls his fifteen pounds skyward, only to fall back with a sullen, heavy splash. A moment afterward another, then another beyond. We

"A half circle to the left."

"Follow more acrobatics."

"His helpless nose is brought above water."

change our course a couple of points to pass in front of the slow-moving school, calculating nicely so that the whirling spoons a hundred feet astern and the moving salmon host shall reach the crossing point of the courses at about the same time.

Another fish breaks water—astern this time, and before he falls back into his element my reel yells like a fiend and the line pays overboard as though it were taken by a sounding whale.

Instantly my oars are drifting idly and I am on my feet, rod in hand, and using the drag for all it will stand. The reel sings on; ten fathoms of line gone on top of the original hundred feet and still going like a race-horse! Suddenly it stops dead, and shortly, away astern there, a brilliant glittering flash of silver reflects mirrorlike the lazy sun, and my captive is in the air. Such tactics! Four feet high—a clear leap, then the splash of his falling body, and back into the air again five or six times before the shower of spray has a chance to settle. Do you hear the rattle-te-bang of the three-inch spoon against his gill covers as he savagely shakes himself to get rid of the thing that is fast in his jaw?

No use! Now he splits the water in wild, swift running leaps that scatter the spray and carry him in a half circle to the left, a rush that vies with the doings of a frightened porpoise, and you begin to wonder why we didn't think to get tackle twice as strong!

He is fast and the struggle brings him no results, so down he goes, down, down, down, the line paying out grudgingly under the drag, but all the same paying out, until 200 feet are gone—250 feet, and the drag no longer complains. A moment of suspense and then he shoots into the air like a rocket away off to one side—always in an unexpected quarter—and the surface fight is on again. In and out of the water, hither and yon, straight away and straight back at you; under the boat and circle again, into the air and down to the limit of pressure and the thing in his jaw never lets go, never goes slack for the fraction of an instant.

Now he sulks; he refuses to break water and allows himself to be towed up to within thirty feet of the boat. Another wild, unreasoning rush as he sees the craft and then into the air again, and follow more acrobatics! Did you ever fight a fifteen-pounder that way for twenty minutes?

At it again! My arm aches with the strain—but his rushes are shorter though just as savage. The pace has begun to tell. Another ten minutes and he cannot overcome the drag of the rod against his strength. He swims strongly and always heads away from the boat—if it wasn't for that thing in his jaw he could show speed yet—but that handicap has worn the best of his wildness down, sandpapered it thin and his finish is in sight.

By-and-by his helpless nose is brought above water. He objects strenuously and has a tremendous flurry like a bass, plunges unreasonably, walks on his tail and pitches his great, gleaming body out of the water recklessly and regardless of anything but the effort at getting the hook from his jaw—and he will, too, if he can gain a quarter of an inch of slack! No use! Again he swims round and round; just a steady strong swim now like an athlete picking up his second wind. I read the signs, reel him in still closer, hoist his gasping nose above water so he will smother down the quicker by breathing too much air.

When I get him alongside I reach downward for my twenty-two caliber rifle to finish him. I use no landing net because I prefer to shoot the fish through the spine and so finish him in the water. He bleeds well in this manner and does not tangle things up disagreeably in the boat. It makes a clean finish.

He is led alongside and duly shot just back of the gills about the line of the spine, whereat he obligingly quits, quivers along his entire length and the battle is won. The dead captive floats alongside, only to be lifted in and deposited along the boat bottom on a piece of clean canvas. A cleaner, better warrior never died.

The watch says it took forty-four minutes to beat his game and there are uncounted thousands like him in the bay free for the taking, if you can hold up your end of the bargain with an eight-ounce rod. Depend upon it his brothers and sisters need no help and they will deal you trouble in bunches as fast as you can get to them. They are free lances, each and every one, wild as the wastes they come out of, travelers for these past seven years or more, now just homing to the boisterous rivers where

"He is led alongside and duly shot."

they were born. Just coming in to spawn and then—die.

It is hard to understand why Nature demands the enormous toll of life that she does demand from the salmon hordes, but it is an undisputed fact that the Pacific salmon live a space of years in the deep sea to reach maturity, and that they only come back to the natal stream to spawn and die.

When you troll here under the trades of forty-seven degrees north and lure these mailed warriors from the blue wilderness of a hundred fathoms of clean salt water, you cannot help it if you have some pangs of regret for the seemingly unneeded death of the schools that you know awaits between the deep sea and those white-robed mountains yonder—only a short thirty miles away. Yet the Ruler has decreed that every one of these splendid fish, now so full of strength, so vigorous, so warlike, must make this little pilgrimage up the river, spawn there and then perish miserably and drift back seaward, a foul carrion that at last serves no other purpose but to enrich the river valley with its carcass, as the spring freshets spread their scattering bones amid the muck and ooze of the river bars.

Just now we can forget the end that the river holds, and we can pull a measured, slow stroke across the incoming tide with a glittering spoon whirling astern, sure in the knowledge that the uncounted warriors that ride the tide will send a member of their hosts to capture and fight that strange glaring, whirling bit of metal, the like of which has been unknown in their deep-sea life off the coast.

In all the catalogue of war there is no such bold fighter or one endowed with such vigor and savagery measured inch for inch. None is there that fights so joyfully, so long, so furiously. None who dies so sullenly; and therein is that charm which spells "go again" after you have fought your first fight with a clean, full-muscled salmon, fresh from the blue mystery of the deep sea.

Come then, Fellows of the Brotherhood of Anglers, from the four corners of the world, for there is a multitude here such as you know not of, and though you numbered ten score for each one who now wields a rod there would still be salmon for the late comer when you were finished, and still

more salmon to make the pilgrimage and die, so be not afraid of a lack of warriors waiting. Come, you men who know the tarpon's leap, and when you have done with the first season here the tarpon will have lost his charm. Come, you of the division of maskalonge fighters from the far north and cross tips with a warrior worth the fighting. Come, you who cast among the sedges and the lily pads for your favorite black bass, and when you are done know that your so-called king has been only a prince of the blood and not the real thing.

Pound for pound, inch for inch, there is no swimming equal in the whole wide world, none so fierce, so full of wild free courage, none that die on the end of a line like the silver mailed salmon, king of kings from the blue deep sea, and the battle ground of the host is Puget Sound. You have not lived until you know the thrill that comes up the line and quivers in the rod you hold in your hand as you feel out the messages of quick war that is going on there under water.

You think the tarpon is a warrior—he is but a yokel. The bass is short of wind and soon weary. The maskalonge is only a beginner. The trout too dainty, though a good enough fighter for his inches. But one other fish can be mentioned with the silvered warrior of the north waters—that is the bluefish and he is the victim of his appetite, not a free lance who would go to war for the simple love of the game. There is the difference, and such a bravo is surely worth his kill, is he not? I have tried to tell you why, but I find that many sensations have no word for conveying intelligence to others and am forced to say that the English language is weak. No man can tell to you the joys of this wild sea room fighting under the mists, while snow-robed mountains east of you and west of you set the scene fittingly.

The great white Mt. Rainier reflects, peak downward, across the shimmering water, and the dark, silent firs back up against the near-by hills—a setting worth the play, a part of the out-door magic that goes with fighting salmon and makes your red blood redder, your years roll back and conjures youth from the grayness of the past.

34
The Lunge
of
French River
(1910)

THE 'LUNGE of FRENCH RIVER

Paul L. Haworth

Illustrated with Photographs by the Author

"BIG baggage!" grunted grizzled old William Du Some as he surveyed the heap of boxes and "turkeys" piled on the wharf at Parry Sound. "Big baggage!" echoed stalwart young Henri Michaux, significantly rubbing the back of Pierre the cook.

There was reason for their exclamations. The Publisher, who had looked after outfitting our little party, is a strong believer in luxurious roughing it. Though for a score of years he has hearkened annually to the wild world's whisper, he has never acquired the art of cutting down impedimenta. He wants all the comforts and appliances of civilized life, even in the wilderness. It is enough to say that he brought two fountain pens and bulkier articles in proportion.

The Rare Book Man, who was having his first camping experience, carried with him a bundle of clothespins and a pair of shoe trees. All four of us indulged in the luxury of pneumatic mattresses and sleeping bags.

It is astonishing, however, how much baggage a thirty-five-foot Mackinaw boat like the *Genesee* can swallow. In half an hour all our belongings had disappeared in her capacious maw, and, with our three rowboats in tow, we were sailing out of the harbor. There was hardly a breath of air stirring, and all day we beat slowly up the coast at a snail's pace among the countless rocky, evergreen-covered islands.

About five o'clock we landed on one of these islands, pitched our tents, and then, two in a boat with a guide in each to row, set out to pick up some fish for supper. In half an hour the Doctor of Philosophy caught two bass, and his companion, the Treasurer, one,

NORTHWARD BOUND.

averaging about a pound and a half, while the other boat was equally fortunate. They were the first fish and no others caught on the whole trip tasted half so good. Next morning the scholastic landed three more, one of them a three-pounder, by still-fishing from the rocks.

But it was not until we passed Point-au-Baril and camped at the mouth of the Naiscootyong that real fishing began. South of the Point, as those who have threaded the mazes of the Thirty Thousand Islands are aware, there are many summer cottages and hotels, and the water is somewhat fished out. Even there, however, catches are easily made that would cause the ordinary angler to sit up and rub his eyes. Beyond Point-au-Baril one can go twenty miles without seeing a house or a person, and the fishing is consequently better than farther south.

We reached Naiscootyong one day just before noon. That afternoon old William rowed the Publisher and the Doctor of Philosophy to a narrow inlet that fairly swarmed with bass. After getting a few strikes we landed on some shelving rocks, and in less than an hour the Publisher landed ten bass weighing from one to three pounds, while the scholastic went him five better, notwithstanding the fact that he broke his rod subduing his biggest fish. When we stopped at last, it was not because the fish had ceased to bite, but because it had ceased to be sport and was merging on murder.

Such catches are by no means exceptional. Henri says that the record catch is ninety-six in a single day. A party of about thirty Pittsburgers who were at Naiscootyong in a large houseboat caught over four hundred in a day. Their largest weighed four and a half pounds—which is large for a bass. Such catches—I learned later—are unlawful, eight bass per rod being the maximum

FIGHTING OUR WAY THROUGH THE LOG JAM.

number allowed per day by the laws of Ontario.

With us, however, bass fishing was a mere incident. Our hearts were set on bigger prey, so, after one night at Naiscootyong, we ran northward toward the Peak of Killarney until one afternoon there loomed ahead a line of everlasting granite. In its walls appeared an opening like the mouth of some fossil monster out of which issued French River, brown with ooze from rotting leaves and trees and roots. Leaving the *Genesee* moored at French River Village, a quaint little lumbering place with two stores, a mill, and an assorted population of French, English, Indians, and half-breeds, we set off next day up the river in our three rowboats on muskellunge intent.

The task before us was no easy one, which partly accounts for the fact that so few sportsmen visit these waters— unsurpassed though they are both for fishing and for natural beauty. The French River is ordinarily a broad, deep

NOW WE PASSED AMONG PINE-TUFTED ROCKY ISLANDS.

stream, or rather labyrinth of *chenails,* lakes, and bays where a stranger might wander aimlessly for weeks. In places, however, the ever present rocks contract the river into a narrow torrent, with rapids and falls that must be portaged around.

The first of these rapids was only two miles above the river's mouth—no gentle ripple but a spot where the water plunged over rocky ledges, gurgled under drifted trees, boiled in rugged chasms, and filled the wilderness with its unceasing ravings. As we made the portage the mosquitoes pounced upon us in swarms, but luckily the season was too late for that tiny black pest—the " No-see-'em-bite-'em-damn-'em " of the Indians.

No sooner were we around the rapids than we ran into a great log jam, containing thousands of logs from camps far up toward Lake Nipissing. Jumping the boats over the half-submerged booms in a way that made the Rare Book Man wish himself safe at home, we pushed and shoved our way through the logs beyond. Much of the way our guides were out upon loose logs, and now and then one of them, in reconnoitering, ran a hundred yards or more over them in a manner that would have made an old-fashioned Harlem billy goat turn a delicate green with envy. After all, however, the feat, as those of us who tried it discovered, is by no means so difficult as it appears. The secret lies in springing lightly from log to log with such rapidity that they do not have time to sink, pausing only on the very largest.

Still, it is dangerous work, for a slip means a fall into the water, and once underneath the logs, the chances of getting your head up into the air again are none too good. Considering the fact that a large proportion of Northern lumbermen are unable to swim, it is astonishing that more are not drowned.

For two days, trolling from time to time and catching many bass and pike, we battled against logs and current. Now we passed among pine-tufted rocky islands, where patriarchal fir trees,

ONE OF THE FIVE-MILE RAPIDS.

shaggy with pendant mosses, cast black shadows, while in the water below the bleached limbs of some fallen monarch of the woods formed an ambush for voracious finny monsters waiting for their prey. Again we passed between walls of gneissic granite, in whose crevices the bearded cedar clung with snake-like roots, while aloft the rock maple, the aspen, and the glistening birch reared their light green foliage beneath the towering white pine.

Anon we saw where some rushing fire

in the three hundred years since Champlain, the Father of New France, passed through it to behold for the first time the *Mer Douce,* the Fresh Water Sea of the Hurons. In that day, owing to the ubiquity of the dreaded Iroquois about Erie and Ontario, the French River, Lake Nipissing, and the Ottawa formed the great aboriginal route between east and west, and along the portage tracks the solid rock was worn smooth by untold generations of moccasined feet.

To the Doctor of Philosophy, who

CONTENT WITH THE WORLD.

had scorched the rocks and left dead, blasted trunks standing amidst the blackened stumps and prostrate bodies of comrades half consumed. From behind lichen-clad rocks the stealthy lynx watched us as we glided by; the awkward porcupine waddled leisurely with rustling quills into the thicket; the loons dived into the brown water; and startled deer, come down to drink in some reedy cove, bounded off like huge rabbits.

We were passing through a primeval wilderness which has changed but little

loves his Parkman as men ought to love their wives, it required but little effort of the imagination to behold flotillas of canoes manned by befeathered savages and care-free *coureurs de bois* in gay capotes and gaudy sashes or hunting-shirts of smoked deerskin, bordered with fringes and the quills of the porcupine. In an effort to make the illusion more complete, he more than once asked Henri and old William to sing that beautiful but endless *chanson à l'aviron,* or boat song, of the *voyageurs,* "The White

Rose." For some reason, perhaps it was bashfulness, perhaps the reserve inbred with their Indian blood, they could not be induced to comply. After all, 'twas little matter, for he knew many of the verses by heart:

" Mais je n'ai trouvé personne
    Que le rossignol, chantant la belle rose,
    La belle rose du rosier blanc!
    Qui me dit dans son langage
    Marie-toi, car il est temps, a la belle rose,
    A la belle rose du rosier blanc! "

dividing into three streams, pours itself with unceasing roar into a foaming caldron. Camping upon the brink of the falls, we were ready next morning to begin the chief business of our journey— fishing for 'lunge.

The muskellunge, or muskellonge, or maskinonge—three of the forty different ways the gentleman's name is spelled —is, as probably most readers are aware, first cousin to the pike, that is, both belong to the genus *esox,* the pike being of the species *lucius,* the 'lunge of *nobilior.*

THE GRAND RÉCOLLET WHERE THE RIVER POURS ITSELF INTO A FOAMING CALDRON.

At evening we pitched our tents on the shelving rocks. The sun soon dropped behind the rugged hills, but the after-glow of the North long furnished light. Far into the night our fire of resinous wood glared against the dark trees and cliffs and shone far out over the river, while we sat and listened to the weird cries of the loons from the outer blackness.

Late one afternoon we entered a deep gorge, some miles up which we came to the Grand Récollet, where the river,

The 'lunge, however, is infinitely gamier than the pike, is much better eating, and is the tarpon of Northern waters. He who after a fair fight lands a big 'lunge has performed a feat that he will probably tell to his children's children.

Early next morning the Doctor of Philosophy, rising with unwonted promptitude, slipped to the brink of the falls and began casting his number five spinner into the swirling eddies in the hope of stealing a march on his companions. But an eight-pound pike and a

HOMEWARD BOUND.

two-pound bass were the only fruits of his labor. If there were any 'lunge about, they disdained his efforts.

Breakfast over, we trolled, two men to a boat, in the rapids below the falls. Bass and pike bit freely, and the Rare Book Man and the Doctor of Philosophy both caught twelve-pounders of the latter variety. To tell the truth, however, we would have much preferred that these fish, which we immediately threw back, should leave our hooks alone; but unfortunately no hook or bait (we used number five spinners baited with six inches of white pike-gut) has yet been devised which is equivalent to a sign: "For 'Lunge Only; No Others Need Apply." Perforce we had to haul in whatever chanced to bite, praying meanwhile that the next strike would be a 'lunge.

Toward noon, as William's boat, containing the scholastic and the Rare Book Man, was passing slowly across the mouth of a little cove, there came such a tremendous tug at the scholastic's line that he knew that *esox nobilior* had at

last accepted the challenge. But his fond hopes were quickly dashed. A sunken log gave the fish an opportunity of which he was not slow to take advantage. In five seconds the line was snarled about the log and the lucky fish was free again.

While William was disentangling the line, the other boat came up and lay to close by. Suddenly the Publisher emitted a yell, his reel began to play a lively tune, and presently far down the stream a great finny form rose to the surface for a moment but did not break water.

"It's a 'lunge!" yelled the Publisher; "and he's the biggest fish I ever hooked!"

Then followed a battle royal. Henri rowed the boat slowly about in the center of the river, while the Publisher matched the angling arts gained by twenty years of fishing experience against the 'lunge's weight and cunning. For half an hour the contest continued, and then, thoroughly exhausted, the fish was dragged into the boat by Henri. A crack on the head with a club, and the king of

ON THE WOLSELEY BRANCH OF THE FRENCH.

northern game fishes lay quivering in the bottom of the boat.

The "king" in this instance, however, proved to be a *queen,* but she made up for it in weight, pulling the scales down to twenty-six and one half pounds. On one side of her mouth—which was far bigger than a lady's should be—was a fresh wound, made doubtless by the scholastic's hook, and the envious Doctor of Philosophy realized, as he gazed at it, that that log had probably caused him to lose the chance of a lifetime.

Numerous pike and bass succumbed to our prowess during the remainder of the day, but not another 'lunge took hold. Next morning we set out once more up the river and camped that night on an island above the first of the Five-Mile Rapids. In the morning we fished far up the river, portaging around the rapids, but a nasty rain set in and at one o'clock we returned to camp without having made the acquaintance of any more 'lunge. Late in the afternoon the weather cleared, and we rowed up a wide bay about two miles long whose mouth was near the camp.

One for the Doctor of Philosophy

As the boat containing the Publisher and the scholastic was moving slowly along near one shore, the latter was suddenly aroused from his reverie by a tremendous tug on his line.

"'Lunge!" grunted Henri. "Keep the line tight and the rod down."

Standing up in the boat, the Doctor of Philosophy did his best, for it was doubtful if he would have another chance. Suddenly, forty yards away, a great fish shot four feet into the air, gave a vicious shake, and fell with a resounding splash back into the river. But the taut line held the hook firmly fixed in the bony mouth, so the fish changed his tactics and began a series of rushes.

He was wonderfully active and seemed absolutely tireless. For more than thirty minutes by the watch he kept up the game of seesaw. First he would allow himself to be reeled in toward the boat; then he would take the hook in his teeth and go dashing away with a force that meant: "Give me line or I will break it!" At last, however, he was drawn, still struggling, into the boat.

His wonderfully game fight had led us to expect an exceptionally large fish, but he brought the scales down to only seventeen and one half pounds. "But he is the prettiest, best-proportioned 'lunge I ever saw," said the experienced Publisher.

An hour later the Publisher landed a smaller 'lunge after a comparatively short fight. Then, while the two boats were lying close together in a small cove and no one was pretending to fish, another 'lunge came right to the surface of the water and seized the Publisher's carelessly dangling hook. But the line snarled over the end of the rod, and in a moment broke like a cobweb. That bay, in fact, seemed alive with 'lunge, for next day the Treasurer landed a twenty-pounder, while others were seen swimming about. Nevertheless, the Rare Book Man was unable to get a single strike, though he fished persistently at every opportunity, all the way back to French River Village. Ordinarily, however, any tyro can catch at least one 'lunge, though the recent completion of two railroads across the French, by rendering the fishing grounds more easily accessible, will probably soon change all this.

At present the whole French River region is, in very truth, a paradise for fishermen. Game, too, is abundant. "Partridges," i. e., ruffed grouse, are plentiful. There are still a few moose; the Doctor of Philosophy one day found a dead one, a two-year-old bull with the horns still in velvet—killed probably by some hungry Indian. Bear signs were seen several times, and deer, I verily believe, are thicker than sheep in Ohio and Indiana. This was, of course, not the open season for game, although some fishermen take the position that if a deer jumps into a boat the occupants have the right to defend themselves. We, fortunately, did not have such an experience —either literally or metaphorically. Consequently our menu was not varied by "forest lamb."

For other purposes than sport the country is comparatively worthless. The whole region is one rugged mass of gneissic granite, covered over in places with scrubby pine and some hardwood timber growing in crevices of the rocks. In the whole one hundred and sixty miles from the Five-Mile Rapids back to Penetanguishene at the southern end of Georgian Bay we did not see a piece of soil large enough for a moderate-sized garden, nor are there any sand or gravel beaches worth mentioning. Fish, game, timber, blueberries, and cranberries are the chief products and are likely to continue so.

When the hundred-million-dollar ship canal projected through the French River to the Ottawa is constructed—if it ever is—these rugged shores will witness an endless procession of vessels carrying —to Buffalo's loss—the wheat and other products of the remote Northwest. This will spoil some of the choice 'lunge fishing spots, but the region in general will always remain a labyrinthine wilderness of innumerable rocky islands, hills, bays, rivers, and lakes, a paradise. for the sportsman and the nature lover.

35
Some
Truths About
Trouting
(1902)

35
Some
Truths About
Trouting
(1902)

SOME TRUTHS ABOUT TROUTING

By EDWYN SANDYS

IT is wonderful how the first warm moist breath from the south affects an old trout fisher. Even in that infernal city cañon—a cobbled street between sheer cliffs of soulless brownstone, mortgaged and otherwise, and inhabited by a brand of cliff-dweller whose favorite form of angling is the playing of suckers—the magic of the south wind can assert itself.

Through my open window streams God's glorious oxygen, and upon the floor is a huge square of gold, painted by that mighty brush which traces the velvet shadows of huge trunk and hair-like twig upon the failing drifts and glassy surface-pools of the North. Perched upon the very sash is a cock-tailed, bull-headed thoroughly British sparrow, and he eyes me with a saucy impertinence which would be exasperating and which might earn for

him a small, cold bottle that lately held ink
were it not that I love every feathered
thing from ostriches to oars. The rascal
knows it, too, and besides, he is full of
spring and absolutely irresponsible. I
know what his heart craves of me. There
are some foolish strips of paper bearing
nothing more valuable than a mere writer's
brief notes, and possibly (?) a few shreds
of yarn are dangling from the right cuff
of the hard-worked jacket. Such things
make a fine mess, when packed conspicu-
ously against some inaccessible stone work,
and the naturalized citizen wants them
with that keen craving which seems to
possess the majority of citizens.

The song of the beggar is as exasperating as his insolent small person. He
seems to say " *Chir-ruff-chir-chir-chir-up*,"
but woven through it is an undertone
which distinctly says: "Ow! come out o'
that, you bloomin' beggar; chuck away
that bally pen; quit meddlin' with that
blawsted stationery; its spring out 'ere."

Only the oldtime teaching that not a
sparrow should fall keeps me from flicking
at him with the trout tackle. And, as if
he were not sufficiently aggravating, there
also is the everlasting New York boy,
proud of new rubber boots and a handy
puddle. I'll bet two dollars on that boy:
one that he wishes he was a centipede so
he could demand a whole lot more boots,
and the other that he attended the late
sportsman's show. Do you see that
motion with the bit of lath? That's his
idea of fly-casting. In his mind that
lath is nine feet long, tapered, jointed,
and reeled like the things he saw at the
sportsman's show. To his ghost-wand is
attached a silken dream-line, and that
puddle is foam-flecked and thrilling with
stream music. That one out-of-plumb
cobblestone is a big rock, and that bit of
banana-peel is a trout—a two-pounder,
mind you!—and that silent, earnest, wading boy is going to get him. When, do
you ask? Never mind when. Some time
—perhaps in the Adirondacks, Maine, Wisconsin, or Quebec—the dream will come
true. How do I know all this? Because
that boy is allowed to come over and play
with me two mornings each week, and I
never yet played with a boy without pois-
oning his young mind to the limit. "Spare
the rod and spoil the child" may be true,
but there's an old rod which can be spared

for him, so soon as I can get him pried
loose from his mother long enough for an
easy trek nor'ard.

There is no whisper of lewdness or any
evil in the syren song of the stream, nor
is there one germ of harm in its hurrying
flood. The heavenly jingle of the bobo-
link's golden bell as he shakes it hither
and yon above the sun-kissed, scented
meadows is only rivaled by the mirthful
chuckle or rippling laugh of the hurrying
trout stream as it plays its ceaseless
game from sun to shade on its magic way

I believe that boys and girls should be
given every opportunity and encouragement to fish, because scientific angling is
one of the cleanest, most instructive, and
most fascinating of all our outdoor
sports. It appears to embody the true
poetry and refinement of sport, and this
without any approach to the over-delicate
or unmanly. Keen devotee of the gun as
I am, yet I would hesitate to rank shooting as a refined sport above angling. It
is possible, by the strictest observance of
the true sporting code, to so elevate shooting that it becomes no unworthy rival of
angling; but, unfortunately, too few men
ever attempt to make work with the gun
the clean, wholesome, educational thing
it ought to be. As a rule, there is far
more killing and much less scientific study
than there should be.

But to the trouting. Now is the accepted time, and fortunate indeed is the
man who is so situated that he can slip
away even to comparatively nearby waters.
Your old hand knows that the first few
days after the snow-water has once run
out are apt to be the best. He also knows
that it is possible to get a bit of sport
on Long Island; better sport and more
of it in the Adirondacks and some parts
of Pennsylvania, and the best of all the
Northern States in Maine. Beyond that
are the almost innumerable Canadian
waters of New Brunswick, Quebec, and
Northern Ontario. These offer sport unsurpassed amid the wildest of romantic-
ally wild scenery, and there are leagues
upon leagues of rare good waters.

The north shore of the St. Lawrence
alone offers ample scope for a lifelong
study of the brook trout and his ways, and
few indeed are the men who have thoroughly tested the cold, swift streams of
even the one stretch of the north shore

between Montreal and Quebec, to say
nothing of the vast wilderness extending
from a bit north of Quebec to and all
around Lake St. John. Then there is the
grand north shore of Superior, with its
storied Nepigon and its dozens of minor
lakes and short streams, the latter fairly

tumbling down the rock-bound slopes into
the huge, ice-cold basin, which floats no
dead to its sternly hewed strand.

Among the huge network of waters
flung over the country from Maine to
Labrador; from Atlantic tidewater to
the snowy northward surf of the Great

His First Trout.

"The wise man does not let his shadow shift over the pool."

Inland Sea; from the wonderful new country of the upper Ottawa down to the long-settled hillsides of the lower, one can find trout fishing unsurpassed in the world and perhaps only rivaled by the cream of the sport of the cloud-swept tarns and glacier-born streams of the huge mountain ranges of the far West. Thousands of miles of trout waters in all, and many of them practically unfished; but there are rods in pickle for some of them this year, or I'm no prophet. To the raw hand at the game I may address a few words of advice.

In the first place, don't imagine that all, or half, or for that matter one-eighth of the easily accessible waters offer unlimited facilities for all sorts of long-distance casting, for they do not. For really artistic fly-fishing one needs must have plenty of space behind as well as in front, for the back-cast really is the difficulty. Here and there, in some of the forest lakes, are reefs and shallows where one may wade and find plenty of room, but as a rule, some craft, or raft, is necessary to

The Crucial Moment.

enable you to get away from the shore. On the stream one finds room for action by wading up or down, and few, indeed, are the streams which may be properly fished from either bank. Hence, trout fishing means wading, which demands a proper equipment, unless the fisher be one of that Bravo Brigade who foolishly take unwise chances in the matter of getting wet and chilled.

The wise man knows that long-continued wading in cold water is very bad for the human machine—that what may be laughed at to-day may be heard from again later on, when the rich sporting blood has cooled a bit. It is all very fine to depend upon that broken reed, the flask, or that much-abused and seldom-understood thing, the constitution. Both fail at times. A distillery couldn't remedy some of the possible damages which may result from foolish exposure, while the constitution of the United States would be no guarantee against the effect of rashly taken chances. That a few men have been wet time and again, for hours at a stretch, is no proof that *you* can stand the same ordeal, and the trouble is that you have to do the sum to prove it. If you moved into a house just vacated by a doctor and found a small vial containing some unknown substance, would you swallow it just to learn if it were deadly or harmless ?

Because wading is the best way to get trout, and down stream the best way to wade, I do both, but before starting to wade I do several other things, and all are important. The first of these is to put on all-wool underwear and thick woolen socks, because a man seldom chills or takes cold in such dress. Over the woolen wear should go a gray flannel shirt or sweater and any old pair of gray trousers. If the weather demands it, an old gray coat should be added, while for the head there is nothing so good as an old, soft, gray felt hat—an old "Fedora," or "wide-awake," is the very thing. Either of these will properly shade the eyes and at the same time furnish a convenient place for the supply of hooks. For the feet, especially during the early season, there is nothing better than the ordinary rubber waders, which come well up to the fork, and fit close to the thigh. These may be turned down to below the knee, if desired,

which enables a man to cool his legs upon a warm day.

Here, then, is the man dressed in a workmanlike and thoroughly comfortable suit, which, because the tree trunks beside the stream, and also the rocks, present a general grayish tone, admirably blends with the surroundings, and fairly melts into the shadows early and late in the day. The next best color is the "dead grass" shade of the regulation shooting suit, but for the stream the gray is unrivaled. And I firmly believe the matter of costume is of more importance than some anglers are willing to admit. Long ago I made a study of the subject of shooting gear, and from geese and other wary gentry I learned the true value of closely matching the costume with the natural surroundings. Later, the color scheme for trout was taken up, and certainly results have proved that close attention to these fine points is good medicine. It is quite true that men garbed any old way can kill trout in some waters, but that by no means applies to all waters, especially if the waters in question happen to be low and crystal-clear. There are fool trout and educated trout, and the man who craves the valedictorian trout, or the sweet girl graduate trout, will do well to observe the common sense rule, which reads: dress as inconspicuously as possible.

A man who had killed his fair share of trout once asked me if " I *really* believed in the importance of correct dressing," which implied that fish "could see out of the water." I knew what he meant, and wondered, for that same man invariably used the finest of tackle, and had killed perhaps hundreds of trout, which had leaped inches above the stream after his flies. Apropos of "seeing out of the water," I have seen a small trout not only jump for, but hook itself, in its effort to seize a fly which for the time was left hanging against the side of a mossy bowlder and several inches above the water. The eye is not always reliable, but I gravely suspect mine has seen a big trout gather in a white moth a foot or more above the stream. This would not only suggest an ability to see out of the water, but also an ability to see infernally well, for a moving mark the size of a miller demands deadly accuracy. Furthermore, the neatness and dispatch displayed by a

Where Expertness is Needed.

big trout in getting to deeper water the instant a man appears upon the bank, shadow or no shadow, is strongly suggestive of ability to see.

The advantage of fishing down stream is two-fold—*i. e.*, the fly, or bait, comes to the fish with the stream, as the fish has learned to expect prey to come, and to meet which he is lying with his nose to the current, which can be made to assist in getting the lure where wanted; also, the man on any ordinary stream should have the needful room behind, while retaining the power to cover every yard of water below. The sole disadvantage of fishing with the stream is that accidental disturbances of stones, etc., may be carried to fish directly below, while sometimes one's extended shadow may cause trouble. The wise man, of course, does not make a habit of letting his shadow shift over every pool he comes to, but the trouble with the shadow of man and rod may be overcome by moving from side to side as occasion demands.

In regard to lures, the simple truth is that only a small proportion of early fish are taken with the fly. It is true that a host of anglers glorify fly fishing and damn bait, but it is equally true that a number of those very men use bait and artificial lures upon those numerous days when trout are not keen for the fly. I have not the slightest desire to belittle fly fishing, nor have I any hesitancy over saying that I have used every likely bait that I could get my hooks on, or get on my hooks. Unquestionably, when fly fishing is good, it is preferable to bait fishing in any form, but unfortunately, it is not always good, or even fair; nay, more often than not it is utterly unreliable, perhaps impossible. At such times, instead of fretting and stewing about it, I go get bait and, incidentally, trout.

It is all very fine to sneer at bait, but with all due respect to the stickler for flies, the bait fisher frequently is the real expert. To use bait on fine tackle requires the fly fisher's knowledge and something more. The expert bait fisher must know what the trout are taking and why, and also where that thing is to be obtained and how. He has more to do than to reach for his hat or his book, and if he cannot procure the exact thing, he must know of one, two, or half a dozen possible substitutes, and just where and how they are to be obtained at short notice, which is apt to mean that he must procure them for himself. After the fish is once hooked, the same skill is required to play and land it, no matter if it rose to a hackle, a worm, a grub, a young mouse, a natural insect, or even to that oft-used, old reliable—a small section of some soulful sow. Hence, the reading tyro will do well to remember that it is not all of fishing to catch fish, with or without the fly, nor is it all of good sense to go without fish when you want 'em, simply because the

poetic method of taking trout is by means of a bunco bug fashioned out of barbed wire and millinery, and bearing only a questionable resemblance to any honest insect.

But when the water, surroundings, day, and fish are what they should be, then indeed is fly fishing the artistic and fascinating thing of which enthusiasts have raved ever since the dawn of the day of fine tackle and its necessary fine art. The trail of the trouter must penetrate the picturesque—nay! it is one long gallery hung with the scenic masterpieces of East and West. Forever before one winds, or spreads, the silver pathway of the brook—the flashing shield of the lonely lake. Forever in one's ears is liquid melody of cold, sweet water, always singing to woody aisles of silence, or breaking in merry music about the feet of stony sentinels whose everlasting duty is to guard the gem-like lakes of all the forested North.

But trout fishing is not always the delicate play of fairy tackle upon baby streams and bantam lakes. Where the grand purple battlements of Superior's northern shore repel the white-maned cavalry of the queen of fresh water seas there is trout fishing unequaled for scope and grandeur of setting.

Where a big bay curves in behind the outer cliffs and leaves the tumult of surfy assault to leap, break, and retreat from its hopeless task, I have stood of a summer evening and wondered. A full half mile of calm, crystal-clear water, cold as the tears of a dying glacier, was ringed and dimpled here, there, and everywhere by the play of the rising trout. And to avoid the possibility of a misunderstanding, let me say that brook trout are meant, and not fat, lazy lake trout, or "lakers." In the bays, coves, and along the North Shore for a stretch of many miles, the brook trout find congenial haunts. The "height of land" is but a comparatively short distance inland, hence all the best streams of that side of Superior are short, as they chiefly are the outlets of small, nearby lakes. Even the famous Nepigon River, which may be termed the continuation of the St. Lawrence beyond Lake Superior, is only thirty-one miles long from its hasty exit from its parent, Lake Nepigon, at Flat Rock, to its final plunge to the level of Nepigon Bay.

36
The Lord
of
Lackawaxen Creek
(1909)

THE LORD OF LACKAWAXEN CREEK

BY ZANE GREY

INDING among the Blue Hills of Pennsylvania there is a swift amber stream that the Indians named Lack-a-wax-en. The literal translation no one seems to know, but it must mean, in mystical and imaginative Delaware, "the brown water that turns and whispers and tumbles." It is a little river hidden away under gray cliffs and hills black with ragged pines. It is full of mossy stones and rapid ripples.

All its tributaries, dashing white-sheeted over ferny cliffs, wine-brown where the whirling pools suck the stain from the hemlock roots, harbor the speckled trout. Wise in their generation the black and red-spotted little beauties keep to their brooks; for, farther down, below the rush and fall, a newcomer is lord of the stream. He is an arch enemy, a scorner of beauty and blood, the wolf-jawed, red-eyed, bronze-backed black-bass.

A mile or more from its mouth the Lackawaxen leaves the shelter of the hills and seeks the open sunlight and slows down to widen into long lanes that glide reluctantly over the few last restraining barriers to the Delaware. In a curve between two of these level lanes there is a place where barefoot boys wade and fish for chubs and bask on the big bowlders like turtles. It is a famous hole for chubs and bright-sided shiners and sunfish. And, perhaps because it is so known, and so shallow, so open to the sky, few fishermen ever learned that in its secret stony caverns hid a great golden-bronze treasure of a bass.

In vain had many a flimsy feathered hook been flung over his lair by fly casters and whisked gracefully across the gliding surface of his pool. In vain had many a shiny spoon and pearly minnow reflected sunglints through the watery windows of his home. In vain had many a hellgamite and frog and grasshopper been dropped in front of his broad nose.

Chance plays the star part in a fisherman's luck. One still cloudy day, when the pool glanced dark under a leaden sky, I saw a wave that reminded me of the wake of a rolling tarpon; then followed an angry swirl, the skitter of a frantically leaping chub, and a splash that ended with a sound like the deep chung of water sharply turned by an oar.

Big bass choose strange hiding places. They should be looked for in just such holes and rifts and shallows as will cover their backs. But to corral a six-pounder in the boys' swimming hole was a circumstance to temper a fisherman's vanity with experience.

Thrillingly conscious of the possibilities of this pool, I studied it thoughtfully. It was a wide, shallow bend in the stream, with dark channels between submerged rocks, suggestive of underlying shelves. It had a current, too, not noticeable at first glance. And this pool looked at long and carefully, colored by the certainty of its guardian, took on an aspect most alluring to an angler's spirit. It had changed from a pond girt by stony banks, to a foam-flecked running stream, clear, yet hiding its secrets, shallow, yet full of labyrinthine water-courses. It presented problems, which, difficult as they were, faded in a breath before a fisherman's optimism.

I tested my leader, changed the small hook for a large one, and selecting a white shiner fully six inches long, I lightly hooked it through the side of the upper lip. A sensation never outgrown since boyhood, a familiar mingling of strange fear and joyous anticipation, made me stoop low and tread the slippery stones as if I were a stalking Indian. I knew that a glimpse of me, or a faint jar vibrating under the water, or an unnatural ripple on its surface would be fatal to my enterprise.

I swung the lively minnow and instinctively dropped it with a splash over a dark space between two yellow sunken stones. Out of the amber depths started a broad bar of bronze, rose and flashed into gold. A little dimpling eddying circle, most fascinating of all watery forms, appeared round where the minnow had sunk. The golden moving flash went down and vanished in the greenish gloom like a tiger stealing into a jungle. The line trembled, slowly swept out and straightened. How fraught that instant with a wild yet waiting suspense, with a thrill potent and blissful!

Did the fisherman ever live who could wait in such a moment? My arms twitched involuntarily. Then I struck hard, but not half hard enough. The bass leaped out of a flying splash, shook himself in a tussle plainly audible, and slung the hook back at me like a bullet.

In such moments one never sees the fish distinctly; excitement deranges the vision, and the picture, though impressive, is dim and dreamlike. But a blind man would have known this bass to be enormous, for when he fell he cut the water as a heavy stone.

The best of fishing is that a mild philosophy attends even the greatest misfortunes. To be sure this philosophy is a delusion peculiar to fishermen. It is something that goes with the game and makes a fellow fancy he is a stoic, invulnerable to the slings and arrows of outrageous fortune.

So I went on my way upstream, cheerfully, as one who minded not at all an incident of angling practice; spiritedly as one who had seen many a big bass go by the board. The wind blew softly in my face; the purple clouds, marshaled aloft in fleets, sailed away into the gray distance; the stream murmured musically; a kingfisher poised marvelously over a pool, shot downward like a streak, to rise with his quivering prey; birds sang in the willows and daisies nodded in the fields; misty veils

hung low in the hollows; all those attributes of nature, poetically ascribed by anglers to be the objects of their full content, were about me.

I found myself thinking about my two brothers, Cedar and Reddy for short, both anglers of long standing and some reputation. It was a sore point with me and a stock subject for endless disputes that they just never could appreciate my superiority as a fisherman. Brothers are singularly prone to such points of view. So when I thought of them I felt the incipient stirring of a mighty plot. It occurred to me that the iron-mouthed old bass, impregnable of jaw as well as of stronghold, might be made to serve a turn. And all the afternoon the thing grew and grew in my mind.

Luck favoring me, I took home a fair string of fish, and remarked to my brothers that the conditions for fishing the stream were favorable. Thereafter morning on morning my eyes sought the heavens, appealing for a cloudy day. At last one came, and I invited Reddy to go with me. With childish pleasure, that would have caused weakness if any but an unscrupulous villain, he eagerly accepted. He looked over a great assortment of tackle, and finally selected a six-ounce Leonard bait-rod carrying a light reel and fine line. When I thought of what would happen, if Reddy hooked that powerful bass, an unholy glee fastened upon my soul.

We never started out that way together, swinging rods and pails, but old associations were awakened. We called up the time when we had left the imprints of bare feet on the country roads; we lived over many a boyhood adventure by a running stream. And at last we wound up on the never threadbare question as to the merit and use of tackle.

"I always claimed," said Reddy, "that a fisherman should choose tackle for a day's work after the fashion of a hunter in choosing his gun. A hunter knows what kind of game he's after, and takes a small or large caliber accordingly. Of course a fisherman has more rods than there are calibers of guns, but the rule holds. Now to-day I have brought this light rod and thin line because I don't need weight. I don't see why you've brought that heavy rod. Even a two pound

Fishing in the Lackawaxen.

bass would be a great surprise up this stream."

"You're right," I replied, "but I sort of lean to possibilities. Besides I'm fond of this rod. You know I've caught a half dozen bass of from five to six pounds with it. I wonder what you would do if you hooked a big one on the delicate thing."

The brown water that turns and whispers and tumbles.

"Do?" ejaculated my brother. "I'd have a fit! I might handle a big bass in deep water with this outfit, but here in this shallow stream with its rocks and holes I couldn't. And that is the reason so few big bass are taken from the Delaware. We know they are there, great lusty fellows! Every day in season we hear some tale of woe from some fisherman. 'Hooked a big one—broke this— broke that—got under a stone.' That's why no five or six pound bass are taken from shallow, swift, rock-bedded streams on light tackle."

When we reached the pool I sat down and began to fumble with my leader. How generously I let Reddy have the first cast! My iniquity carried me to the extreme of bidding him steal softly and stoop low. I saw a fat chub swinging in the air; I saw it alight to disappear in a churning commotion of the water, and I heard Reddy's startled: "Gee!"

Hard upon his exclamation followed action of striking swiftness. A shrieking reel, willow wand of a rod wavering like a buggy-whip in the wind, curving splashes round a foam-lashed swell, a crack of dry wood, a sound as of a banjo string snapping, a sharp splash, then a heavy sullen souse; these, with Reddy standing voiceless, eyes glaring on a broken rod and limp trailing line, were the essentials of the tragedy.

Somehow the joke did not ring true, when Reddy waded ashore calm and self-contained, with only his burning eyes to show how deeply he felt. What he said to me in a quiet voice must not, owing to family pride, go on record. It most assuredly would not be an addition to the fish literature of the day.

But he never mentioned the incident to Cedar, which omission laid the way open for my further machinations. I realized that I should have tried Cedar first. He was one of those white-duck-pants-on-a-dry-rock sort of a fisherman anyway. And in due time I had him wading out toward the center of that pool.

I always experienced a painful sensation while watching Cedar cast. He must have gotten his style from a Delsartian school.

One moment he resembled Ajax defying the lightning and the next he looked like the fellow who stood on a monument smiling at grief. And not to mention pose, Cedar's execution was wonderful. I have seen him cast a frog a mile—but the frog had left the hook. It was remarkable to see him catch his hat, and terrifying to hear the language he used at such ordinary angling event. It was not safe to be in his vicinity, but if this was unavoidable, the better course was to face him; because if you turned your back an instant, his flying hook would have a fiendish affinity for your trousers, and it was not beyond his powers to swing you kicking out over the stream. All of which, considering the frailties of human nature and of fishermen, could be forgiven; he had, however, one great fault impossible to overlook and it was that he made more noise than a playful hippopotamus.

I hoped, despite all these things, that the big bass would rise to the occasion. He did rise. He must have recognized the situation of his life. He spread the waters of his shallow pool and accommodatingly hooked himself.

Cedar's next graceful move was to fall off the slippery stone on which he had been standing and to go out of sight. His hat floated downstream; the arched tip of his rod came up, then his arm, and his dripping shoulders and body. He yelled like a savage and pulled on the fish hard enough to turn a tuna in the air. The big bass leaped three times, made a long shoot with his black dorsal fin showing, and then, with a lunge, headed for some place remote from there. Cedar plowed after him, sending the water in sheets, and then he slipped, wildly swung his arms and fell again.

I was sinking to the ground owing to unutterable and overpowering sensations of joy when a yell and a commotion in the bushes heralded the appearance of Reddy.

"Hang on, Cedar! Hang on!" he cried, and began an Indian war-dance.

. . . and threaded the familiar green-lined towpath toward home.

The few succeeding moments were somewhat blurred because of my excess of emotion. When I returned to consciousness Cedar was wading out with a hookless leader, a bloody shin, and a disposition utterly and irretrievably ruined.

"Put up a job on me!" he roared.

Thereafter during the summer each of us made solitary and sneaking expeditions, bent on the capture of the lord of the Lackawaxen. And somehow each would return to find the other two derisively speculative as to what caused his clouded brow. Leader on leader went to grace the rocks of the old bronze warrior's home. At length Cedar and Reddy gave up, leaving the pool to me. I fed more than one choice shiner to the bass and more than once he sprang into the air to return my hook.

Summer and autumn passed; winter came to lock the Lackawaxen in icy fetters; I fished under southern skies where lagoons and moss-shaded waters teemed with great and gamy fish, but I never forgot him. I knew that when the season rolled around, when a June sun warmed the cold spring-fed Lackawaxen, he would be waiting for me.

Who was it spoke of the fleeting of time? Obviously he had never waited for the opening of the fishing season. But at last the tedious time was like the water that has passed. And then I found I had another long wait. Brilliant June days without a cloud were a joy to live, but worthless for fishing. Through all that beautiful month I plodded up to the pool, only to be unrewarded. Doubt began to assail me. Might not the ice, during the spring break-up, have scored him from the shallow hole? No. I felt that not even a rolling glacier could have moved him from his subterranean home.

Often as I reached the pool I saw fishermen wading down the stream, and on these occasions I sat on the bank and lazily waited for the intruding disturbers of my peace to pass on. Once, the first time I saw them, I had an agonizing fear that one of the yellow-helmetted, khaki-coated anglers would hook my bass. The fear, of course, was groundless, but I could not help human feelings. The idea of that grand fish rising to a feathery imitation of a bug or a lank dead bait had nothing in my experience to warrant its consideration. Small, lively bass, full of play, fond of chasing their golden shadows, and belligerent and hungry, were ready to fight and eat whatever swam into their ken. But a six-pound bass, slow to reach such weight in swift-running water, was old and wise

and full of years. He did not feed often and when he did he wanted a live fish big enough for a good mouthful. So, with these facts to soothe me I rested my fears, and got to look humorously at the invasions of the summer-hotel fishers.

They came wading, slipping, splashing downstream, blowing like porpoises, slapping at the water with all kinds of artificial and dead bait. And they called to me in a humor actuated by my fishing garb and the rustic environment.

"Hey, Rube! Ketchin' any?"

I said the suckers was bitin' right pert.

"What d'you call this stream?"

I replied, giving the Indian name.

"Lack-a-what? Can't you whistle it? Lack-awhacken? You mean Lack-afishin'."

"Lack-arotten," joined in another.

"Do you live here?" questioned a third.

I modestly said yes.

"Why don't you move?" Whereupon they all laughed and pursued the noisy tenor of their way downstream, pitching their baits around.

"Say, fellows," I shouted after them, "are you training for the casting tournament in Madison Square Garden or do you think you're playing lacrosse?"

Good fellows all! The laugh that came back proved the joke on them, and that it would be remembered as part of the glorious time they were having.

July brought the misty, dark, lowering days. Not only did I find the old King at home on these days, but just as contemptuous of hooks and leaders as he had been the summer before. About the middle of the month he stopped giving me paralysis of the heart; that is to say, he quit rising to my tempting chubs and shiners. So I left him alone to rest, to rust out hooks and grow less suspicious.

By the time August came the desire to call on him again was well nigh irresistible. But I waited, and fished the Delaware, and still waited. I would get him when the harvest moon was full. Like all the old moss-backed denizens of the shady holes, he would come out then for a last range over the feeding shoals.

At length a morning broke humid and warm, almost dark as twilight, with little gusts of fine rain. Of all days this was the day! I chose a stiff rod, a heavy silk line, a stout brown leader, and a large hook. From my bait box I took two five-inch red catfish, the little "stone-rollers" of the Delaware, and several long shiners. Thus equipped I sallied forth.

The walk up the towpath, along the canal with its rushes and sedges, across the meadows white with late-blooming daisies, lost nothing because of its familiarity. When I reached the pool I saw in the low water near shore several small bass scouting among the schools of minnows. I did not want these pugnacious fellows to kill my bait, so procuring a hellgamite from under a stone, I put it on my hook and promptly caught two of them, and gave the other a scare he would not soon forget.

I decided to try the bass with one of his favorite shiners. With this trailing in the water I silently waded out, making not so much as a ripple. The old familiar oppression weighed on my breast; the old throbbing boyish excitement tingled through my blood. I made a long cast and dropped the shiner lightly. He went under and then came up to swim about on the surface. This was a sign that made my heart leap. Then the water bulged, and a black bar shot across the middle of the long shiner. He went down out of sight, the last gleams of his divided brightness fading slowly. I did not need to see the little shower of silver scales floating up to know that the black bar had been the rounded nose of the old bass and that he had taken the shiner across the middle. I struck hard, and my hook came whistling at me. I had scored a clean miss.

I waded ashore very carefully, sat down on a stone by my bait pail and meditated. Would he rise again? I had never known him to do so twice in one day. But then there had never been occasion. I bethought me of the "stone-rollers" and thrilled with certainty. Whatever he might resist he could not resist one of those little red catfish.. Long ago when he was only a three or four pounder, roaming the deep eddies and swift rapids of the Delaware, before he had isolated himself to a peaceful old age in this quiet pool, he must have poked his nose under many a stone, with red eyes keen for one of those dainty morsels.

My excitation thrilled itself out to the calm assurance of the experienced fisher-

man. I firmly fastened on one of the catfish and stole out into the pool. I waded farther than ever before; I was careful but confident. Then I saw the two flat rocks dimly shining. The water was dark as it rippled by, gurgling softly; it gleamed with lengthening shadows and glints of amber.

I swung the catfish. A dull flash of sunshine seemed to come up to meet him. The water swirled and broke with a splash. The bass' broad black head just skimmed the surface; his jaws opened wide to take in the bait; he turned and flapped a huge spread tail on the water.

Then I struck with all the power the tackle would stand. I felt the hook catch solidly as if in a sunken log. Swift as flashing light the bass leaped. The drops of water hissed and the leader whizzed But the hook held. I let out one exultant yell. He did not leap again. He dashed to the right, then the left, in bursts of surprising speed. I had hardly warmed to the work when he settled down and made for the dark channel between the yellow rocks. My triumph was to be short-lived. Where was the beautiful spectacular surface fight I expected of him? Cunning old monarch! He laid his great weight dead on the line and lunged for his sunken throne. I held him with a grim surety of the impossibility of stopping him. How I longed for deep, open water! The rod bent, the line strained and stretched. I removed my thumb and the reel sang one short shrill song. Then the bass was as still as the rock under which he had gone.

I had never dislodged a big bass from under a stone, and I saw herein further defeat; but I persevered, wading to different angles, and working all the tricks of the trade. I could not drag the fish out, nor pull the hook loose. I sat down on a stone and patiently waited for a long time, hoping he would come out of his own accord.

As a final resort, precedent to utter failure, I waded out. The water rose to my waist, then to my shoulders, my chin, and all but covered my raised face. When I reached the stone under which he had planted himself I stood in water about four feet deep. I saw my leader, and tugged upon it, and kicked under the stone, all to no good.

Then I calculated I had a chance to dislodge him if I could get my arm under the shelf. So down I went, hat, rod, and all. The current was just swift enough to lift my feet making my task most difficult. At the third trial I got my hand on a sharp corner of stone and held fast. I ran my right hand along the leader, under the projecting slab of rock, till I touched the bass. I tried to get hold of him, but had to rise for air.

I dove again. The space was narrow, so narrow that I wondered how so large a fish could have gotten there. He had gone under sidewise, turned and wedged his dorsal fin, fixing himself as solidly as the rock itself. I pulled frantically till I feared I would break the leader.

When I floundered up to breathe again the thought occurred to me that I could rip him with my knife and by taking the life out of him, loosen the powerful fin so he could be dragged out. Still, much as I wanted him I could not do that. I resolved to make one more fair attempt. In a quick determined plunge I secured a more favorable hold for my left hand and reached under with my right. I felt his whole long length and I could not force a finger behind him anywhere. The gill toward me was shut tight like a trap door. But I got a thumb and forefinger fastened to his lip. I tugged till a severe cramp numbed my hand; I saw red and my head whirled; a noise roared in my ears. I stayed until one more second would have made me a drowning man, then rose gasping and choking.

I broke off the leader close to the stone and waded ashore. I looked back at the pool, faintly circled by widening ripples. What a great hole and what a grand fish! I was glad I did not get him and knew I would never again disturb his peace.

So I took my rod and pail and the two little bass, and brushed the meadow daisies, and threaded the familiar green-lined towpath toward home.

The line trembled and straightened.

37
To the Shores
of the
Mingan Seigniory
(1897)

TO THE SHORES OF THE MINGAN SEIGNIORY

BY FREDERIC IRLAND.

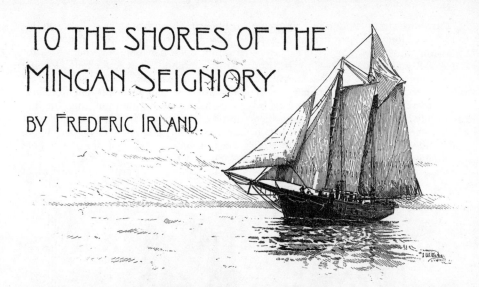

IN whatever murky American city one's lot may be cast, the earthly paradise of a perfect summer day is never very far off, as the wild duck flies. When the walls and pavements of New York are blistering under the August sun, it is but a night's journey to the cool green May which, on the Gulf of St. Lawrence, lasts until the beginning of autumn. During the worst of the heated term of 1896, when people died of sunstroke by the hundred in every great city of the United States, the boy and I, in ulsters and mittens, joyously trod the deck of a gulf schooner, while the Saguenay sailors worked her against head-winds blowing fresh from the innumerable ice-cold lakes of Labrador and the primeval solitudes of the Laurentian Mountains.

The vast country north of the Gulf of St. Lawrence is, to the uncommercial explorer, the most interesting region on this continent, if not in the world. For nearly four centuries the ships of civilization have sailed by it, yet, except at the very water's edge, there has been no intrusion upon it. The rivers which pour forth from every opening in the hills bear witness that the back country is a net-work of lakes and water-courses. Ask the Commissioner of Crown Lands of the great Province of Quebec to-day what his department knows of that region, and he will tell you that it is the least known portion of North America; that only a few of the lakes have been surveyed; that two exploring parties have

recently crossed the peninsula; that a handful of fishermen's houses fringe the gulf; that for the rest of it, the wandering Montagnais Indians are the only tourists who traverse half a million square miles of territory. Steamers go up the Saguenay. Lake St. John is reached by rail. But away to the northeast is a tremendous tract of country, from whence issue streams greater than the Hudson, the headwaters of which no white man has ever seen. How many Americans, if asked to mention the beautiful rivers of the continent, could give even the names of the Bersimis, the Outardes, the Manicouagan, the Misticapin, the Moisie, the Mingan, the Romaine, the Natashquan, the Olomonosheeboo, the Meccatina, the Esquimaux? Only a few salmon fisherman, who are the most indefatigable of sportsmen, would recognize them.

It was to view this neglected summer seacoast that the boy and I left Quebec last summer, to go to Tadousac by a steamer as fine as any floating hotel of the Sound, and to proceed beyond Tadousac by such means as could thereafter be devised. We went for a lazy cruise, and to see some of the wonderful salmon streams of that country.

Before leaving Quebec we had secured a permit from the Crown Land Office "to fish in the waters not presently under lease, or in which the fishing rights belong to the province, on the north shore of the Gulf of

405

St. Lawrence, from Pointe de Monts up to Blanc Sablon. Said permit shall be good for two months."

"And if you fish in all those rivers," said the smiling Deputy Commissioner, "you will not come back this summer, or the next, either." We found this to be true, because only a small part of the fishing rivers of that shore were under private lease in 1896, and a beautiful stream breaks through the mountains about every ten miles.

It was evening and low tide when we clambered up the slanting gang-plank at

it being midsummer and a dull season, we soon chartered the ship, her cook, her captain bold, her mate and her crew, for $180 a month. That was enough for one evening. The missing Robitois, sailor at $8 a month, went ashore to postpone wedding-bells, which now would not ring for him until our return. Besides, the tide must be waited for, and we slept at the hotel, the last one this side of the north pole along that coast.

The six hours of northern summer night soon passed, and then we swung out with

On the Sunny Deck.

Tadousac, and stood on the dock, as high as a cottage roof above the water. Just around the point, in the deep little bay, two or three schooner-lights blinked and nodded in a sleepy way, as the vessels swung at anchor on the gentle swells. Tadousac is somewhere near three centuries old, and it has fully twenty houses already. The mountains rise in grandeur behind the place, and the Saguenay, six hundred feet deep, pours copiously at its feet.

The owner of one of the schooners was at home, for his vessel had just returned, after a highly successful delivery of lumber from St. Anne des Monts to Quebec, and,

the tide, and sailed away through the morning mist to Rivière du Loup, on the South Shore, where Henry Braithwaite, guide extraordinary, all the way from New Brunswick, with provisions and birch-bark canoes, and silent Malicete Indians, waited to be taken aboard. On the way across the wide St. Lawrence a summer thunderstorm broke, but the forty-foot sails were not reefed; the yacht-like freighter heeled till her deck was like the roof of a house, and she made the twenty-four miles in two hours, while the porpoises puffed and blew, and arched their sinuous white backs all around us.

If you want to go to heaven before you

die, visit the northeastern Canadian coast in summer, under the personal conducting of good guides. The faithful Braithwaite had planned for weeks. We had projected this invasion of the North a whole year before, while searching for the elusive moose of the Miramichi; and when we made fast at the dock at Rivière du Loup, all was ready. Canoes and bundles and Indians

In Tadousac Harbor.

were soon on board, and away we flew, between the dim blue hills that mark the receding shores of the great river of Canada, every breeze and every turning tide bearing us prosperously farther north and east.

It was a polyglot crowd on that schooner. There were Canadian sailors who spoke no English; the Indian, Baptiste, who spoke French and Malicete; Francis, from Old Town, Me., whose Malicete

and Abenaki were beyond criticism, and whose careful English was a reminder of the speech of the Honorable Thomas Brackett Reed. So, for any complicated message, there was a tortuous channel, via Francis and Baptiste, to the Canadian skipper's French and back again; and the Lord knows how the translations fared in transit.

What a gambler's game a sailing vessel plays. Some days we sailed and sailed. Sometimes we went to bed with a headland in sight, and in the morning, after hours of seeming progress, it had been an undecided contest between wind and tide, and we were still there. One day a southwest gale swept us over galloping green hills; while the next the sails flapped and clattered as the schooner reeled helplessly on hummocks of leaden water, without a breath of air stirring.

One great charm about this region is

Portaging on the Mingan.

the fact that you have left the space-destroying railroad train far behind you, and the steamer, too. The ocean liners from Quebec run to the south of Anticosti Island, and only one little coaster, the Otter, makes a fortnightly trip down the north shore to carry the mail, during July and August, to the few hundred cod fishermen scattered here and there. If there were a railroad, a train like the Empire State Ex-

with his black dorsal fin four feet in the air, and his head as big as a wine-cask. Farther down the Gulf we were seldom out of sight and hearing of the whales, of which we counted twenty-seven one day. At night the phosphorescence of the sea left a wake of green fire streaming from the rudder, and when we invaded a school of little fish, they seemed, as they darted away, like hundreds of submarine shoot-

Salmon Pool on the Jupitagen.

press, or the great transcontinental flyer of the Canadian Pacific, could run from Quebec to Blanc Sablon in a day; but as it is you are in the country where no one hastens. You wish to go a hundred miles. If the wind blows, you go. If not, surely it will blow to-morrow, or some other day. Then let us be content that all is well.

There is an endless variety of new sights to see. The lower St. Lawrence swarms with sea-life. There are the seals, bobbing up their heads, and dodging down at the least alarm; the porpoises, always snoring; often the evil shape of a grampus,

ing stars. All day long the gulls kept trying to determine the precise limits of shotgun range. We had a fine collection of the mistaken ones, ready for the taxidermist; and the family of rats on the schooner were no doubt grateful for the change from ship-fare, for they ate everything but the feathers.

On warm, sunny days, when the world went well, it was most comfortable to bring the mattresses from the cabin, place them on top of the deck-house, lie down and do nothing but breathe. It was a subject of continual surprise how short the time was between meals.

A "Strike."

We had no permit to stop and fish in any of the streams west of Pointe de Monts. This is the place where the St. Lawrence River widens out into the gulf. There are several fine fishing rivers west of the point, but, as they are within three hundred miles of Quebec, they are under lease. The three great rivers between the Saguenay and Pointe de Monts are the Bersimis, the Outardes and the Manicouagan. The Bersimis is a deep and dark lake-fed stream, and the salmon in it do not rise to the fly. The Outarde is effectually blockaded against the entrance of the sea-going fish, by impassable falls at its mouth. The Manicouagan also has a fall at the gulf which the salmon cannot climb, and yet its upper waters are filled with these noble fish during their spawning season. This paradox is accounted for in a curious way. About forty miles east of the Manicouagan the little Godbout, one of the most famous salmon rivers in Canada, discharges into the St. Lawrence. For a generation its fishing-right has been controlled by the Gilmours, of Ottawa. Far back in the interior this stream has its source in a lake which has two outlets; one emptying into the Godbout, the other into a tributary of the Manicouagan. So the salmon ascend the Godbout, cross the lake, descend the other outlet into the Manicouagan, and go on their way rejoic-

A Happy Boy.

ing to their trysting-places on the gravelly shallows of the upper river.

Either one of these streams is large enough to irrigate a whole Western arid State. The course of the Manicouagan is marked by lakes of great size. More and more, as one becomes acquainted with the coast, and sees the clear, cold floods which pour through every chasm in the mountains along the shore, is he impressed with the aqueous wealth of the interior.

From Pointe de Monts to the Bay of Seven Islands, there are a hundred miles of shore which the schooner fleet of lower Quebec shun and fear. There is no good harbor from Trinity Bay to the Bay of Seven Islands, and there is a tale of shipwreck for every rock along the coast. Several rivers come in, the largest being the Pentecôte or Mistacapin, the Rivière des Rochers, and the Marguerite. I talked with the surveyor who first explored the Rivière des Rochers in 1895, and he assured me the stream was filled

Gaffing a Salmon.

with trout of great size. " From twenty to thirty inches in length " were his figures. I have no reason to doubt this. But trout are at a discount in the salmon country. The whole of lower Quebec is better adapted to fish culture than any other purpose, except the manufacture of ice-water and scenery.

At Trinity Bay, and at the Bay of Seven Islands, are telegraph stations ; for the Dominion Government maintains a wire all the way down to Esquimaux Point, where

it crosses to Anticosti Island. In all the scattered offices along the shore, one may see the old-fashioned paper-tape machines, by which the eye may read what an unaccustomed ear could not follow. This telegraph line is in lieu of a life-saving service, on one of the roughest and most dangerous of coasts. If shipwrecked sailors get ashore alive, they may notify their friends by wire. Trinity Bay is a pilot station, where, if the weather is thick, the incoming ship may take on guides for the voyage up river ; but most of them wait till they get to Rimouski.

Sailor-men cannot propel their floating homes without wind, and when we reached the Bay of Seven Islands there came a calm. Little did we care, for, as we rode at anchor, with the canoes and the Indian guides lying about the deck, the bright sun overhead, the mosquitoes paying us friendly visits from the land, it seemed but little different from any dull day in camp on shore when the fish would not rise. This Bay of Seven Islands is a circular, land-locked sheet of water, six miles across. A group of island mountains rise out of the sea and guard it from the waves. On the shore of the bay is a little village, just a row of fishermen's houses, with the scrubby forest behind them. The storehouse of the Hudson Bay Company is the largest building, and the home of the agent, Mr. Walter Colvile, is the most comfortable house. In front of all the fishermen's houses are platforms of sticks, upon which countless cod-

Mouth of the Magpie River.

fish and halibut dry in the sun, and dese-
crate the pure summer air.   While waiting
for favoring gales we went ashore.   And
here we saw the daily life of a little community the like of which cannot be found
anywhere except on this coast.   Mr. Colvile, gentleman and diplomat, the representative of a great commercial organization which once dominated half a continent, was the little king.   On one side of
him stretched away the thin line of fishermen's cottages ; on the other were the
newly purchased white tents of fifty Montagnais Indian families, down from the
interior with their season's catch of furs.
While he talked to us of things in the outside world he so seldom saw, a little boy
waited to buy a quart of kerosene oil, and
two big-eyed Indian girls discussed the
price of red handkerchiefs.

Along the sandy beach, the tide being
out, big dogs of the wolfish, sled-drawing
breed patrolled the water's edge, getting
their dinners from the little stranded fish,
and other unlucky inhabitants of the water.
One dog found a lobster, and at once there
was a dispute with other dogs, in which the
lobster was promptly torn claw from claw.
Another dog tried to steal a codfish from
a drying-platform, and the boy sentinel

berated the dog in French and belabored
him with a club.   By the side of the nearest
house two women bent over their wash-
tubs ; and out beyond the islands, on the
swells which tumbled without a wind to
shape them, the little fleet of cod-fish-
ing boats crept slowly home, laboriously
dragged by the long sweeps which furnished the ashen breeze.

Another schooner, almost like our own,
drifted in on the tide.   That night there
was a good deal of shouting and singing
among the fishermen.   Some time after
midnight a cottage burned.   In the morning many empty brandy bottles, bearing
French labels but no revenue stamps, lay
about the shore, and the trading schooner
had passed on.   Such are the craft that
make business for the revenue cutter Caroline, which prowls up and down that coast,
and occasionally confiscates a cargo.   The
contraband stuff comes from St. Pierre
and Miquelon, those tiny islands below
Newfoundland, all that remain of the
once mighty French dominion on this continent.   If a convulsion of nature should
engulf those troublesome resorts of smug-
glers, the revenue service of Canada would
not mourn.   One fisherman was building a
tiny schooner, too big for a fishing dory and

Salmon Leaping a Fifteen-foot Fall.   (From a photograph.)

too small for a freighter.   In reply to the question as to what he was building it for, he smilingly said, " O, I tink I go down to French Saint Peter dis fall."   And if the Caroline did not catch him, he no doubt made a good profit on bad French liquor.

Below Seven Islands the Moisie River empties itself into the gulf.   This is, perhaps, the finest salmon stream on the coast. It is the " Big River " of the Montagnais, for it rises farther back in the interior than the rivers east of it, and thus forms a more convenient highway to the Indians' distant hunting-grounds.

With the morning came the wind, and the clatter, clatter of the horizontal windlass, weighing the anchor.   We sailed on by the Moisie, for it is a leased river; past the river of Trout, because the salmon cannot climb the rocky rapid at its mouth ; on down the harborless coast a day's sail, till we reached the Manitou River, where are the wonderful falls.   At the mouth, high on the shore, lay the grisly bones of a fine American schooner which had ventured too near when the wind was light, and then was pushed to her doom by the remorse-less tide, while her anchors dragged over the smooth, rocky bottom.   Our little French captain did not relish a similar fate, so we sailed on five miles to the rocky harbor of Chaloupe River, and came back to the solitary grandeur of the Manitou falls by canoe.

This cataract, two miles from the mouth, is noteworthy, even in a land of waterfalls. If it were accessible, it would be much visited.   The whole river, as wide as the Potomac at Harper's Ferry, but of much greater volume, plunges over a precipice one hundred and thirteen feet high.   The surrounding cliffs are covered with the fir and spruce which mostly constitute those endless forests.   The tumult of the water in the gorge below is such that a canoe cannot approach very near ; there is no path or trail over the thickly overgrown rocks ; and the rage of the plunging river must be conquered before the truly majestic beauty of the virgin fastness may be beheld.   The roar of the fall can be heard long before one approaches it, though the rising spray may be seen from a considerable distance out in the gulf.   The cata-

Another Snap-shot at a Leaping Salmon.

ract of the Manitou, away on the lonely North Shore, is of no commercial interest. It attracts no sight-seers. The sailors fear the coast in its vicinity. But since the days when the world was young it has poured over those flinty rocks, the spray in summer forming a fresh rainbow every shining moment, and in winter freezing into myriads of beautiful ice-palaces, whose glistening pinnacles have borne witness through the centuries, as seasons have come and gone, that human eyes are not the only things for which the beauties of this world are made.

When we had done looking at the waterfall, and returned to the gulf, there was such a heavy sea running that the canoe could not live, and the Indians had to carry it back over the rocks for five miles. They did not seem to mind the burden much. When we reached the schooner, the waves were roaring in at the narrow harbor entrance, chasing each other in ceaseless cavalry charges, and we lay all that night, proud of the rock that stood between us and the angry sea. A fisherman, steering for the harbor, ran aground be-

tween two small rocks outside, and was rescued when the storm went down, his boat meantime breaking in two.

Our own schooner, which was one size too big for the harbor mouth, could only run out when the tide was high, and after waiting two tides for a fair wind, all the fishermen in the place, about a dozen, turned out in their dories and towed us through to the open gulf, the towage bill of three dollars being considered high by our loyal Captain Joe.

The next large river east of the Manitou, coming out of this unknown country, is the St. John. There are at least five St. John rivers in Canada, but this is distinguished as the St. John of the North Shore. It is a great salmon stream, but in 1896 it was unleased. The first fall, more than twenty miles from the mouth, is the nearest point where the fish stop. Thirty years ago the commander of a Canadian Government vessel, who was doing the same thing we did last year, discovered a most remarkable thing at this fall. There was a rock in the channel, so shaped that when the fish jumped against it, many of them

A Characteristic Shore Formation.

fell into a cavity on the other side, from which, in low water, they could not escape. In this way myriads of noble salmon had, through countless years, lost their lives; and so well known to the neighboring bears was the fact that, when the commander was there, he found the remains of hundreds of the fish scattered about the rocks, where the bears had dragged them. He carried up a keg of powder, and blasted out a fish-way, since which this curious fish-trap has not been of any benefit to the bears.

Thirty miles below the St. John are the Mingan Islands, between the mainland and the western end of the island of Anticosti. The shores of these islands present a geological formation which is frequently found in this part of the world, and which was the cause of the many wrecks suffered by early explorers. At high tide perpendicular rocks seem to rise from the water's edge; but at low tide flat ledges, extending far out from the cliffs, are laid bare. In many places these shelving ledges extend for miles, and a person caught on them in a rising tide would be in great danger, as he could not ascend the face of the rock wall. Most of the three-hundred-mile coast line

of Anticosti Island is thus grimly guarded. On the shelving rocks the seals love to sleep at low tide, and once, when we were rambling along the shore, we surprised a herd of horsehead seals, each animal ten or twelve feet long, and heavy as an ox. The speed with which these great creatures slid splashing into the water was surprising. Soon two or three of them cautiously raised their heads above the water, snuffed the air, to be sure what we were, and then we saw them no more.

The islands are the nesting-places of thousands of birds, and in some places the young gulls and other fluffy infants with untrained wings would prowl about under our feet in the most awkward and ridiculous fashion, while hundreds of alarmed parent birds filled the air with their cries as they circled overhead.

Our careless wanderings thus far had carried us, by easy stages, nearly five hundred miles northeast of Quebec. We were opposite the mouth of the Mingan River, and as I wished to see my bright young companion wrestle with a big salmon, we concluded to say good-by to the schooner for a few days, and ascend the river.

That was where the canoes came in, and the guides, who had sunned themselves on the deck for days, made ready to depart.

At the mouth of the Mingan, for more than two hundred years, a settlement of the same name has been recognized on all the maps. At present there are two families who reside there the year round; that of Mr. Scott, agent of the Hudson Bay Company, and that of Mr. Malony, telegraph operator and warden of the river. One would little guess to look at the peaceful scene, that this place was the centre of one of the most protracted legal controversies the world has ever known. But it was. The whole coast of the gulf, from the Seven Islands to Blanc Sablon, more than four hundred miles in length, and six miles in depth, was claimed as the feudal holding of the Mingan Seigniory. The grant under which this claim has always been maintained was made to François Bissot, in 1661, by the Company of New France, deriving its powers from the French Crown. This grant was indefinite in terms, and gave vague rights to establish hunting and fishing stations, and to take the necessary timber and lands, down the coast, to "the Great Bay toward the Esquimaux, where the Spaniards usually fish." The short story of a controversy extending through two centuries is that the successors of the Sieur Bissot, while never secure in title, camped persistently on the land, and always claimed everything. Every time

Four Montagnais Indians.

there was a disturbance between France and England, the buildings at Mingan were pretty sure to be burned, by one side or the other. It was an easy thing to stop in the beautiful little harbor among the islands, and apply the red torch of war. Promptly after the cession of Canada to Great Britain in 1763, the Mingan seigniory folks laid before that government their claim of proprietorship. It was always disputed for uncertainty; but finally, in an unguarded moment, the Legislature of the Province of Canada, in 1854, admitted that there was such a thing as the Mingan seigniory, and in 1892 the Privy Council of England adjudicated the limits of it to be from Cape Cormorant to the river Goynish, a distance of about one hundred and fifty miles, and six miles deep from the coast. This right is now held by the Labrador Company, of Montreal, and it gives them absolute control of the fishing in the lower six miles of the sixteen rivers which cross the Mingan seigniory on their way to the gulf. The only ones which the Labrador Company consider worth watching, however, in a country where only the best fishing-waters are looked at, are the Mingan and the Romaine. In the other streams, either the salmon are barred by the falls, or they do not stop inside the six-mile limit, and above that the Province of Quebec holds control.

The courtesy of the Labrador Company had been extended to us to kill a few salmon at the first fall in the Mingan.

A Heavenward Pilot on an Earthward Voyage.

Here may be seen one of the most remarkable annual exhibitions of the rough course of true love to be found in all the world.

The first fall on the Mingan is about three miles from the mouth. It is forty-six feet high, in three pitches about equal in height and with seething pools between. The spawning beds of the salmon are on broad, gravelly bars far up the river. They must surmount this fall once a year in order to reach them. We camped on a sandbar below the fall, and watched the struggle. The broad pool below the fall was so full of these royal fish, that their tails and dorsal fins could constantly be seen sticking out of the water. Every minute one or more fish would make a rush from the depths below, spring far into the air, every fibre quivering, and time after time fall back, only the most powerful and determined occasionally succeeding in passing the first pitch. Above that, every nook and crevice in the rocks where the salmon could obtain a resting-place, was crowded. Great monsters they were, weighing from twenty-five to forty pounds. How they ever made the second and third pitches I do not know, for there was not the good starting chance that they had in the deep hole below the first pitch.

Well, the boy took a ten-ounce trout-rod, with a hundred yards of line on it, and cast out among the fins and tails in the soap-suds below the fall. The canoe was ready, and in a few minutes the rod was nearly jerked from the youngster's hands. The men shoved him into the canoe and paddled for dear life after the running fish, which had impulsively started for the open sea. You may suppose that the salmon broke loose; that he smashed the tackle; that he overturned the canoe. But he did not. Those guides knew their business, and so did the boy. The fish towed the canoe two miles down stream, and one hour and seventeen minutes after the trouble began, Braithwaite grabbed the salmon with the gaff-hook and threw him up on a sand-bar.

The next day we went up the river. Twelve miles from the falls, and after making six or seven smaller ascents, we reached a place where the stream came through a deep gorge. Here, again, we pitched our tent. On the morrow we climbed the mountain, and looked down into the cañon, far below, filled with great rocks, riven from the precipice by the frost. In the crevices beneath our feet lay the unmelted ice of last winter, or of no one knows how many winters, untouched by the August sun. There was a general air of ruin about those cracks, and we could not help wondering if the next rock to fall might be the one beneath our feet, and if this was its day for falling.

Climbing the highest peak in sight, the country beyond stretched away for miles beneath our gaze. Above the chasm the river spread out into lake-like expansions, filled with green islands. Far to the north rose the next low range of the mountains, and through a distant notch the thread of the shining river was lost to view. The low clay bottoms were covered with a thick growth of small evergreens, while the highest rocks, in their interstices, sheltered the ground hemlock and many other forms of verdure. As far as we could see, the world was gray and green ; and, though the animals were noticeably less abundant than in Maine or New Brunswick, yet we knew that the glimmering river was full of vigorous life, and that the quiet fresh-water seas beyond the hills in every direction were the homes of myriads of beautiful creatures that knew not the fear of hook and line. In a little depression we found the skeleton-like lodge poles where, earlier in the season, some family of Montagnais had lived while on a spring bear-hunt. Away to the north, in the country " beyond the Height of Land," as the Hudson Bay people call it, we saw, in imagination, the bands of caribou, gray-necked and patri-archal, which are the standard winter food of these Indians.

I do not know how other men would feel on the top of that mountain, looking over into the depths of the Labrador wilderness ; but to me that day all its voices sang a siren's song, and the myriad faces of the hills and lakes smiled a glad welcome. People are accustomed to think of that vast and far-off wild as a death-like, forbidding place. It is not so. In winter, cold and severe, no doubt ; in summer it is God's own land of beauty. But we could not tarry, and in a few days we left the fish in peace, and returned down the river to Mingan.

The Hudson Bay people tell me that a Montagnais family will often bring down, as a season's catch, a thousand dollars worth of furs. Sometimes, if the wandering caribou shift their winter feeding-grounds, the Indians are in danger of starvation ; but if things go as they should the natives do very well. Each spring they come in their canoes down the river

to the coast. At Mingan, where there is always a summer colony of them, many have permanent cabins. Fully a score of those who summer there own trim little sail-boats of American make, for which they pay one hundred dollars apiece. They trade their furs for what they need or fancy, and no one sells better supplies than the Hudson Bay Company. During the summer the Indians visit each other, do up their religious ceremonies for the year —they are all good Catholics—and build new canoes for the return trip. It is very difficult to procure good birch-bark on the North Shore, and of late years the Hudson Bay Company have been furnished a fine grade of canvas for the outer covering of canoes. It was very interesting to see the splendid, workman-like manner in which the canoe builders did their work. Their canoes made our Malicete birch-bark affairs seem ill-shapen and clumsy by comparison.

When we returned to Mingan we found the graceful yacht of the Jesuit missionary in the harbor. This devoted man and fine sailor had come from a more distant point down the coast, and there was great activity among the Indians. Down by the shore a new canoe, white as snow, was raised on a little platform. The missionary came out from one of the tents, in the vestments of his sacred office, stood before the assembled Indians, held his hands aloft, and chanted the service of blessing the canoe, in a fine, sonorous voice that could be heard at least half a mile. The holy water was sprinkled, and then the solemnity of the occasion was a little marred by the Indians producing their guns, bedecked with ribbons, and firing a scattering round of shots as a finale.

It was at Mingan, too, that we saw a little more of the vicissitudes which beset the dauntless pioneers of the Church. It was about time for a pastoral visit from Father Bouchard, the spiritual shepherd of the fishermen. While we were in the harbor a man appeared on the nearest island and shouted loudly for help. Being rescued, he was found to be Father Bouchard, wet and miserable. While he had slept, the man accompanying him had run his boat aground near one of the islands, the night before. The good Father, who had nothing to eat, waited for high tide to float him off ; but the hope was vain.

Then he waited until low tide, waded across half a mile of shoal water and followed the beach of the island around for four miles, until he came opposite the post. Then his shouts were heard, and he was relieved from further impersonation of Robinson Crusoe. We took him into our big dining-room and kitchen in the hold, where he devastated the food in an appalling manner. While he slept in the cabin Mr. Malony and his son went to see if they could get Father Bouchard's boat off the rocks. They succeeded, for the boat and its luckless pilot overtook us down the coast two days later. In the meantime the priest slept, ate, indulged in rough and tumble games with my boy friend, and took his turn at the schooner's wheel for hours at a time. Strong as a pugilist, cheerful as a cricket, all things to all men, Father Bouchard was a fine example of the wisdom displayed by the Catholic Church in the selection of the men to fulfil its arduous tasks. He insisted on our anchoring at his little home village of Magpie, where on Sunday afternoon he had the idle fishermen catch and harness his winter dog-team, to exhibit the means by which, when winter filled the gulf with ice, he travelled from one end of his long parish to the other. The dogs knew there was something wrong about being hitched to a sled in August, so they entangled their harness, pulled awry, and fought like demons. We heard them howling as we sailed away with the tide.

One might write about the wonderful fishing rivers east of the Mingan ; of the Romaine, the great Natashquan, and a score of other streams. But we did not sail that far. As Deputy Commissioner Tache had told us at Quebec, if we had visited those distant waters, we should not have come back that summer. As it was, we flew homeward before a northeaster that howled over the gulf and blew away some of our sails, and shot us into the harbor of Grand Metis, on the South Shore, where, at low tide, the water all went out of the bay and let the schooner down on her side. The bilge water ran over the bunks of the guides who were asleep forward ; the boy rolled out of his berth in the cabin ; the dishes fell off the table, and there were French imprecations in the darkness. But in the morning our schooner was right side up again, floating on the high tide as though nothing had happened.

We went ashore and found a man who loaded our baggage on a little two-wheeled red cart, and we followed him over the hills, driving a horse which refused to recognize the command to " Get up," but which cheerfully responded to " Marche donc ! " Six miles of this brought us to the railroad station at St. Flavie, on the Intercolonial Railway, and two days later we were sweltering in a belated hot spell which swept over the Northern States like a furnace-blast. Then we wished we had tarried on the edge of Labrador.

38
A New Hand
at the
Rod
(1890)

A NEW HAND AT THE ROD.

BY C. R. C.

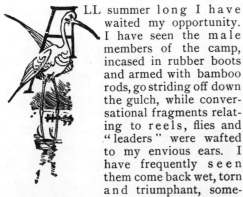

ALL summer long I have waited my opportunity. I have seen the male members of the camp, incased in rubber boots and armed with bamboo rods, go striding off down the gulch, while conversational fragments relating to reels, flies and "leaders" were wafted to my envious ears. I have frequently seen them come back wet, torn and triumphant, sometimes loaded with fish, and sometimes not, as luck favored them; but always with stories. I have heard all about the big one that fell back into the water; about the bigger one that got caught in the bushes and jerked off the hook, and about the biggest one of all, "regular Jumbo, by George!" that gave one flop just as he was being dropped into the bag and —vanished!

Why should I not have the privilege of shaping some of these romances?

The camp is deserted.

The brothers and husbands and visiting cousins have all gone to town.

The fish poles lean invitingly against a pine.

"Woman's hour has struck."

I will go fishing.

The selection of a pole becomes the first difficulty and that arises not from the superiority of one pole over another, but from the question as to which man's wrath I can most safely provoke. Lose his knife, break his pipe, mislay his papers, slander his wife, but keep his jointed rod holy, is the eleventh commandment of the amateur fisherman. This smaller rod seems the least elaborate; it is also light and easy to hold—besides it belongs to a cousin's friend, who, if anything happens, will have to look pleasant whether he feels so or not. So, Mr. Jones, by your leave, while you are in town getting the mail or ordering provis-

ions, or going to the circus, or whatever it is that takes the men off in a body, leaving the camp to the women and children and chipmunks—by your leave, I say, I will borrow your rod. So that matter is settled, only it would be simpler and pleasanter if you had not put two hooks on the line; one at a time is enough to catch in one's hair.

Now for something in which to bring home the fish. The game bag, to be sure, and here it hangs on a branch. Ugh! how it smells! I really cannot hang that thing around my neck. Strange how impervious men's faculties are to disagreeable odors. A basket would answer the purpose, but in this benighted valley of the Arkansas there is no such thing as a splint basket, the want of which we have discovered to be one of the small housekeeping difficulties of this region. A tin pail would answer the pur-

"WHAT A STEEP PATH!"

pose, but it would not be sportsmanlike, look at it in any light you please. The kitchen tent offers nothing else in the way of a receptacle except a deal cracker box with a picture of Pike's Peak on the end ; clearly unavailable. Nor will I degrade to such uses my burnt alligator satchel or the case to my camera.

Ah ! a handkerchief. Silk, and a large one ; I hope it is not Mr. Jones'; but he will forgive me if I bring it home full of trout. A knot in each corner and it will hold a dozen easily. See ! And yet they say that women have no adaptability.

* * * * *

What a steep path it is down into this gulch ! I say path, but there is not a

rushes and swirls and quarrels with the boulders ! See that smooth, green slant of water, curving over a granite shelf and breaking into foam below like a Kodak view of Niagara. The color is entrancing ; it is not emerald (there is too much ochre in the rocks), but a restful brownish green with an unexpected touch of blue at intervals which can only be a reflection of the Colorado sky. Surely a reflection, for here, in the only quiet portion of the troubled surface, I see the inverted outline of Sheep Mountain as it stands block-

"AM I TO SIT HERE ALL DAY?"

sign of one except a foothold here and there on a pine root or a bunch of soap weed ; elsewhere boulders and long steep stretches of loose gravel. As I dig my heels into the soil, sliding frantically downward, grazing my elbows and peeling the leather in strips from my best shoes, I long unspeakably for an old pair bestowed weeks ago on an ungrateful washerwoman. My scramble comes to an end at the brink of the Cottonwood River, foaming among the rocks at the bottom of the gulch. Steep, chalky cliffs rise on either side and all around the stately pines keeping guard over the solemn fastnesses of a Rocky Mountain canyon. Ah ! this lovely river. How it

ing the view toward the head of the canyon.

I will paraphrase Wordsworth :

Three voices are these : one is of the sea,
One is of the mountains, another of a trout stream,

which, if you don't vex yourself unduly about the metre, is a very good version. This pool has a bass voice, a double diapason ; the one above, where I can see the pebbles on the bottom, gives out a shallow soprano tinkle as the water ripples lazily along. The silence of this hushed auditorium is further broken only by the wind in the pines and the occasional hoarse call of a magpie or a blue jay. Song birds do not venture above the valleys when the valleys themselves are 8,000 feet above sea level.

However, all this is not fishing, and what will the camp say to an empty game bag at supper time? As soon as I have unhooked the brown fly from my hat and the white fly from my hair I will begin.

Now, let me see; what are the rules of the game? I must stand "up stream" and "cast" down, letting the fly lie as near as possible on the surface, then draw it slowly toward me, so. Then repeat the operation.

This is called "whipping" the stream. One learns a great deal in this world by careful observation, and the camp talk is bearing fruit. Yes, trout fishing is delightful and not at all difficult if only this rock would not tip so. It destroys my equanimity as well as my equilibrium, and one needs both in a trout stream.

*   *   *   *   *

It seems as though I ought to have a bite by this time. I have been "repeating the operation" for fully twenty minutes; the sun is hot, and the rapid water makes my head dizzy. I wonder what the men do at this stage?

Ah! I remember. According to the professional lingo the fish are not "rising" in this pool, and I must go farther up stream, which I proceed to do as soon as my skirts are tucked up a little more securely. How I regret my incapacity to wear those big rubber boots that fasten around the waist! They would be just the thing for this swampy place.

There! One foot is wet —the other also! Dear me! It would have been wiser to go out on the road and come back to the stream farther on. Still, let me be philosophical. One can no more have trout than fame or riches without some accompanying disadvantages. Emerson says in his essay on compensation——

Is that a fish? Surely—there—to the right, just under the shade of that rock!

See him, with his head up stream, his tail lazily waving in rhythm with the water, his pink-spotted sides flashing in the sunlight! Oh, you beauty! how delicious you will taste, served up in bread crumbs with a dash of lemon (or Worcestershire sauce?) and a garnish of watercresses! Do have this nice little brown fly, or the nicer white one at the end. See, I drop them just over your nose and dangle them invitingly. "Will you walk into my parlor?"

Ah! he is gone, and strange to say I did not see him go, though my eyes were on him. That is too bad, but not an uncommon experience if I may judge from our dinner-table talk. Our authoritative angler (alias the Camp Liar) says if you "whip" a pool and the fish sees you there is no use staying in that place any longer.

Now, who would give a trout credit for so much discernment? This one saw my hat and my general get-up, and,

"WHAT IN THUNDER!"

like a sensible fish, he took himself off directly.

I must now try my luck farther up stream. This trout fishing is a perpetual "movin' on;" as arduous as poor Jo's peregrinations, and with as little result.

*   *   *   *

Oh, for one more safety pin! That last jump loosened my dress skirt, and now there is an appalling rent in the front breadth, the result of the interference of a dead branch. What is to be done? Ah, of course—a hairpin!

There, that will last a little time, and in the meanwhile I will see what is in this pool; it looks trout-full. Or, on second thoughts, I will not. Just on the opposite bank is a cow, and she is looking this way. If it was just an ordinary Ohio cow I would pay no attention to her, but these range cattle have a gaze that would freeze the blood in one's veins.

Shoo! I will move on.

Here at last is the place. A glassy sheet of water surrounded by lichenous purple rocks; a volume of foam pouring in from above and spreading out into ripples below; a dead pine spanning the stream from bank to bank, and cushions of moss meeting the placid water on all sides. Could there be a more ideal spot for fishing or meditation? All around is a grove of quaking asp (first cousin to the poplar). A refined, gentle tree with whispering leaves and lady-like attitudes.

The change is refreshing, for pines, be they ever so poetical, are grim and monotonous, and their blackened trunks covering the side of the mountain speak of fire and storms, snowslides and the roar of beasts in the night. That they should be succeeded in Nature's plan by these clean, white-stemmed trees is a silent allegory. *Post tenebras lux.*

Beneath the trees and among the rocks grow the vivid Colorado wild flowers; not such pale beauties as we find in April in New England and the Middle States, but gorgeous, scarlet, yellow and rose pink blossoms, like dabs of pigment on a palette. I really would not dare to carry this bit of scenery home in a water color, except to show to people who have been here. It would seem like an attempt to improve on one's subject.

Now I am going to do something that will show great strength of nerve and will. I am going out on that log. You see it is directly over the pool, and I can throw the fly just where it ought to go. The case is perfectly clear; heretofore I have not been in the proper position. Those men who wear big boots, climb right into the water up to their knees, and, of course, they catch trout—who couldn't?

*   *   *   *

Well, here I am, safe and sound, looking down into the very depths of the stream, where I am confident there is a whole panful of trout waiting yearningly for my flies. Not in the least difficult getting out, either, and if one of the gentlemen had been here he would have thought it necessary to help me.

What's the matter now? I can't move my pole; the hook is fast in that tree. Dear, dear, how stupid of me to carry it over my shoulder as Mr. Winkle did his gun! Come off there! I do not wish to be slangy, but really——

No, it won't stir; neither this way nor that! Now, I don't wonder that men "say things" when they have such provocation as this. What do they say, anyway, and when they say it how does it work? I would like to make any kind of a remark that I thought would loosen that hook. I have heard Mr. Jones in the remote seclusion of his own tent say, "Gee whang it!" but that is his own particular property, and to borrow a man's jointed rod and his expletive, too, is stretching a privilege in a way my conscience won't allow * * * Am I to sit here all day? * * * I wonder what a steady pull would do—like *that.* I don't dare to be very forcible for this log is quite round and—I'll try a series of coaxing jerks with an emphatic yank to finish with.

Ah! there it comes, with the air of saying, "I was not caught at all, only fooling."

Nevertheless the brown fly is left up in the tree, where, it is to be hoped, he will lead a useful and prosperous career. Now, if the trout will only be persuaded that the flavor of this white fly is as fine as that of the brown one, I'll catch a string of fish that will prove me entitled to a rod of my own. No hurry, however. The camp timepiece is Mt. Harvard. When the sun drops behind that wall of granite which towers above us to the West we know it is a quarter to 5. Long before that time chilly shadows fill the gulch and creep up the cliff, and the South Park Range takes on a cold gray, then deepens to purple, while the three snow peaks of Mt. Princeton glow with rosy pink against the evening sky.

According, then, to signs and omens, it must be about half past 3 o'clock, and as long as the sun continues to warm up this particular nook I am going to sit and swing my feet over the water. It is comfortable and romantic, and I don't care so much about fish after all. To tell the truth we have had salmon trout for dinner every day for the past two weeks and are thinking of sending to Buena Vista for ham or bacon or some such delicacy for a change. So why should I cast flies?

What are those beautiful lines of Whittier's addressed to Monadnock? They begin with something about a painter and "for her sake." I do not quote readily. I wish I did. Let me see.

> First a lake
> Tinted with sunset ; next the wavy lines
> Of far receding hills, and yet more far
> Monadnock. * * *

Shades of Izaak Walton, was *that* a bite? That earthquake, that cyclone, that terrific tug that is bending the pole into a letter C and lashing the water into suds. It is never a trout ; it is nothing less than a sturgeon, or perhaps a sea serpent, and it is pulling me off the——

* * * * *

Something must always be left to the imagination of the reader. When the Russian poet Pushkin is carried beyond the force of language his emotions explode into a shower of stars. So I find nothing but asterisks will express my situation. Up to my waist in the Cottonwood ; the water sweeping my skirts around me ; my head dizzy and my hat floating rapidly off toward the Arkansas ! But the trout? Ah, yes! Here he is ; I seized him with both hands as I took my plunge and he shall *not* get away. He is not so large as I expected. Indeed, quite inside the law ; hardly worth cooking for a camp of nine people. Still he is my first trout, and I'll not surrender him to any fish commissioner.

I steal up to camp the back way, and after leaving the rod with its fellows against the tree I seek my own tent.

As the 6 o'clock horn sounds I hear Mr. Jones' footsteps going supperward. Will he stop at the pine tree?

He does.

I hear the click of the metal reel and then a growl—

"What in thunder ! "

BASS FISHING ON RIDEAU LAKE.

BY J. W. LONGLEY.

I HAD reached forty without having cast a line, an unusual experience in this country among men who have any means or leisure. When a boy, armed with hook and line and limber rod, cut from the bushes, and with a worm for bait, I essayed to lure the trout and other small fishes from a stream near my paternal home. I would angle for hours, noting in the clear water whole swarms of little fish surrounding my hook and nibbling the bait at will. Terrible jerks made I, but to no purpose. Weary and vexed at ill luck I was induced to surrender my rod to a little darky boy about half my size, who would forthwith begin pulling up the fishes by the dozen. I took a violent dislike for fishing. It was clearly not an intellectual diversion. It seemed unworthy of a man possessing any mental endowments.

Then came college life, the study for a profession and its pursuit. Laborious literary labors were interlarded, and thus the years passed. Boyhood gradually merged into manhood and youth crept along until the gray hairs and thin patch and the rude awakening of the fortieth birthday gave solemn warning that the vernal equinox was passed and life would know no more the odors of its first spring. During all these busy years, entirely absorbed in the pursuit of knowledge, fame and fortune, I looked with pity upon the deluded mortals who were wasting their time and energies on any such paltry and purposeless pastime as fishing. Among the mere pleasure-loving crowd I regarded these excursions as the fitting complement of an aimless life ; but when I saw strong-minded men, possessing brains and ability and advancing rapidly in business, professional practice and public life, deliberately collecting together an elaborate kit and gear and starting out on a fishing excursion, I could not help feeling that they were the victims of a mild form of insanity.

This bit of very unimportant autobiography is given merely as a prelude to a narrative—a sort of quiet and sombre background for the little picture that is to follow.

During the summer of 1889 I was urged by a friend residing near Brockville, Ont., to come for a visit, and among other inducements offered was a week's fishing on the Rideau Lakes. He had just discovered the beauties of this region and its merits, and had erected a hotel on one of the numerous islands, with the intention of making the place a favorite summer resort. If my dear friend could have known of the good-natured contempt that such a proposition awakened in my mind I fear his invitation would not have been given. But, to shorten matters, I was finally induced to go to Brockville for a little visit, but with many misgivings and painful anticipations of boredom. Out of good nature, and to avoid the appearance of churlishness, I also consented to go to the lake one Tuesday afternoon, spend the night at the hotel, and the next day start for home. With secret cunning I inwardly reflected that this would preclude the possibility of protracted boredom.

Off we started one Tuesday afternoon late in August. The day was beautiful. We took the new line of railway from Brockville—the Brockville, Westport and Sault Ste. Marie—and in a short time were at Westport, a little town situated at the head waters of the Rideau system of lakes. It was now dusk, and entering one of those charming little steam yachts that are so common along the St. Lawrence and its tributary waters we had a pleasant sail of ten miles, and then landed at Long Island, and were soon made comfortable in the hotel—one of the model summer structures of the period, built, as usual, of boards nailed to a frail framework—no shingles without and no plaster within. As you lie on a very comfortable bed, moonlight or sunlight works away in through little apertures in the wooden walls, and your fellow guest in the room above makes his presence felt on the board floor over your head a trifle more

distinctly than if he were in your own room. Broad verandas of course surround the house, and it is altogether an ideal summer lodging. I spent my first night in the deliberate pursuit of absolute rest and pleasure, it having been determined before retiring that we were to be up at 5.30 in order to indulge in one fishing tour before I took my departure. I accepted this as a compromise, and felt an inward sense of pride and self complacency at this tribute to my good nature and self sacrifice.

The morning broke radiantly clear, as only an August morning in Ontario can break. There was not a cloud in the sky, but the sun's brilliant rays were tempered by a thin, dreamy haze, which so often lends a subdued charm to the beauties of an early autumn morning. I did not need to be awakened; and, taking a hasty bath and throwing on my clothes, I stepped out upon the veranda. The scene was truly superb. Long Island stands in the centre of the lake, and all about and in every direction are smaller islands covered with rich foliage, and here and there are newly-built summer cottages that wealthy persons have erected. These are the advance guard of numbers which will appear when the beauties and advantages of the place become better known. My host soon appeared, together with the genial Dr. M., who accompanied us on the tour. Turning to the water's edge, I saw the boatmen already at work making the preparations necessary for the fishing excursion. Presently the rods were brought forth, the reels adjusted, the lines prepared and the hooks attached.

I was presented with the gear that I was to use and started with the rest of the party for the boats, feeling certain every moment that I would either break the rod by some blundering or contrive to get the hook neatly imbedded either in my clothes or my flesh; but we got safely on board the boats. My host and I occupied one, the doctor and his friend the other. Each boat was admirably fitted up with all conveniences. Two heavily-cushioned seats were prepared for the fishers, while the boatman sat in the bow and rowed, and had, in addition, the care of a kettle of live minnows, our bait, and a landing net, which was to contain the many trophies of our prowess. Thus it was that for the first time in my life I started on a fishing excursion. The boatman gave his first pull at the oars. "What a piece of hopeless idiocy," thought I, "and for grown-up men!" My self respect was well nigh extinguished, and the minutes were counted until it should be safely over and I once more back to sensible pursuits and among rational beings.

We soon reached the "fishing ground." Massie — that was our boatman's name, and he was a thorough expert—dropped his oars. The tin can was opened, a bright and lively minnow was fastened to the end of my hook, and, following the example of my host, with a sigh of self contempt I threw the line out. I saw it sink into the water, and as Massie said it was deep and we should require thirty or forty feet of line, I began mechanically to pay it out. The click of the revolving reel was the only sound that broke the impressive silence of the sun-illumined waters. Thus sat we, my friend's line on one side of the boat, my own on the other, and I smiled to myself as I recalled the epigrammatic definition of fishing by some cynic: "A fish at one end of the line and a fool at the other," the only thing wanting, in my thought, being the fish.

Aye! What was that? Heigho! Something tugging at my hook. Quick as a flash I was upon my feet. "You've struck him" cries Massie, perfectly cool. How could a person be cool in such a case was the thought that darted through my brain. How can I describe everything that was crowded into that one moment? The little rod in an instant was bent and the whole hidden depths of the lake seemed to be in commotion. Instinct instantly taught me to keep the line taut, and so I began furiously to wind up the reel. I had at least forty feet out, a few feet had been wound in, when the enemy made a plunge, and to save my rod the line was paid out again. Then I began to reel in once more. I just held him and slowly wound in the line. Soon, at a little distance from the boat, I saw him—a perfect beauty! His next move was toward the surface, and with a sudden dash he leaped out of the water and into the air. My! Now I feared I should lose him. I kept a steady grip and he passed through the acrobatic ordeal without escaping me.

I resumed my work of taking in line. He tugged away gallantly and then made a dive under the boat; but, with an instinct which years of education could not have instilled, I instantly adjusted the rod to the changed conditions. My foe was evidently getting tired of the struggle. Click!

went the winding reel. He was drawing near the surface. Again I could see him at a nearer view.

"A beauty!" exclaimed Massie, as he seized the landing net. Click! went the reel, but who could repeat the wild monologue I kept up during this intoxicating performance. Every second was bringing him nearer the surface. The landing net was already in the water and near to the struggling beauty. I gave him a little tip and Massie dexterously got beneath him. In a flash I saw him safely landed, and gave forth a shout that echoed to the remotest recesses of this isle-studded lake.

Thus was landed my first fish—a beautiful, fat black bass weighing four pounds! Oh, what a revolution! How life had changed in five short minutes! The cold cynic of forty winters — where was he? Gone! and in his place stood an enthusiast, his eyes beaming, his heart palpitating with delight, his pulse dancing, and his whole soul alive with rapture. What cared he for law or politics? What mattered it that constituents might grumble, newspapers rave, and opponents inveigh? Begone, vain world! What are all the dreams of ambition, the yearnings for power, the thirst for fame? Did he not recall the well-worn lines of—I think—Oliver Wendell Holmes?

Ah, what are the treasures we perish to win
Compared with the trout we first caught
    with a pin?

To veteran fishermen all this will, no doubt, seem turgid and ridiculous; but, perchance, memory will enable them to go back to the sunny hours of childhood when they felt the ecstasy of the first fish. Multiply these sensations in a man of forty and then be charitable.

The morning wore quickly away, and this bass was not my sole trophy. Again and again the delightful sensation of a tug at the end of the line was repeated, and, one after another, a fine collection of black bass was safely deposited in the tin drawer which was fitted up as a receptacle in our boat. My host is an experienced fisherman, an enthusiast, and has always been regarded as both expert and lucky. But, by one of those concatenations of events that no fellow can understand, though he diligently dangled his line, he got nothing, while I was keeping Massie continually employed with his landing net and the fastening of fresh minnows on my hooks.

Eight o'clock came and we started for

"AYE! WHAT'S THAT?"

home and breakfast. We reached the little landing cove almost simultaneously with the doctor and his companion. They had had some luck, and got a few small ones, but nothing compared to mine ; and as we walked up to the hotel, Massie bearing before us my pan of stunning big fish, there was not a prouder or happier man in the Dominion of Canada.

And what an appetite for breakfast ! How delightful the fresh air of the morning ; how uplifting was the beautiful scenery ; how exhilarating the captivating sport ! All the cares and worries of life seemed to have been thrown aside and a complete rejuvenation taken place. My heart was light, my spirits were buoyant. Ah, Mr. Brown-Séquard, methinks your elixir of life will prove an ephemeral renewer of youth beside the never-failing joy of a summer holiday, heightened by the exhilarating charms of fishing sport.

After a satisfactory breakfast and a composing pipe, seated on the veranda, in the most comfortable of chairs, my host reminded me that the time was approaching when we should have to take the steam yacht for Smith's Falls in order to catch the train for Halifax.

"I am afraid it will be inconvenient for you to leave to-day," I timidly and insinuatingly suggested. "I know you do not want to lose the whole day's sport."

I thought I saw a wicked smile pass around as I glanced at the faces of the company.

"I see it," said my genial host. "You want to stay another day ! By all means. You have not half seen the place. Stop until to-morrow."

He had hit the idea completely. The individual who once counted the minutes that should bring an escape from boredom was now enthusiastically looking forward with consuming eagerness to more of the unspeakable delights of the rod and line. And let it be said here that not the next day nor the day following saw my departure from this interesting spot. Once the sweets of sporting life were tasted, no few hours would suffice to satisfy my growing appetite for more.

I rapidly overcame my long-cherished belief that to abandon my post of duty in the thick of business affairs for a single day would unhinge the whole machinery of the universe. Indeed, one morning's success with rod and reel converted me from an elderly, serious, plodding worldly worker into a modified savage, content to let men come and go at their own sweet will, while I enjoyed the keen thrill of playing a frisky black bass through the clear waters of that Canadian lake. How many men — and among them men of wealth — there are, who live devoid of a true knowledge of the real joys of existence, and probably shorten their days by reason of an inexorable sense of the supreme necessity of their personal attention to all the details of their affairs. If once the door could be opened and they could be induced to look in upon the feast that nature spreads for the weary and overworn in so many places on this great continent of ours, with its lakes and rivers, its forests and its streams, they would soon begin to partake, life would be sweeter as well as longer, and they would presently discover how marvelously well the world manages to wag along without the personal superintendence of any of us.

The trip to Smith's Falls having been abandoned by unanimous consent, of course another fishing excursion was in order. Other grounds were visited. My host and I were companions as before, and once more luck perched upon my rod. My friend managed to secure one fish while I succeeded in getting a half dozen, and back we came to luncheon. We fished with excellent luck in the afternoon until

the shades of night began to fall. At last we wound up our reels and prepared to return to the hotel. The sun was down. The day had been clear and warm. As the sun departed and the twilight began to deepen into dusk came the delicious coolness of an August evening. There was scarce a breath of wind and the whole surface of the lake was like one vast mirror. Far as the eye could see were lovely vistas of island and water in every direction, the foliage reaching to the very edge of the lake.

As I lay back in the cushioned seat, the whole scene seemed the most beautiful and uplifting I had ever beheld. Supreme quiet and peace rested over the whole lake, save when broken by the weird echoes of the distant loon. Long Island is divided by an inlet on both sides. Entering either north or south by a narrow passage, one presently opens out into a beautiful little lake within the island completely overshadowed with a luxuriant growth of hardwood. Once upon the bosom of this little inland lake in the gloaming of a summer twilight the scene is beyond description. The mirror-like surface is darkened by the shades of night, and from its unruffled surface is reflected everything near of earth and sky

"AND BACK WE CAME TO LUNCHEON."

with such perfection that it is impossible, even on the most intent observation of material objects, to determine whether you are gliding through water or sky. Everything is unreal and mystic, and all the early dreams of fairyland seem realized.

Suddenly from the tall maples above our heads came the plaintive notes of a whippoorwill. It was the first time I had ever heard the strains of this love-fabled bird, and amid such surroundings and under such influences, is it any wonder that rooms of the heart, long closed and locked with rusty keys, were opened, and the soft and delicious impulses known only when love plays upon the tender chord of youth came back for the moment in great torrents of sentiment? I could not but recall then and there one especially suggestive verse of the old song of the whippoorwill, that I had always cherished, but which now filled me with its meaning as never before :

It is said that whatever sweet feelings
  May be throbbing within a fond heart,
When listening to whippoorwill's singing
  For a twelvemonth will never depart.
Oh, then we will meet in the woodland,
  Far away from the hurrying throng,
And whisper our love to each other
  When we hear the first whippoorwill's song.

But let me not drift into sentiment. It is well sometimes to have the soul stirred up a bit, and these reflections were the wholesome results of a first day's fishing. Amid these happy dreams the boat glided along, and soon we were at the landing place. With an appetite not etherealized by the beauties and glories of the scene we were soon partaking of a substantial dinner. Not, indeed, a formal affair, with courses of dainties designed to tempt a cloyed appetite, but a toothsome collection of substantials, fresh bass caught by our own hand, served hot and sweetened by that most effective of sauces—a healthy appetite, born of outdoor exercise, freedom from care and the uplifting influences of nature. This, indeed, was living! This was getting out of one's self—out of the ruts of monotonous routine and restoring tone to body and mind.

After dinner how delightful the pipe tasted as we again seated ourselves on the veranda to enliven an hour with tale and gossip, and how soon, nature having free scope to assert herself, we felt a sweet drowsiness which told us that bed was the place for us all. Not after midnight and with nightcaps and other noxious inventions, but early in the evening, the system all aglow with health. We arranged for another tour at half-past 5 next morning, and soon we were all in bed, and with a delightful sense of healthy exhaustion the world and consciousness began to fade out of sight.

That sleep was undisturbed by restless dreams ; but in the balmy slumbers of the night came to me pleasant sensations of a tug at the line. In visions I was holding the rod once more, and felt what the fisherman so longs for and starts with delight in finding—the rapturous tug at the hook which indicates a bite, and, in many cases, a capture. Here was the enthusiast of a day completely carried away with the sport, and continuing the happy exercise in dreams. But what sportsman who has whipped a stream all day for salmon, and been rewarded by landing a thirty-pounder before the day was over, has not gone over the exciting scenes in the silent watches of the night? It was as the scarred veteran of a hundred fights recalls the stirring incidents of some infantry charge when the enemy's stronghold was stormed, and the old flag was planted on the deserted battlements of the foe amid battle's roar and his comrades' cheers.

Day after day passed, each filled with its quota of sport and pleasure. My exceptional luck continued, and though the party was increased by fresh arrivals I still remained each day *facile princeps*— the new meteor in the piscatorial heavens. The longer I remained the more indifferent I became to all that was occurring in the outer world. Rest and renewed health were the guerdons of each day's experience. But all things must come to an end, and the time necessarily arrived when I was to take my last look at Rideau Lake and go back to newspapers, letters, telegrams and business. Thus endeth the story of my first—but I hope not last — fishing expedition, which had been postponed by the accidents of fate for forty years. Once more I am in the old routine, but with renewed vigor and energy. The prosaic now surrounds and prevails. But amid the din of duty it is pleasant to go back to such scenes as I have been describing. They brighten up one's life, and some other unfortunate old boy who like myself has not indulged in sport, because it was undignified, may be roused from his lethargy while reading these pages and become what I now am, an enthusiastic, though I hope a sensible, sportsman.

39
Virgin Streams
and Lakes
for Sport
(1891)

Virgin Streams and Lakes for Sport

BY ERNEST INGERSOLL.

THE Mackinaw Straits and Island, St. Mary's River and the lake country of Northern Wisconsin and the south shore of Lake Superior have long been names suggesting unlimited fishing and an ample variety of almost all the other recreations familiar to those who love to spend their vacations out of doors. The means of reaching these localities and moving about there, however, have been so greatly improved of late that some particular information in reference to this northern country should be given to the readers of OUTING.

The natural approach is by way of Mackinaw, where several lines of railway converge more conveniently than is generally understood: for instance, "solid" trains are run through in summer from Cincinnati to Mackinaw City, and others from Detroit and Toledo. Or one may go from Cleveland or Detroit by steamer. At any rate, Mackinaw City is the main gateway, and the first point of stoppage will be Mackinac Island, a few miles out in the straits.

Mackinac is one of the most charming places in all this charming region, and there is abundance of excellent summer-hotel accommodation for all comers. The drives about the historic old island; the many quaint and curious objects of nature which are present; the exquisite landscapes to be formed out of the rocky and cedar-grown foreground of half-ruined cliffs, the middle distance of blue, sail-flecked water and the background of distant shore; the various forms of aquatic amusements and exercises; the interesting legends and relics of the turbulent past which remain to be studied, and the glorious climate and sunshine, all form a combination rendering Mackinac entertaining and profitable in an extraordinary degree to the weary city man.

The angler, however, need expect little satisfaction on the island itself. If he sails or rows across to the Chenaux archipelago (or "The Snows," as the people call it) he may take bass, pike and muskallonge in the channels between the islets, and perhaps he will make a good catch. While the fishing there is not what it used to be, the enjoyment of exploring the labyrinth of waterways that intersect this picturesque group is just as keen now as to the first man who let his Indian guide thread their defiles. It is, however, an easy matter to go over to the northern mainland by ferry to St. Ignace, get a day's fishing and return in the evening, and this is what visitors at Mackinac do.

From St. Ignace a railway (Duluth, South Shore and Atlantic) runs straight north to Lake Superior, crossing at Trout Lake, some forty miles inland, the Minneapolis, St. Paul and Sault Ste. Marie Railway, popularly styled the "Soo Line." The trains of the latter road afford a means of readily reaching many excellent ponds and streams eastward to Sault Ste. Marie and westward to Rhinelander and the Wisconsin lakes. On the other hand the Northwestern sportsman, by coming East this way, is able to experiment with the whole list of river and lake fishing, and then proceed directly east either by

IN THE REACHES OF THE PIKE RIVER.—P. 232.

way of Mackinaw or over the Canadian Pacific's Sault line to Montreal.

Sault Ste. Marie, upon the St. Mary's River, which connects Lake Superior with Lake Huron, occupies not only a naturally advantageous situation for a commercial city, but one of singular attractiveness in summer. Before her sweeps the broad stream, just escaped from Lake Superior, and rushing, emerald green and foam white, down the splendid rapids for which we have kept the old French name *Sault* —a leap. Behind her circles a range of gentle hills, their crests fringed with forest. Opposite is the Canadian town of the same name, connected with the American city by the long and graceful spans of the huge "international" bridge, and the sky line there, again, is ragged with wooded hills. Northwestward the river widens into the blue and glistening plain of the great northern sea, always alive with shipping approaching and departing from this gateway of inland commerce, through whose massive locks, during a comparatively short season of navigation, passes annually an amount of tonnage greatly exceeding that of an entire year through the Suez Canal. Eastward the St. Mary's gradually curves out of view among pretty islands.

Here the earliest explorers found Indians encamped and fishing in great numbers, and here the pioneer traders built

their block houses and bartered with the redskins, who brought furs from far and near. Here grew up a half-way station on the great Northwestern canoe trail by which the Hudson Bay Company kept up communication between its headquarters in Montreal and its posts in Prince Rupert's Land, far north and west of Lake Superior. Here, almost as soon as the United States assumed its independence, a garrison was placed to hold a strategic point, and here a military post is still maintained, and is soon to be greatly enlarged. Later, as commerce developed, this land was beaten hard by the most important carrier trails in America; and later yet the United States constructed the ship canal which for thirty years has been a pathway around the rapids free to the commerce of all nations.

As these events happened one by one a quiet little town grew up on each bank, but from the first this one on the Michigan side was the more important, because here was the tramway carry, then the canal, then the landings for the fishing industry. Half a dozen years ago this town awoke into new life. Railroads had pressed nearer and nearer, both in Ontario and in Michigan. Commerce demanded more room for passage than the locks afforded, and the Government began the grand new canal now constructing. Far-seeing capitalists perceived that by bridging the

PLAYING A TROUT IN THE ST. MARY RAPIDS.

SAMPLES FROM THE SNOWS.

rapids and joining into one the railway systems east and west a through line between the Atlantic ports of Canada and New England and the grain, lumber and mineral tracts of the Northwest could be made much more direct than anything then existing.

All this came about within four or five years of intense activity, and the quaint little town sprang at a bound into a populous city. When the plans had been accomplished the city was left, able to advance unaided save by the energy of its six or seven thousand people. Fine buildings of every description have been erected, excellent—really excellent—hotels exist, and every appliance of civilization and comfort has been acquired.

The northern latitude of Sault Ste. Marie and its site upon a peninsula between the three greatest of the "great" lakes give it a summer climate of remarkable salubrity and coolness, and it becomes one of the most delightful of vacation resorts for those who are unwilling to go into the wilderness and yet desire to escape the expense of "the season" at some very fashionable watering place. Here is an excellent and cultivated society made up of the citizens, supplemented by the officers of the army post, the engineers in charge of the canal works and various professional men more or less temporarily resident here. The place is easily accessible by either water or rail from every Western and Southern locality, and it affords a great variety of "things to do"—driving, sailing, steamboat excursions, shooting, and, most important of all, superb fishing. The latter feature is the only one upon which this brief review has space to be particular.

Sault Ste. Marie is the centre of a wide circle of trout waters of every variety, from reefs in the open lake to streams so hidden under roots and brush that you can only hear, not see, their gurgling currents. Before the extensive excavations upon the two new canals had soiled the waters near shore, the local anglers used to wade into the edge of the rapids and cast their flies for trout right into the swift river. This will be done again when the works are completed and the water resumes its customary limpidity. But the rapids fishing is properly done from a boat, with Indians to paddle. Two of them and their boat—a strong, admirable craft, clincher built, but canoe shaped—will pole you up the boiling torrent, flashing snowy and green under the sunlight, and upon reaching a place which they think desirable will skillfully hold you poised upon the surface as the fish hangs poised near the bottom of that same crystal current.

Your hook is baited with a live and lively little fish something like a bullpout, which the Indians call cockadoosh, and this bait may be taken or it may not, for the trout of the rapids are frequently fastidious feeders and not always hungry. But if one does seize the hook you will immediately understand that it is a big one. Your line will fly out in a way that will astonish you and your rod will bend to its utmost tension, for it is strained not only by the desperate struggles of a char that will weigh from three to five pounds, but one which has a terribly swift and powerful current to help him pull against your bamboo and silk. But if you are skillful and lucky you will get him, and then what exultation will fill your heart. One would think that such fishing would require extra stout tackle, but the most experienced local anglers told the writer that for years they had been catching big fellows—four pounders, for instance—with a nine-ounce rod and a No. 5 line. A good many of these break, to be sure, and it often takes an hour to exhaust your plucky captive and bring him in, but in such a scientific conquest as that what man would begrudge an occasional loss of tackle. He has given the fish an even chance and has won a fair share of the battles.

These big fish of the rapids are true

MID STREAM BELOW THE BRIDGE.

brook trout which have come down out of the hill brooks and grown in the larger waters until they are able to stem the cataracts and go where they please. Their flesh is sometimes as pink as that of a salmon and their backs as black as old leather. In the nooks and holes along the quiet lower reaches of the St. Mary's many a one has been tempted from his lurking place fully their equal, and many another still remains to challenge the angler. Two Indians (and a boat), trained to the work of fishing in the rapids, will charge $3 for an afternoon, or $5 for all day. When a fly is used in the St. Mary's one of the Rangeley Lake style is most effective.

Another local means of enjoyment is to go to the north shore of Lake Superior, by which is here meant the Canadian side of the outlet of the lake, from twenty to sixty miles distant from Sault Ste. Marie. Whitefish agencies exist over there, and in summer an opportunity is presented every three or four days to go across in one of the little steamboats engaged in this business. A pleasanter way, however, is to make up a party, take tents and provisions, hire a sailboat and a couple of Indians with small boats and birch-bark canoes, and go over prepared to spend a week or more.

Into the lake at that part fall a number of rapid creeks, every one of which abounds in speckled trout. They are wading streams, and may be followed up for miles, and there are ponds and spring holes hidden among the rocks that will yield a basketful apiece.

At the mouths of these streams, and along the Canadian shore of the lake generally, many half-submerged points of rock and outlying reefs form a barrier between the outer lake and the strand. Among these rocks lurk trout of large size and the highest quality, which can only be taken with a well-cast fly. Here the angler can display his skill and get his highest reward ; and, though the excitement of his work will not be so great as when standing in the midst of the rushing Sault, the scene and the work together on these reefs will lack nothing in invigorating enjoyment. A sportsman would deny himself a great privilege who should neglect to take this trip to the north shore and try these reefs as well as the rivers there. The St. Mary's and Detour rivers below (east of) the city are extremely attractive to the summer vacationist. They are dotted with wooded islands which make the scenery beautiful, keep the waters quiet, offer charming camping places and afford excellent grouse shooting. Big and little trout lurk everywhere, and at the Neebishes, a dozen miles below town, the waters are famous for bass, both the big mouthed and small mouthed, which take a fly eagerly. It is strange that more yachts and canoe clubs do not come cruising to these island-protected waters, whose defiles may be threaded

GAME TO THE LAST.

through a great triangle which stretches from the Straits of Mackinaw on the south to the Sault, and thence east to the further side of Georgian Bay. In summer small steamboats traverse them and the trip is most interesting.

Half a dozen trout streams within a few miles of Sault Ste. Marie invite you to test their quality. In most of these ordinary casting is out of the question; they are only tortuous little brooks that you may leap across in many places (yet having deep holes), and are closely shut in and canopied by brush for a large part of their length. The work must be done, therefore, mainly with bait worms, but when a fish strikes it is just as much fun to get him into your creel in good style as though he had a London-made fly in his jaw. One gentleman told the writer that he had taken trout in these woods where he could not see the water at all, by letting his line down through a tangle of cedar roots. Perhaps the best stream within the compass of a day's excursion is Bear Creek, which flows southward into Lake Michigan. It has been fished but little yet, and is alive with fish. Pine River, somewhat more distant, is larger, and both are covered by the railroad, which has stations on their banks.

The south shore of Lake Superior within 100 miles of the Sault is a favorite fishing resort of not only local anglers, but of many Southern sportsmen who have been well advised. Here scores of streams and lakes are accessible along the line of the Duluth, South Shore and Atlantic Railway. Two Hearted River, the Grand Marais region, the rivers that flow into Munising Bay and the reefs that lie along that shore and form a part of the Pictured Rocks, are all locally famous for excellent fishing of various kinds. Grand Marais

Lake yielded a party of three, last summer, 500 trout, the weight of which would average a pound apiece, while some were twice that or more.

This district, however, has been well covered in OUTING heretofore, and needs to be referred to here only to connect it with the angling resources of the St. Mary's region.

From Sault St. Marie westward to Minneapolis by the "Soo" line is a journey of more than 500 miles right through the wilderness. Except the group of port towns upon Lake Michigan, Manistique, Gladstone and Escanaba, and Rhinelander, in Central Wisconsin, there are no villages of any account, only small stations and supplying points for the lumbering which goes on in all parts of this vast forest. The lumbering operations, however, make roads and trails in all directions and provide, along almost every river, stopping places at the camps of the woodsmen, while in many counties, particularly along the shores of Lake Superior, stage lines connect towns not reached by rail and afford a means of getting to excellent fishing waters between them.

An hour's run west of Trout Lake brings one into the Manistique Valley, where the rivers abound in trout and the lakes in pike, or bass, or trout, according to the characteristics of each. West of the Manistique waters, and before the Eagle waters are reached, however, the country is more barren, though all the streams look tempting. Some have been trout brooks in the past; others have never, so far as is remembered. Lately, however, the State Fish Commission, through Mr. Shepard, of Rhinelander, has placed in most, if not all, of these creeks hundreds of thousands of fry, which will

NOON AT THE CAMP.

begin to show themselves after a year or two. At present Pike River is the only one worth fishing ; but this is very worthy of attention indeed. The station for it is Dunbar, a mere hamlet without any hotel. It would be necessary, therefore, for the persons who mean to explore this stream to bring a tent and provisions with them, prepared for immediate service. The Pike is a shallow river, suitable for wading, and the best plan, probably, would be to ascend it, since its capability is not to be judged by trials close by the railroad crossing, where naturally it has been overfished. It is better to go up stream than down, because a large space below the railroad is controlled by a Chicago club of anglers who would be likely to expel any trespassers in short order. A road runs along the bank, or near it, by which camp equipments could be carried as far as desirable, and a pleasant camping place may be found at almost every bend of the stream. Many of its tributaries will lead him who follows them under the overhanging greenery to the sequestered ponds of which they are the outlets, and in these ponds dwell the largest and strongest and gamiest fish. The Pike is a good river, but with this exception the angler is advised not to halt until he reaches Rhinelander, the county seat of Oneida County, where the railroad crosses the Wisconsin River.

Rhinelander is a flourishing village of two thousand five hundred or three thousand people, and is one of the principal supplying points for the hundreds of lumbering camps and mills scattered throughout Northern Wisconsin. Here everything needful can be obtained in the way of outfit, so that a person or a party of persons who did not choose to bring a camp equipment could procure a tent, sleeping materials and provisions of all kinds. Here, too, men thoroughly familiar with the woods, able to guide a party anywhere, arrange and manage boats, cook and care for the camp, may be hired at about $2.50 a day.

Rhinelander is the proper gateway to the lake region of Northern Wisconsin, where are hundreds of rock-bound bodies of water fed by springs and limpid brooks and the fountains of beautiful streams, which connect them into a chain, or lead their waters into the Wisconsin. The map of Oneida and Forest counties is so spotted with them that there seems hardly more land than water.

A railroad north from Rhinelander and another one north from Gagen, a junction point a dozen miles eastward, passes through the very heart of these lakes and ponds and makes access to them easy, besides which there are wagon roads, trails and canoe routes. Some of them are very well known, such as Tomahawk, the St. Germain (Big and Little), Flambeau and Trout lakes (these two on the head waters of the Chippewa), the congeries of ponds and brooks called " Eagle Waters," the Pelican lakes and many others.

Upon some of them hotels exist, such as those at Minocqua, Scott's and Conklin's, at opposite ends of Tomahawk Lake, and a few others. These are frontier taverns, to be sure, but a great many tourist sportmen find them acceptable. It is said that a thousand visitors may be found sometimes at hotels or encamped around the Tomahawk lakes alone. Scattered all through the woods, and almost invariably standing upon the bank of some lake, may be found the substantial camps of the lumbermen. One or two men, not over-fastidious in the matter of fare, could make one of these camps their home very well. But a better way would be to pitch a tent close by, have their own provisions and avail themselves of the camp cook's oven for baking, and otherwise profit by the conveniences and sociability of the lumbermen's home. If the visitors were " good fellows" they would be welcomed.

The average party, however, will prefer to be away by itself. Providing itself with complete equipment for camping, and perhaps taking its own canoes, it will be driven out from Rhinelander, or some station nearby, to a lake the guide knows of, the shores of which have not yet resounded to the " rare domestic sound " of the lumberman's axe, nor been desolated by fire. Many such can be found buried in the heart of the virgin forest, where not a sign of man's intrusion breaks the exquisite harmony of nature. No keel but that of the wild duck's breast has parted those sky-like waters, and the splash of the pike, as he leaps and dives, or the falling of a dead branch alone disturbs the serenity of sound.

Here the shore is scanned for a point jutting out into the lake and exposed to the breeze. Upon the larger lakes many such are found which have been occupied as camping places by the Indians since time immemorial. At the hidden tarn which has been imagined the point must be cleared of underbrush (if you are the first camper), so that the wind may blow freely underneath the great pines that shade your tent and waft away the flies and mosquitoes, which are the pest of the woods wherever the brush is thick and the breeze hushed. Ideal camping places like this are never far to seek. Under the magnificent trees the moss lies like a deeply-piled carpet, and before you the blue plain of the lake stretches to its picturesque bounds. Your firewood is at hand, your boat rocks at its moorings close by, your spring, crystal pure, is only a rod or two away, the air is laden with balsamic odors, and growing leaves overspread the world for hundreds of miles around you. It is a delight and an invigoration merely to exist in such a place, yet you can add to it as fine fishing as North America has to show.

The sport here—that is, in waters tributary to the Wisconsin — is with muskallonge, wall-eyed pike, pickerel, bass and some small fry, like perch and whitefish. You must leave these and cross over to the Chippewa waters, such as Trout and the Flambeau lakes, if you want trout. This it is easy to do by road or by canoeing and short carries.

Pickerel, pike and bass are almost everywhere, and in many lakes the bass are extremely abundant, of large size and game quality. One of the best places for bass, by the way, is in North Pelican Lake, which is directly upon the "Soo" line, a few miles east of Rhinelander. The station is North Pelican. Out of this lake runs the Pelican River ; and where it begins, at the foot of the lake, is a lofty cataract, in and about which lurks a fine kind of bass, locally regarded as quite distinct from the ordinary species.

It would be a most delightful run, by the way, to put a canoe into the lake at North Pelican, skirt the pretty shores, carry around the falls and descend the rapid outlet to Pelican River. Then, if you pleased, you could go up a few miles to Pelican Lake, which is three or four miles in diameter ; or you could keep on down to the Wisconsin. This river is full of rapids, just made for "shooting," and has a sinuous, picturesque course of the most delightful kind. Its mouth is only a few miles below Rhinelander, to which you could return. This is only an example of a great number of water routes to be followed, and a canoe club would

find here an ideal country for an exploring tour.

These lakes are probably the only places where muskallonge are still numerous and of large size. In some of these, like Pelican and the lower Tomahawk, they have become rare, but in a hundred others which any guide can indicate, or your own experiments will discover, it is possible to take them daily. Last summer hundreds were caught exceeding twenty pounds in weight, some three times that, and when you have one of those big fellows on the end of your line, with teeth an inch long, you think you have caught a shark big enough to swallow Jonah. There is no doubt that more and larger and better muskallonge and bass can be caught here than anywhere else in the country.

The best time to enter this country is from the middle of May to early June in respect to fishing. The fish bite well then, the flies and gnats are not so bad as later, the air is cool at noonday and in the evening the comfort of a big fire can be enjoyed, the forest is greenest and most odorous, the weather is clear and bright. Another charming season is during September and into October, before the rains begin, and it is doubtful which of the two ends of the summer is to be preferred.

After the fishermen have left the lakes in the fall the deer hunters come to the country. The law says no deer shall be shot before October 15 nor after the last day of the ensuing November. Unfortunately the game laws are not very well enforced in this wilderness, but as a matter of fact little harm is done, since most of the men here are too busy to do much shooting. In regions where wolves are abundant more fawns are killed in the spring by these brutes than all the shooting of the year amounts to.

However, deer are still abundant all through this lake country, and every autumn dozens of parties of hunters come from the cities to get them, and hundreds are shipped away to their friends. Thus far little market shooting has been done, and there seems to be no serious diminution in the deer census from year to year. Deer hunting in the fall has a bit of spice here, too, in the liability to run upon a bear (or have one run upon you) at any moment. They are numerous, certainly, but nobody seems any more afraid of them than of the wolves or wild cats. It is not easy, in fact, to find anything one of these woodsmen is afraid of. Fur-bearing animals of all kinds are numerous; gray rabbits abound in unlimited profusion, and red squirrels and chipmunks are common, but gray or black squirrels rather scarce.

From Rhinelander west nearly to St. Paul and Minneapolis, the road passes on through the same continuous forest of mixed timber. For the most part this is "old cuttings," or areas from which the available timber has been taken out; but here and there large patches of virgin forest yet remain, where one may see the tall white pines towering head and shoulders above the hard woods, the hemlocks and the spruces, and pleasing the eye of the lumberman as he passes them, as the whisking away, now and then, of a covey of grouse brings the smile to the face of the sportsmen on the train.

Some twenty-five miles west of Rhinelander the imperceptible "height of land" between the Wisconsin and the Chippewa rivers is passed, and the train begins to cross many clear and rapid streams, winding their way down to the latter great watercourse, which empties itself into the Mississippi at the foot of Lake Pepin.

This is the river for trout. All its almost numberless sources, which gather the drainage of almost one hundred townships, contain brook trout, and the lakes that feed it—though these are far fewer and less important than those which nourish the superior Wisconsin—are the home of lake trout which the lumbermen (many of whom come from Maine) regard as identical with those of the Rangeley and Moosehead lakes.

This Chippewa River and its branches are ideal for canoeing. The various larger streams have carried logs for many years and have been cleared of obstructions until their currents flow almost as open and steady as canals. Beautiful camping places abound along their banks, and the woodsmen know how, by short carries, to go from one to the other, or to find hidden lakes and tumbling branches, where trout are nosing the cataracts and seeking the utmost springs for the deposit of their roe.

In this upper Chippewa country there is good work for the gun in the fall. Each autumn parties of sportsmen come north from Chicago and various other southern points, bringing full camping equipments and indulging themselves in a fortnight's shooting with most satisfactory results. Now and then a black bear falls to their guns, but most of these are shot later in the season in an accidental way by the woodsmen and farmers whose provisions they incautiously approach. Not long ago a big fellow stalked out on the railroad just ahead of a train, and, ignorant or defiant of danger, was run down and ignominiously tossed into the bushes by the locomotive.

As for birds, there are always plenty of grouse—"pheasants" they call them here —but the country is scarcely open enough for prairie chickens, which, however, are creeping northward with the advance of clearings. The same is true of the quail. Ducks abound during the season of migration upon every lake and along all the streams, especially where they expand into marshes, and include a long list of varieties, but geese are less common and swans almost unknown.

All things considered — fishing, shooting, canoeing, camping — it is doubtful whether one could go anywhere more easily and more profitably in search of an outing.

40
A Day
on the
Stream for Trout
(1891)

A DAY ON THE STREAM FOR TROUT.

BY WAKEMAN HOLBERTON.

THE little village of Ralston, Pa., was an ideal spot for an artist and angler to dwell in, and I was in the habit of spending my summers in this wild secluded valley in search of studies and sketches for backgrounds to my trout and game pictures, though I think that the good fishing had the most to do with it. The narrow valley through which rippled the fair Lycoming River, surrounded by high hills covered with virgin hemlock forest in which deer and bear were easily found by the sportsmen in the fall, and often seen by the angler on a quiet evening, has unfortunately been somewhat marred by the bark peelers and lumbermen.

I had been hard at work for some weeks at my painting and began to feel that I deserved a holiday. The water was in prime condition, the forest fresh and green and the air sweet with the perfume of the wild grape. In short, it was perfect weather. So before going to bed I got everything ready for an early start; filled

the alcohol lamp in readiness to boil an egg and make a cup of hot coffee, put tobacco in my pouch and laid out my fishing suit and hobnail shoes, not forgetting to put a couple of light leaders to soak in my leader box.

It was barely daybreak when I awoke next morning, and let me remark that early rising is a virtue that sportsmen must learn to cultivate, and, though it comes hard at first, it is astonishing how soon one gets used to it, and even learns to like it after a while. My simple meal was soon finished, and a substantial lunch rolled up, first in a napkin and then in a bit of oiled silk, so it could be carried in the bottom of my creel without harm, and for company put with it a pint of good claret.

As I stepped out of doors into the fragrant fresh air I could hear the rustling of the stream that ran but a stone's throw from the house, yet though it contained good trout I was not going to disturb it to-day, but try some new waters

" over the hills and far away." I crossed the stream over a rustic bridge and followed an old, deserted wood road up the mountain. This path, once used by miners, was almost overgrown with the brushes and brambles, while on each side, as far as the eye could see, the hemlock forest towered upward toward the blue sky. The woods were cool and sweet and alive with the melody of many birds, chief among which I could hear the soft, flute-like note of the wood robin, while now and then a ruffed grouse darted away with much noise and bustle, or a gray or black squirrel greeted me with an angry chatter. Mile after mile I trudged along, until finally I descended the hill toward the stream tumbling among the rocks below.

When I reached it I discovered it was not the trout stream I expected to find, but only a little tributary and unfit for fishing. I followed this down for half a mile and a very rough trip it was too, when suddenly, as I pushed through a bunch of laurel, I found myself on the banks of a lovely stream. The little brook which had been my guide tumbled into the magnificent pool worn out of the solid rock by the action of the water. I put down my creel and rod and bathed my face and hands in the cold spring water. After a few minutes' rest and a smoke I put the little rod together, attaching a fine nine-foot leader to my line for a cast, a great dun as a stretcher, a brown hen for a first dropper and a grizzly king for a hand fly, and commenced fishing over a promising looking pool, but without success. Just below, just under the bushes, I had my first good rise and killed a handsome eight-inch trout on the great dun. The water was very clear, and oh ! how cold, the fish shy and not over plenty ; still every little while there was a splash, a short, sharp struggle and the quivering rod brought a victim to the landing net.

After wading down stream for a couple of hours or so I came to quite a fall, and had to take to the woods to get around it. Just below was a big, dark pool with flecks of white foam floating on the black water. Carefully approaching I sent my flies out close to the foam, and instantly a good twelve - inch trout took the stretcher, and soon after another fastened to the hand fly. The spring of the rod told after five minutes' heavy strain, and I gradually worked them in reach of my

net, but had to wade ashore to get them into my creel. Well, that was something like ! But unfortunately at the next cast a fish took half my leader, and I had to go ashore for repairs.

It was hardly time for luncheon, but the long walk and early breakfast had made me feel very anxious about the contents of my napkin ; so I gathered some dry wood and soon had a good fire under the bank, first putting the claret in the stream to cool. What a comfort a fire is, particularly when one is alone in the forest. It almost takes the place of a companion. While the fire was burning down, I cleaned my trout and washed out my creel, packing the fish carefully back in fresh grass, except a few of the smaller ones ; these I wrapped in buttered paper, seasoning them with salt and pepper, then dipped them into the stream and placed them under the coals, just like Uncle Thad Norris used to do at Jim Henry's on Brodhead's Creek.

In fifteen minutes or thereabouts they were done, and when the paper was peeled off looked very inviting, and they tasted as good as they looked. The meal over, I kicked the dishes into the stream where they came from, and, leaving the scraps to the birds and squirrels, stretched at full length on the ferns to enjoy a long, lazy smoke and take what I call solid comfort.

A splash in the pool, made by a good-sized trout, recalls me to business, and I remember it is yet a long way to the deserted mill where I am to wind up the day's sport. So I wade again into the cold water and proceed on my way down stream, casting into every likely spot as I go. The stream looked beautiful as it twisted and turned, now rippling over shallows and then tumbling into a dark amber colored pool, overhung with the branches of laurel and rhododendron. The sun here and there brightened up the water, but in the narrow valley it dwelt not ; already many of the best reaches were lying in cool shadow.

It was quite late by the time I reached the old deserted mill pond where I hoped to kill a few big trout ; nor was I disappointed, for, by the time I rigged a fresh cast of a coachman and ginger palmer, the fish were already dimpling the water, quietly sucking in some unlucky miller that was struggling on the smooth surface of the pond.

After lighting a fresh pipe I waded in

as silently as possible, and as soon as the ripple had subsided I began casting. Here I enjoyed great sport, killing several good-sized trout that made my rod creak and bend in a most alarming manner. My last fish was a particularly fine one, and I had all I could do to keep him away from the sunken logs at the bottom of the old mill pond. He measured sixteen and three-quarter inches long and weighed one and three-quarter pounds. This was the largest trout, with one exception, I had up to that time killed. So I was content to stop, particularly as I could hardly crowd the big one into my creel. I unjointed my rod and soon found the old wood road. It was quite dark and gloomy under the big trees; the song birds were hushed, the melancholy note of the whip-poor-will and the hoo-hoo-hoot of the great horned owl had taken the place of their sweet notes. Tired but contented I trudged along with a basket of trout that any angler might well feel proud of and soon I could see the distant lights in the windows of Chetmeyer's hospitable tavern, which had become a second home.

Drawn by Senyard.   THE DESERTED MILL POND.

41
The
Fun of
Fishing
(1910)

THE
OUTING
MAGAZINE

VOLUME LVI APRIL, 1910 NUMBER I

THE FUN OF FISHING

by Dr. James A. Henshall

United States Bureau of Fisheries

Illustrated with Photographs

NGLING is as old as civilization. We read in the classics that in A.D. 230 the Macedonians fished the river Astræus with the artificial fly. The first book on angling in the English language was printed at Winchester, England, in 1496. Its author was a woman of noble birth, Dame Juliana Berners, prioress of a nunnery near St. Albans. She gave explicit instructions in the art, with directions for making rods and tackle, and gave the formulas for the tying of artificial flies for each month in spring and summer, many of which are in use to this day under various names.

The love of angling has ever gone hand in hand with the love of Nature. For, should the angler catch no fish, Dame Juliana quaintly says: "Yet atte the leest he hath his holsom walke, and mery at his ease. A swete ayre of the swete savoure of the mede flowers; that makyth hym hungry."

So, as one of the incentives for an occasional outing is a love of angling, it should be remembered that "it is not all of fishing to fish," as George Dawson aptly expressed it. Rather, it is the opportunity that angling affords for a realization and enjoyment of Nature's resources, with the subsequent compensation of renewed health and strength. The cares and anxieties and perplexities of everyday life are forgotten as the angler wades the merry stream and casts his flies on the flashing water. He is wholly obsessed with his pursuit and has unbounded faith in his methods.

And while the eager expectancy of a response to his lures absorbs his every faculty, he enjoys, at the same time, in a subconscious way, the bounties of Nature surrounding and investing him. The voices of the stream are ever in his ears—the lapping and purling of the

451

Photograph by Mrs. C. S. Taber.

IN THE GOOD OLD SUMMER TIME.

water as it sparkles on the riffle or whirls in the eddies. He is alive to the song of the birds, the hum of insects, and the whispering of the leaves as the sunlight filters through them.

But it does not follow that one must be a fly fisherman to obtain the full measure of enjoyment of such an outing. Mother Nature is equally kind to all who seek her solitudes. Even the boy angler, with bent pin and earthworm bait, is conscious of her moods and expressions, though he does not realize it at the time; in after years there will suddenly flash on memory's mirror that very scene of his boyhood.

He can scent the pungent odor of the mint that grew on the bank and remember the flash of the butterfly's wing that went sailing by, the rustle and quiver of the leaves overhead, and the cool and grateful sensation as he laved his bare feet in the stream. All this he remembers distinctly, even though he fails to recollect whether it was a minnow or a sunfish that he caught, or how many of them.

But better than an occasional outing is to camp for a week or a month beside a tumbling mountain stream, a brawling river, or a placid lake. The pleasures of angling can then be diversified by sauntering through the woods, climbing the hills, or rowing and sailing on the lake. Everywhere, on every hand, there is always something worth while—gathering and studying the wild flowers, observing the characteristics of the trees, collecting insects, or watching the amusing antics of the birds—enough to occupy all one's time during the day.

Then at night one can view with wonder and delight the starry canopy overhead, where the stars shine with more brilliancy and in greater numbers than are seen in the haunts of men. Perhaps then only does the city dweller see the flaming belt of Orion, the big and little dippers, and the Pleiades in the full glory of their surroundings.

Though there are degrees in angling, he of the first degree, the still fisher with alder rod, enjoys the sport with as much genuine love and zest as the mas-

WHERE THE TROUT STREAM WINDS THROUGH A WOODED VALLEY.

ter of angling with his slender wand of split bamboo and fairylike flies. Even the colored brother, with his hickory pole and crawfish bait, finds sport galore in yanking out a channel catfish. The outdoor environment and the voices of Nature appeal to each one the same. All are brothers of the angle.

The expert fly fisher who offers his silken gage of a Jock Scott fly to the lordly salmon, a polka fly to the gamesome black bass, a coachman to the brook trout, or a gray hackle to the graceful grayling, is, perhaps, to be envied. For, although his address to each fish requires various methods and much modification of his tools and tackle, he is equally at home with all—the fifteen-ounce rod for salmon, the seven-ounce for black bass, the six-ounce for trout, or one of five ounces for grayling. So, also, as to the caliber of his line and leader and the size of his flyhook; each must be commensurate with the size and gameness of his quarry.

In legitimate angling the Atlantic salmon is lord of all. His capture requires the skill and finesse of the fin-ished angler, and the use of the most approved tackle, which is the outcome of the experience of centuries. The wild leap for freedom of the hooked fish, his stubborn resistance, his fierce fighting, his sulking, and his final gaffing have been extolled by eminent and expert fishers for hundreds of years, and recorded by the pens of ready and enthusiastic British writers. At the present day, in America, fortunes are spent yearly in his pursuit, for verily it is an expensive sport which can be had only on leased Canadian rivers and to a limited extent on one or two streams in Maine.

The several species of Pacific salmon do not rise to the artificial fly, more's the pity, and are of no interest to the fly fisher. During the days of " 54—40 or a fight" an old Scotch official and salmon fisher said: "Dom the country; the saumon will no rise to the fly; let the Yankees have it."

On the other hand, the favorite American game fish, the black bass, which now has a local habitation and a name in every State of the Union, as well as in

EXPECTATION.

Canada and Mexico, can be fished for without money and without price, so far as the waters are concerned. The large-mouth black bass was caught by the first English colonists of Virginia, the Carolinas, and Florida, who bestowed on him the names of "salmon" and "trout" as a tribute to his gameness. The early French *voyageurs* knew him intimately and well, while the small-mouth black bass was the favorite game fish of enthusiastic anglers of the Middle West fully a century ago. But it was not until fifty years later, when the black bass was introduced into the waters of the Eastern States, that he came into his own as an acknowledged peer among game fishes.

The life histories of both the large-mouth and small-mouth bass are now common knowledge. All over the length and breadth of our land, from Maine to California, wherever there is a lakelet, the large-mouth bass may be found sunning himself among the water lilies and bulrushes, while the small-mouth bass rears his spiny crest and flashes his bronze armor in almost every stream from New York to Arkansas. No other game fish is now so eagerly sought by the tens of thousands of anglers of every degree as the black bass, and no other game fish is so accessible on lake, pond, or stream, either by wading or fishing from a boat or from the bank.

In the Eastern States no other game fish is so well known and prized as the brook trout. Perhaps no other is held in such veneration by the veterans of the angling guild, who view with sorrow and regret its passing from many of its native streams. And though it is being replaced with the English brown trout and the Pacific rainbow trout, no other can ever win the same love and affection with which the ruby-studded living arrow of the crystal waters is regarded by the old-timers. They hark back to the days of long ago, when barefooted they trudged along the brookside, their pathway adorned with trailing arbutus, their ears attuned to

REALIZATION.

the song sparrow, but with eyes ever alert for the trout under the bank.

And how this is all lived over again as their children and grandchildren go back to the old home, during the vacation months, and fish the same brooks and gather flowers and health. Or perhaps it is the old pond where the bullpout or even a pickerel may still be found and the water lilies still bloom.

If one cannot visit the haunts of the salmon, black bass, trout, or grayling, there are always other fishes to claim the attention of the true angler, who with the lightest tackle can still enjoy the pleasures of the sport. It is not so much the character and esteem of the fish itself as the spirit with which the angler enters into the game. With a rod of three or four ounces and midge artificial flies, the rock bass, white bass, crappie, perch, blue gill, or even the common sunfish will afford as much real sport, *per se,* as more pretentious fishes. And for camp fare there are no better dainties for the camper with a camper's appetite.

A FAVORITE TROUT POOL.

WHERE THE ROAD CROSSES THE RIVER.

LUNCH TIME IS NOT THE LEAST PLEASANT PART OF THE DAY'S SPORT.

In this country of abundance in both species and numbers of fishes, many real game fishes are apt to be ignored. In England, on the contrary, where there are comparatively few species, thousands of anglers who are debarred from preserved waters, or who cannot afford the expense of salmon or trout fishing, are just as enthusiastic in pursuit of such coarse fish as roach, dace, rudd, bream, or barbel, all members of the minnow family, none of which is equal in gameness to our chub or fallfish. We have a minnow in the streams of the Pacific slope three or four feet long that takes bait freely and rises to the artificial fly, but it is not a game fish and is not much sought except by the Indian. And then, unfortunately, we have the German carp, which by some is considered a game fish in England, but in this country is anathema, and justly so.

If one is not a fly fisher he can still use bait, minnows, crawfish, worms, grubs, and grasshoppers. It makes little difference as to the lure employed, for the chief object is to capture the quarry, and it is all one to the fish whether it succumbs to an artificial fly or to the humble and lowly earthworm.

In salt-water fishing bait is almost universally used, as shrimps, crabs, clams, sand- and blood-worms. And what a joy it is to the men, women, and children of the cities to leave behind the dusty streets, the stifling heat of brick and mortar, for the seashore, to find relief in fishing, bathing, and beach combing. Even a single trip on an excursion steamer to the fishing banks affords a day of real pleasure long to be remembered.

During the summer blackfish or tautog, bluefish, striped bass, and weakfish may be taken in most places along the coast of the Middle States. The bluefish, however, is rather uncertain in its advent, and may be scarce or plentiful. Like the coyote, it hunts its prey in company, sometimes in countless numbers, and roams along the coast in quest of the schools of small fry, on which it descends like the Assyrian of old, its cohorts, however, gleaming in blue and silver instead of purple and gold. Even the flounder, scup, or cunner are not to be altogether despised should the "tide-runners" refuse to bite. It is only their familiarity with his bait that breeds the contempt of the fastidious angler.

With his boat rocking gently on the incoming tide, the angler, apart from

AND WHEN THE DAY IS DONE SORT OUT THE CATCH AND COMPARE RESULTS.

his fishing, is conscious of the white sails shimmering in the offing, the long streamer of smoke from the funnel of an outgoing steamer, and is not unmindful of the erratic flight of the sea gulls as they scream and hover over the shining water and dash into it occasionally for some tidbit of flotsam. He pauses from his fishing once in a while to admire the beauty of the graceful trophies in his basket—their pearly tints and silvery sheen, their jeweled eyes and shapely fins—while the salt breeze fans his cheek as he "loafs and invites his soul." Surely the angler has chosen the better part in the catalogue of outdoor sports.

In the ethics of true sportsmanship there are several things in relation to angling that it may be well to remember: Always kill the fish outright as soon as unhooked; whether using natural or artificial bait never, under any circumstances, employ more than a single hook; and never take more fish than your needs demand. The methods of the fish hog are not for us. Rather let us ponder the advice of good Dame Juliana Berners, as applicable now as four centuries ago:

"Also ye shall not be ravenous in takyng of your sayd game as to mooche at one tyme. . . . As whanne ye have a suffycyent mese ye sholde covet no more at that tyme. Also ye shall beysye yourselfe to nourysth the game in all that ye maye, and to dystroye all such thynges as ben devourers of it. And all those that done after this rule shall have the blessynge of God and Saynt Peter, whyche he theym graunte, that with his preecyous bloode vs boughte."

42
The Lake
of the
Abounding Trout
(1910)

THE LAKE OF THE "ABOUNDING TROUT" by Kirk B. Alexander

Illustrated by D. C. Hutchison

UNQUESTIONABLY, the lake was out there (and unquestionably still is) somewhere in the heart of St. Ignace Island. We were as sure of that as we were of the facts that St. Ignace Island blocks the entrance to Nipigon Bay, Lake Superior, and that we were camping on St. Ignace Island. Michael and Joe and Nish-i-shin-i-wog, being all amiable redmen and experienced guides and eager ever to impart cheering information, to be corrected or retracted under ultimate compulsion, were perfectly sure that they knew just where to put their hands on that lake.

In the first place, the map showed the lake plainly and alluringly. Moreover, being a garrulous and candid map, even as Canadian maps go, it grew confidential, giving the lake's length—six miles —and its population and "principal products" — to wit — "abounding in speckled trout." We wanted very much to find that lake; first because we aspired to see just how utterly shameless in its mendacity the map could be; second, because we wanted to extend an angler's greeting to those trout which had been "abounding" all these fifteen years of that map's misled life with little or no encouragement; and, third, because we calculated that we had at most but two days left of a month's playtime in the wilderness. The little pulp-wood steamer, *J. C. Ford,* might come poking her snub-nose into the cove to-morrow and whistle us arrogantly back to starched linen and the kindred horrors of civilization.

So the Camp Boss arose from his H. B. blanket, stretched himself toward the white northern moon, kicked a log back into the camp fire, and said: "Well— how about it? Who goes after the lake?"

Of course he might have said "to the lake" and been more grammatical, but being a north-woodsman, the Camp Boss knew well the elusiveness of which lake and map in conspiracy were capable. He knew that we'd have to surround that six-mile lake and tire it out and trip it up and sit upon its heaving chest before we could properly call it our own.

The verdict for a sunrise departure lake-ward was unanimous; that is, virtually unanimous. The Indians didn't vote at all, because this business of discussing and consulting a roll of paper with ridiculous lines and letters on it disgusted them. Steve was asking himself in what coat-pocket or in whose tent or on what rock he had left his pipe and didn't hear. At least, he pretended not to hear. He felt about the entire project of the lake-trip precisely as the Indians felt about the map—and if that could be translated into good, pure Chippewa idiom it might be printed here with propriety. Steve could get all the exercise and adventure he really craved by carrying his rod and fishing-box from his tent to the beach or strolling over to the grub-tent. Had he been given the power to arrange such matters, he would sit on a rock and cast, Kaiser-like, while the pick of Superior reef-trout were driven up to his busy dropper-fly.

Billy said something sotto voce to Steve. It was something stinging and stimulating and subtly contemptuous. Steve sprang to his feet and thundered: "I'll show you whether I'm a quitter or not." And when we had disentangled them it was perfectly evident that Steve was "going after the lake."

"Gee-sus" in stunning splendor was coming over the eastern rim of Superior and screaming gulls were deep in the serious and ceaseless business of getting fed, when we tumbled out of blankets and raced to beach and bath, while the nipping air made speed and comment unavoidable. When the third relay had successfully brought Steve to the open, still clinging to his blankets, we breakfasted; then made up packs, sought out compass, fly-rod, and steel-rod, flies for those for which the map prepared us and spinners for those which lurk in green lake bottoms where trout are not—and they are the piratical pike.

Also we took a shot-gun for foolish spruce-hens, buck-shotted shells for an inhospitable bullmoose, a camera for the log-keeper, and a hatchet and spikes for raft-building. Michael and Joe carried, in their packs, a skillet, a tea-pot, bread, bacon, salt, a culinary equipment rudimentary in the extreme. Nish-i-shin-i-wog remained to guard the camp against bears and itinerant fishermen.

We began the ascent on the ridge which rose from the water like some giant lizard emerging from the deep and swept away upward to its radial center, "Old Baldy," miles inland. "Old Baldy" we believed to be the head-stone of the six-mile lake. It's ridiculously simple to walk up one of those Superior ridges. It gives you a maximum appreciation of your own ability and acumen and a minimum comprehension of the obstacle to be overcome and that is always bad. This particular ridge, after about half a mile, grew wearied and bored with being a ridge and tried being a mountain, letting another promontory on the far side of a deep, thick valley take care of the ridge business for a while.

It is curious how all the sprawling, tangled, obstinate, cunning, fun-loving, congested, and cussed bushes of that flora insisted upon settling in the valley bottoms and leaving the airy realty of the ridges and hill-sides without a market. Steve noticed it first, which, of course, was quite inevitable. He had scorned· our warning to disjoint his trout-rod for the trip. More than that, he had three vivacious and clinging flies on his leader. Also he had a landing net hung around his neck with an elastic, which would cling to a twig and then,

released, slap him smartly between the shoulder-blades. He had a net helmet enveloping his features and gauntlets against the black-flies who loved him dearly.

When three flies, landing-net, and netting helmet enmeshed themselves simultaneously in the vegetation, Steve would seize the opportunity to tell us frankly and fully what he thought of the whole "fool jaunt" and the procession would take out time to dissociate Steve from his environment. When he was shorn of all, save headnet and gauntlets, we began to make time.

Out of Steve's hearing we all remarked upon the obvious inequalities of the going. Of course, there was no trail, save those which moose and deer and caribou had made and those trails led everywhere and anywhere. With hats pulled over our eyes we pushed gropingly through dense spruce, hemlock, juniper, swamp-willow, and tag-alder thickets. We climbed over wind-rows and sank into great logs that looked sound and were but dust. We plodded through caribou-moss to the knees and floundered through tamarack-swamps.

Steve's head-net early confirmed his judgment and established its own efficacy. It incarcerated all the black-flies and deer-flies along with Steve and distracted their intentions from us entirely. They seemed to think it a lure intended for their exclusive divertisement and sportive tastes. When Steve discovered the effects of this fatuous interpretation, he wrathfully hung his head-net upon a tag-alder bush. We often speculate even now how badly that bush has been bitten.

We emerged from that rank valley and nimbus of flies at last and regained the ridge-radiation. Joe stopped us and we heard the music of trickling water, and between two Norway pines, deep at their roots, we found the crystalline depths and wondrous refreshment of one of those enchanted springs with which a bountiful providence has equipped the northern forests.

On across the plateau we moved, Steve's resting-respites growing more frequent, needful, and protracted. We broke through a hedge of red birches and trailing pine and then a great marvel and an expanse of surpassing loveliness burst out upon us. We had come upon a country of giant cedars and spruces, stretching away, on a slight incline, to the misty mountain which loomed up, perhaps four miles away. Wild roses made gay the whole wild color scheme of predominant green, with blue hare-bells in the rocks and yew and juniper and moose-maple. The country was open and wonderfully park-like in its exquisite composition.

Our expressions of admiration were awed whispers—save Steve's, who, breath and utilitarian instinct returning together, declared fervently:

"There's a half-million feet of timber without a knot-hole."

And we fell upon him.

There were blue-berries there, too. And such blue-berries!— the average the size of a Malaga grape. They nestled in the shadows of the rocks and swept away, a sheen of misty blue, as far as the eye could reach. Bear tracks showed we were not the only appreciators of this luscious bounty.

Joe nosed about, while we gorged upon blue-berries and smoked and baited Steve. Indians always do that—nose about, I mean. When we were coasting Lake Superior, Joe and Michael would disappear while we lunched and return triumphantly with a rabbit or a wolf-trap or an abandoned moccasin or a rotting dog-sled—or some other priceless trophy.

It was lunch time when we heard the brook. Of course Michael heard it first. Else what prerogatives are there in patriarchal dignity—and Michael eighty now at least? Joe had started the fire in a place so formally beautiful in its arrangement of cedars and shrubs and gay flowers that it left us with the uncomfortable impression that we were picnicking on somebody's million-dollar country estate—somewhere between the formal garden and the tennis lawn. Trout for lunch, obviously, is preferable

STRETCHED HIMSELF TOWARD THE WHITE NORTHERN MOON.

to bacon. The Camp Boss and Steve hearkened to the call of the brook, gurgling there somewhere in the green shadows. It was curious and stimulating, the way Steve threw off complete exhaustion, nay, paralysis of mind and body, when he heard the word "trout."

The water was boiling and Michael's cunningly-made tea-cups of birch-bark were ready, when we heard shouts, first of exultation, second, of apprehension— then shrill cries for help. Of course, they were Steve's cries. We rushed to the brook. It was a versatile and many-mooded little brook—here and there a deep, green, mysterious pool—and then a stretch where the giggling water scarcely covered the stones. The Camp Boss had stationed Steve at a pool with his rod and told him to do his worst.

Steve's first cast was, undoubtedly, an invitation to the largest and most democratic social event that pool had ever known. They rushed from all nooks and corners. Steve said he counted 398, fighting for his flies. The survival of the fittest was quickly adjudicated and Steve found himself hooked up with two very big, thoroughly frightened trout. That was the cry of exultation. Then those two fish did an untraditional and most reprehensible thing. They should have circled round and round the pool until we could find Steve's net for him. Instead of that, they started down the brook. That was the cry of apprehension.

Steve followed on, being the only thing he could do. Moreover the pace was killing, because even a trout half out of water, sliding along on its side over moist stones is no laggard. For fifty yards down that brook, falling down, getting up, screaming for help, Steve went, paced by those two trout. The trout knew the turns better, but Steve was making a pretty race of it, plucky and spectacular, when we reached the bank.

Once he sprinted and overtook his pace-makers with a splendid burst of speed. He tried to kick one into a clump of alder bushes and grasp the slippery body of the other with palsied fingers. Then he sat upon one, obviously to smother it, and hurled shuddering curses upon the other, as he struck savage blows at it with a crooked stick. Michael netted them and Steve accepted congratulations and "entertained at lunch."

The lake, the six-mile lake, the lake of our dreams and the lake of the mapmaker's mendacity, wasn't far—after that. In fact, Steve had had, I think, but two rests when the blue sheen and sparkle of it burst out upon us, as we rounded a sentinel-rock upon a shoulder of "Old Baldy." Little time was squandered in congratulations. There was no unfolding of the starry banner or exchange of appropriate, dramatic, and maudlin sentiment. We had work to do—specifically, a raft to build. We wanted to see just how expectant and appreciative "speckled trout" can be when they have been "abounding" for

generations without the interference of the "race-suicide" proponents and the census-man.

We started out sanely with the purpose of having a raft "built for comfort, not speed." After the first official test there was some logical conjecture even about the "comfort." We had two very brilliant young engineers among us—men "sure to be heard from"—you know the kind. Billy, for instance, had built numberless million-dollar railroad bridges, but the mechanical problem of the raft baffled him. Indeed, in a half hour more engineers-in-chief resigned from the job than have come home from Panama for a presidential spanking. At last we turned it all over to Michael and Joe, just as each of us had felt from the first to be inevitable. They did it in, perhaps, fifteen minutes—and it was declared seaworthy and ample for three.

I don't know why Billy, Harry, and I were elected the prize-crew, but we were. Harry took Steve's trout-rod and leader of flies. He meant to get at the bottom of this "abounding" rumor. Billy equipped himself with a steel rod and a "spinner." I manned a paddle of grotesque design and we were off amid cheers from the reviewing-stands. The work of keeping afloat—above the knees—and dodging Harry's hopeful back-casts engaged our minds for the first few minutes. It was a nice point whether I preferred Harry's flies or Billy's spinner-hooks, but I decided that, if I had any latitude of choice, I'd stick to Harry and his flies as a gratuitous decoration of my ears or back-hair or cheeks.

We had swept out majestically a hundred yards from shore when it became evident that, if there was any "abounding" being done in that lake, it wasn't the "speckled trout" that were doing it. We were discussing this further mendacity on the part of the map—when the answer came. Billy had just made a record-cast and was throwing rhetorical orchids at himself. He gave voice to a muttered exclamation and started over the side of the raft in response to a vigorous summons that seemed to come along his line. We grappled with him. Then Billy's steel-rod and reel and

WE CLIMBED OVER WIND-ROWS AND SANK INTO GREAT LOGS THAT LOOKED
SOUND AND WERE BUT DUST.

HE HAD US TIED UP LIKE LAOCOON AND SONS.

parently, for a moment supposing that the condition of being so closely en rapport with a forty-pound 'lunge could make any possible difference with such splendid insouciance as ours. Without this hypothesis, they must have thought we were doing a Virginia reel or something on that raft from sheer lightness of heart.

Harry tried to get his leg out of Billy's loop and stow his own line simultaneously. He didn't really make a success of either. He got two of his flies into my trousers and his line around Billy's neck. That seemed to stimulate the musky to fresh feats of agility and daring. He began cutting figure-eights and spirals around the raft and under it and, I think, over it. He had us tied up like Laocoon and sons in the grasp of the encircling snakes, when Billy, attempting a quick turn, went through the raft to his arm-pits. I tried to help him and pried off a log or two. Then the spikes began coming out.

Each rush of the musky took away an integer in our factor of buoyancy. When the moment of final disintegration came, Harry and I began swimming. Billy, however, straddled the biggest log and bade the muskellunge lead on which the muskellunge forthwith did. Had it not been for canvas hat and briar pipe clenched in his teeth, Billy would have passed very well for Aphrodite being towed Olympus-ward by dolphins from her radiant bath. Harry and I wanted to stick around and enjoy the water-fête, but we had a hundred-yard-swim ahead of us. Presently Billy turned his rod over to that avaricious musky and joined us.

Of course, we could have built a fire

line and spinner opened up a surprising course of spontaneous action. The rod doubled, the reel shrieked, and the end of the line went chassé-ing around the lake. Billy was very pallid. Then the fish broke water—off about forty yards—and we looked at one another with wonder, even terror in our eyes. It was Monsieur Muskellunge that had been doing all this geodetic "abounding." Evidently, the 'lunge saw us when we saw him—and, equally evidently, he was glad to see us. He started for the raft with no further ceremony or shenannigan. Billy couldn't reel in fast enough, so a loop of the line got around Harry's leg. It must be remembered how thoroughly congested our quarters really were.

The reviewing-stand ashore had heard the splash the muskellunge had made and began telling us all about it—never, ap-

and stripped and dried our clothes. But the black flies were showing much too much enthusiasm. We decided to abandon the secret of the "abounding" rumor and break the cross-country records for camp. Soaked flannels do not make wilderness-going easy, but they do provide a potent sort of incentive. The Camp Boss regretted that we hadn't thrown Steve into the lake.

Michael gave us a very impressive exhibition of wood-craft when we were ready to start. He took a look at the setting sun, at the top of "Old Baldy," and, then, at the far-away cove on Lake Superior and that coveted camp-fire, where Nish-i-shin-i-wog's dinner was simmering and dry clothes and hot things and great good cheer were waiting. Then Michael grunted and started briskly down the hill-side, already shadowing in the approach of evening. He went straight, over hills, through dark valleys, cañons, and swamps, we stumbling after the old patriarch, and at last we emerged from the thickets—within ten feet of the crackling camp-fire which a huge boulder had entirely screened from our view as we approached.

There was little political, ethical, esthetic, or piscatorial discussion about the fire that night—no post-prandial oratory. Billy was too tired to bait Steve and Steve was too tired to resent it, if Billy had. We staggered to our blankets from a stupendous dinner and dropped straightway into that profound, dreamless sleep of the northland.

It is a terrific shock to be awakened when one is sleeping the delicious sleep of complete physical exhaustion. I never can forget that shock. At last I realized that it was the Camp Boss's voice that I had been hearing for centuries. He had me by the leg—and he was saying—and repeating many times:

"Up, lads, quick. The *Ford's* out in the cove—whistling for us."

I sat up in my blankets and had an attack of vertigo—just the nervous shock and terrific mental effort to grasp it all after a brutally abrupt return from oblivion. The camp-fire was still burning low. The moon, too, was low and ghostly in its faded brilliance. We built up the fire and lighted lanterns. It is not nice to strike a five-tent camp at 2 A.M.; to dress in the unbelievable cold; to pack wet clothes with your bedding; to take down your rods and untie hard knots and collect scattered kits with numb fingers and sleep-deadened minds, while an impatient lake-captain blows hurry-up whistles out there in the blackness of night-cloaked Superior with only his port light to show his sympathy.

The sun was just piling up over the reefs and the sea-gulls were awakening to another work-day, when the last boat-load—the Camp Boss and Joe and I—after a last look around, pulled out of that sanctified cove and went up on the davits of the *J. C. Ford*. That last look around was tragic but vastly disillusioning, because, contrasted with the horrors of an abandoned camp-site, even civilization is bearable. Then a bell in the engine-room sounded the knell—the knell of another play-day ended and another summer-idyl gone—that's the real tragedy of it—gone forever.